CRITICAL THINKING IN CLINICAL PRACTICE

Eileen Gambrill

CRITICAL THINKING IN CLINICAL PRACTICE

Improving the Accuracy of Judgments and Decisions About Clients

Jossey-Bass Publishers

San Francisco • Oxford • 1990

CRITICAL THINKING IN CLINICAL PRACTICE
Improving the Accuracy of Judgments and Decisions About Clients
by Eileen Gambrill

Copyright © 1990 by: Jossey-Bass Inc., Publishers
350 Sansome Street
San Francisco, California 94104
&
Jossey-Bass Limited
Headington Hill Hall
Oxford OX3 0BW

Library of Congress Cataloging-in-Publication Data

Gambrill, Eileen D., date.
    Critical thinking in clinical practice : improving the accuracy of
judgments and decisions about clients / Eileen Gambrill. — 1st ed.
        p.   cm.—(The Jossey-Bass social and behavioral science
series)
    Includes bibliographical references.
    ISBN 1-55542-198-9 (alk. paper)
    1. Clinical psychology—Decision making.   2. Counseling—
Decision making.   I. Title.   II. Series.
    [DNLM: 1. Decision Making.   BF 441 G192c]
RC457.G28   1990
616.89′1—dc20
DNLM/DLC
for Library of Congress   89-24660
                                                                 CIP

Manufactured in the United States of America

The paper in this book meets the guidelines for
permanence and durability of the Committee on
Production Guidelines for Book Longevity of the
Council on Library Resources.

JACKET DESIGN BY WILLI BAUM

FIRST EDITION

Code 9007

The Jossey-Bass
Social and Behavioral Science Series

Contents

Preface   xi

The Author   xix

1. The Need to Refine Clinical Reasoning Skills:
   Problems and Prospects   1

2. Sources of Influence on Decisions That
   Clinicians Make   26

3. Content and Procedural Knowledge: Deciding
   How to Work with Clients   53

4. Reasons and Reasoning: The Heart of Making
   Decisions About Problems and Solutions   88

5. The Influence of Language and Persuasion Strategies   116

6. Formal and Informal Fallacies: Mistakes
   in Thinking and How to Avoid Them   140

7.   Classification, Pseudoauthority, and Focusing
on Pathology: Additional Sources of Error   162

8.   Collecting Data: Factors Affecting What People
See and Report   190

9.   Causes of Clients' Problems: Making Accurate
Assumptions   223

10.   Predictions About Clients and Treatment
Effectiveness: Improving the Odds   264

11.   Enhancing the Quality of Case Conferences
and Discussions   296

12.   Overcoming Personal Obstacles to Critical Thinking   325

13.   Maintaining Critical Thinking Skills   350

References   367

Name Index   413

Subject Index   423

Preface

Critical Thinking in Clinical Practice is for clinicians who want to think more clearly about the decisions they make and the context in which they make them. It will be of value to all professionals who offer services to clients, including psychologists, psychiatrists, social workers, and counselors. Clinical practice is an uncertain enterprise. Much still remains unknown about what works best with which client toward what aim, and individual differences exist among clinicians in terms of how they carry out their practice. Indeed, the very criteria that should be used to evaluate outcomes are in dispute. These characteristics make mistakes inevitable. However, even in uncertain problem areas such as clinical practice, some decisions are better than others. The percentage of those that are better can be increased by avoiding frequently occurring sources of error.

The spirit in which this book is written is illustrated by the author of *Straight and Crooked Thinking: Thirty-Eight Dishonest Tricks of Debate* (Thouless, 1974). The purpose of learning about sources of error is to enhance clear thinking skills, to learn to recognize sources of error and acquire remedies so that mistakes can be avoided. The emphasis here is on offering readers additional decision-making tools they can use to improve the accuracy of their clinical judgments. Clinical decision making is approached as a set of general and specific skills that can be improved with practice. Beliefs, attitudes, and interpersonal skills that influence the effectiveness with which knowledge of content and procedures are used are reviewed.

Surprisingly little attention is devoted in professional training programs to many sources of error that can lead clinicians astray. For example, little attention is given to informal fallacies that may result in questionable decisions. Some clinicians approach clinical practice as an art, rejecting as irrelevant empirical research related to practice concerns. However, in many areas empirically based practice knowledge is available that can be put to good use both at the individual level of practice and in seeking larger social changes. Critical thinking and an empirical approach to practice are closely related; both involve a spirit of inquiry and acceptance of error.

Development of the Book

A number of influences led to the writing of this book. One was the discovery of common errors in thinking among clinicians in different countries: Examples include being overly reliant on small biased samples, not recognizing pseudoexplanations, and having a false sense of accuracy in predicting future events. Another was puzzlement about the success of colleagues who use weak rather than strong strategies when trying to influence others: Examples include using straw person arguments, misrepresenting positions, and begging the question. A third was the discovery of books such as *Straight and Crooked Thinking* (Thouless, 1974)—a well-written book describing a range of common errors as well as remedies. A fourth influence was research concerning human judgments that has been pulled together in sources such as *Human Inference* (Nisbett & Ross, 1980) and *Judgement and Choice* (Hogarth, 1980, 1987). Books such as *The Protection of Children* by Dingwall and his colleagues (1983) that describe the decision-making process in case conferences provided a fascinating supplement to studies of clinical decision making by individuals. Research and theory in the area of teaching people to think were also of value.

Overview of the Chapters

Chapter One describes the role of decisions in clinical practice, the kinds of clinical errors that may occur, and sources of error. The influence of information-processing strategies in making clinical decisions is highlighted, and ways in which these may lead to errors are noted (for example, discounting conflicting information in exploring the accuracy of clinical assumptions). Clinical reasoning is viewed as a skill, and differences between experts and novices are reviewed. Finally, the costs and benefits of critical thinking are reviewed.

Chapter Two describes sources of influence on clinical decisions. Readers are encouraged to take a broad view of such influences—to consider the influence of political, structural, and economic factors on what is defined as a personal or social problem and what are considered suitable intervention options in relation to different kinds of problems. The influence of agency variables is also discussed because many clinicians either work in an agency or have contacts with agencies—perhaps through services that are contracted out. In addition, psychological factors that influence clinical judgments are reviewed, including sources of behavioral confirmation that may result in leading clients as well as premature acceptance of initial assumptions.

The importance of knowledge (data that decrease uncertainty) is discussed in Chapter Three. Research shows that domain-specific knowledge as well as procedural knowledge is required in making accurate clinical decisions. This chapter emphasizes the key role of clinical training programs and the value of learning-how-to-learn skills.

Reasoning is at the heart of clinical decision making—forming hypotheses about presenting concerns, gathering data to evaluate the accuracy of different views, offering arguments for assumptions, and evaluating the quality of these arguments. Chapter Four provides an overview of different kinds of reasons (for example, hot and cold), suggests some helpful distinctions (for example, between facts and beliefs), and describes different kinds of arguments and explanations.

The influence of language and social-psychological persua-

sion strategies are discussed in Chapter Five. The interview is the
context in which most counseling efforts are carried out, and
language plays a crucial part in what transpires there. Sources of
possible error that are related to language are described in this chapter, including "bafflegarb," use of emotional words, and conviction
through repetition.

Rarely are clinicians trained in the various kinds of formal
and informal fallacies that may occur in clinical practice and thus
compromise the quality of decisions. Informal and formal sources
of fallacy may involve overlooking, evading, or distorting facts.
Although most clinicians may be familiar with some of the sources
of fallacy described in Chapter Six, they may not be familiar with
others that may result in clinical errors, such as inappropriate use
of analogies and circular reasoning. Chapter Six shows how learning to identify and remedy informal fallacies can improve the quality of clinical decisions.

The topics of classification, pseudoauthority, and pathological set are discussed in Chapter Seven. Classification is inevitable
in clinical practice. This chapter describes sources of error that may
result from it, such as an incorrect classification of clients and treatment methods. Pseudoauthority is singled out for special focus because it represents a substantial source of error in clinical practice.
For example, clinicians may accept knowledge based on inappropriate appeals to consensus or traditional wisdom. A pathological
set also is singled out for special attention because clinicians tend
to focus on pathology and ignore positive attributes of clients.

Chapter Eight describes options for collecting data. Sources
of assessment information are described, as well as their advantages
and disadvantages. The chapter also discusses factors that influence
what clinicians see and report (such as vividness, motivation, and
insensitivity to sample size).

Clinicians make decisions about causal factors related to
presenting problems and desired outcomes. Factors that influence
selection of causes (such as similarity between effects and presumed
causes and the availability of preferred practice theories) are reviewed in Chapter Nine, and guidelines are offered to enhance the
accuracy of assumptions. These include helpful rules of thumb,

such as paying attention to sources of uncertainty and examining all four cells of a contingency table.

Making choices and predictions is a routine part of clinical practice. Predictions are made about how clients will behave in the future and about the effectiveness of intervention methods. Sources of error that may decrease the accuracy of clinical predictions are described in Chapter Ten, and steps are suggested that can be used to increase accuracy (such as taking advantage of statistical tools and decreasing reliance on memory).

Clinical decisions are often made in case conferences, particularly when decisions are difficult ones that involve high costs if errors are made. Tendencies in such contexts that may decrease the quality of decisions (such as the belief that all contributions are equally good, and confusion between the consistency and differential weight of signs) are discussed in Chapter Eleven, and guidelines are provided for enhancing the quality of discussions.

Personal obstacles that may get in the way of developing and using critical thinking skills are discussed in Chapter Twelve. Examples include a disinterest in critical thinking, a preference for mystery over mastery, unrealistic expectations of success, and a fear of discovering errors. Social anxiety may decrease willingness to express opinions that differ from those of others. Moving beyond weak arguments requires accurate identification of errors and knowledge of remedies, as well as effective interpersonal skills for diplomatically neutralizing weak influence attempts and highlighting the real issues.

Guidelines for maintaining critical thinking skills are described in Chapter Thirteen. As with any other skill, having the skill does not mean that it will be used, and many influences can erode critical thinking skills.

Purpose of the Book

This book is not meant to be read at one sitting but is designed to be sampled over many readings. This will provide the reader with leisurely opportunities to catch errors that I no doubt have made in my thinking. Writing a book about critical thinking is a daunting prospect, given the inevitability of revealing crooked thinking. However, the book is written in the spirit that we all make errors and that the task is to learn to recognize and correct them.

It is important to note what this book attempts to do as well as what it does not do. This book *does* attempt to draw on a range of areas that are pertinent to critical thinking in clinical practice and to draw these together in a format that makes sense to clinicians and that can be used to enhance the quality of clinical practice. It does not attempt to offer incisive reviews of the many fields that are touched on here as they relate to clinical decisions. Many streams of research and theory relate to clinical decision making. The teaching of thinking is as old as philosophy itself, and entire domains of inquiry have been concerned with this subject. Material related to the area of clinical decision making lies in sociology, social psychology, psychology, rhetoric, philosophy, education, and popularized presentations of formal and informal fallacies, such as *Straight and Crooked Thinking* (Thouless, 1974). The potential arena of relevant resources has been a challenge of manageability. This book is not for those who are looking for a state-of-the-art presentation on artificial intelligence or who seek in-depth discussions of one of the many topics mentioned in this book. Entire books could be (and have been) written on many, if not most, of the topics discussed in this book. References are provided throughout the book to sources that offer more detail.

Strong differences of opinion exist about many of the topics discussed in this book, such as statistical versus clinical prediction and the most useful way to pursue knowledge. The sources of error described here, especially those resulting in confirmation of favored views, will encourage biased misreadings of some of the content. There has been a historical reluctance to make clinical assumptions explicit so that their accuracy can be carefully examined. Efforts in this direction, even though described with the utmost tentativeness, often have been greeted with vigorous negative reactions that are based on misreadings of what has been presented. Consider, for example, the ongoing discussion concerning the use of actuarial methods for making clinical decisions. Even though the advantages of such methods may be described in measured terms (as an adjunct to the use of clinical intuition), positions may be distorted as arguing for the general superiority of such methods.

Acknowledgments

I am indebted to the many authors of the excellent material from which I have drawn liberally. I wish to thank the participants of my workshops on making clinical decisions in both the United States and Britain, who greeted this material with such enthusiasm and inspired me to continue working in this area. These workshops supported my impression over the years that most clinicians are open to examining their reasoning processes in an atmosphere of constructive inquiry. I also want to extend my thanks to reviewers of earlier drafts of the manuscript, including William E. Henry and Gracia A. Alkema of Jossey-Bass, who have been consistently supportive yet were critical in nudging the manuscript toward clarity and in considering the topic important.

Perhaps the most intimate dialogue concerning the material in this book occurred with my most severe critic—one of the reviewers who wrote lengthy responses to drafts of the manuscript. It is a better product because of this dialogue, in terms of getting a clearer picture of obstacles to critical thinking and presenting material in a manner that will encourage readers to become engaged with the material.

Finally, I wish to extend a special note of appreciation to Sharon Ikami for her excellent typing and consistent warmth and good will.

Berkeley, California Eileen Gambrill
April 1990

The Author

Eileen Gambrill is professor of social welfare at the University of California, Berkeley. She received her B.A. degree (1956) from the University of Pennsylvania, her M.S.S. degree (1961) from Bryn Mawr School of Social Work and Social Research, and her Ph.D. degree (1965) from the University of Michigan in social work and psychology. She has been a visiting scholar at the University of Oxford and Tel Aviv University, and she served as external examiner for the Department of Social Work at the National University of Singapore from 1984 to 1988.

Gambrill's main research interests include social skills training, decision making in child welfare, and the application of behavioral methods in social work practice. Her books include *Behavior Modification: Handbook of Assessment, Intervention, and Evaluation,* (1977), *Children in Foster Care* (1978, with T. J. Stein and K. T. Wiltse), *Casework: A Competency Based Approach* (1983), *Supervision: A Decision-Making Framework* (1983, with T. J. Stein), and *Taking Charge of Your Social Life* (1988, with C. A. Richey).

Gambrill served as editor of the newsletter of the Association for Advancement of Behavior Therapy (1974 to 1977) and as a representative at large of this association from 1979 to 1981. She was editor-in-chief of *Social Work Research and Abstracts* from 1984 to 1988. She also maintains a private practice and has served as a consultant to a variety of groups.

CRITICAL THINKING IN CLINICAL PRACTICE

1

---◇◇◇◇◇◇---

The Need to Refine Clinical Reasoning Skills: Problems and Prospects

---◇◇◇◇◇◇◇◇◇◇◇◇◇◇◇◇◇◇◇◇◇◇---

Decision making, whether explicit or implicit, is at the heart of clinical practice. Decisions are made at many different levels of complexity. In addition to complex ones that involve collecting, processing, and organizing diverse sources of data, scores of smaller decisions are made in the course of each interview. For example, moment-to-moment decisions are made during an interview about how to respond. Options include questions, advisements, reflections, interpretations, self-disclosures, and silence (Goodman & Doley, 1976). Decisions are made about whether to accept clients for treatment, what concerns to focus on, what information to gather, what intervention methods to use, and how (or whether) to evaluate progress. The judgments that must be made are difficult ones, requiring distinctions between causes and secondary effects, problems and the results of attempted solutions, personal and environmental contributions to presenting complaints, and findings and evidence (links between clinical assumptions and findings). The usefulness of different outcomes must be weighed, the risks of different options must be evaluated, and probabilities must be estimated. Errors may occur both in structuring problems and in drawing inferences.

Judgmental tasks include describing clients and situations, deciding what causes presenting problems, and making predictions about outcomes. For example, a clinician may have to describe a

1

child's injuries and decide whether these were a result of parental abuse or were caused by a fall (as reported by the mother). She will have to decide what criteria to use to make this decision, what type of data to gather, and when she has enough material at hand. If a decision is made that the injuries were caused by the parent, a prediction must be made as to whether the parent is likely to abuse the child again. Clinical errors that may occur include

- Errors in description (Example: Mrs. V. was abused as a child [when she was not].)
- Errors in detecting the extent of covariation (Example: All people who are abused as children abuse their own children.)
- Errors in assuming causal relationships (Example: Being abused as a child [always] leads to abuse of one's own children.)
- Errors in prediction (Example: Insight therapy will prevent this woman from abusing her child again [given that this is not true].)

There is no doubt that clinical decisions can be improved. The histories of the mental health industry, psychiatry, psychology, and social work are replete with the identification of false causes for personal troubles and social problems. The exposure of clinical errors is a topic of concern to journalists as well as investigators in a variety of fields, as illustrated by recent media coverage of children who died at the hands of their foster or adoptive parents. Reviews of the psychiatric enterprise reveal a long list of intrusive and misguided interventions to cure mental illness (see, for example Sedgwick, 1982; Szasz, 1961, 1970). Epidemiologists bring to our attention different rates of use of certain kinds of interventions, such as the higher number of hysterectomies in the United States as compared with Britain. Such differences may reflect actual need, or they may result from influences that are in direct conflict with client interests (such as an overabundance of surgeons or a tendency to think for clients rather than inform them fully and let them make their own decisions). What would be considered an error today might have been considered common (and good practice) years ago. For example, many people who entered a mental hospital in the fifties and spent the rest of their lives there should not have been hospitalized in the first place. Current clinical practice can be likened to a broad slice of psychiatric history in terms of what is offered to clients. Some clinicians carry out their practice with little or no effort to take advantage of new data concerning what seems to be effective with different kinds of problems with different kinds of clients. Popular reviews of psychotherapy, such as *The Shrinking of America* (Zilbergeld, 1983), encourage the view that it makes no difference whether clients receive what they came for—they are still glad they came.

Clinical errors may result in (1) failing to offer help that could be provided and is desired by clients, (2) forcing clients to accept "help" they do not want, (3) offering help that is really not needed, or (4) using procedures that aggravate rather than alleviate client concerns (that is, procedures that result in iatrogenic effects. See, for example, Kessler, 1978; Mays and Franks, 1985; Morgan, 1983). One of the few books devoted to a description of failures in therapy (Foa & Emmelkamp, 1983) attributed lack of progress to a variety of clinical errors, including misclassification of clients, inadequate interventions (for example, too short, omitting important components), lack of relapse prevention, and negative therapeutic relationship. Errors in judgment may result in misattributing client problems to internal mental disorders; overlooking pathology; selecting weak or ineffective intervention methods; or predicting incorrectly suicidal potential, need for hospitalization, or future recurrence of violent acts. That is, judgments made may result in clinical errors. Criteria for detecting errors include information concerning future behavior—intervention programs are not successful, or predictions about future actions are not borne out. The recurrence of a problem may or may not reflect clinical errors in judgment. A problem may recur because a contributing factor was overlooked (an error) or because environmental conditions recurred over which there was no control (not an error). Examples of errors identified by Blau (1988) include being overenthusiastic, giving advice (when this would be a mistake), and allowing interviews to drift.

Robertiello and Schoenewolf (1987) identify 101 therapeutic blunders. Factors that Strupp and Hadley (1985) describe as being associated with negative effects include mistakes about goals, such as not reaching mutual agreement on goals and selecting goals that are not in the client's best interest. Other kinds of errors include false assumptions about the effectiveness of therapy (especially the assumption that it is all-powerful), technical rigidity, getting too close to clients (or remaining overly aloof), and misuses of interpretations (encouraging excessive attention to the pursuit of insights) and the creation of dependency on the part of clients. These authors note a variety of negative effects that may result from clinical errors, including embracing therapy as an end in itself, using therapy to rationalize feelings of superiority, seeking to achieve goals that are too difficult in order to please the therapist, as well as a general loss of hope and an increase in negative attitudes toward all forms of help.

Blau (1988) suggests the following as indicators of errors due to "the psychotherapist's conflicts":

- The behavior (of the therapist) is distressing to the client.
- The behavior is repetitive.
- The clinician feels guilty about what has been done or what has been omitted.
- The client questions or objects to the repetitive behavior.
- The clinician is uncomfortable with the client.
- The clinician apologizes or acknowledges the behavior but continues to make the therapeutic error.

Objective criteria for detecting errors are not as available in the fields of psychology, social work, and psychiatry as they are in the field of medicine, where anatomical or histological indicators may be found by a pathologist. Still, there are many indicators as described above (see also Chapter Ten). Clients may not and probably do not know when an error occurs, since they usually are not informed about different assessment and intervention options. Clients may not know, for example, that the intervention methods suggested by a clinician are not those that have been found to be most effective and do not offer much potential for attaining outcomes the client desires. Nor may they realize that selection by clinicians of certain problems to address may involve an error; in that the choice made may not address the clients' real needs (although it may serve other ends—see Chapter Two).

Errors may occur in all three phases of clinical practice: assessment, intervention, and evaluation. Errors may occur in the assessment stage by overlooking important data or attending to irrelevant data, in the intervention stage by selecting weak rather than strong intervention methods, and in the evaluation stage by reviewing progress loosely rather than carefully. If an irrelevant or inaccurate source of data is relied on for assessment, the result may be an incorrect and irrelevant account of a presenting problem and related factors and a consequent recommendation of an ineffective intervention method. Important factors may not be noticed. For example, a clinician may overlook the possible role of physiological factors in presenting problems of depression. Depression is a common side effect of birth control pills and is also related to hormonal changes among middle-aged women. Failure to consider physical causes may result in inappropriate treatment decisions. Clinical errors also occur during intervention. An irrelevant intervention method may be selected rather than one that would help clients attain valued outcomes. Even though selection of any method may provide some gain, the question is, what method will provide the most gains and the greatest likelihood of maintenance of those gains? Selecting an intervention method that will provide only modest positive outcomes and thus forgoing methods that would yield marked progress is one type of clinical error. Clinical errors also may occur because intervention procedures are not implemented correctly. "Treatment fidelity" is of concern when gains can be maximized by following a prescribed protocol. Adherence rates of health care professionals are often low, even when clear instructions are provided and clinicians report that they intend to carry out recommendations (Meichenbaum & Turk, 1987).

The incorrect assumption that gains will be maintained (when in fact they will not) is another kind of clinical error. Errors may result from selection of irrelevant or invalid progress indicators. A common error in evaluating progress is accepting a feeling of what is working rather than arranging for ongoing feedback based on client-selected relevant progress indicators (see Chapter Ten). A clinician may decide to end counseling because self-report by the client indicates that objectives of counseling have been met. Inclusion of other sources of data may indicate that this is not the case and that intervention may have been ended prematurely. What is needed is a description of the kinds and frequencies of errors that occur in clinical practice.

The very nature of clinical practice leaves room for many sources of error. Some errors result from a lack of information about how to help clients. Empirical knowledge related to clinical practice is fragmentary, and theory must be used to fill in the gaps. Other errors result from ignorance on the part of individual clinicians—that is, knowledge (defined here as information and procedural know-how that reduces uncertainty) is available but is not used. This lack of knowledge and skill may be due to inexperience or inadequate training. Errors also result from lack of familiarity with the political, economic, and social functions of professions such as psychiatry, psychology, and social work and with the influence of social-psychological variables in the therapeutic context. The interpersonal context within which counseling occurs offers many potential opportunities for mutual influence of responses (see Chapter Two). Errors may occur because of personal characteristics of the clinicians, such as an excessive need for approval (see Chapter Twelve).

Decisions must be made in a context of uncertainty; the criteria on which decisions should be based are in dispute, and empirical data about the effectiveness of different intervention options are often lacking. A desire to decrease uncertainty is another source of error. There are many pressures on clinicians to act more certain than they are, including the rhetoric of professional organizations that oversells the feats of clinicians, clients who seek more certainty than exists, peers who support exaggerated claims of certainty, and journal articles that misrepresent findings. A reluctance to consider errors as inevitable in clinical practice may result in overlooking sources of uncertainty.

The strategies used to make decisions may also result in errors. Although these may often result in sound judgments, the task here is to identify ways in which they are not correctly used so that clinical errors can be avoided. Judgmental strategies are not necessarily used consciously, which is another reason it is helpful to be familiar with them. However, familiarity with sources of error is not enough. If this were true, certain kinds of errors would not recur in clinical practice. For example, many writers have argued that mental health professionals are too focused on pathology, that stereotypes interfere with making balanced clinical decisions that reflect what a client can do as well as what he cannot do (see, for example, Hobbs, 1975). However, some clinicians continue to focus on individual pathology, neglect client assets, and overlook environmental causes of personal troubles.

Given the role of decision making in clinical practice and the variety of factors that influence the quality of decisions, it is surprising that more attention is not devoted to this content in professional training. Although students in clinical training programs learn to attend to some sources of error (such as factors that influence reliability and validity) and are cautioned to avoid mistaking correlation for causation, they are not exposed to the range of formal and informal fallacies described in this book—and about the conditions that encourage the use of these fallacies and that make it likely that their influence on clinical decisions will slip by unnoticed. Clinical students may not be exposed to sociological perspectives concerning psychological and psychiatric concepts (for example, see Goffman, 1961; Scheff, 1984a, 1984b): that the labeling of attributes or actions as symptoms or psychopathology is intimately associated with political and economic concerns and social conventions; that therapists function as "moral managers" (Sedgwick, 1982, pp. 141 & 147) (see Chapter Two). The topic of clinical decision making has not been ignored in professional sources. For example, Meehl's book *Clinical Versus Statistical Prediction* appeared in 1954. The classic "Why I Do Not Attend Case Conferences" (Meehl, 1973) identifies the kinds of errors and tendencies in groups that dilute the quality of decisions. The influence of illusory correlations on clinical observation was explored in the late sixties (see, for example, Chapman, 1967; Chapman & Chapman, 1967, 1969). The tendency of clinicians to attribute problems to the person and overlook the role of environmental factors has been a topic of interest for some time (see, for example, Rosenhan, 1973).

Barriers to making accurate decisions are described below, followed by an overview of tendencies that result in incorrect decisions. Recently, there has been a flowering of interest in human judgment and the factors that influence this. A discussion of thinking as a skill is then presented, and the differences between effective and ineffective thinkers and between novices and experts are discussed. The costs and benefits of thinking are then reviewed.

Barriers to Making Sound Judgments

Some barriers, such as selective perception, are common to all judgmental tasks. Others, such as the lack of agreed-on criteria for determining the accuracy of decisions (see, for example, Wilkins, 1986) and the intrusion of everyday language, are more problematic in clinical contexts than they are in the hard sciences or in activities such as car repair. Some of the biases that influence judgments are the result of limited information-processing capacities. Because a great many things cannot be considered at once, perception is selective; clinicians do not necessarily see what is there to be seen (see Chapter Eight). We tend to process data in a sequential manner, although a network or web approach to the associations between variables may result in more accurate judgments. Although strategies used to simplify judgmental tasks and decrease effort may usually work well in making accurate judgments, at other times they may result in errors. In addition, memory capacity is limited and accessibility of information (data that decrease uncertainty) is selective. It is difficult, if not impossible, to be sure that beliefs are compatible with one another, since they often are difficult to recall and may be implicit rather than explicit.

Because only a limited number of hypotheses can be considered at one time, those that are overly general tend to be retained, and exaggerated importance may be assigned to some findings to justify retention of a favored hypothesis. Lack of knowledge and interfering attitudes are other limiting factors (see Chapters Three and Twelve). Judgments and decisions must be made in the face of uncertainty; even if all could be known, typically not enough time would be available to know all, nor could the human mind deal with the multitude of dimensions that might be involved. Yet another barrier is the effort required to make sound judgments.

There is often no agreed-on criterion against which to check the accuracy of decisions in clinical practice in psychology, social work, and psychiatry—unlike medical practice, in which the reports of a pathologist can often verify clinical assumptions. Economic and political interests influence decisions in the area of interpersonal helping as they do in other fields, such as medicine (see Chapter Two). Clinicians may not be aware of how these larger influences affect the very definitions of clinical and social problems and recommendations for intervention. Because many clinical tasks involve the same kinds of judgments made in everyday life, replacement of empirically based information by unsupported hunches is especially easy. For most clinicians, "practice theory" is probably a mix of common knowledge, hunches, and scientific knowledge (Bromley, 1986, p. 219).

Tendencies That Decrease Accuracy

People show a remarkable tendency to believe in initial judgments, even when they are informed that the knowledge on which they based their judgments was arbitrarily selected, for example, by the spin of a roulette wheel (Tversky & Kahneman, 1974). Clinicians tend to form impressions of clients quickly; these first impressions influence their expectations about outcomes (Barocas & Vance, 1974), which in turn may affect how they respond to clients and so confirm their original impressions. As Snyder and Thomsen (1988) note, the view that these initial judgments are accurate is questionable, since different therapists may form quite different impressions of the same client (Houts & Galante, 1985; Strupp, 1958). Not only are initial beliefs resistant to new evidence, but they also are remarkably resistant to challenges of the evidence that led to those beliefs. Primacy or anchoring effects may be a result of the tendency to generate theories that bias the interpretation of additional material. Premature commitment to a position and insufficient revision of beliefs, as well as a tendency to believe (often falsely) in the consistency of behavior, all contribute to the primacy effect.

Evidence in support of preferred theories tends to be accepted, and evidence contrary to these tends to be discounted; different standards are used to criticize opposing evidence than to evaluate supporting evidence. Moreover, data that provide some support for and some against preferred views, increase the confidence of holders of both views. For example, students who read studies supporting and critical of their views about capital punishment were more confident of their initial position than they were before they had read any evidence (Lord, Ross, & Lepper, 1979). The generation of data, as well as the retrieval of material, is influenced by causal assumptions. Clinicians have a tendency not to search for evidence against their views; this tendency often results in errors. The more biased clinicians are in favor of an argument and the more unaware they are of these biases, the less likely they will be to weigh (or even identify) points against an argument as carefully as they do points in favor of it.

Clinicians who believe that they can do well in a specific situation will probably act differently from those who believe they will not be effective. Expectations tend to be self-fulfilling: assumptions about how clients will respond encourage reactions that are compatible with these beliefs (Snyder & Swann, 1978). Snyder and Thomsen (1988) have written an excellent description of the many opportunities for behavioral confirmation in therapeutic exchanges; they draw on literature in psychotherapy as well as in other areas of study (see also Swann & Guiliano, 1987). These authors, as well as others (Pyszczynski & Greenberg, 1987), note the many stages at which confirmation may take place; assumptions in earlier phases influence actions taken in later phases. For example, a clinician may have read a report describing a client as schizophrenic. This data may then color subsequent processing of information; that is, there may be a selective search for evidence in support of this assumption and a selective ignoring of evidence that does not support the assumption of mental illness. The behavior of clients, their histories, and relevant current situations are scanned selectively for confirmation of initial assumptions, and data that are not compatible with such assumptions are ignored (not inquired into). That is, data collection may be in the interest of confirming initial assumptions rather than in the interest of exploring the accuracy of assumptions.

Errors may occur because certain logical-statistical principles are ignored, such as the size and representativeness of samples, the importance of base-rate data, and the importance of considering relative frequencies in assessing covariations (see Chapters Nine and Ten). The tendency to attribute problems to dispositional (personal) characteristics of clients and to ignore environmental factors is common in clinical practice.

The tendencies described above may influence decision making in all phases of both private and agency-based clinical practice (for example, describing clients and their concerns, making inferences concerning causal factors, and making predictions about the effectiveness of different kinds of treatment methods). Specific examples of their influence are given in later chapters of this book. The spirit in which they are discussed is that being forewarned is being prepared—that the more familiar clinicians are with sources of error that compromise the quality of decisions, the more easily they can avoid them. Many of these biases result in too little thinking in contrast to too much thinking—that is, a "premature cessation of search" (Baron, 1985a, p. 208).

Clinical Reasoning as a Skill

A skill-based metaphor for reasoning is popular today. It is assumed that critical thinking requires a repertoire of strategies: for example, strategies for memorizing content, anticipating questions, and focusing on key information (Sternberg & Kagan, 1986). Research showing that mathematical problem solving, reading, and invention can be improved by teaching tactics supports the accuracy of this approach (Schoenfeld, 1982). Successful managers, for example, seek concrete information when faced with ambiguity, obtain information from a range of sources, and identify useful analogies to explain a situation (Klemp & McClelland, 1986). As skill is acquired in an area, knowledge tends to be stored in larger chunks, and these chunks are run off in a more automatic fashion. For example, consider the difference between skilled and unskilled drivers. The ability of chess masters to quickly identify effective moves depends on pattern recognition—that is, the ability to recognize large chunks of information (Chase & Simon, 1973).

Components of practical intelligence tend to be learned on the job. The goal of practical intelligence is to accomplish tasks in real-life settings. Different kinds of practical intelligence include managing emotions, developing and using interpersonal skills, responding to setbacks and failures, and dealing with procrastination. A skill analogy suggests certain distinctions and concepts, such as the difference between general and specific skills. There is relatively little consensus about what distinguishes unskilled from skilled thinkers. "While some may see inept thinkers as limited by their repertoire of operations, others may find their encoding impoverished, while still others locate the difficulty in inadequate goals, or inadequate monitoring of them" (Nickerson, Perkins, & Smith, 1985, p. 651). Whether there are general skills is a topic of controversy.

Many investigators (see, for example, Baron, 1981; Sternberg & Wagner, 1986) believe that intelligence is best understood through understanding of general coping processes rather than through the investigation of correlations among test scores. IQ tests concentrate on academic skills and have limited predictive value in relation to everyday performance (Sternberg & Wagner, 1986), as well as limited prescriptive value in terms of offering guidelines to enhance performance (Campione, 1989). There is thus an interest in "metacognitive" skills, which involve managing cognitive resources and monitoring cognitive performance (Nickerson et al., 1985, p. 142). Examples of such skills include planning and strategizing, monitoring and evaluating knowledge and performance, and recognizing the utility of a skill. These metacognitive skills involve reasoning about reasoning. Research showing that the value of strategies is typically context bound (related to a particular kind of problem) is a strike against the "economy hypotheses," in which it is proposed that great benefit can be derived from learning a few general strategies. The importance of domain-specific knowledge including both facts (knowing what) and know-how (knowing how to carry out certain procedures) is supported by research that shows that physicians who made accurate clinical decisions in their area of expertise were not as likely to do so when they were considering problems in another specialty (Elstein et al., 1978) (see chapter Three).

Thinking occurs in a particular social and physical context that influences the nature of the interaction between individuals and problems to be resolved. That is, "different situations are more or less conducive to learning and thinking" (Greeno, 1989, p. 134).

The analogy of thinking to a set of skills calls forth concepts such as rules, moves, strategies, and so forth. Rules can guide clinicians as to when a given skill can be used to advantage. For example, physicians who make accurate medical assessments pay attention to information that contradicts a diagnosis (Elstein et al., 1978). Some writers disagree with a focus on the importance of rules; they argue that just because a person has certain rules of inference does not mean that they will be used and that their effectiveness will depend on the model drawn on in reasoning (Johnson-Laird, 1983). Analyses of lapses in reasoning in arguments given by three hundred subjects about social issues showed that the most common ones involved failures to evaluate or elaborate the model offered—for example, counterexamples were overlooked (Perkins, Allen, & Hafner, 1983). So, both rules and models seem important. A clinician may have a certain model in mind when offering an argument but fail to use (or not have available) rules to evaluate its accuracy.

A rich literature is available describing efforts to teach thinking skills and improve performance (see, for example, Nickerson et al., 1985; Anderson, 1981; Chipman, Segal, & Glaser, 1985). Research in a variety of areas relates to this topic (problem solving; creativity; and teaching of reading, writing, and reasoning). An ambitious effort was initiated in Venezuela, where a program was developed to increase intelligence through the education of large segments of the population, including school children, the military, and civil servants (Machado, 1980). There is no doubt that reasoning skills can be enhanced. Thinking ability and intelligence are only partially related; either can be modified independently of the other—that is, how people use their intelligence can be altered. For example, high intelligence is no guarantee of creativity (Weisberg, 1986); even though people may be highly intelligent, they may not have learned good thinking strategies. Simply knowing about a strategy is not enough. Other requirements include knowing (1) how to apply it (necessary background knowledge and specific means of putting the strategy to work are needed), (2) when to apply it, and (3) automatization (strategies need to become automatized) (Perkins, 1985, p. 352). The way in which strategies are viewed (for example, perceived plausibility), as well as other factors such as forgetting, influences the application of strategies.

Do Novices Differ from Experts?

The answer to the question "Do novices differ from experts?" depends on the nature of the judgmental task. Research in the areas of problem solving in physics and mathematics indicates that experts differ from novices both in quality of outcomes achieved (experts are superior) and in processes used. Experts do not necessarily perform better than novices in unstructured problem areas such as psychology and psychiatry (Johnson, 1988). For example, Goldberg (1959) compared the ability of psychiatrists with that of their secretaries in diagnosing brain damage by using the Bender-Gestalt test. There was no difference between these two groups. And no relationship was found between individual diagnostic accuracy and degree of confidence. People, whether familiar with a domain or not, have difficulty integrating diverse sources of information as is required in clinical decisions and tend to make certain kinds of errors (such as being inconsistent in how data are combined), which decreases the accuracy of judgments. Clinicians as well as lay people often have incorrect views about chance. Experts as well as novices may be prey to a variety of illusions, such as the illusion that one can have control over an outcome when this is not possible.

Effective reasoning requires identification of relevant features of a situation. Ineffective reasoners may fail to note relevant features or may attend to irrelevant ones. Useful operations are also required, such as dividing a problem into subproblems and relating a problem to analogous ones. The importance of understanding a problem is stressed by all writers: before starting to think about how to solve a problem, it is important to identify the goal and to structure the problem in a useful way. Differences found between experts and novices include the following (Glaser & Chi, 1988; Nickerson et al., 1985, p. 69):

- They know more (for example, more strategies).
- They know that they know more.
- They demonstrate superior performance mainly in their own areas of expertise.
- They know better how to use what they know; they are faster than novices at solving problems.

- What they know is better organized; knowledge is arranged hierarchically, enabling recognition of large patterns.
- They represent problems at a deeper level compared to novices.
- What they know is more accessible; they have superior short-term and long-term memories.
- They have better learning skills.
- They are more likely to carry out an "executive review" of their reasoning process—to assume simultaneously the roles of doer and observer.
- They approach problems in different ways than do novices; they devote more time to analyzing a problem qualitatively.

Experts develop skill at metareasoning—planning their problem-solving approach, considering competing hypotheses, asking questions that will prime the use of helpful data, and reviewing assumptions in terms of their consistency with the evidence at hand. For example, expert physicists categorize problems by using essential information required to discover a solution, whereas novices attend to the superficial aspects of physics problems (Chi, Feltovich, & Glaser, 1980). Experts learn about possible causes associated with a given behavior, sign, or syndrome; this has been referred to as the "logical competitor set" (Feltovich, Johnson, Moller, & Swanson, 1984). Expert problem solving takes advantage of new possibilities as they arise; it is opportunistic (Lesgold et al., 1988).

Interviews of experts have been used in learning how they arrive at judgments. The information derived is used to develop computer expert systems; judgments given are codified into rules, which are referred to as the "knowledge base." A program is then developed that will simulate and (it is hoped) improve on human inferential reasoning (see, for example, Groen & Patel, 1988). Expert systems have been used to diagnose disease, to select antibiotics, and to play chess. In his review of the *Encyclopedia of Artificial Intelligence* (Shapiro, 1987), Medin (1989) notes major gains that he believes have resulted from the development and evaluation of artificial intelligence systems. These include encouraging clear description of the processes involved, appreciation of the complexity of judgmental tasks, the importance of common sense and knowledge of the everyday world, and the importance of controlling relevance.

Dreyfus and Dreyfus (1986) argue that artificial intelligence systems have not lived up to their promise because experts do not use rules to arrive at their decisions; therefore, it will do little good to interview the experts because they cannot describe how they arrive at their decisions. Thus, the experts themselves do not know what they know and therefore cannot tell it to investigators eager to identify the judgmental rules that are used in order to construct an expert system. Instead of using rules, Dreyfus and Dreyfus believe that the expert is recognizing "thousands of special cases" (p. 108). They argue that when experts are asked how they arrive at their decisions, they are forced to abandon the thinking system that they use as experts and to revert to the level of novices and describe rules they no longer use. Dreyfus and Dreyfus go further in their argument—experts may not even have access to these rules any longer. It is important to keep in mind that these authors are talking about unstructured problem areas—those in which the goal, the relevancy of information, and the effects of decisions are unclear (p. 36); these are the kinds of problems clinicians deal with. Skill in solving unstructured problems seems to require a great deal of experience with the domain. Experience permits the building of an "immense library of distinguishable situations" (p. 32). Chase and Simon (1973) estimate that a chess master can recognize 50,000 types of positions (Chase & Simon, 1973). Not only may these positions have no names, but they do not seem capable of being described verbally. Thus, Dreyfus and Dreyfus (1986) argue that expert behavior is not governed by rules and that it is not abstract. Some other investigators share this view; they argue that the basis of diagnostic expertise is the possession of a large memory store of symptom patterns, each of which is associated with a diagnosis and a course of action (see, for example, Feltovich et al., 1984). Practice alone, however, will not necessarily result in improved performance (see discussion of the limits of experience in Chapter 3).

Experts do not outperform novices under all circumstances. This finding (that, in unstructured problem areas, experts may make the same errors as novices) gave additional impetus to research concerning judgmental processes (see discussion of influences on clinical judgments in Chapter 2 and discussion of sources of error in causal analysis and prediction in Chapters 9 and 10).

The Costs and Benefits of Thinking

Like anything else, thinking carefully has advantages and disadvantages; there are long-term benefits for short-term investments (Hogarth, 1980). The tendency to overemphasize immediate costs in relation to future gains (Ainslie, 1975) is one obstacle to clear thinking. The benefits of thinking depend on individual goals and expectations. An interest in enhancing clinical competence as well as curiosity (valuing the search for evidence) and a desire to make decisions that are morally right encourage clear thinking.

The Benefits of Thinking. Baron (1985b) argues that characteristics that contribute to good citizenship should be valued and that rationality of thinking is one of these traits. "If rationality helps us to hold true beliefs and make good decisions, and if we concern ourselves with beliefs and decisions relevant to society, then rationality will help society make good collective decisions on the basis of available beliefs" (Baron, 1985b, p. 236).

Thinking more carefully about practice beliefs and judgments will increase the accuracy of clinical decisions. Informal fallacies and weak rhetorical appeals will be less likely to be influential, and clinicians will be more aware of biases that influence their judgments. Enhancing the quality of reasoning will offer new problem-solving skills that are useful in making clinical decisions, such as deciding which questions to ask, which data to gather, and which factors to relate to clinical problems. Selection of weak or ineffective intervention methods may be avoided by a search for alternative views of presenting problems. Clear thinking skills and empirically based content and procedural knowledge can be used to avoid errors, such as the fundamental attribution error in which environmental factors related to presenting problems are overlooked. For example, steps can be taken to decrease this source of error by paying greater attention to the role of significant others and involving these individuals in assessment and intervention. (Significant others are those who interact with clients and therefore influence their behavior.) This new focus often will prevent disruption of plans by significant others because these people will be involved in assessment and intervention.

Clarifying vague terms (such as *addiction, abuse, dementia,* and *self-determination*) will prevent misunderstandings between clinicians and their clients, as well as among clinicians, and will help avoid the "patient uniformity myth," in which clients and their problems are incorrectly assumed to be identical (Kiesler, 1966). Only when desired outcomes are clearly described, may it be obvious that, given the resources available, some are unattainable or conflict with other valued outcomes. Another benefit of clear thinking is clarification of values and preferences. Only when more thought is devoted to exploring preferences, may these be discovered. For example, a clinician may believe that she prefers behavioral assessment methods; however, inspection of her clinical practice may indicate otherwise.

Careful thinking about a decision will minimize regret. If advantages and disadvantages of alternative courses of action are identified at an early point, they are not as likely to come as a surprise after an option has been selected and acted on (Janis & Mann, 1977). Enhancing clinical decision-making skills will be helpful in recapturing a sense of discovery and curiosity in maintaining the positive challenges of clinical work and in encouraging an attitude of "constructive discontent" (Koberg & Bagnall, 1976). No doubt most clinicians find the process of clinical decision making fascinating and challenging. Others may lose this sense of positive challenge over the course of their careers as they labor in environments in which the match is not optimal between resources and either skills required or challenges offered. A sense of curiosity and discovery may be replaced by a mindless approach to work that is dull and dulling (Chanowitz & Langer, 1980).

Familiarity with persuasion strategies and informal fallacies will be helpful in upgrading the quality of clinical decisions made in all contexts: interviews with clients, case conferences, discussions with colleagues. I was quite mystified when low-level appeals were often successful in swaying colleagues. After becoming familiar with persuasive tactics and the variety of fallacies that may occur, as well as reasons for their effectiveness, I not only understood their popularity, but I was also better prepared to handle them. Argument-analysis skills are valuable in focusing on key assumptions and identifying the problems with a position. An emphasis on rationality—on arriving at accurate accounts—will encourage a collaborative approach to decision making and decrease the frequency of weak appeals and adversarial tactics.

Increasing content and procedural knowledge related to clinical decisions, as well as clear thinking skills and styles, increases the probability of selecting effective intervention methods. Clinicians are then in a better position to assess whether given outcomes can be pursued successfully. Some clinicians may believe that, because of the disparity between resources required to help some of their clients and the available resources, their hands are tied. In some instances, this may be true; at other times, there may be options for change. If options are available, then perceived constraints are artificial. It is disturbing to hear clinicians say "nothing can be done" when, in fact, if they were familiar with available content and procedural knowledge, they could do something. It is also distressing to see clinicians using personal counseling methods that have little or no impact on their clients' problems because other intervention methods will be required for their resolution. Although saying "nothing can be done" relieves clinicians of personal responsibility, it also leaves them helpless and leaves clients without the benefit of state-of-the-art methods.

Some clinicians believe that helping people is an art—that there is little if any empirical knowledge that can be used to increase the accuracy of clinical decisions and that, therefore, taking the time to become familiar with and to draw on this is not only a waste of time, it will diminish the quality of service because it will interfere with the spontaneity that is the heart of effective helping. Actually, there is evidence in many areas of clinical practice that certain decisions are better than others in terms of helping clients achieve desired outcomes (see, for example, Falloon, Boyd, & McGill, 1984; Sacco & Beck, 1985). What role should spontaneity have in clinical practice? Perhaps clinicians should ask themselves, "In what areas would I want my dentist or doctor to be spontaneous?" Spontaneity does have a role in selecting a method from several different methods to achieve a given outcome, when all the methods may be equally effective. For example, during a workshop with Salvador Minuchin, a member of the audience asked him, "How did you know to use that particular method at that exact time?" Minuchin replied that there were many different actions he could have taken at that point—that the important question was the objective sought; a variety of different methods could be used to attain it. People usually do not "optimize" (choose the best of all possible alternatives) but rather "satisfice" (seek a satisfactory option). Simon (1983) refers to this approach as "bounded rationality." There is indeed a role for responsible spontaneity in clinical practice. The role of creativity in reasoning is emphasized throughout this book.

Considerable time may be spent thinking about problems that are unsolvable (that is, there is little or nothing that can be done that would make the slightest difference). Conversely, too little thinking time may be devoted to problems that are resolvable. Increasing clear thinking skills will result in a wiser allocation of thinking time. Additional knowledge of different kinds of decision-making strategies and the situations in which these can be used most profitably will be available. In many situations, it may not be cost-effective to spend time trying to identify the optimal alternative since it may not make much difference what is done; that is, there may be a range of indifference within which any one of a number of options would be satisfactory. For example, perhaps any of several specific methods can be used with equal effectiveness to enhance client participation; then, trying to select the optimal one is a waste of time.

The Costs of Thinking. A review of the presumed costs of thinking reveals why so many people do not think carefully about their beliefs and the tasks they confront. There are social, psychological, and practical costs of thinking. The costs of thinking are usually overemphasized. For example, many people (including clinicians) falsely believe that only experts can understand what is going on in a field. The media perpetuate this belief, and scientists do too little to make their efforts accessible to those outside their field. In fact, many of the basic principles of an empirical approach are quite straightforward and easy to understand, even though these are not generally taught (Miller, 1987; Stevens, 1988). Consider the tendency of clinicians to search their memories for one or two supporting examples when they are asked about the accuracy of an assumption and to believe that these examples provide satisfactory evidence for their beliefs. It takes little training to realize that the case is far from settled (see Chapters Nine and Ten). An overestimate of the costs of thinking often is combined with an underestimate of the value of further thinking and an overconfidence in the thinking already done. These tendencies result in impulsive decision making (Baron, 1985). Reliance on a "makes-sense epistemology" (Perkins et al., 1983) encourages impulsive decisions (see discussion of empathic explanations in Chapter Four).

Making accurate clinical decisions may require additional time and effort in questioning initial hypotheses, gathering data to explore assumptions, and encouraging colleagues to consider alternatives. It often takes longer to refute an argument than it does to state a position. The benefits of thinking are usually in the future, whereas the costs in time, effort, and lost opportunities are usually immediate (Baron, 1985). Learning to question inferences requires the cultivation of compatible goals and beliefs (see Chapters Twelve and Thirteen). Effort will also be required to master knowledge that is a necessary adjunct to clear thinking. The time and effort involved in increasing clear thinking skills can be substantially reduced by using effective learning skills and helpful tools, as well as by encouraging compatible beliefs about knowledge, thinking, and learning that will make the process efficient and enjoyable rather than difficult and boring. Once statistical tools are mastered, using them to increase the likelihood of accurate decisions will take less time than will the usual intuitive means of making decisions (Nisbett, Krantz, Jepson, & Kunda, 1983).

Any extra time and effort devoted to clear thinking will be saved many times over in increased accuracy of clinical decisions. Errors in assessment or intervention may be discovered. Examination of practice assumptions and clinical reasoning processes may reveal beliefs that are poorly supported or inaccurate. An interest in protecting self-worth is a key factor in avoiding information that is not self-serving. Thinking requires a suspension of certainty; a tolerance for doubt. If self-efficacy is low, this tolerance probably has a narrow edge, resulting in neglect of sources of bias and disconfirming data. Belief that current preferences and judgments are fine "as is" is helpful in maintaining self-esteem and value in the eyes of others. Our biases and prejudices and patterns of thinking have served us well—at least so we think. Thinking about problems and issues entails the possibility of having to admit error.

Suggesting positions and questioning the views of others carries the risk of negative reactions from colleagues. Clear thinkers "act unsociably"; they want to question assumptions that "their peers take for granted" (Adler, 1987, p. 250). If self-efficacy is low and the desire for social approval is greater than the interest in identifying the best answer, divergent perspectives may not be shared. Even though clear thinking skills are used with consummate diplomacy, negative reactions may result. Complementing clear thinking skills with effective interpersonal skills and creating an environment that encourages high-quality clinical decision making will decrease the probability of negative reactions.

Careful consideration of options and assumptions may reveal additional sources of uncertainty. The complexity of the tasks clinicians confront challenge the clearest thinker. Dilemmas include (1) the tension between the need to act despite uncertainty and the desire for certainty and (2) the attempt to not impose personal biases while pursuing objectives to increase client options (Lenrow, 1978). Estimating the probability that an intervention method will be effective may reveal that it is relatively low. For example, in child protective agencies, social workers may have to tackle problems even though they realistically estimate the chances of success to be low. The likelihood that a parent may curtail the use of cocaine that interferes with adequate parenting of her child may be 10 percent, given available intervention options and resources. Still, the effort may have to be made in a context of permanency planning, in which other goals such as termination of parental rights can be pursued only after services have been provided to a parent and these have failed to alter problems. Being aware of the slim probability of effectiveness in this larger context should be helpful in highlighting the necessity of this step as well as in preventing clinicians from blaming themselves for lack of success, given that they have offered the best services possible. Not recognizing situations in which chances of success are slim is probably one factor that is associated with burnout (Maslach & Pines, 1979).

Most decisions involve costs as well as benefits. Thinking about a decision may reveal tradeoffs that have been ignored. People, clinicians included, are engaged in two tasks: (1) they seek to know more about the world and (2) at the same time, they wish to protect themselves from the world—especially from information that might prove upsetting (Rokeach, 1960). As the need for defense against disturbing information gets stronger, curiosity gets weaker.

Yet another cost is the time needed to critically review practice theories. Many clinicians accept practice beliefs without asking questions such as "Is it true?" "Is there any evidence that this assertion is correct?" "Would another explanation offer greater leverage in helping this client?" Not asking these questions saves time and effort. Also, if clinicians do not have facilitating beliefs and understanding about knowledge, thinking, and learning (see Chapter Three), avoiding these questions protects them from the frustration of seeking answers. Use of clear thinking skills will increase responsibility for providing the help that can be offered to clients and decrease tendencies to blame clients for resistance. Increased responsibility in the absence of skills to act effectively is unpleasant. No wonder so many people opt for answers based on inappropriate authority (see Chapter Five)—they do not realize that doing so limits their freedom (Fromm, 1963). The flip side of responsibility is freedom; giving up responsibility entails giving up freedom. Thinking clearly increases freedom from the unwanted influence of other people. Clinicians will move beyond acceptance of arguments simply because they "make sense" realizing that what makes sense is not necessarily true; uncritical acceptance of practice theories leaves clinicians at the mercy of what someone else thinks. One of the basic choices in life is whether to look or not look. Clear thinking skills increase a willingness to risk looking.

How Skeptical Should Clinicians Be?

A thoughtful approach to clinical decision making requires a skeptical attitude. How skeptical should clinicians be? They should be as skeptical as they have to be in order to arrive at accurate clinical decisions within a required time frame. Decisions must be made in spite of uncertainties. "Practitioners are asked to solve problems every day that philosophers have argued about for the last two thousand years and will probably debate for the next two thousand. Inevitably, arbitrary lines have to be drawn and hard cases decided" (Dingwall, Eekelaar & Murray, 1983, p. 244). As Thouless (1974, p. 166) points out, "What we do is more important than what we think." "So important is action that we can reasonably condemn as crooked thinking any device in thought which has as its purpose the evasion of useful or necessary action" (p. 166). People could not get through a day if they questioned every judgment. They cannot offer evidence for every belief that they hold. They must trust the "experts" for many of their beliefs—that is, they cannot offer evidence for many of the everyday decisions they make. The case is different for clinicians: they should be able to offer cogent reasons for selection of methods of assessment, intervention, and evaluation.

Summary

Decision making is at the heart of clinical practice. Decisions must be made on many different levels, including classifying clients into categories, making causal assumptions, and making predictions about the effectiveness of different kinds of interventions and future behavior of clients. Research suggests that errors occur because of misuse of generally effective information-processing strategies. Tendencies that decrease accuracy include discounting conflicting evidence, failing to search for disconfirming evidence, and holding a bias toward dispositional explanations. Clinicians who are psychoanalytically oriented tend to search for and attend to different factors than those who are behaviorally oriented; these selective searches influence clinical decisions. Clinical practice requires the integration of information from diverse sources, which places a strain on memory and on capacities to combine different kinds of data. Unique barriers to making sound decisions arise in clinical practice because of disagreements about criteria to be used to assess the accuracy of decisions, the cultural relativity of the definitions of personal troubles and social problems, and the gaps in knowledge about how to achieve given clinical outcomes. Research suggests that thinking skills can be enhanced and that helpful strategies for improving accuracy can be acquired. Decision making is viewed as a set of skills accompanied by beliefs and understanding about knowledge, thinking, and learning, which can be improved through guided practice.

Clear thinking involves long-term benefits for short-term investments. The benefits from enhancing clear thinking skills will far outweigh the costs if skills are used judiciously and diplomatically and effective learning skills are used. The benefits include increasing accuracy, recapturing a sense of discovery, and acquiring new reasoning skills. Other benefits include avoiding problems, increasing personal freedom, and allocating thinking time more wisely. Costs include the discovery of faulty beliefs and areas of uncertainty. Using clear thinking skills may result in negative reactions from colleagues and may increase personal responsibility because more accurate distinctions are possible between artificial and real constraints on achieving desired changes. Making the obscure less obscure requires time, effort, and skill. On the other hand, the costs of not devoting this time and effort are substantial. "In exchange for the time saved, clinicians must preserve and encourage unwanted complacency, unverified dogma, and self-perpetuating error" (Feinstein, 1967, p. 310).

Increasing the quality of clinical reasoning skills may encourage a reconsideration of the value and potential of pursuing valued goals that may have been abandoned; it may also result in a change of preferred practice theories. Most importantly, it enhances the quality of services offered to clients.

2

Sources of Influence
on Decisions
That Clinicians Make

Either a broad or narrow view can be taken concerning factors that influence clinical decision making. The narrowest view focuses only on the interaction between clients and clinicians—how they influence each other within the clinical interview. Considerable research has been conducted in this environment focusing on micro components of client-therapist interchanges. Truax's work (1966) demonstrated that, despite Rogers's (1957) statement that the nondirective therapist provides a nonevaluative reflective mirror, even nondirective therapists influence clients. An understanding of the variables that affect clinical decisions requires a much broader exploration of environments—past, present, and future; it is not enough to confine attention to the clinical interview. Decisions made in clinical interviews are influenced by past environments (such as clinical training programs and the social-historical conditions within which practice theories and service-delivery systems emerge), current environments (such as the organization in which many clinicians work and the current milieu in which social problems are defined), and future environments (hoped-for futures). Only by understanding how these environments influence clinical practice can the nature of clinical decisions be understood and changed in major ways (see, for example, Burnham, 1988).

Psychotherapy is a highly political enterprise. Given the relativity of the definition of problems and differences of opinion about what kinds of help should be offered, it could not help but be so. That is why it is so important for clinicians to be informed about the history of psychiatric treatment, which illustrates the value-laden base of psychotherapy. Political, social, and economic considerations influence which problems are defined as "in need of treatment." For example, as the number of clinicians has expanded so, too, has the number of "conditions" that need treatment.

The particular settings in which clinicians work influence the kinds of clients and problems encountered. Both private and agency-based practice exist in a larger environment that influences decisions. Concerns about funding and the need to respond to and consider reactions of outside pressure groups are influential in agency-based practice. Beliefs about the "overall task environment" play an important role. A psychiatrist may believe that working-class clients are not as likely to respond well to insight-oriented approaches as more educated middle-class clients are and so may recommend different treatment approaches for working-class clients. Clinicians have "scripts" for gathering information from different kinds of clients. The nature of feedback provided is influenced by these initial beliefs that may, in turn, alter the task environment. For example, if clinicians believe that poor, relatively nonverbal clients are not good candidates for counseling, they may not try as hard to engage such clients, and, as a consequence, clients may drop out (prematurely terminate treatment). This may confirm original beliefs. Diagnostic labels must often be applied to clients, and these labels may influence subsequent reactions.

It is not surprising that clinicians may believe that what they do when with clients and how clients think, act, and feel during clinical interviews is influenced solely by the nature of the transactions during clinical interviews. Clinical training may not provide students with an understanding of historical and structural factors that influence the development of professional practice (Mills, 1959). The attention of clinicians on a day-to-day basis is on individual clients and families; it is easy to forget to step back to view the larger picture within which clinical practice takes place. It is always difficult to step outside our usual way of viewing things and consider different perspectives. New perspectives often diverge considerably from currently accepted views making it a challenge to accurately understand other views so that one is in an informed position to decide whether to accept or reject them. The day-to-day concerns of practice easily lull even informed clinicians into complacent acceptance of societal definitions of personal troubles, social problems, and proposed solutions, forgetting the relativity of these definitions and preferred approaches to resolving problems. Consider, for example, the social pressure on women who are overweight (according to our societal definitions) to shed pounds and the acceptance of this goal by clinicians. Why not concentrate on altering how significant others respond to excess weight?

Socioeconomic factors directly influence the problems of drug abuse. Is it odd that crack cocaine is so widely used among poor, unemployed people? "A 42-year-old mother struggling to escape her addiction to crack cocaine warned members of the San Francisco Board of Supervisors yesterday about the terrible power of the drug, which is threatening the economic and social health of the city. [She] told the board's Health and Human Services Committee that she began using the potent form of cocaine as an escape from a life of abuse and poverty in one of the city's public housing projects. 'Crack cocaine was my doctor, my lawyer, my lover,' she told the supervisors. 'It became everything to me because I didn't have to think about the pain any more'" (Gordon, 1989, p. 1). Should the focus of drug problems be on users rather than on environmental conditions that encourage substance abuse? Isn't this like waiting until people are exposed to asbestos poisoning and then treating them (Sedgwick, 1982)? Who would lose and who would benefit from decriminalizing use of controlled substances (Best, 1988)? Lack of attention to the larger picture encourages blaming personal problems on individuals rather than realizing that political, economic, and social factors are responsible for many personal problems.

Another situation in which the big picture is ignored is that of individuals who are encouraged to seek treatment for their "alcoholism" while environmental factors that contribute to drinking (such as poverty, unemployment, and the multimillion-dollar advertising of alcoholic beverages) are often ignored. (In 1988, a total of $1,340 million was spent on alcohol advertising. [Marinucci, 1989, p. D-1]). Who benefits and loses from acceptance of a disease model of alcoholism, in which attribution for the problem is placed on the individual? What is the impact of such an attribution on the alcohol industry, the way in which resources are distributed in a society, and the mental health industry? Who benefits from blaming the problems of unemployment among black youth on these individuals themselves?

One of the purposes of this book is to encourage clinicians to consider the social and political functions of psychiatric and psychological ideologies—to move beyond preferred practice theories to ask: Where do these theories come from? What particular views of reality do they espouse? Which views do they obscure or actively suppress? Who benefits from a given view of pathology and health? What consequences will occur if a given view is accepted or rejected? Asking these questions will help guard the values of freedom and reasoned consideration of key issues (Mills, 1959). It is the question that is not asked that poses the greatest danger to freedom. Freedom is not just choosing among the alternatives; it is having a say about what alternatives are considered (Mills, 1959).

The Role of Political, Economic, and Social Factors

Clinicians as well as clients are influenced by the historical epoch in which they live and work; they are influenced by this in the definition of both personal troubles and social problems, as well as in proposed resolutions. Only by understanding the structural and political preconditions within which the current mental health system developed and is maintained can the nature of clinical decisions be understood and the limitations and potential of the helping professions be accurately assessed. Without such an understanding, the relativity of clinical decisions will not be appreciated, and questionable decisions are likely to be made. For example, decisions to intervene may be made when there is no justifiable reason to do so, a decision may be made not to intervene when intervention would help clients to enhance the quality of their lives, or ineffective intervention methods may be chosen.

A historical understanding of the different ways in which deviance has been defined reveals the value-laden basis of definitions of individual troubles and social problems: consider, for example, the movement from calling certain individual variations in behavior sinful, then criminal, then indications of mental illness (Scheff, 1984a, 1984b; Szasz, 1970). Studies of clinical decision making suggest that decisions are often based on beliefs about the moral character of clients rather than on objective accounts based on empirically grounded theories of behavior. There is a close relationship between explanation and evaluation (see discussion of empathic explanations in Chapter Four). Decisions must often be made concerning the intentionality of an act. The question of intention highlights the moral aspect of decisions—that is, the client "knowingly" selected one way to act from a variety of options. The choice made characterizes the kind of person the client is; that is, it is a reflection of moral character. The relation between judgments of moral character and ascriptions of deviance is emphasized by sociologists and often neglected by clinicians.

Imputations of moral character (as distinguished from objective descriptions) may be conveyed in the way clients and their actions are described as well as in treatment methods selected. A concern with whether applicants for services are worthy of receiving aid has a long history in the helping professions (Leiby, 1978). The ascribed nature of deviance is shown by changing definitions of deviance and different perspectives concerning society's responsibility in relation to groups such as the homeless, the poor, the sick, the abused, and the neglected. If deviance is an ascribed rather than inherent status, then there is room to build a case for or against ascriptions. The allegation of a certain kind of character may rest on a retrospective analysis of past behavior and predictions of future behavior as well as descriptions of current behavior. The manner in which a case can be built is illustrated in the example given in Chapter Eleven.

The development of a discipline (for example, psychology) or profession (for example, social work) occurs in a particular political, economic, and social context that influences what is created. Social work has long been concerned with its second-class image in relation to psychiatry and has been influenced by this concern, for example, by buying into the psychiatric view of human behavior. Psychology has been occupied with establishing and defending its scientific credibility and its objectivity. Morawski (1987) notes, "The drives for cooperation, organized research, integration, and unified science undoubtedly served economic ends" (p. 168). Badinter (1980) proposes that the notion of "mother love" arose only recently when it became necessary to convince mothers that care of their children was critical in order to provide needed human resources to maintain the state and that the modern-day concept of mother love stemmed from idealization sponsored by the state. This view is quite different from psychological discussions of mother love.

It has been argued that the modern concept of the self is also relatively recent in origin, being dependent on reliance on the clock (Verhave & Van Hoorn, 1984). Thus, industrialization needs of the state and technology encourage the development of certain views about people. Clients who have trouble getting to work on time or arriving at clinical interviews on time may have views of time different from the employers or counselors. An interest in psychological factors is more prominent in rights-based cultures, such as the United States, than in duty-based cultures, such as the Hindu (Shweder & Miller, 1985). In rights-based cultures, emphasis is placed on personal decision making; in duty-based cultures, moral actions are defined as those that are compatible with the natural order. Both clinicians and clients in the United States live in an intensely psychological era in which alternative therapies have expanded enormously, in which therapy as entertainment or as spectacle is common. Hundreds may attend a lecture by a famous clinician. Hundreds of thousands of psychological self-help books are sold every year. A focus on the individual is a hallmark of what Beit-Hallahmi (1987) calls the "non-symptomatic psychotherapy subculture," which consists of those who seek counseling not to alleviate symptoms but to facilitate self-understanding and self-improvement. "A subculture of psychotherapy exists when a significant minority of individuals in any society are committed to secular psychotherapy as a way of finding meaning to their lives. This is shown by the commitment of time and money, and the emotional investment involved" (p. 481). This subculture is especially prominent in large urban centers in the United States, such as Boston, New York, and Los Angeles.

An important byproduct of critical school analysis has been greater sensitivity to the value implications of psychological theory (Gergen, 1987; Scheper-Hughes & Lovell, 1987). Take, for example, Gilligan's work (1982) on sexist bias in psychological theory and Sampson's argument (1977) that psychological theory supports individualism and discourages recognition of our interdependency. Lack of knowledge about the intellectual history of different psychological conceptions limits awareness of the value biases inherent in given views. Not considering the larger picture leaves clinicians open to influence by concepts and perspectives that they may reject if they considered the social and political repercussions of such concepts. Knowledge about the intellectual history of a discipline or practice perspective will increase appreciation on the part of empirically oriented clinicians that complete objectivity is impossible and, on the other hand, will correct misunderstandings among intuitive clinicians about potential contributions of a scientific approach to practice. Lack of familiarity with the intellectual history of a field leaves clinicians prey to repeating rather than building on past debates. For example, some writers contend that current discussions of the role of thoughts are largely repetitions of earlier ones. In a more concrete example, those who recommend the expansion of private prisons often do not mention that there were many private prisons in the early part of this century, but they were closed and care of prisoners was returned to the state because of poor and brutal treatment of prisoners (D'Iulio, 1988).

Some have argued that the prime function of mental health professionals is to encourage the values compatible with a capitalistic culture (Ehrenreich & Ehrenreich, 1977). Critics of the mental health services such as Basaglia (in Scheper-Hughes & Lovell, 1987) believe that many people (including clinicians) do not understand economic requirements of capitalistic societies such as the United States and the effects of these requirements (such as invalidating and controlling individuals who do not contribute to productivity: the unemployed, the disabled, and the elderly, to name but a few). Clinicians are viewed as conscious or unconscious functionaries involved in imposing an ideology of health care and treatment on clients; social scientists are viewed as offering legitimation and jus-tification for such practices that, although they seem to be universal for all citizens, meet the needs of the dominant group and control or restrain the needs of the dominated groups (Scheper-Hughes & Lovell, 1987, p. 155). Clinicians are quite right to reject and to be skeptical of this inappropriate use of science (see also discussion of the scientific method in Chapter Three); "collective social problems are redefined as smaller, localized community problems, giving peo-ple a false perspective about where the problems originate and how they might be resolved. When superficial changes are made on the community level, the larger social and political issues that are at the root of the oppression and the deviance of marginal groups are depoliticized and atomized" to protect the interests of dominant vested interests (Scheper-Hughes & Lovell, 1987, p. 99; see also Man-ning, 1985; Berger & Luckman, 1966).

Mental health services expanded during the community mental health movement, and the number of mental health profes-sionals increased greatly. Critics argue that this expansion was not really in the interests of the clients served but, on the contrary, was in the interests of expanding boundaries of attempted imposition of normative values and containment of unproductive deviance. Basa-glia wrote, "Otherwise, there is no explanation for the overempha-sis on health services rather than on the quality of the treatment provided" (Scheper-Hughes & Lovell, 1987, p. 155). "If the reha-bilitation goals of both institutions [prisons and asylums] were genuine, one would find rehabilitated patients and prisoners rein-tegrated into society" (pp. 207–208). Illich (1976) argues that hos-pitals and drugs harm more people than they cure. Sources of human misery that are related to environmental factors and that create deviant behavior are falsely attributed to individual charac-teristics ("mental illness") and thus encapsulated. Special service-delivery systems can then be created for these individuals, and these systems become a source of jobs for professionals. In fact, when a service is created for a given group of people, the number of members who are in need of such services increases rather than decreases; "any new service should reduce illness, since it was created to meet an unfilled functional need. Instead, like every in-stitution within the productive cycle, the new service can only look to its own survival. Its goal is production and the patient becomes an object in its grip and not the subject for whom the service was created" (Basaglia in Scheper-Hughes & Lovell, 1987, p. 114).

Decisions about who should receive services and what services should be provided are influenced by available resources both in private as well as agency-based practices. Resources available are directly related to political, economic, and ideological influences in a society. For example, some people believe that few resources were initially provided to prevent and find a cure for acquired immunodeficiency syndrome (AIDS) because this problem primarily affects minority populations. Three options are possible when resources are scarce. One is to widen the definition of a resource. This often occurs in private practice. For example, a clinician in private practice may decide that since no relapse-prevention program is available in his geographical area that would be best for a client with a substance-abuse problem, he will offer another kind of intervention. Widening the definition of resources may work for or against clients; it works against them if the new resources selected are not as helpful. The second option is to increase the threshold for deciding that treatment is required. This often occurs in agency-based practice. One of the major conclusions made by Dingwall and his colleagues (1983) following their observation of work in British child protective agencies was the reluctance of staff to identify child maltreatment. That is, professionals tailored their decisions to the resources available. These authors highlighted the relativistic nature of clinical decisions, noting that social workers are continually admonished to consider the individual needs and norms of different groups: that what may constitute child abuse in one group may not in another and that this relativistic view prevents the system from being overwhelmed by new cases. Often, neglectful circumstances were excused even when clients did have some control over them.

A third option when resources are scarce is to focus on problems for which resources are plentiful (see Chapter Nine). Clinicians do not have the resources to alleviate severe material deprivation and so often focus instead on problems that they can help resolve, such as interpersonal concerns. This may result in undue attention to factors such as client compliance and cooperation as indicators of moral character (Dingwall et al., 1983). A large gap between what can be done and what is needed (whether due to lack of skills on the part of clinicians or lack of community resources) may encourage negative reactions toward clients (if their presence is a reminder of a limited ability to be of help), or problems of secondary interest to clients may be focused on. The second and third options have been carried to an extreme in the case of homelessness. Denial is at a peak in terms of citizens (clinicians among them) passing homeless people sitting, lying, or begging on the street every day. According to Sedgwick (1982), too often a request for greater resources "amounts to a request for some form of tardy and individualized intervention in a problem that should be met in preventative terms implicating the wider social and political system" (Sedgwick, 1982, p. 195).

Professional organizations influence clinical decisions in a variety of ways both in terms of what they do and, perhaps even more importantly, in what they do not do. They influence both private and agency-based practices by helping to set standards for licensing—they therefore influence who is allowed to practice. They also influence practice by engaging in political activities to protect and expand their turf, as shown by the intense struggle between psychologists and psychiatrists about who should have control over diagnosis and treatment of clients (see, for example, Buie, 1987; 1989). The American Psychological Association has a "Defense Fund" that distributed sixty awards totaling $286,000 in 1984–1985 (staff, *APA Monitor,* August 1985, p. 57) (see also discussion of Newsspeak in Chapter Five).

Assumptions made by Western clinicians may be quite inappropriate when applied to non-Western clients. Sharp differences are seen in the expression of a problem like schizophrenia, and other differences include the greater role of physical complaints among Asian clients, differences in how children are raised (making children sleep alone is seen as a punishment in India or Japan), and differences in the sense of an individual self (much less among Asians than among Americans) (Bond, 1986; Lock, 1982). Seeking help from a mental health center is more likely to be viewed as a stigma in Asian cultures, whereas experience in therapy is the norm in some Western communities. Problems such as agoraphobia are rarely seen in non-Western countries, and problems such as "koro" (panic reactions due to fear that one's penis or nipples will retract into the body and cause death) that occur among the Chinese are unknown in the West. If these differences are not recognized, quite inappropriate clinical decisions may be made concerning non-Western clients.

Confining attention to the clinical interview when attempting to understand sources of influence on clinical decisions is like trying to understand the circulatory system from the perspective of a single red blood cell. If clinicians are informed about the economic, social, and political factors that influence practice, they are less likely to ignore environmental factors related to personal troubles and social problems.

The Influence of Agency Variables

The nature of the practice setting, private or agency-based, influences options for increasing the quality of clinical decisions. It is generally accepted today that behavior is influenced both by personal as well as environmental factors (Bandura, 1986). Both sources of influence should be considered when thinking about how the environment influences clinical decisions. Many practitioners work in some kind of organization such as a community mental health center or hospital (see, for example, Berger, Jurkovic and Associates, 1984). Increasingly, public agencies contract out services to private practitioners. An understanding on the part of private practitioners about factors that influence agency-based practice will be helpful in understanding the constraints and options that exist in such practice. Qualities of agency environments that influence decisions include preferred views of clients, status and power differences, social and time pressures, and beliefs about the importance of different kinds of tasks. Whether clear thinking skills are used depends in part on the incentives provided in clinical contexts.

Although there is an overlap in the factors that influence decisions in private and agency-based practice, there are differences as well. Professionals in private practice can control whom they see; they can filter out clients they do not want to work with. In a recent dialogue among social workers in private and agency-based practices, one private practitioner proudly announced that she refused to see anyone who had a cocaine or alcohol problem—telling them to "get rid of their habit" and then she would see them. The situation is quite different in agency-based practice, in which practitioners have much less control over whom they will see. Special considerations arise in contexts in which involuntary intrusion into individual or family life occurs, such as in child protective services or enforced hospitalization of mentally ill patients. Decisions are influenced by the constraints and options that are uniquely created by compromises made by participants in the decision-making process, such as the state, the community, and the professionals who carry out the supposed intent of society's position. Sources of influence on decisions made in agencies include the following:

- nonvoluntary aspects of the context (for example, criminal justice and child welfare settings)
- different kinds of professionals involved
- clarity of agency policy
- preferred-practice theories
- funding sources
- procedures related to accountability
- vulnerability to scandal (newspaper stories)
- training of staff
- power differentials among professionals

Research investigating decisions made in the criminal justice systems (for example, Emerson, 1969), commitment hearings (Decker, 1987; Pfohl, 1978), and child protective services (for example, Dingwall et al., 1983) reveal biasing factors that influence decisions.

Status and Power Differences. Power differences between agency staff and clients favor staff, especially in nonvoluntary settings. This difference allows staff and their representatives (such as attorneys) to have an influential role in the negotiation of clinical decisions, such as whether to return a child to the parents' care. Jacobs (1985), for example, presents a case in which parental and agency reports of what would be in "the best interests of the child" differed greatly. The court had to decide who had the authoritative version. The mother wanted her daughter returned to her care. Jacobs argues that the agency's power and status were used to create a credibility for its version that was greater than the credibility of the mother's version and that this was accomplished through "strategic written maneuvers in constructing the official court report," so that the mother's version of the best interests was discredited and the agency's version was viewed as the correct account (p. 80). Identical factual evidence was given quite different interpretations consistent with the goal of the person presenting the view. Those with power in an agency are often interested in retaining it and may view attempts to share power as threatening. An objection to a more systematic method for clinical decision making may actually reflect a more basic concern with keeping privileged positions.

The history of psychiatric care is replete with examples of the invasive exercise of power by staff over hospitalized patients. Alleviating punitive environments for mental patients who are under the control of psychiatric staff has been the major aim of antipsychiatric politics (Sedgwick, 1982).

Limited Access to Information. Access to some environments is at the discretion of those who inhabit them, as in the case of health care visitors who can only enter clients' homes with the permission of parents. Clumsy efforts to do so may result in a complete lack of access to the premises. Although some factors that limit access to information are insurmountable, others are discretionary or self-imposed. For example, a clinician may decide not to collect observational data in real-life settings, even though there is time to do so and such data would be helpful. Different kinds of professionals have access to different kinds of information. A physician in an emergency room, especially one who is not familiar with the local community in which a client resides, may ignore or not have information about a family's social situation that may be helpful in making a decision about the cause of a child's injuries (Dingwall et al., 1983). The physician may have access to medical evidence of child abuse but no data about social evidence or even moral evidence (data about the moral character of clients).

Agency policy concerning record keeping and evaluation influences the quality of information that is available. Vagueness rather than clarity may be preferred. Clinicians may find it difficult to continue careful evaluation in a climate that favors sloppy evaluation.

Preferred Views of Clients. Settings differ in the views of clients that are encouraged. Strong (1979) studied decisions made in pediatric outpatient clinics and found that parents were assumed to be honest, competent, and caring and that the disorders of their children were assumed to be natural events. If the physicians discovered evidence that contradicted this view, they engaged in exchanges designed to reconceptualize the parent's character. Today, child abuse and neglect has received increased attention, and different assumptions may be made. The opposite tendency may now be present, in which parents are under excessive suspicion concerning a child's injuries or failure to thrive. Whether this suspicion is acted on may be tempered by the "rule of optimism" (defined below). Studies of workers in welfare offices reveal that clients are often viewed as liars and manipulators (Blau, 1960). Wills (1978) argues that this occurs because workers make personal attributions about the cause of client behaviors; they overlook the influence of the situation, in which applicants are dependent on the decisions of the social worker. Clinicians prefer clients who are manageable and treatable (see later section). Clinicians' views of clients are also related to the match between staff, clients, and preferred-practice theories.

Favored or Tolerated Appeals and Political Tactics. Clinicians differ in the kinds of appeals and political maneuvers that they favor or tolerate. Such preferences will influence the quality of decisions in agency-based practice. Just as there are a variety of methods that can be used to discourage change, there are many that can be used to increase the likelihood of a change. The term *stratagem* refers to cunning methods of achieving or maintaining an end (that is, trickery). One strategem that may be used is manipulation of information. Only some alternatives may be presented, data can be displayed in such a way as to obscure rather than clarify what is actually happening (see, for example, *How to Lie with Statistics,*

Huff, 1954). Doubts about a disliked position can be created by spreading rumors. "Once suspicions, apprehensions, or misgivings are created, people will be misled by the old adage 'where there is smoke there is fire!' However, both the smoke and the fire may be illusory" (Michalos, 1971, pp. 100–101).

Negative labels may be applied to people who raise questions. Rather than thank a colleague who questions a diagnosis, labels such as "uninformed" or "naive" may be applied to the "questioner" to discourage unwanted influences. Consider, for example, how whistleblowers are often treated. If negative labels and innuendos stick, staff may avoid the troublemaker, not wanting to be guilty by association. Stonewalling can be used to block change; verbal statements in favor of a decision may be made without doing anything to implement it. Administrators may reaffirm their agreement with an idea by setting a specific date to accomplish a certain task but take no steps to put it into effect. The maneuver of stonewalling occurs anytime someone grants a request but fails to deliver.

Another stratagem is staff reorganization. This deflects attention from other matters and may juggle responsibilities so that people with opposing views are in less advantageous positions. There are many other stratagems available for use. An administrator may request a study to gain more data relevant to a decision; this may preclude action for weeks or months. In an appeal to no precedent it is assumed that if something has not been done by now, there is no good reason it should be done; the idea is that we (or you) would have discovered and corrected it by now if the disputed practice is a poor one. No evidence for or against the wisdom of the proposed change is offered. Tokenism refers to making minimal, unsatisfactory efforts and acting as if they are adequate. Impossible deadlines may be insisted on, thus restricting time for careful consideration of alternatives. Agreement on a small decision may be sought that can then be appealed to make subsequent larger decisions. It is often argued that the end justifies the means, that even though there are disadvantages to the route suggested, it provides a way to achieve valued outcomes and is therefore justified. It may be argued that even though the use of aversive methods are objectionable, these are used to achieve the valued end of decreasing assaultive behavior—

even though it has not been shown that positive methods have been tried and have failed to achieve this goal. It may be argued that because an idea is new, it is ipso facto good. This stratagem is the converse of the no-precedent fallacy. People who use this tactic may attempt to portray an advocate of other positions, especially those that have been or are being used, as a stick-in-the-mud who is not au courant.

Power relations in an agency may be concealed or denied. This is one way in which a given ideology is maintained (Thompson, 1987). For example, in an agency, there may be an "old boys group" or "old girls group" that makes all the important decisions. However, this may be denied by members of this group. One of the oldest ways to dilute competitive power is to divide and conquer—to create divisiveness among potentially competing groups. As long as they are busy arguing with each other, they will not pose a threat.

Other Factors. Clinical settings differ in terms of what behaviors are reinforced, ignored, or punished—that is, in terms of the contingencies in effect. Often, no positive feedback is provided for competencies that enhance the quality of clinical decisions. Helpful behaviors may even be punished, as when clinicians are criticized for evaluating their work by collecting self-monitored or observational data or are considered obsessive because of an interest in setting clear objectives. Administrators and supervisors often attend to behaviors they do not like, neglecting behaviors they want to see more often; they focus on catching staff doing something wrong rather than catching staff performing competently. Supervisors may ignore approximations to desired outcomes, such as asking particular questions, doing a task correctly even though it is late, or completing part of a task correctly.

Settings differ in the social pressure to conform to the majority view. For example, there may be only one psychoanalytically oriented clinician in an agency in which most staff members prefer a behavioral approach. Alternative views concerning presenting problems may be dismissed immediately rather than explored by weighing the evidence for different views. Attempts to present divergent accounts may gradually wane. Clinical decisions are often made in a very brief time—especially in view of the consequences that ride on such decisions. Studies of psychiatric commitment hearings show that only a few minutes are devoted to each decision (Decker, 1987; Scheff, 1984b). It is no wonder that decisions are not optimal in noisy offices with ringing phones and constant interruptions—the environment in which many practitioners carry out their daily work: These distractions interfere with concentration. Although some clinicians may flourish under such conditions, others will be adversely affected. Whether performance is compromised depends on the skills required to carry out a task (Hockey, 1984). "Kant did some of his best thinking in bed with blankets wrapped around him in a special way; Dr. Johnson needed a purring cat, orange peel, and tea; and Schiller filled his desk with rotten apples" (Yinger, 1980, p. 27).

Personal beliefs, as well as generally accepted views within an organization or profession, influence the perceived importance of different kinds of clinical tasks. Dingwall and his colleagues (1983) noted that physicians considered conducting assessments as "a rather low grade use of medical time" (p. 51). This view may decrease the care with which assessments are conducted and thus the quality of decisions made. Pressures to act quickly may result in an underestimation of the importance of careful assessment. Staff turnover also compromises the quality of decisions. In agency-based practice, a family may have many different workers during one year. Rather than building on what has gone before, new staff members often approach a case as a tabula rasa, with little regard for prior data collected or recommendations made. Earlier decisions often are not honored by new workers who do not know the entire case history. The initial tendency is to think the best about a family (the rule of optimism) and then to become disillusioned over time as efforts fail (Dingwall et al., 1983, p. 76).

Ignorance is not bliss in relation to the understanding of how the environment influences feelings, thoughts, and behaviors. Lack of appreciation for the influence of environmental factors results in misattributions for lack of success, which poses a significant obstacle to improvement of clinical decisions. Clinicians may blame themselves for faults that have little or nothing to do with the quality of their clinical skills but everything to do with the society in which they practice; clients may be blamed; or all blame may be mistakenly placed on environmental limitations, and options for altering these constraints may be overlooked. Not identifying the true obstacles, the clinician is unlikely to take effective action. Rather, a bad situation is accepted prematurely. Procedures, policies, and habits that interfere with effective decision making may be accepted as a fait accompli when, in fact, change is possible.

Psychological Factors That Influence Clinical Judgments

Clinicians are influenced by their emotional reactions in their day-to-day work with clients. Emotional reactions affect what clinicians notice, what they recall, how they organize information, and the predictions they make. Even small changes in mood and arousal level may influence judgments. For example, male subjects rated nudes as more attractive after a vigorous workout on an exercycle than they did before the workout (Cantor, Zillmann, & Bryant, 1975). Subjects who received a small gift rated TVs and cars more positively than those who received no gift (Isen, Shalker, Clark, & Karp, 1978). Descriptions of familiar people given while subjects were happy were charitable, loving, and generous compared with the fault-finding descriptions given when subjects were angry (Bower & Cohen, 1982). Affect also influences memory; events are recalled that match current mood (Teasdale & Fogarty, 1979). We tend to think positive thoughts when we are in a good mood and tend to think of negative experiences when we are depressed (Isen et al., 1978). Depressed people have a greater tendency to focus on themselves, to make internal attributions for negative events, and to give up after failure (Pyszczynski & Greenberg, 1985).

These sources of influence may affect clinical judgments. For example, clinicians remember better those events that match their current mood and ask more questions about such events. If clinicians are sad, they may attend more to risks and negative events than if they are happy, in which case they may underemphasize risks and obstacles. The clinician's mood is influenced by the client, as well as by external factors such as an argument with a significant other or an arduous commute in heavy traffic. (For a review of the effects of mood on a clinician's memory, see Salovey & Turk, 1988.) Negative affect related to fear of failure or a seemingly insoluble problem may disrupt performance. Clinicians differ in their style of approaching problems and in their dispositions toward handling uncertainty and risk (Brim & Hoff, 1957). Positive affect facilitates learning and problem solving; it seems to promote flexibility, which is an important aspect of creative thinking (Isen, 1987). Being aware of such influences increases the likelihood that they, and their possible effects on decisions, will be identified.

Decisions are influenced by motivational variables as well. For example, the likelihood of preferred outcomes is overestimated. Janis and Mann (1977) describe many disastrous results of the influence of motivational variables on decisions, such as the 1941 failure to take preventative action despite the concrete evidence that Pearl Harbor would be attacked. Tuchman (1984) discusses other historical examples of the influence of motivational variables on judgments, such as the decision by the Trojans not to examine the wooden horse before allowing it into their city. Clinicians differ in their beliefs about degree of personal responsibility for problems and solutions (McGovern, Newman, and Kopta, 1986). Negative events may be more likely to be attributed to environmental factors when clients and clinicians are similar than when they are different (Jordan, Harvey, & Weary, 1988).

Information-processing strategies influence decisions, and many writers emphasize these as a key source of judgmental errors. Clinicians must go beyond the information at hand in making decisions because they rarely (if ever) have all relevant data. Simplifying strategies must be used to manage the data on hand. Two tools that are used for this are knowledge structures (theories and preconceptions) and judgmental strategies (heuristics) such as availability (the accessibility of events and concepts in our perceptions, memory, or imagination) and representativeness (the extent to which events appear to resemble each other) (Tversky & Kahneman, 1973, 1974; Kahneman and Tversky, 1973). An example of the influence of resemblance criteria is the tendency to predict the likelihood of given outcomes on the basis of the similarity of a predictor to an outcome. For example, if a psychologist finds that a client has a high D (depression) scale on the Minnesota Multiphasic Personality Inventory (MMPI), he may make a diagnosis based on this indicator since the predictor seems representative of (similiar to) the criterion.

However, elevated D scores have little predictive validity when used alone. An example of the influences of availability on judgment of causal relationships (Kahneman & Tversky, 1973) is the tendency of observers to attribute behavior to characteristics of the person rather than to situational factors; the actor's behavior is more noticeable compared to more static situational events. We are influenced by the relative ease of recalling instances or behaviors or events when we try to estimate frequency.

Nisbett and Ross (1980) argue that most inferential and judgmental errors are due to the overuse of generally correct intuitive strategies (such as the application of preexisting knowledge) and the underuse of certain formal, logical statistical strategies (see Chapters Nine and Ten) "In ordinary social experience, people often look for the wrong data, often see the wrong data, often retain the wrong data and often make wrong inferences on the basis of their understanding of the data" (Nisbett & Ross, 1980, p. 12). Investigators differ in how prevalent they believe such tendencies to be in real-life contexts; however, there is general agreement that they are of concern (Jungermann, 1983; Wallsten, 1983). Motivational and informational sources of error interact in various ways. Clinicians are most likely to miss biases in situations in which they are biased for (or against) a certain point of view and the informational source contains the same bias. Bias can intrude at any point in the judgmental process and may also occur because of interactions between different stages of data processing (Hogarth, 1980). "First, the acquisition of information from both the environment and memory can be biased. The crucial issue here is how certain information does or does not become salient. Second, the manner in which information is processed can be biased; for example, if the individual simplifies the judgmental situation by using an inappropriate mental strategy. Third, the manner in which the person is required to respond can induce bias . . . Finally . . . outcomes of judgment can induce bias in both: (1) interpretation of their significance (for example, is the outcome attributable to one's actions or simply a chance fluctuation?); and (2) learning relationships for predictive validity" (Hogarth, 1980, p. 158).

Preconceptions and theories influence how client problems and possible resolutions are conceptualized. Clinicians could not function without preconceptions, and often these are helpful. At other times, they involve systematic errors (errors in the direction of some bias in contrast to random errors that may cancel each other out) and result in incorrect inferences. "The impact of preconceptions is one of the better demonstrated findings of twentieth-century psychology" (Nisbett & Ross, 1980, p. 67). Preconceptions can lead to incorrect inferences when (1) a theory is held on poor grounds (there is not adequate reason to believe that it is relevant); (2) a theory is used unconsciously; and (3) use of the theory "preempts examination of the data" (Nisbett & Ross, 1980, p. 71). All three bases are common in clinical practice. Practitioners often hold theories that have no empirical support as dearly as theories that do have support, are often unaware of preconceptions that influence their decisions, and often do not check out their preconceptions by examining outcomes. Overconfidence in and availability of a theory increase the likelihood of biased preconceptions. The more ambiguous the data are, the more the descriptions are influenced by preconceptions. Clinicians differ in how open they are to examining their beliefs and decisions. Dispositions that influence critical thinking, such as curiosity and open-mindedness, are as important as clear thinking skills (see Chapter Nine).

Clinicians are influenced by the vividness of material in collecting, organizing, and interpreting data. Vivid information is more likely to be remembered than pallid information, thus it is more available (Nisbett & Ross, 1980; Taylor, Fiske, Close, Anderson, Ruderman, 1979). Factors that contribute to vividness include emotional interest of material; the extent to which it provokes imagery and is concrete; and its sensory, temporal, or spatial proximity. For example, consider the vividness of case material compared with that of statistical information. This may be one reason why many research reports are of little interest to practitioners; the reports lack vividness. Data from firsthand experience are more vivid and more likely to influence judgments than secondhand data. Practitioners often appeal to their experience: "I have seen this in my own practice." Clinicians may continue to use certain tests despite their questionable reliability and validity. In a survey of 500 clinical psychologists, they indicated that, in decisions about using a test, personal clinical experience with a test was more important than were data on reliability and validity (Wade & Baker, 1977). These clinicians emphasized the "subjective, insightful and experiential nature of the testing process" (p. 874). They gave more weight to their personal clinical experiences than to experimental evidence. Vivid information can be misleading, especially when duller but more informative material is not considered. "The vividness of information is correlated only modestly, at best, with its evidential value" (Nisbett & Ross, 1980, p. 60). Statistical information concerning hundreds of individuals may be discounted in favor of one vivid case example that supposedly contradicts this information.

People are not necessarily aware of what influences the decisions they make. The role of unconscious influences on judgments is one of the better supported findings within psychology—that is, influences on thoughts and actions that are not noticed or appreciated (Bowers, 1984). Noticing an event does not mean that its influence is appreciated; appreciation requires awareness of a cause-effect relationship. Lack of comprehension of such relationships is perhaps the major reason that people remain unaware of why they act as they do (Bowers, 1984, p. 244). Biasing influences may not be remembered—that is, "the influence of some event need not depend upon memory for its initial occurrence" (Bowers, 1984, p. 238). If clinicians are not aware of their biases, they are less able to counter those influences.

The Interaction Between Clients and Clinicians

A great deal of research has been devoted to exploring the influence of client characteristics on choice of intervention methods and outcomes and on attributions about and attitudes toward clients. The match between a helper and a client influences the decisions that are made and the resulting outcomes. Houts (1984) found that "psychodynamic clinicians" were less pessimistic in their prognosis concerning a client when the client's explanatory bias for the problem was consistent with a psychodynamic orientation. Clients "who approach treatment passively appear to fare better with a dominant-controlling therapist than with a more passive-following therapist" (Abramowitz, Berger, & Weary, 1982, p. 371).

Clinicians like clients who are treatable and manageable, clients who participate in the helping process, and who offer counselors success: clients who get better (Wills, 1978). Views about the treatability of clients influence decisions about whether to accept a person for counseling. "Implicit treatability criterion" include evaluations of clients' likability and manageability (Fehrenbach & O'Leary, 1982). Research suggest that helpers prefer helpless clients; this fits with the demand characteristics of a helping encounter—helpers are supposed to offer help, and clients are expected to need and want it. This can work against clients in the long run; helplessness in the face of an inability to offer help can become burdensome and result in the avoidance and escape behavior seen in burnout (Cherniss, 1986; Maslach & Pines, 1979).

Evaluations of interpersonal attractiveness influence the decisions clinicians make to accept clients or to continue to see them. The preference for young, attractive, verbal, intelligent, and socially adept (YAVIS) clients is well know: in a survey of 421 psychiatrists, psychologists, and social workers, Goldman and Mendelsohn (1969) found that helpers preferred YAVIS clients. These clinicians reported that they worked best with clients who displayed little pathology. Such clients are more likely to be manageable and treatable than are those clients at the opposite ends of the pole (old, unattractive, nonverbal, intellectually limited, and socially backward). YAVIS clients are more likely to behave in ways that are consistent with someone who needs help and with "the clinician's role as a helper (through compliance with treatment expectations and behavior change) [which] are likely to result in increased perceptions of interpersonal attractiveness" (Fehrenbach & O'Leary, 1982, p. 32).

Clinicians' views of people are less favorable than are lay persons' views; that is, professionals tend to focus on negative traits of individuals. The focus on negative qualities increases with increasing experience (Wills, 1978). "Experience produces an increased emphasis on negative characterological aspects, particularly an increased perception of maladjustment, and a less generous view of clients' motivation for change" (p. 981). (See discussion of the sick-sick fallacy in Chapter Seven.) Are professionals more accurate in their negative views? Research suggests that they are not; "in general, there is no difference in judgmental accuracy between professionals and lay persons" (Wills, 1978, p. 981). Trained helpers tend to selectively scan for negative information, whereas lay people do not have this negative focus. Views based on a negatively biased sample will obviously not be as favorable as those based on a balanced consideration of both assets and deficits; the negative views result in more pessimistic predictions concerning outcomes.

Research has consistently shown that lower-class patients are less likely to be accepted in treatment, less likely to receive intensive psychotherapy, and more likely to end therapy prematurely (e.g., Hollingshed & Redlich, 1958; Parloff, Waskow, & Wolf, 1978). When patients are assumed to be lower class rather than middle class, they receive more severe psychiatric diagnoses (see, for example, Abramovitz & Dokecki, 1977). Some writers argue that this is a direct result of the fact that clinicians reflect the values of the dominant middle class, but their clients are often working class (Scheper-Hughes & Lovell, 1987). This is especially true in many agency-based practices. Research investigating effects of race and gender is not conclusive; different methods yield different findings. Archival research shows that black clients are less likely to be referred for individual psychotherapy and are more likely to drop out of treatment (Abramovitz & Murray, 1983). Both class and race are related to manageability and treatability. Field studies suggest that male and female therapists respond differently to male and female clients (Davidson & Abramovitz, 1980). Wakefield (1987) has recently argued that sex bias in the diagnosis of primary orgasmic dysfunction results in inflated estimates of incidence for women, inaccurate accounts of female psychosexual vulnerability, and overconfidence in the effectiveness of sex therapy. (For a recent discussion of race, gender, and class as they influence practice, see Davis & Proctor, 1989.)

Over time, the views and values of clients tend to match those of their therapists because of the interactive nature of clinical practice. Statements that match the therapist's conceptualizations are reinforced, encouraging increasing congruence between views of the therapist and those of the client (Truax, 1966; Frank, 1974; Snyder & Thomsen, 1988). Some evidence indicates that clients tend to report content from their dreams that is consistent with the counselor's conceptualizations (Whitman, Kramer, & Baldridge, 1963).

The therapeutic enterprise involves an interaction between clients and therapists; it involves a social influence process in which the reactions of one party influences the reactions of the other (Snyder & Thomsen, 1988; Wills, 1982). The social nature of therapy renders this enterprise subject to all the kinds of influences that occur in any social exchange. It can be argued that clinicians learn about these influences and, in addition, acquire the skills to avoid sources of bias and error that influence everyday interactions. It can be argued also that sources of bias and error are especially likely to occur in this context because of the unequal status of the participants. A variety of negative effects that are directly associated with how clinicians relate to their clients have been described (Herron & Rouslin, 1984; Strupp & Hadley, 1985). Both clients and therapists arrive at the first interview with preconceptions concerning what is a problem, what it is related to, and how it may be resolved. Clients tend to bring problems to agencies that match the orientation of the clinic from which they seek help (Kadushin, 1969). Thus, some clients may already be disposed to screen their presentation of problems and related causes in accord with the theoretical orientation of agency staff. As soon as the exchange begins, a trajectory may be initiated on the basis of initial preconceptions that supports and stabilizes initial conceptualizations. Research has shown that therapists' views of clients are formed relatively swiftly and remain stable over a long period (Meehl, 1960). How clinicians structure problems affects what they inquire about, which in turn affects what their clients report. The type of information focused on differs among therapists of differing theoretical preferences (eclectic, cognitive-behavioral, psychodynamic, and family systems) (Kopta, Newman, McGovern, & Sandrock, 1986). Given the tendency to search for evidence that confirms initial preconceptions, the clinician is unlikely to note data that point to competing views of problems. That is, once a clinician arrives at a point of view of what the problem is and what factors are related to it, he or she may search selectively for additional information to confirm their views in the client's history, current situation, and behavior. Because counselors typically sample only a minute portion of the client's repertoires (behavior in the interview), they are unlikely to discover behavior that is not consistent with prior expectations.

Summary

Many environments affect the quality of clinical decisions in both private and agency-based practices, including past (for example, structural factors influencing the development of the mental health industry), present (for example, the clinical interview and current service-delivery systems), and future (anticipated changes in service delivery). Only by understanding how these many environments influence clinical practice can the nature of clinical decisions be understood. Studies of clinical decision making suggest that decisions often are made on the basis of beliefs about the moral character of clients rather than on objective accounts based on empirically grounded theories of behavior. Practice theories and professions develop in a particular historical period in which political, social, and economic factors affect their nature. The resources provided to address particular personal and social problems are closely related to these larger structural variables. What is considered a psychological problem differs at different times and in different ethnic and cultural groups. Not considering the larger picture leaves decisions open to influences that clinicians may reject if they do consider their social and political repercussions.

The particular setting in which decisions are made influences those decisions. In agency-based practice, the quality of clinical decision making may be compromised by large caseloads, lack of clear agency policy concerning priorities, and contradictory demands from diverse sources. In both private and agency-based practices, preferred views of clients, available resources, and social and time pressures affect decisions. Other influences include the perceived importance of clinical tasks, access to information, and the current contingency system. Competencies that enhance the quality of decisions, such as keeping track of progress, may be ignored, and reactions that compromise the quality of decisions, such as nattering (complaining without assuming any responsibility for creating desired changes), may be reinforced.

Certain kinds of errors tend to occur due to misuse of generally effective information-processing strategies. Clinicians are influenced by the availability of information and theories. A psychoanalytically oriented clinician may attend to different factors than one who is behaviorally oriented. These selective tendencies influence predictions made. Clinical practice requires the integration of information from diverse sources, which places a strain on memories and capacities to consider different sources of data. Motivational and emotional reactions may also bias judgments. Data that are vivid are especially likely to be misleading. Attention may be focused on bizarre symptoms, and data that are less vivid (but nevertheless important) may be ignored. Tendencies that decrease accuracy include discounting conflicting evidence, failing to search for disconfirming evidence, and being affected by a bias toward dispositional explanations. The particular match between a client and a clinician also affects the decisions that are made.

Familiarity with the many sources of influence on clinical decisions increases the likelihood that errors are avoided and that practice theories are chosen that will protect and expand client options.

3

Content and Procedural Knowledge: Deciding How to Work with Clients

Clear thinking skills are not enough to make accurate clinical decisions—specialized knowledge is also needed (Chi & Glaser, 1985). Accurate clinical decisions are defined as those that enhance the quality of services provided to clients; they increase the likelihood that problems of concern to clients and significant others will be resolved or alleviated and that the overall quality of life of clients and significant others will be enhanced rather than diminished. (See Chapter One for additional description of kinds of clinical errors.) The term *knowledge* here refers to information that is valuable in decreasing uncertainty and in answering clinical questions. Not all data that are gathered are informative. The importance of knowledge of content was one of the major findings of the study of diagnostic decision making among physicians (Elstein et al., 1978). The "possession of relevant bodies of information and a sufficiently broad experience with related problems to permit the determination of which information is pertinent, which clinical findings are significant, and how these findings are to be integrated into appropriate hypotheses and conclusions" were critical components related to competence in clinical problem solving (p. x). However, specialists who make accurate decisions in their area of expertise may not display expertise when making clinical decisions outside of their field (Patel, Arocha, & Groen, 1986). "Reasoning does not occur in a vacuum. Although logic has to do with the forms of argument as distinct from their content, the arguments one encounters in real life have content as well as form, and being able to judge the truth or falsity of that content, clearly a knowledge-based ability, is essential to effective reasoning in any but the most abstract sense" (Nickerson, 1985, p. 359).

Knowledge that is helpful in making accurate inferences includes knowledge of content or topical knowledge (facts related to a domain and concepts that are helpful in defining and understanding problems), knowledge of procedures ("how to") as well as self-knowledge (personal assets and limitations in gathering and processing information). For example, a knowledge of dysfunctional and constructive communication patterns in families offers a conceptual framework for translating concerns such as "poor communication" into a framework that clarifies the nature of the problem.

Is Knowledge Important in the Field of Psychotherapy?

Research concerning decision making in medicine highlights the importance of knowledge in a specialized area (see, for example, Elstein et al., 1978). Are there similar studies in psychiatry, psychology, counseling, or social work? Psychology and psychiatry, especially, claim to be based on a scientific approach. However, some research findings indicate that neither specialized content nor clinical experience is related to success with clients. For example, consider studies comparing the relative effectiveness of "lay helpers" (people with no specialized training in interpersonal helping) with trained practitioners; lay helpers were as effective as professionals (see, for example, Durlak, 1979). Failure to find differences between professionals and untrained individuals is probably related to common "nonspecific factors" shared by many kinds of helping efforts, such as "having a positive approach to people" (Wills, 1982, p. 383). Modeling such an approach for clients may be "a significant and largely unobserved source of therapeutic gain in informal helping relationships" (p. 387). Wills (1982) notes that these kinds of nonspecific factors are often not taught in graduate clinical training. Trained clinicians and naive subjects share sources of bias that consist of assumed associations between certain signs and symptoms. For example, Chapman and Chapman (1969) found that reports of undergraduate students concerning the covariations of symptoms with signs in "clinical data" that contained no systematic relationship duplicated those of experienced clinicians. Both naive subjects and clinicians reported that patients who were suspicious of others tended to distort drawings of the eyes; that dependent clients tended to make feminine or childlike drawings, and that impotent clients drew figures with broad shoulders.

Such data seem to raise questions about the need for specialized content and experience. Would the same results be found today when more practice-related research is available? If similar results were found, would this necessarily mean that specialized content does not play a role in success in psychotherapy? In order to answer these questions we would have to examine the studies in question to determine whether the professionals included really were experts in their area and whether there was enough knowledge in an area to enable someone to be an "expert." For example, there has been a great deal of clinical research concerning agoraphobia (see, for example, Barlow & Waddell, 1985). It is thus unlikely that a college professor of English who is friendly and supportive but who has no specialized training in working with agoraphobic patients could attain the same results with such clients as could a recognized expert in this area. However, to my knowledge, such a study has never been done. In contrast, if little is known in an area, there might not be much difference in effectiveness between trained and untrained helpers. So-called "nonspecific" factors may assume preeminence and eliminate differences in effectiveness between professionals and nonprofessionals. Untrained helpers may even have an edge because graduate training tends to encourage a focus on pathology (see Chapter Nine).

On the other hand, when specialized knowledge is available, its use, combined with nonspecific helping skills, will give the edge to professionals who are familiar with this knowledge and who possess related skills. The less that is known about how to help clients achieve given outcomes—that is, the less domain-specific knowledge is available—the less important it is to use this knowledge in clinical practice. Conversely, the more empirically based domain-specific knowledge is available, the more important it is to consider this in making decisions. For example, knowledge about the degree of effectiveness of different kinds of therapy in relation to achieving a given outcome will decrease the likelihood that potential success will be underestimated or overestimated.

Science and Pseudoscience

A good part of the prestige of psychiatry and psychology rests on the supposed scientific base and approach within these fields. This does not represent the practice of some clinicians or researchers who, knowingly or not, embrace a pseudoscientific perspective (Bunge, 1984) (see Table 1). The picture presented to the public in terms of what is known by clinicians often far exceeds reality (Colman, 1987; Gardner, 1957; Kohn, 1988; Medawar, 1979). Basaglia argues that the ideology and "trappings" of science are used to "pull the wool over people's eyes in suggesting credibility of claims that does not exist" (Scheper-Hughes & Lovell, 1987). Clinicians, in their role as part of the "public," are not immune from the influence of rhetorical presentations in the mass media as well as in professional sources. The battle for acceptance of the scientific method that has been won in the physical sciences and in many areas of medicine has not yet been won in psychotherapy. For example, Medawar (1984, p. 58) argues that quasi-scientific psychologies "are getting away with a concept of truthfulness which belongs essentially to imaginative literature" and that this represents "a style of thought that will impede the growth of our understanding of mental illness." He describes this approach as "poetism," which "stands for the belief that imaginative insight and a mysteriously privileged sensibility can tell us all the answers that are truly worthy of being sought or being known" (p. 60). (See also the recent discussion of transpersonal approaches by Ellis & Yeager, 1989.) Within this style of thinking it is assumed that because there is uncertainty in the world, there is no difference between different degrees of credibility. The sometimes bitter and always spirited disagreement between those who favor a scientific approach to practice and those who favor an intuitive subjective approach is partially related to status and economic advantage; clinicians with subjective approaches dominate clinical practice and have vested interests in

Table 1. Comparison of Attitudes and Activities of Scientists and Pseudoscientists.

Typical Attitudes and Activities	Scientist			Pseudoscientist		
	Yes	No	Optional	Yes	No	Optional
dmits own ignorance, hence need for 1ore research	X				X	
inds own field difficult and full of oles	X				X	
dvances by posing and solving new roblems	X				X	
'elcomes new hypotheses and ethods	X				X	
roposes and tries out new hypotheses	X					X
ttempts to find or apply laws	X				X	
herishes the unity of science	X				X	
elies on logic	X					X
ses mathematics	X					X
athers or uses data, particularly 1antitative ones	X					X
ooks for counterexamples	X				X	
vents or applies objective checking cedures	X				X	
ttles disputes by experiment or mputation	X				X	
lls back consistently on authority		X		X		
ippresses or distorts unfavorable ta		X		X		
odates own information	X				X	
eks critical comments from others	X				X	
rites papers that can be understood anyone		X		X		
likely to achieve instant celebrity		X		X		

Source: From "What Is Pseudoscience?" by M. Bunge, 1984, *The Skeptical In-uirer*, *9* (1), p. 41. Copyright 1984 by Committee for the Scientific Investigation of Claims the Paranormal. Reprinted by permission.

maintaining this privileged position—and act on this interest—consciously or unconsciously.

Lack of understanding of and misrepresentation of the scientific method is also responsible for this disagreement. Many critics of a scientific approach do not seem to understand the basic principles of such an approach. Some confuse this with scientism, "the belief that science knows or will soon know all the answers, and it has the corrupting smugness of any system of opinions which contains its own antidote to disbelief" (Medawar, 1984, p. 60). Lack of understanding is responsible for the "sterile study fallacy" in which a study is disregarded because it focuses on a narrow aspect of some subject. This criticism reflects a lack of appreciation for the incremental development of knowledge; one study represents but one step among many that will be required to understand a problem, such as substance abuse. Removing a study from this developmental perspective may misrepresent its role in the overall picture. (Critics can, of course, selectively pick out studies that do not contribute much, if anything, to knowledge development and ignore those that do.) An understanding of the scientific method is not usually available to the public. "It itself is esoteric knowledge" (Stevens, 1988, p. 382). "There is a grave crisis in science education. The basic principles of the scientific method are not being taught in a manner that enables otherwise well-educated people to apply them to problems in their daily experiences" (Stevens, 1988, p. 385). Science educators often emphasize deterministic models rather than the uncertainty involved in understanding the relationship between variables (Shaughnessy, 1983). This limits experience in "probabilistic thinking" and discourages a useful view of uncertainty (as indicating limits of understanding) and encourages a common distortion of "science" as deterministic in a dogmatic sense. Clinicians are not immune from this educational deficit, which is so common in our culture and which accounts in large part for the ready acceptance of proposed causal factors without any evidence that they are relevant. Consider, for example, the uncritical acceptance of phenomena such as past lives, spirit guides, auras and the occult (Miller, 1987; Singer & Bernassi, 1981; Stevens, 1988). Even quite elementary knowledge of scientific ways of weighing the value of evidence would call such claims into question.

Hallmarks of a scientific approach toward clinical practice include looking for alternative explanations, updating knowledge, and selecting assessment and intervention methods based on what has been found to be most effective through systematic investigation rather than on appeals to authority or on what "feels right." It is assumed that there are many unsolved questions in clinical practice and that advances can be made by posing and exploring new questions. It is also assumed that questions cannot be answered unless they are cast in a refutable form. There is an interest in theories that are refutable (it is possible to test them in terms of whether they are more or less accurate than alternative explanations in making explicit predictions) (see Chapter Four). It is assumed that nothing is ever proven, that rather there are increments of confirmation in terms of evaluating the accuracy of any clinical assumptions (Medawar, 1984; Popper, 1963). Thus, a true scientific approach is quite the opposite of the characteristics often attributed to it such as "rigid," "dogmatic," "closed," "trivial." Within a scientific approach, it would be just as ill advised to claim that some people are psychic as it would be to claim that there is no such thing as "psychic abilities" without confirming evidence. "Scientific investigation of controversial topics involves the search for more, better, less ambiguous, and more interpretable data" (Jensen, 1989, p. 147).

A scientific approach is often criticized on the grounds that it cannot capture the full meaning of psychological experiences— that scientific accounts often are trivial, unrepresentative accounts. A trivial account, by definition, cannot account for events of interest. A scientific approach to practice requires use of a broad range of methods that faithfully represent significant aspects of the phenomena under investigation. There is no doubt that social science and professional journals are replete with research reports that are irrelevant or distort the events under investigation (see for example Armstrong, 1980; Lipton & Hershaft, 1985). This does not mean that an empirical approach is not useful. It does indicate that, like anything else, it can be appropriately or inappropriately applied. For example, inappropriate use is often made of a group design in the investigation of the clinical effectiveness of different methods. Clients may be randomly assigned to different groups, overlooking critical individual differences that call for selective matching of clients to particular groups. Statistics are often used inappropriately. Thus, there is good science and bad science: science that reflects events accurately and science that distorts the events and yields outcomes such as "patterned falsehoods" (Thorngate, 1986). It is not this kind of science that is advocated here.

Professionals are wise to be skeptical of trivializing applications of the scientific method to the creation of practice knowledge. Accurate understanding of the hallmarks of the scientific method is needed to distinguish between helpful and trivializing or bogus uses of this approach (Gardner, 1981). Bogus uses refer to the use of scientific ideology to reaffirm and maintain current service definitions of problems and service-delivery systems that may, in reality, hinder rather than achieve a higher quality of life for clients. Scientific theories "can be incorporated into a purely ideological language which serves to justify the current stagnation" (Basaglia in Scheper-Hughes & Lovell, 1987, p. 118). Classification of clients into psychiatric categories lends an aura of "scientific credibility" to this practice, whether or not there is any evidence that this is warranted or that it is helpful to clients in meeting their needs. Clinicians become disenchanted with the scientific method because of being confronted repeatedly with trivializing or bogus examples of its use in professional newsletters and social science journals. Because of this, they may discard a method that is useful, if not essential, in finding out how to help clients. The usefulness of the knowledge that results (information that helps clinicians make accurate decisions) depends on the astuteness of the questions posed and the appropriateness of the methods used to explore the questions (Popper, 1963).

The tendency to doubt the value of empirical research may result from lack of knowledge about useful research or from disappointment that more knowledge is not available. Studies in the field of medicine show that published research often has little influence on practice (Banta, 1984) and that improved treatment methods are often not adopted (Light, 1980). Some hope for certain answers when these cannot be offered. Some writers still ask "Is psychotherapy effective?" As others have noted, this is like asking "Is medicine effective?" As in medicine, questions concerning effectiveness are only meaningful when particular problems are considered. Reviews of psychotherapy often omit many areas in which considerable progress has been made and documented (see, for example, Zilbergeld, 1983). We do know more today about what works (or does not work) with certain types of clients than we did many years ago, especially in certain areas in which there has been considerable research based on empirical inquiry into clinical practice and its effects. Examples include working with autistic children (Howlin & Rutter, 1987), anxiety (Mavissakalian & Barlow, 1981), agoraphobia (Barlow & Waddell, 1985), prevention of relapse (Marlatt & Gordon, 1985), parent training (Dangel & Polster, 1984), and family treatment of schizophrenics (Falloon, Boyd, & McGill, 1984), to name but a few.

The Limits of Experience

Experience does not necessarily result in improved performance. In fact, it may have the opposite effect. Experience does not offer systematic data about what works with what clients and what problems. It may decrease rather than enhance the identification of creative options, as shown in a study by Johnson (1972) in which people who did not work in a spark-plug factory identified more alternative uses for spark plugs than personnel who worked in the factory. Thus, learning may become "context bound." Expertise is not necessarily a monotonic function of experience. For example, third- and fourth-year residents do not perform as well as either first- or second-year students or experts in interpreting some X-rays (see Lesgold et al., 1988). Possible reasons for such findings include vacillation between old (but inaccurate) representations of problems and new (perhaps "untrusted") views about what is accurate (Strauss & Stavy, 1982). Experience alone may not offer the tactical guidance and necessary representation of problems that is required for practice to be beneficial (Brehmer, 1980; Einhorn, 1980b; Perkins, 1987). Even if some improvement does occur without tactical coaching, it will not match the potential gains of what would be possible with guidance. Clinical practice is a highly personalized professional endeavor that allows a wide range of individual discretion on the part of counselors: how to structure problems, what outcomes to pursue, when to stop collecting information, what risks to take, what criteria to use to select intervention methods (individual or family intervention), and how to evaluate progress. Short-cuts may be taken that may or may not enhance accuracy. This characteristic, as well as the high degree of privacy of clinical practice (rarely is it observed by other clinicians), allows unique styles, which may or may not enhance accuracy of clinical decisions, to be cultivated through experience. Use of vague or confirming evaluation procedures may serve to maintain styles that are not optimal.

Clinical Training Programs

A number of changes could be made in clinical training programs to upgrade the quality of decision-making skills. Some sources of error that influence clinical judgments are universal, and no doubt students bring unique dysfunctional habits from their personal lives into their professional lives. Still, why isn't more of the content described in this book included in clinical training programs—including skills that can be used to maintain clear thinking skills even in hostile environments? One reason is that practice theories focused on often favor empathic and ideological explanations. Instructors in clinical training programs may not be familiar with sources of fallacy or may embrace an intuitive in contrast to an empirical approach to practice and the clear thinking skills that go along with this (see, for example, Medawar, 1984, pp. 58-60). Although instructors may say they draw on practice-related research in their work with clients, observation of their practice and their lectures may not support this statement. In some training programs, structural and political factors that influence how personal and social problems are defined and handled have been downplayed.

Clinical internships may not offer trainees sustained tactical guidance. In no way could many clinical training programs be considered true apprenticeships, in which students have the benefit of guided performance and learning based on conditions known to be important for learning (Dillon & Sternberg, 1986; Gagne, 1977, 1987). As Stevenson and Norcross (1987) note, "clinical training in an academic environment is often just that—academic—long on teaching by exposition and short on teaching by practice" (p. 78). Important conditions of learning include the following:

- Clear identification of objectives (what is to be learned)
- Clear description of content and procedural knowledge already available
- Sequential steps that match available skill levels
- Clear, relevant means of monitoring progress
- Model presentation accompanied by instruction concerning skills to be learned, the reasons for using these, and the conditions under which they are useful
- Practice opportunities
- Immediate feedback concerning accuracy

Clinical supervisors may rely on indirect measures of trainee's skills in the form of process notes, brief written reports, or descriptions during supervisory meetings or case conferences forgoing opportunities to listen to tape recordings of interviews with clients or to observe trained staff working with clients. Too rarely do trainees have opportunities to observe trained staff working with clients (Barth & Gambrill, 1984), although such observation without tactical guidance may provide little help in any case. That is, model presentation without explicit instructions about the principles modeled may be ineffective (Palincsar & Brown, 1984).

Clinical programs should provide a high-quality mentoring experience in which mentors share information about *how* they arrived at decisions as well as what the decisions are so that novices have access to a model of the clinical reasoning process "in action." Helpful questions to ask during assessment and intervention should be modeled by experts when training novices, both questions asked of clients and questions asked covertly—that is, the process as well as the product of reasoning should be modeled. Research suggests the importance of an active coaching role on the part of instructors, including offering guidance as well as requiring explanations and evaluating progress (Campione, 1989). Wise selection of cases can facilitate learning also (Collins, 1985).

Clinical supervisors often reconstruct their thinking process "after the fact" during supervisory discussions, and such reconstruction may not portray the reasoning process that actually occurred. Within a traditional psychoanalytic framework, novices undergo a lengthy experience of psychoanalysis themselves. It is assumed that through this experience, clinicians will become aware of their own transference and countertransference tendencies and so will be less likely to impose these unknowingly on clients. This experience can be viewed as a kind of unique mentor experience in that an "expert" models the manner in which clinical work is conducted. One problem with this approach is that the supervising analyst does not "think aloud" in the presence of the analysand (quite the reverse) in relation to why certain actions (or inactions) are taken at a given point, so the novice is not privy to the reasons for these (Dewald, 1987). Detailed feedback may not be offered based on observation of interviews.

An educational environment in which controversial issues are routinely discussed and in which conflicting points of view are aired in a constructive manner would encourage critical reasoning skills. Discussing the pros and cons of different proposed courses of action and different alternative accounts encourages clinicians to welcome spirited discussions in an atmosphere in which participants take responsibility for identifying and supporting clinical assumptions and recommendations.

Few programs require students to develop expertise in contingency analysis: skill in identifying and altering the relationships between environmental events and behaviors of interest. They are thus handicapped in understanding how the environment (including the reactions to other people) influences behavior and tend to misattribute outcomes and behaviors that are the result of environmental consequences to personal characteristics. Lack of knowledge and skill in contingency analysis is one of the main causes of the dispositional bias that is so common among clinicians (see Chapter Nine). Programs vary considerably in how they train students to evaluate their work with clients, ranging from reliance on global methods to reliance on ongoing monitoring using specific progress indicators. Ongoing evaluation of specific progress indicators is most useful for making timely clinical decisions.

Many obstacles to clear thinking (such as lack of motivation, impulsive decisions, and procrastination) are related to a lack of self-management skills. Research concerning the differences between effective and ineffective problem solvers highlights the critical role of self-regulatory skills, such as monitoring performance and seeking feedback. Self-management, as well as contingency management skills, will be required to maintain and enhance clear thinking skills in work environments that do not support or are actively hostile to the use of such skills. Students should emerge from clinical programs with expertise in the area of self-management, including skills in self-reinforcement and planning of self-change programs to attain desired goals.

Professional development requires continued learning. Thus, learning-how-to-learn skills are critical for clinicians but are often not taught in clinical training programs. Rather, students may be supported in an excessive reliance on unguided experiences. Clinical students should learn how to spot and counter "stratagems," and they should acquire political skills, such as how to form coalitions that would help them to achieve desired changes and maintain positive environments. A lack of such skills is one of the reasons for the sense of helplessness and hopelessness among many clinicians in agency-based practice.

Content knowledge is emphasized in many clinical courses: learning what rather than how. Such information is of limited value if it is not complemented by procedural knowledge—how and when to use content knowledge in practice and how to automatize procedures so they can be used efficiently. Understanding difficult content "is a highly procedural matter" (Perkins, 1985, p. 346). Content covered in classroom instruction may be quite different than content covered in clinical internships. Clinical students may take courses emphasizing an interactional perspective in which there is an emphasis both on environmental and personal factors related to presenting problems, and then they may be placed in internships in which there is a strong dispositional bias (see Chapter Nine). For example, such an agency may recommend play therapy for a seven-year-old child referred for classroom management problems without observing interaction in the classroom to explore the possible role of significant others such as peers and teachers in contributing to "problems."

Assessing Practice Knowledge

The effectiveness of a clinician may be limited by lack of knowledge, especially knowledge of material in professional literature that describes nonpreferred, even disliked, practice orientations. Awareness of what one knows and does not know is one of the ingredients of expertise. Practice-related facts and beliefs differ among many dimensions, including how well they can be empirically supported. The degree of certainty possible depends on the issue. There can be uncertainty about something that can be determined such as the existence of Freud or uncertainty about the exact indeterminancy of an event that is determinate (for example, the probability of a coin that is unbiased coming up heads is .05). However, it may be impossible to decide an issue because it is outside the rules of the system (for example, what kind of chairs chess players should sit on) (Johnson-Laird, 1983; see also Kahneman and Tversky, 1982). Clear thinking skills can be used to increase the percentage of accurate data acquired relative to unsupported or incorrect data.

A clinician's content and procedural knowledge in an area can be reviewed to find out what proportion can be supported with evidence and what percentage of useful knowledge is at hand compared with what is available. Comprehension is a matter of degree. A clinician may have complete understanding of some practice concepts, a moderate degree of comprehension of many, and perhaps no understanding of others. Clinicians may be familiar with only a modest percentage of knowledge that is potentially available concerning a presenting problem and how to resolve it—not because of any inherent limitations on their part, but because of the kinds of learning environments they have arranged and encountered, including graduate training. Each of these environments offered only some percentage of knowledge that would be helpful in clinical practice and, in the bargain, probably offered some misinformation also.

Clinicians differ in the criteria used to assess the accuracy and completeness of knowledge. Possibilities include "what feels OK"; "what seems to work"; "how knowledge compares with that of colleagues," and "what's possible to know given the constraints of time, energy, and competing priorities." Some prefer an intuitive approach in which content is valued if it seems relevant on the basis of face value (that is, without any empirical validation) and if it is compatible with preferred practice theories: if it "feels" right. Others believe that research can offer helpful guidelines about what "works" and thus prefer a scientific approach in which content is valued if it has some degree of empirical support—if there is some research-based evidence that it is correct. The dangers of selecting material on the basis of what "feels right" or what matches preferred practice theories are that material will be selected that matches preconceptions and biases, resulting in inaccurate clinical judgments. One obstacle to shifting from an intuitive to a scientific approach to practice is misinformation about a scientific approach offered in clinical training programs, as well as in the professional literature. If little is known about a topic, there's not much to learn. Large discrepancies in what is known and what can be known occur when a great deal of knowledge is available, as in the areas of parent training, depression, and anxiety (to name but a few). Both are active areas of inquiry with a rich empirical literature concerning the effectiveness of different kinds of programs.

Deciding What to Read/Listen to

Clinicians make decisions about what to read, how to read, what to discuss, what workshops to take, and what lectures to attend. These decisions influence what is offered to clients. Thus, the reading done by clinicians is more than a personal matter; decisions made influence the nature of the services provided to clients. It is thus important to consider the different criteria that may be used to select and weight material. Clinicians approach reading with different goals. Goals in reading the professional literature may include discovering

- How client participation can be encouraged
- How to implement helpful assessment measures
- What effective intervention methods to use with a specific kind of problem
- How to prevent relapse

- How to involve significant others
- How different presenting problems can be distinguished (for example, agoraphobia, generalized anxiety, and panic)
- What to check if a procedure is not effective

Clinicians select material that reflects their preferred practice framework or methodology; that is, decisions are influenced by what is already known and favored. Behaviorists tend to read articles written by behaviorists. Psychoanalysts read articles in psychoanalytical journals, attend psychoanalytical conventions, and speak to other psychoanalysts. These preferences, if acted on, protect clinicians from contact with alternative views—not always a happy outcome for clients. Selection of what to read will be influenced by judgments about credibility, which are influenced by social and circumstantial factors as well as by personal preferences. Criteria that influence decisions about which kinds of knowledge to seek and which kinds to ignore are discussed below.

Comprehensibility

The importance of clarity depends on our goals. Many writers have pointed out that we often value what we cannot understand (see, for example, Thouless, 1974). We tend to believe that if we cannot understand something, it is profound—that what is clear is simple-minded. One reason is that obtuse knowledge can be used to impress our colleagues; appearing knowledgeable about subjects others know little about can have many indirect benefits (Thorngate & Plouffe, 1987). Clinicians often do not realize how little they do understand about material—accepting empathic explanations (see Chapter Four) and not testing their utility in terms of applying this knowledge. Both the media and professional sources are full of descriptions that appear informative but really are not. For example, social problems may be attributed to obscure social conditions without description of these conditions or the factors responsible for maintaining them. (See later discussion of active versus passive reading.) Burnham (1987) makes a persuasive argument that the popularization of science by journalists in fragmented bits and pieces is one of the major reasons for the widespread acceptance of superstitious beliefs.

Credibility

Credibility refers to degree of belief. Clinicians differ in the criteria used to assess the credibility of knowledge (the truth value of facts or beliefs). (Degree of conviction is not necessarily correlated with the truth value of a statement.) Possibile criteria include the following:

- Authority: believed because of who said it (for example, Freud, Skinner, Kohut, your supervisor)
- Liking: believed because your friends believe it
- Consensus: believed on the basis of the dominant view in a field
- Fear: believed in because of fear of being different or left out
- Empathy: believed because it feels right (see discussion of empathic explanations in Chapter Four)
- Scientific criteria: believed because of empirical support

Mysticism. Knowledge may be accepted on the basis of criteria such as divine revelation, altered states of consciousness, or inspiration (see discussion of empathic explanations in Chapter Four). Some subsample of knowledge classified here may reflect an inability to describe cues that we do detect but cannot verbally describe. Knowledge based on mysticism lacks "a high degree of intra- and inter-judge reliability (Thorngate & Plouffe, 1987, p. 67). However, there may be a high degree of consensus within groups (not between groups) because of conformity and habit (rather than common mystical experience). Reliance on variations of mysticism by people in all walks of life is striking, as illustrated in any issue of the *Skeptical Inquirer.* "Consider the number of scientists who pray for inspiration and insight rather than perspiration or foresight to guide them" (Thorngate & Plouffe, 1987, p. 75). Reliance on mystic authority is quite popular, as illustrated by the many young people who flock to cult groups.

Rationalism. The credibility of a claim can be tested in relation to "logical derivations of knowledge previously assessed as credible" (Thorngate & Plouffe, 1987, p. 67). Rationalism comprises a significant part of scientific reasoning. "Conclusions that are derived from credible premises or axioms are credible; otherwise they are not" (p. 67). Premises are assessed as credible by scientists through observation and measurement. Many premises are not intuitively obvious nor are they verifiable by observation and/or measurement (such as, "Freud would have changed some of his major conceptions if he had access to research over the past twenty years.").

Empiricism. The credibility of information may be assessed by checking it against what is seen, heard, touched, tasted, or smelled. Most clinicians reject scientific empiricism in favor of anecdotal empiricism: "a claim to knowledge is assessed as credible if it is similar to, or congruent with, recalled anecdotes from personal experience; otherwise it is deemed incredible" (Thorngate & Plouffe, p. 69). Anecdotal empiricism, as Thorngate and Plouffe (1987) point out, takes much less time to learn than does scientific empiricism, which requires years of labor. One reason that reliance on this form of empiricism results in errors is that the vividness of particular experiences may have little or no correlation with the true frequency or importance of an event (see Chapter Nine).

Analogy. Credibility may be assessed in terms of how well the structure or form of the claim, rather than its content, agrees or is compatible with knowledge that has been judged to be credible or incredible. Clinicians have a great tendency to anthropomorphize what they see, or to mechanize things. Different kinds of analogies include metaphors, similes, and models. Advantages of analogies include their value in understanding new events, thoughts, or ideas (see Chapter Six for a discussion of their disadvantages).

Authority. Most knowledge is not firsthand as in the four sources mentioned above—it is secondhand, and thus the source of the knowledge should be considered in determining credibility. One way to evaluate the credibility of an authority is to use one or more of the other four criteria. Authority may be ascribed on the basis of irrelevant variables such as gender and number of degrees (see

Chapter Five). Whether the claim of an authority should be accepted depends on how important a topic is to us. Gullibility serves some important functions, such as preserving a sense of optimism about people, accepting knowledge as entertainment, and avoiding time spent on checking claims that really are not important.

Individual preferences alone do not determine selection of knowledge base; the nature of the claim must also be considered. Metaphor, mysticism, and rationalism will not be of much value in checking the claim that a client has been hospitalized for schizophrenia on two occasions. Empiricism will not be of much use in assessing the credibility of the claim that "life is like a tree" or "one bird in hand is better than two in the bush." Convenience is also a criterion. Often, more than one criterion is used as when the credibility of a claim based on authority is assessed by appealing to another source such as empiricism. Conflicts may occur between the head and the heart (mysticism and rationalism), and between what we see and whether it makes sense (empiricism and rationalism). Choice is further complicated by conflicts within as well as between epistemologies; for example, conflicting data often are generated within an empirical framework.

Importance

Both psychological and pragmatic importance influence consumption of knowledge. If material is not considered useful, it probably is not sought. Psychological importance must be considered also. "Knowledge can also be important because it promotes understanding, provides a sense of order, continuity, elation or peace, establishes a focus for the expression of emotion, inflates or guards the ego, develops or maintains a favored (usually positive) self-image" (Thorngate & Plouffe, 1987, p. 79). We seek information that allows us to compare ourselves with others.

Interest—Knowledge as Entertainment

Clinicians are more likely to read material they find interesting. Motivation is a key variable in learning; interesting presentation of material encourages clinicians to read or listen. "The consumption of knowledge is much like the consumption of food. Valuable knowledge should be digestible (comprehensible), edible (credible), nutritious (important)" (Thorngate & Plouffe, 1987, p. 85). Psychological knowledge, at least that described in professional journals, is not likely to have these characteristics. Rather it "is by tradition, if not by necessity, stripped of its wonder, ground to an emotional pulp, and distributed in plain brown envelopes. It is food for the cortex not the soul. It is meant to bypass the senses and the passions. It has the subtlety and all the excitement of weak tea" (Thorngate & Plouffe, 1987, p. 88). Here, too, this does not have to be. Scientific reports can and should be written in an engaging yet informative manner.

To Read or Not to Read

Some clinicians rarely read research reports relevant to their practice. Fifty-six percent of a large sample of social workers reported that "they did not consult research material when confronted with a difficult practice situation" (Kirk, Osmalov, & Fischer, 1976, p. 122). There are sound and unsound reasons for neglecting valuable sources of knowledge. Plausible but surmountable excuses include it takes too much time; I cannot find good articles or books; I do not remember what I read; and I do not know how to acquire procedural knowledge to complement knowledge of content. Poor excuses are usually based on overgeneralizations such as the research is flawed (some is and some is not); the writing is bad (often but not always true); nonclinical samples are used (findings will usually be relevant for clinical samples as well, Bandura, 1978); they do not know what they are talking about (they often do); and some research is fabricated (most is not).

Is reading (or listening or thinking) always a good idea? On the basis of decision-making research, one might conclude that sometimes not reading is better, since clinicians select material that supports their biases, are influenced by irrelevant material, and alter their memories on the basis of inaccurate information they hear about later. So reading is not necessarily a help; it depends on what and how we read.

Active Versus Passive Learning

Clinicians differ in their preferred learning styles—in the quality of their learning skills and in their beliefs about knowledge, thinking, and learning. This does not mean that they are all equally effective. Recent research reveals the importance of personal and social beliefs about knowledge, thinking, and learning (Greeno, 1989). Views about knowledge and understanding differ greatly, as can be seen in the discussion of different criteria for assessing the credibility of knowledge. Some clinicians may test claims against relatively unanalyzed personal judgments. Others rely on "procedural knowing," in which it is assumed that knowledge results from an "intellectual process" (Greeno, 1989). Other clinicians view knowledge as a form of "received truth" that relies on authority. Biases in considering material, such as the tendency to interpret what is read (or heard) in accord with preferred views, emphasizes the value of active versus passive reading. Clinicians are no more immune to the influence of the confirmation bias than any other group.

The introduction of new material may be followed by the statement "It doesn't feel right." Here we have a learning style that screens material based on whether it "feels right" (whether it fits prior preconceptions). This is not a helpful style; feelings about what is true are not necessarily good guides to what is true. Some clinicians believe that they learn best through experience; just getting in and working with clients. This preferred style is usually not complemented by arrangement of conditions that must be present for experience to be helpful (see prior discussion of the limits of experience). Many writers in the area of teaching clear thinking skills have commented on the close relationship between problem solving and learning how to learn—that problem solving involves a learning process. Thus, learning styles are closely related to difficulties in acquiring content and procedural knowledge. A great deal is known about the conditions required for effective learning (Gagne, 1977). Faulty beliefs about the conditions that facilitate learning will get in the way of keeping up with new information and putting this to use in clinical practice. It is surprising that clinicians are often not trained in the use of effective learning conditions since clinical practice involves helping clients to learn new skills as well as continue learning to upgrade clinical skills. Use of ineffective learning skills is one of the greatest sources of self-censorship.

Reading or listening can be active or passive. More will be learned and remembered if it is an active process in which relationships between previous knowledge and new information are explored (Weinstein & Rogers, 1985). The prevalence of the confirmation bias (the tendency to accept views that match preferred views) emphasizes the value of active learning (a deep approach to learning) versus passive learning (a surface approach). The differences between these approaches are shown below (Entwistle, 1987, p. 16).

The deep approach involves

- Intention to understand
- Vigorous interaction with content
- Relation of concepts to everyday experience
- Relation of new ideas to previous knowledge
- Relation of evidence to conclusion
- Examination of the logic of the argument

The surface approach involves

- Intention to complete task assignments
- Memorization of information
- Failure to distinguish principles from examples
- Treatment of the task as an external imposition
- Focus on discrete elements without integration
- Nonreflectiveness about purpose or situation

Surface approaches encourage assimilation of new material in which new concepts are integrated into existing frameworks with relatively small changes in overall views. Deep approaches are needed for accommodation in which large changes in conceptual views take place (Prosser, 1987). Conflict which is more likely to be created in deep approaches is important in the development of concepts (Dewey, 1933; Sigel, 1979).

Passive learning often results in "inert knowledge" (Whitehead, 1929). There are two kinds of inert knowledge. One kind is conceptual knowledge unaccompanied by procedural knowledge. This has been referred to as the "parroting problem" (Bereiter & Scardamalia, 1985, p. 65): a principle may be recited but not applied correctly. For example, the correct definition of insight may be given, but examination of clinical work may reveal a lack of understanding of this concept. Only when a clinician is asked to apply knowledge can his or her "procedural understanding" be assessed. The second kind of inert knowledge is data that are available but not used. Knowing when to apply relevant knowledge is one of the characteristics that distinguishes experts from novices. Experts can retrieve useful knowledge from their memories; they have more effective metamemory search skills. The two kinds of inert knowledge represent the difference between a behavior deficit (lack of a competency) and a prompting or motivational deficit (a skill is available but not used). The problem of inert knowledge highlights the importance of seeking high-quality learning opportunities designed to enhance procedural as well as conceptual knowledge. Confusion between the entertainment value of information and its pragmatic value (how useful is it in clinical contexts) encourages the development of inert knowledge.

Active reading differs from passive reading in a number of ways. In the former, the reader is active in posing and answering questions about the material:

- What is the evidence for this statement?
- Is this true for all people (for my client)?
- How can I use this information in my practice?
- Is there anything left out of this argument?
- What is the main point of this section?
- Can I summarize the argument?
- How does this relate to other evidence about this topic?
- How can I remember this information?

Helpful learning strategies are described below. Using these will enhance learning and increase enjoyment of the process.

Comprehension Monitoring

Comprehension monitoring includes asking questions about content, paraphrasing, noting progress, identifying troublesome content, summarizing information, and reviewing the adequacy of explanations offered. Does an explanation provide a plausible account, or does it simply paraphrase the problem to be explained or offer an irrelevant explanation? Self-talk and cues are used to guide comprehension (Meichenbaum & Asarnow, 1979). In programs using this approach students learn basic strategies of "playing teacher." The idea is to enhance learning, retention, and understanding by increasing active involvement with material. Involvement increases the likelihood that appropriate responses will be made to obstacles, such as not understanding a word or sentence. (One common error is to react to difficulties in learning as an occasion to skip material rather than try to understand it.) Comprehension monitoring is especially important in self-learning, since no one else is available to review knowledge acquired (unless an interactive computer program is used). Lack of comprehension often occurs because of a poor match between the knowledge of readers and the text. Compared with novices, experts approach material with a different sense of "true" knowledge. "Experts are probably better able to monitor their comprehension within their areas of specialization than are novices because: (a) systematization of knowledge produces chunks which unite facts into higher order structures; (b) more detailed and organized structures create expectations on the part of the learner; and (c) experts have more explicit knowledge about the organizational principles (structures) involved in a body of knowledge" (Weinstein & Rogers, 1985, p. 621).

Memorization of facts and relationships without understanding is not enough to make use of knowledge. Effective learners "identify and define problems with their ability to understand the significance of new information . . . they *actively* apply particular strategies and *look* at the effects" (Bransford & Stein, 1984, p. 68). Systematic questioning is one of the most helpful learning strategies. Questions to keep in mind when reviewing practice-related research include the following:

- Are concepts clearly defined?
- Are measures used valid and reliable?
- Is it clear how concepts are derived from a theory?
- Is the derivation appropriate?
- Are data collection methods clearly described?
- Is the study design clearly described?
- Are sampling procedures adequate?
- Is the study design adequate?
- Are appropriate control groups included?
- Are data-collection methods free of bias?
- Are data-analysis methods appropriate?
- Are follow-up data available?
- Were changes impressive?
- Are conclusions warranted?
- Are alternative explanations for results likely?
- Can findings be generalized to other situations?

Elaboration Strategies

Elaboration strategies include "adding mental imagery, reading to answer questions, noticing categories, attending to hierarchical structure, and finding examples to illustrate principles" (Nickerson et al., 1985, p. 304). There is an active search for relations, and new content is related to old information. Counterexamples are sought. "Effective learners attend to factual content, but they also try to understand the significance or relevance of facts" (Bransford & Stein, 1984, p. 56). Such strategies increase interconnections among material and so increase options for recall. Personal knowledge and beliefs are introduced through implicit assumptions about material. Readers approach a text with different rules of inference and knowledge; because they have different strategies, they process inferential tasks in different ways (Hagert & Waern, 1986). Thus, "the reader or reasoner constructs his or her own interpretation of the text, which thereby assumes quite a different meaning from that intended by the author" (p. 112).

Avoiding the Confirmation Bias

Data that do not support preferred beliefs and practice theories are likely to be overlooked and may even be misinterpreted as data that support preferred views. Too much credit is given to data that support preferred views. An illustration of this tendency is shown in the study by Lord et al. (1979) in which two studies concerning the deterrent effects of capital punishment (one offering supportive evidence and the other offering negative evidence) were read by Stanford University students who had previously indicated whether they believed in capital punishment as a deterrent to potential murderers. The studies involved two different designs. Regardless of the design used, students found the study supporting their own position to be more convincing and better conducted than the study opposing their position. (Conditions were counterbalanced across direction and belief). Furthermore, after reading both studies, students were more certain of the accuracy of their original position than they were before they read either of the studies. Reading only material that matches assumptions held is unlikely to violate expectations, which is one of the triggers for learning (Hayes-Roth, Klahr, & Mostow, 1981).

Other Helpful Reading Habits

Deemphasizing the answer (or product of thought) and emphasizing the process involved in reaching a solution enhances problem solving (Greenfield, 1979, p. 237). Effective readers attend to hierarchical relations—how content can be organized in terms of multiple linkages. These organizational strategies often involve "deep processing" (in contrast to superficial descriptions) in which key principles are used to structure problems. Tree diagrams are useful in illustrating the relationship among hierarchically ordered events (see Chapter Nine). Identifying goals when reading or listening encourages a focus on material of interest and is helpful in avoiding the distractions of irrelevant details.

One of the best ways to understand new material is to attempt to communicate understanding in writing. Writing involves a process of reflection in which degree of understanding and points of obscurity or error are identified (Murray, 1984). "One difference between experienced writers and novices is the importance each assigns to the process of rewriting. The experienced writer sees writing as a technique for learning and discovery, whereas the novice tends to view it as a chore analogous to 'tidying up' (fixing sentence structure and words)" (Bransford & Stein, 1984, p. 104).

Writing can be divided into two major kinds, both of which are used in clinical practice. One kind involves description of events. For example, a record may contain a description of the interaction between family members. Common deficiencies in this kind of writing include confusion between description and inference and a lack of descriptive detail such as clear examples (see Chapter Eight). The second kind of writing involves presenting positions and making and supporting inferences. Striking deficiencies in this kind of writing have been found. Large studies in the United States indicate that only about 20 percent of students are able to write an acceptable persuasive essay (National Assessment of Educational Programs, 1981). Problems included failure to offer support for positions, making unwarranted generalizations, and lack of illustrative examples. (See section on case records in Chapter Six.) The environment in which reading (and listening) takes place will influence how much is learned. Concentration (and thus comprehension) may be compromised by interpretations, noise, and fatigue.

"The principle of charity requires that we look for the best, rather than the worst, possible interpretation of material" (Scriven, 1976, p. 71). This approach increases the likelihood that useful applications of material are identified and decreases the likelihood that valuable content is prematurely discarded. People often respond to differences in a defensive or rejecting way rather than by viewing differences as opportunities to explore new ideas and discover new options. Often, material is rejected because of the label attached to it. A clinician who is behaviorally oriented might pass by an article with the term *psychoanalytic* in its title; those who are psychoanalytically oriented may feel a cold chill when seeing the word *behavioral*. It is important to look beyond labels to the quality of information that is offered. Labels tell us too little about too much and imply too much about too little (Hobbs, 1975). The ad-

vantages of looking for applications rather than limitations are illustrated by a study in which two groups of engineers were given
different instructions in viewing new material. Engineers who were
asked to focus on how content could be used came up with more
creative ideas than did those who were asked to identify its limitations (Hyman, 1961). A charitable approach is especially important
when reading material that is not representative of preferred practice theories.

Remembering What Is Read

Active reading through use of elaboration and comprehensive monitoring strategies increases the likelihood that material will
be remembered. An event must be noticed before it can enter short-
term memory (STM). We cannot hold much information in STM,
and, without rehearsal, content disappears in thirty seconds or less.
Only some of the material that enters STM enters long-term memory (LTM), which holds content that is stored and can be retrieved.
Rehearsal of information can be used to maintain and transfer contents from STM into LTM. Use of different modes of representation
during rehearsal increases recall.

Many of the problems that are attributed to memory difficulties are due to lapses of attention; how attention is distributed influences what enters STM. Items that appear first and last in a list
tend to be recalled. These effects are known as the *primacy* and
recency effects, respectively. Items in the middle of a list tend to be
forgotten. Depth of processing influences memory (see prior discussion of comprehension monitoring and elaboration, Bower & Karlin, 1974). The manner in which information is arranged in our
memory also influences recall. The more ways there are to index a
piece of information or the more associations we have with it, the
easier it is to remember; that is, our knowledge network is better
integrated.

Content is stored in LTM and must be accessible as needed
during decision making (Brown, 1978; Brown & Campione, 1981).
Loftus refers to this retrieval as rummaging through mental drawers. Experts not only have more drawers to rummage through, they
also have a more elaborate system of interconnections among items

and more rules to help them avoid unpromising drawers (Chase & Ericsson, 1981).

Improving Memory

Access to relevant knowledge increases the accuracy of clinical decisions. Some strategies for enhancing memory, such as rehearsal and elaboration, can be used when information is first encountered. Others are helpful when trying to recall material. The relevance of different strategies depends on the material of interest. Very negative and stressful emotions hinder accurate perception and memory. The nature of a task influences the effects of stress; if a habit is well learned, it is less susceptible to disruption by stress or fatigue. Rehearsal is helpful; repeated description of an experience increases the likelihood that it will be remembered. Deliberately attending to certain features enhances memory for those features. For example, the salience of cues for names can be increased by paying attention to a person's facial characteristics as a name is heard or by trying to distinguish a person's face from other similar faces (Bransford and Stein, 1984, p. 42). Important information can be recorded on notes to be referred to later. Comprehension monitoring and elaboration will increase the likelihood that material will be remembered. Whether knowledge is used is also important. (See other sources for guidelines for improving memory, for example, Higbee, 1977; Pressley, Borkowski, & O'Sullivan, 1984).

Getting Access to Helpful Information

Empirical literature related to clinical decisions has increased dramatically. This complicates the task of keeping up with new developments. For example, there has been a great deal of research related to agoraphobia; assessment protocols are available and intervention methods are described in detail (Barlow & Waddell, 1985). Detailed assessment and intervention guidelines have been described in many other areas as well. Material is of little value if it cannot be located when needed. A good filing system increases accessibility. Current uses of the computer (such as offering lists of abstracts relevant to a selected area) will be as outdated as the wisdom tooth when they are replaced by search-and-display procedures and printout options that are far more useful to clinicians. The computer can be used to gain the following information:

- Developmental norms related to given age groups
- Normal and deviant interaction patterns in relation to given kinds of presenting problems (for example, parent-child interactions)
- Indicators of psychopathology
- Assessment measures and protocols related to given concerns together with information about their reliability and validity
- Descriptions of intervention methods and protocols
- Strategies for enhancing client participation
- Descriptions of factors that maximize the effectiveness of specific intervention methods
- Options for assessing progress
- Procedures for encouraging generalization and maintenance

Electronic newsletters and computer bulletin boards can keep clinicians informed about recent research (Dozier & Rice, 1984; see also Niemi & Gooler, 1987).

Professional organizations could take more energetic steps to inform clinicians about controversial matters and practice related knowledge. One helpful step would be to screen manuscripts carefully for opinions masquerading as facts, strawman arguments, question begging, and the suppression of evidence in favor of preferred views. Authors may be unaware that statements are questionable, that positions are distorted, or that alternative views or conflicting evidence is not presented. The differences between what can be accomplished in the everyday world of practice and idealistic assertions by the leadership of professional organizations may encourage despair and burnout among professionals. Take, for example, a recent statement by a past president of the National Association of Social Workers: "We have before us what some have termed a 'once-in-a-century opportunity' to address and solve the most intractable problems of our youth" ("From the President," 1986, p. 2). Being told clinicians have an opportunity to resolve large social problems encourages only guilt and confusion when such problems cannot be resolved by individual counseling (see Chapter Two) and when there is little or no indication that any changes have occurred or will occur on the structural level to address these social problems. In lieu of a more active role of professional organizations in helping clinicians to be informed, clinicians must take energetic creative steps of their own to assess the quality of their knowledge in a domain and to enhance this. Such helpful steps include testing out the accuracy of beliefs with people who are knowledgeable in an area and seeking recent descriptions of work in an area.

A willingness to examine practice beliefs encourages an openness to new knowledge. The suppression of information, whether intentional or not, is the most insidious of all sources of error—because we cannot know what is omitted. It is not only others who withhold information. Clinicians themselves are a prime source of suppressed information via the decisions made about what to read and whom to listen to; they themselves arrange a large part of their knowledge domain (and the gaps in it). Some information is inaccessible because it is written in other languages, and clinicians must await translations (for example, the essays of Frank Basaglia, who was responsible for transforming the mental health delivery system in Italy, Scheper-Hughes & Lovell, 1987).

Keeping Knowledge Alive

Knowledge will drift away if it is not used. Even when clinicians intend to use knowledge and have correct understandings of procedures, they may not use this in their practice (Meichenbaum & Turk, 1987). Prompts (such as checklists) and incentives will have to be provided to foster use of knowledge (see Chapter 13). Steps that can be taken to prevent knowledge from becoming inert include using it, training others, writing a step-by-step outline, using prompts, offering incentives for its use, and engaging in "deep processing" concerning its importance and rationale.

Learning can be planned or unplanned. Gains in clinical knowledge are more likely if a continuing education agenda is designed that offers access to both high-quality training programs and useful written material. Agency policies and practices concerning continuing education influence the quality of available learning opportunities. For example, training programs may or may not include procedures that encourage generalizations of new skills on the job.

Belief Perseverance

The greatest challenge is giving up old beliefs and replacing these with new ones when new information contradicts old beliefs. We tend to cling to old beliefs—and for reasons that seem and often are good: they have worked for us, they are familiar, and they give us a sense of control over the environment. Beliefs can survive significant logical and empirical challenges. For example, consider the failure of debriefing—that subjects continue to believe in initial estimates of their performance even after they have been "debriefed" about the environmental reason for their performance (Ross, Lepper, & Hubbard, 1975). Subjects were asked to distinguish real from fictitious suicide notes and were provided with false feedback in relation to their performance. All subjects were debriefed following this phase of the study; they were informed that the feedback they had received was false and that they had been assigned to one of three conditions: success, failure, or average performance. Debriefing was not successful in altering perception of performance. Subjects assigned to the success condition continued to rate their performance and abilities more favorably than did the other two groups. Subjects assigned to the failure condition continued to rate themselves as lacking in ability and as unsuccessful. The perseverance effects of initial impressions have been found with observers also.

Why are beliefs so persistent? Here, too, information-processing factors are at work in terms of biased search, recall, and assimilation of evidence (Einhorn, 1980a). Although motivational and emotional factors may play a role, they do not seem to account for the kind of research findings described above. All the tendencies that have been previously discussed come into play such as confirmation bias and ease of discounting contradictory information by offering alternative explanations. Offering explanations for beliefs makes these more lasting. "Thus the subject who suddenly finds herself confronted with evidence of her superior or inferior ability at discriminating suicide notes might search for some aspect of her background or personality that might account for such a talent or deficiency. The seemingly successful subject, for example, may credit her performance to her familiarity with the self-revealing poetry of an author who later committed suicide; the apparent failure may cite her own cheerful and optimistic disposition as an impediment to the empathetic set of task demands" (Einhorn, 1980a, pp. 26-27). Beliefs are more likely to be altered if concrete information based on firsthand experience is provided that is compatible with current knowledge. Here, too, we see the importance of a true clinical apprenticeship that would offer such opportunities. Widely accepted clinical beliefs are likely to receive consistent support from material that appears in professional sources—especially those selectively chosen from the many available. Only by a careful selection of reading material can clinicians discover innovative material that offers divergent views of clinical practice (see, for example, Basaglia, in Scheper-Hughes & Lovell, 1987; Sedgwick, 1982) and preserve less popular views.

Summary

Domain-specific knowledge is helpful (or critical) in making accurate clinical decisions. Knowledge relevant to clinical practice has expanded considerably, which makes personal choices as to whether to use this knowledge more significant in what is offered to clients. Accurate assessment on the part of clinicians of the completeness of their knowledge in an area influences the accuracy of the decisions they make. If a great deal is known on a topic, the possible discrepancies between what a clinician knows and what can be known may be quite large. If a great deal is known but little is used, then what is offered to clients is not empirically based methods but pseudoscience; clinicians as well as the public may be bamboozled into forgetting the difference by the emotive persuasiveness of rhetorical presentations in the media as well as in professional sources. What in fact rests on unsupported proclamation may be placed in the trappings of scientific credibility. Bogus claims are often made for the objectivity of psychiatric classification schemes and service-delivery systems that benefit staff members more than clients.

Decisions made about what to read or listen to are influenced by comprehensibility and credibility of material, as well as by entertainment value and judged importance. Clinicians differ in the criteria used to assess the credibility of material. Some prefer scientific empiricism; others prefer anecdotal empiricism, mysticism, or appeals to authority. Preferences influence what is learned and thus what is offered to clients. Clinicians also differ in the goals they set in selecting material to read and workshops to attend. Some focus on entertainment value. Others focus on acquiring knowledge that can be used to help clients.

Skills in learning how to learn, as well as facilitating attitudes toward knowledge, influence the size of the discrepancy between what a clinician knows and what can be known that would be helpful in arriving at accurate decisions. Active learning skills, such as comprehension monitoring and elaboration skills, enhance learning; these are especially important in view of the tendency in both the media as well as in many professional sources to suppress unpopular views. Use of the principle of charity when reading decreases the likelihood that valuable content will be prematurely discarded. Asking "What's missing?" and "Is there any evidence that this claim is true?" decreases acceptance of bogus claims that limit the quality of services offered to clients. What often seems an overwhelming task today will be substantially eased as computerized search, display, and printout options become more widely used to gain access to domain-specific content.

The nature of clinical training programs influences clinical decisions. Inclusion of a high quality mentoring experience as well as material concerning sources of formal and informal fallacies, contingency analysis, evaluation of practice, and the influence of social, political, and economic influences on the mental health industry—all discussed in an atmosphere that encourages consideration of the pros and cons of different positions—would enhance clinical decision making skills. Training programs should provide students with effective learning and self-management skills they can use to continue their professional development in an effective manner and to overcome obstacles to clear thinking such as lack of motivation, procrastination, and lack of perseverance (see Chapter Twelve). Professional organizations could increase efforts to enhance the quality of clinical decisions by decreasing dysfunctional rhetoric, clarifying vague ethical guidelines related to clinical competence, and presenting both sides of issues discussed in professional sources. The knowledge available to clinicians and the manner in which this knowledge is used is shaped by the particular society in which they live; understanding political and structural influences on the mental health industry allows clinicians to identify underlying values and consequences associated with different practice perspectives.

4

Reasons and Reasoning:
The Heart of Making Decisions
About Problems and Solutions

Clinical reasoning occurs in an interpersonal context (that between therapists and clients) and considerable attention has been devoted to the description of this process and its effects on assumptions made and the outcomes of therapy (see, for example, Garfield & Bergin, 1986; Rice & Greenberg, 1984). Less attention has been devoted to the effects of both formal and informal fallacies on the clinical reasoning process and the resulting arguments presented (although considerable attention has been devoted to the description of reasoning fallacies on the part of clients and this is a major emphasis within rational-emotive therapy, Ellis & Grieger, 1977 and Beck's cognitive behavioral therapy, Beck, 1976).

Clinical reasoning involves making and evaluating arguments, making judgments and drawing conclusions, and forming and testing hypotheses (Nickerson, 1986a). It is "largely the conversion of unconscious judgments, feelings and knowledge into something more explicit" (Scriven, 1976, p. 180). Reasoning is concerned with exploration of the assumptions that are related to premises; that is, a tentative conclusion is drawn and then the assumptions related to the conclusion are reviewed to determine whether the conclusion is warranted. So, the major part of clinical reasoning involves debating with ourselves—identifying options and thinking through the consequences of selecting one of them. The terms *rea-*

soning, problem-solving, decision making, and *thinking* are closely related, and the tasks they involve overlap. Reasoning is an active process involving an interaction between clinicians and the social and physical situations they encounter (Greeno, 1989, p. 135). Far from being a dull, uncreative activity, being reasonable requires skill and sensitivity to the difference between "well supported" and "widely accepted." Being reasonable "takes courage, because it seldom corresponds to being popular" (Scriven, 1976, p. 5). Affect influences reasoning in several ways, as described in Chapter Two.

Views of Intellectual Competence

Discussions about what makes a "good thinker" are as old as philosophy itself. Let's take a look at what a modern day author views as knowledge, abilities, attitudes, and ways of behaving that are characteristic of a "good thinker" (Nickerson, 1987, pp. 29-30).

- Uses evidence skillfully and impartially
- Organizes thoughts and articulates them concisely and coherently
- Distinguishes between logically valid and invalid inferences
- Suspends judgment in the absence of sufficient evidence to support a decision
- Understands the difference between reasoning and rationalizing
- Attempts to anticipate the probable consequences of alternative actions before choosing among them
- Understands the idea of degrees of belief
- Has a sense of the value and cost of information, knows how to seek information, and does so when it makes sense
- Sees similarities and analogies that are not superficially apparent
- Can learn independently and . . . . has an interest in doing so
- Applies problem-solving techniques appropriately in domains other than those in which they were learned
- Can structure informally represented problems in such a way that formal techniques (for example, mathematics) can be used to solve them
- Listens carefully to other people's ideas

- Understands the difference between winning an argument and being right
- Recognizes that most real-world problems have more than one possible solution and that those solutions may differ in numerous respects and may be difficult to compare in terms of a single figure of merit
- Looks for unusual approaches to complex problems
- Can represent differing viewpoints without distortion, exaggeration, or caricaturization
- Is aware of the fact that one's understanding is always limited
- Recognizes the fallibility of one's own opinions, the probability of bias in those opinions, and the danger of differentially weighting evidence according to personal preferences
- Can strip a verbal argument of irrelevancies and phrase it in terms of its essentials
- Understands the differences among conclusions, assumptions, and hypotheses
- Habitually questions one's own views and attempts to understand both the assumptions that are critical to those views and the implications of the views
- Is sensitive to the difference between the validity of a belief and the intensity with which it is held

Reasons

Many kinds of reasons are used in clinical decision making, and different practice theories emphasize different ones. These differences affect how problems are framed and what information is gathered. Examples of fallacies related to different kinds of reasons are offered in other chapters. Clinicians often reason from analogy; that is, they look to what has happened before to discover what to do in novel situations; they seek and draw conclusions from a comparison of experiences. The analogy of psychological problems to illness is perhaps the best known analogy in clinical practice and one that is still widely accepted (as can be seen in acceptance of the disease view of alcoholism and discussions of "sick" families). Comparisons are often made between the functioning of the human mind and computer processing. Arguments based on an analogy depend on the similarity of the cases compared. Questions of concern (Terry, 1973, p. 99) include How many respects are similar? How many respects are dissimilar? Are the bases of comparison relevant to the issue? Is there agreement on the major points? For example, those who do not accept the disease view of alcoholism argue that problematic drinking does not have the characteristic of a disease; for example, drinking does not necessarily become worse without treatment and, for some, it is not true that one drink leads to many (see, for example, Fingarette, 1988). Analogies may be literal or figurative. Literal analogies involve comparison between classes, cases, or objects of the same kind. Figurative analogies involve comparison between unlike categories.

Clinicians generalize from samples to populations. A psychiatrist may interview three Vietnamese families and make assumptions about all Vietnamese families. The accuracy of a generalization depends on the size and representativeness of the sample. Questions of concern include Are the examples relevant? Are enough examples provided? Are the examples typical? Are there any counter-examples?

Making clinical decisions also requires reasoning from signs and symptoms. Observed signs (such as slumped shoulders, downcast eyes, and tears) may be used to infer emotional states such as depression. That is, the signs are used as "signifiers" of a state. Signs may be used also as indicative of a certain history. A recent example is the use of the "reflex anal dilatation test" to evaluate whether children had been abused sexually by their parents (Hobbs and Wynne, 1989). A key question here concerns validity—are the signs really indicators of the state assumed (see discussion of the predictive accuracy of tests in Chapter Ten).

Clinicians also reason by cause—that is, they have assumptions about the causes of particular presenting problems such as anxiety, substance abuse, obsessions, or marital disharmony. The study of attributions made in different contexts and the factors that influence them is an active area of research (see Chapters Two and Seven). Some publications such as the *Skeptical Inquirer* are dedicated to highlighting the lack of evidence for many commonly accepted causes of behavior (such as spirits from past lives). However, lack of evidence for a claim does not mean that it is incorrect.

Nor does lack of evidence discourage people from believing in a claim. Indeed, some clinicians believe in practice theories that have no supporting evidence.

Another form of reasoning is by exclusion. Alternative accounts for a given event or behavior are identified, and the adequacy of each is examined. This involves a search for rival explanations. For example, if a client is referred to a community mental health agency because of intractable depression, one hypothesis may be that this is an unsolvable problem, given modern-day knowledge. A rival hypothesis may be that this client did not receive state-of-the-art intervention and that rapid improvement would follow such intervention. The book *Rival Hypotheses* (Huck & Sandler, 1979) presents 100 different claims and invites readers to evaluate these in order to sharpen their skills in identifying alternative hypotheses. A search for alternative explanations is one of the main strategies that can be used to avoid premature acceptance of an explanation that may be inaccurate (see Chapter Nine).

Hot and cold reasons correspond to two major routes to persuasion—by affective association (hot) or by reasoned argument (cold). Many people try to persuade others by offering reasons that play on emotions and appeal to accepted beliefs and values. Simon (1983) uses the example of Hitler's *Mein Kampf:* "Hitler was an effective rhetorician for Germans precisely because his passion and incentives resonated with beliefs and values already present in many German hearts. The heat of his rhetoric rendered his readers incapable of applying the rules of reason and evidence to his arguments. Nor was it only Germans who resonated to the facts and values he proclaimed. The latent anti-Semitism and overt anti-Communism of many Western statesmen made a number of his arguments plausible to them" (pp. 98–99).

Some Helpful Distinctions

Plausible reasons are much more likely to be offered if distinctions are made between facts, beliefs, and opinions. These and other helpful distinctions are discussed in the section that follows.

Some people confuse the use of logical principles and reasoning. Logic is concerned with the form or validity of deductive arguments. "It provides methods and rules for restating information so as to make what is implicit explicit. It has little to do with the determination of truth or falsity" (Nickerson, 1986a, p. 7). Effective clinical reasoning requires much more than logic; it requires skill in developing arguments and hypotheses, establishing the relevance of information to an argument, and evaluating the plausibility of assertions. That is, it requires a great deal of inventiveness. It also requires a willingness to change beliefs on the basis of evidence gathered. Johnson-Laird (1985) offered this example concerning who committed a murder. The victim was stabbed to death in a movie theater. The suspect was traveling on a train to London when the murder took place. Logically it seems that this suspect must be innocent: one person cannot be in two places at once. However, the only way to guarantee the truth of a conclusion is to eliminate all possible counter examples. "Logic cannot ensure that one has considered all the different ways in which the murder might have been accomplished. Like most everyday problems that call for reasoning, the explicit premises leave most of the relevant information unstated. Indeed, the real business of reasoning in these cases is to determine the relevant factors and possibilities, and it therefore depends on a knowledge of the specific domain. Hence, the construction of putative counter examples calls for an active exercise of memory and imagination rather than a formal derivation of one expression from others" (Johnson-Laird, 1985, p. 45).

Similarly, logic will not be of value in deciding that a client who complains of fatigue and headaches should be screened by a neurologist to determine if there is a physical cause of these complaints; knowledge as well as logic is required (see discussion of formal and informal fallacies later in this chapter).

It is sometimes assumed that reasoning and creativity have little to do with each other. Some poeple believe that engineers are not creative people, that they deal with well-defined relationships that simply require a great deal of tedious study and memorization to master. On the contrary, creativity and reasoning go hand-in-hand, especially in areas such as clinical decision making in which needed information is often missing, and in which there is no one solution and no agreed-on criteria for evaluating success. Cognitive styles, attitudes, and strategies associated with creativity include the following (Greeno, 1989; Nickerson et al., 1985; Weisberg, 1986):

- Readiness to explore
- Readiness to change
- Attention to problem finding as well as problem solving
- Immersion in a task
- Restructuring of understanding; restructuring one's relation to a situation
- Belief that knowing and understanding are products of one's intellectual process
- Withholding of judgment
- Emphasis on penetration and understanding
- Thinking in terms of opposites
- Interest in being original
- Distinguishing the conventional from the original
- Valuing complexity, ambiguity, and uncertainty combined with an interest in finding order
- Commitment as reflected in long hours devoted to work and total engagement
- Valuing feedback but not deferring to convention and social pressures
- Recognition of multiple perspectives on a topic
- Deferring closure in early stages of a creative task

Knowledge is required to evaluate the plausibility of premises related to an argument. Take the following example: (1) Depression always has a psychological cause; (2) Mr. Draper is depressed; (3) Therefore, Mr. Draper's depression is psychological in origin. The logic of this argument is sound, but the conclusion may be false. The cause of Mr. Draper's depression could be physiological. Thus, knowledge is critical in offering cogent arguments.

Reasoning involves the review of evidence against as well as evidence in favor of a position. Rationalizing a belief entails a selective search for evidence in support of a belief or action which may or may not be deliberate. "[It is] easy after having made some choice that is significant in our lives to fall into the trap of convincing ourselves of the reasonableness of that choice. It is also easy to forget, with the passage of time, what the real determinants of the choice were and to substitute for them 'reasons' that make the choice seem like a good one, and perhaps a better one than it actually was" (Nickerson, 1986a, p. 14). When clinicians rationalize arguments, they are interested in building a case rather than weighing evidence for and against an argument. (See discussion of hindsight bias in Chapter Ten and excuses in Chapter Twelve.) This is not to say that there is no interest in persuading when arguments are presented; the difference lies in a balanced consideration of multiple perspectives in viewing possible reasons.

It is helpful to distinguish among propaganda, bias, and points of view (MacLean, 1981). *Bias* refers to an emotional leaning to one side. Biased people try to persuade others but may not be aware that they are doing so. They may use propaganda tactics and faulty reasoning and offer statements in a manner designed to gain uncritical or emotional acceptance of a biased position. Personal biases may make it difficult to identify biases in a statement. *Propagandists* are aware of their interests and usually intentionally disguise these. Here too, messages are couched in a way to encourage uncritical acceptance. Those with a *point of view* are also aware of their interests but sources are described and propaganda devices and faulty reasoning are avoided; statements are made in a manner that solicits critical review. Views can be examined because they are clearly stated. People with a point of view are open to clarifying their statements when asked. (See Ellul, 1965, for an interesting discussion of propaganda).

Reasoning does not necessarily yield the truth. "People who are considered by many of their peers to be reasonable people often do take, and are able to defend quite convincingly, diametrically opposing positions on controversial matters" (Nickerson, 1986a, p. 12). However, effective reasoners are more likely to generate assertions that are closer to the truth than ineffective reasoners. Some assumptions are better (closer to the truth) than are others. The accuracy of a conclusion does not necessarily indicate that the reasoning used to reach it was sound; errors in the opposite direction may have cancelled each other out.

A number of terms reflect the difference between rigorous

logical reasoning and exploratory thinking, between the generation of hypothesis and the testing of hypotheses. Examples include divergent versus convergent thinking, and problem finding versus problem solving. However, as noted in the discussion of creativity and reasoning, a sharp distinction between the two kinds of thinking does not hold.

Assigning appropriate weight to evidence for or against assertions is a key part of what it means to be reasonable. Distinguishing between *consistency, corroboration,* and *proof* is important in assigning proper weight. Clinicians often use "consistency" in support of an assumption; for example, they search for consistent evidence when exploring a depressed client's history of depression. An assertion should be consistent with other beliefs that are held; that is, self-contradictory views should not knowingly be entertained. Of the three criteria (proof, falsifiability, and consistency) consistency is the weakest for offering positive evidence. Two or more assertions may be consistent with each other but yield little or no insight into the soundness of an argument. Saying that A (a history of "mental illness") is consistent with B (alleged current "mental illness") is to say only that it is possible to believe B given A.

Falsifiability is an important characteristic of assertions. Some assertions are not falsifiable; there is no way to determine if they are false. Psychoanalytic theory is often criticized on the grounds that it is not falsifiable—that contradictory hypotheses can be drawn from the theory (Popper, 1963). Proof is a much stronger criterion and since a future test may show an assumption to be incorrect, even one that is strongly corroborated, no assertion can ever be proven (Popper, 1963). However, a theory can be shown to be false given that it is falsifiable. If nothing can ever be proven, the least one can do is to construct falsifiable theories: theories that generate specific hypotheses that can be tested. The points below describe this approach (Popper, 1959, p. 36).

1.   It is easy to obtain confirmations, or verifications, for nearly every theory—if we look for confirmations.
2.   Confirmations should count only if they are the result of *risky predictions;* that is to say, if, unenlightened by the theory in question, we should have expected an event which was incom-

patible with the theory—an event which would have refuted the theory.

3. Every "good" scientific theory is a prohibition; it forbids certain things to happen. The more a theory forbids, the better it is.

4. A theory which is not refutable by any conceivable event is nonscientific. Irrefutability is not a virtue of a theory (as people often think) but a vice.

5. Every genuine test of a theory is an attempt to falsify it or to refute it. Testability is falsifiability; but there are degrees of testability; some theories are more testable, more exposed to refutation, than others; they take, as it were, greater risks.

6. Confirming evidence should not count except when it is the result of a *genuine test of the theory;* and this means that it can be presented as a serious but unsuccessful attempt to falsify the theory.

In an empirical approach to clinical practice it is assumed that the credibility of an assertion is related to the uniqueness and supportive value of the predictions that have been tested. Credibility of clinical assumptions may be assessed using quite different criteria such as authority or mysticism (see Chapter Seven).

It is helpful to distinguish between facts and beliefs. A belief can be defined as "confidence that a particular thing is true, as evidenced by a willingness to act as though it were" (Nickerson, 1986a, p. 2). Beliefs vary widely in credibility. Most clinicians would believe the statement "childhood experiences influence adult development" to be highly credible. There would be less agreement on the credibility of the assertion that "childhood experiences determine adult development." Facts can be viewed as beliefs that are well supported by evidence and therefore as justifying a high degree of confidence. Facts are capable of verification; beliefs may not be. Reasons (good ones) consist of justified beliefs; that is, plausible, sound arguments can be offered for claims made. Some beliefs are matters of definition (for example, 3 + 3 = 6).

Another helpful distinction is between beliefs and opinions. Beliefs are statements that, in principle, can be shown to be true or false, whereas with an opinion, it does not make sense to consider it as true or false because people differ in their preferences and opinions. An example of an opinion statement is "I prefer insight-oriented treatment." This statement appeals to preferences. An example of a belief is "Play therapy can help children to overcome anxiety." Here, evidence can be gathered to determine if this is indeed the case. Additional examples of opinions and beliefs are shown below. The first one is an opinion and the last two are beliefs.

- I like to collect payment for each session at the end of the session.
- Insight therapy is more effective than cognitive behavioral treatment of depression.
- My pet Rotweiler helps people with their problems (quote from psychologist on morning talk show, 4/6/88).

The woman who offered the last statement also described the value of her pet Rotweiller in offering support to her clients during interviews: the pet would sit by the wife when she spoke and move over to the husband and offer support to him when he spoke. We often allow our preferences to influence our beliefs, even though preferences and beliefs should be independent.

Another common distinction is that between deep processing or mindful action in which an active effort is made to understand something and automatic or mindless functioning in which tasks are carried out fairly automatically (see, for example, Chanowitz & Langer, 1980).

Arguments

There are many products of reasoning: arguments are one product. The term *argumentation* refers to the process of making claims, challenging these, backing them with reasons (assertions), criticizing these reasons, responding to the criticism offered (Toulmin, Rieke, & Janik, 1979, p. 13). In clinical practice, this process is often covert; that is, different possibilities of causes for presenting problems are considered during clinical interviews. An argument in this sense refers to the claims and reasons offered for these—that is, "a set of assertions that is used to support a belief" (Nickerson, 1986a, p. 2). This term has a different meaning in everyday use in which it refers to disagreements between two people (for example, "They had an argument about who would go to the store.").

Arguments involve a set of assertions, one of which is a conclusion and the rest of which are intended to support that conclusion. For example, if a clinician argues that, because a client has a history of being hospitalized for anxiety and compulsive hand-washing, current complaints about anxiety and obsessive thoughts indicate that another severe episode of compulsive hand-washing is imminent. The conclusion that another severe breakdown will occur is based on the premise that there is a history of hospitalization for what seem to be similar problems. The purpose of arguments is often to convince someone (or oneself) that something is true or to convince someone to act in a certain way. Another purpose is to explore openly the accuracy of given assertions.

Arguments consist of parts; they can be taken apart as well as put together. They may be strong (convincing) or weak (unconvincing), simple or complex. A complex argument usually involves several assertions in support of one or more conclusions. Assertions may involve statements of fact ("a belief for which there is enough evidence to justify a high degree of confidence," Nickerson, 1986a, p. 36), assumptions, or hypotheses. For example, there may be no doubt that a client was hospitalized. The term *assumption* refers to "an assertion that we either believe to be true in spite of being unable to produce compelling evidence of its truth, or are willing to accept as true for purposes of debate or discussion" (Nickerson, 1986a, pp. 36–37). A hypothesis is an assertion that we do not know to be true but that we think is testable. Assumptions, hypotheses, or statements of fact may be used as premises in an argument—or they may serve as conclusions; that is, an assertion may be a conclusion that is drawn from what precedes it and can also be a premise with respect to what follows it. "The credibility of a conclusion can be no greater than the least credible of the premises from which it is drawn, so a conclusion cannot be considered a statement of fact unless all of the premises are statements of fact. . . . If the conclusion follows from two premises one of which is considered to be a fact and the other an assumption, the conclusion should not be considered a statement of fact" (Nickerson, 1986a, p. 37). Universal assertions that contain words such as *all* or *no* are much more difficult to defend than are particular assertions that contain qualifiers such as *some.* The statement that all children of alcoholic parents have problems as adults would be more difficult to support than the more modest claim that some children of alcoholic parents have problems later.

A key part of an argument is the claim, conclusion, or position that is put forward (see Table 2). In the statement "Mary Walsh is the person who is responsible for the abuse of this child; she had the greatest opportunity," the claim or conclusion is clear. Often, excessive wordiness makes a conclusion difficult to identify; that is, "an eloquent speaker or writer can dress up his arguments in all kinds of ways so as to conceal their deficits and make them attractive to his audience" (Toulmin et al., 1979, p. 106). The claim here is that Mary Walsh is guilty of the abuse of the child. Claims or conclusions are often qualified—that is, some probability is expressed (for example, "I think there is a 90 percent probability that Mary Walsh abused this child"). Conclusions can be further qualified by describing the conditions under which they do, or do not, hold. A clinician may believe that she would only abuse the child "if she were under extreme stress."

A second critical feature of an argument is the reasons or premises offered to support the claim made. Premises can be divided into two parts—grounds and warrants (see Table 2). The grounds (data or evidence) must be relevant to the claim as well as sufficient to support the claim, and that is when warrants are used. Warrants concern the inference or justification of making the connection between the grounds and the claim. The question is: Do the grounds provide support for the claim made?

Warrants may involve appeals to common knowledge, empirical evidence, practice theory, etc. Let's return to the claim that Mary Walsh is responsible for the abuse of a child. The ground is that she had the opportunity to abuse the child. The warrant is probably something of the nature that opportunity is sufficient to yield abuse—clearly an inaccurate assumption. There is no firm backing for the warrant—opportunity does not an abuser make. So warrants purport to offer evidence for making the step from the

Table 2. Toulmin's Six Types of Statement in a Rational Argument.

Label	Name(s)	Logical Function
C	Claim or conclusion	States a claim or a conclusion.
D	Data, evidence, or foundation	Offers data or foundations, i.e., relevant evidence, for the claim.
W	Inference warrant	Warrants or justifies the connection between data (D) and claim (C) by appealing to a rule of inference, such as an operational definition, a practical standard, or an analogy.
Q	Modal qualifier	Qualifies a claim or conclusion (C) by expressing degrees of confidence and likelihood.
R	Rebuttal or reservation	Rebuts a claim or conclusion (C) by stating the conditions under which it does not hold; or introduces reservations showing the limits within which the claim (C) is made.
B	Backing	Backs up, justifies, or otherwise supports an inference warrant (W) by appealing to further evidence (empirical data, common knowledge, professional practice, scientific theory, and so on).

Colloquially speaking:

C	answers the questions 'What are you saying?' 'What is it you are claiming?' 'What is your conclusion?'
D	answers the questions 'What have you to go on?' 'Where is your evidence?' 'What data do you have?'
W	answers the questions 'How do you make that out?' 'What is the connection?' 'Why are you entitled to draw that conclusion?'
Q	answers the questions 'How sure are you?' 'What confidence do you have in your claim?' 'How likely is it that what you say is correct?'
R	answers the questions 'What are you assuming?' 'Under what conditions would your argument break down?' 'What reservations would you make?'
B	answers the questions 'What proof have you?' 'What is the justification for your line of reasoning?' 'Is there any support for the connection you are making?'

Source: From *The Case-Study Method in Psychology and Related Disciplines* (p. 195) by D. B. Bromley, 1986, New York: Wiley. Copyright 1986 by John Wiley & Sons. Reprinted by permission.

grounds to the claim and the strength of the support offered should be evaluated. How reliably does the warrant offer such evidence? Are the grounds necessary or sufficient? For example, opportunity is necessary but not sufficient. The possible combinations of false or true premises and conclusions are shown in Figure 1.

An argument may be unsound for one of three reasons. There may be something wrong with its logical structure: (1) all mental patients are people; (2) John is a person; (3) therefore, John is a mental patient. It may contain false premises: (1) all battering men were abused as children; (2) Mr. Smith batters his wife; (3) therefore, Mr. Smith was abused as a child. It may be irrelevant or circular: (1) kicking other children is a sign of aggression; (2) Johnny kicks other children; (3) therefore, Johnny is aggressive.

The last two arguments contain informal fallacies; they have a correct logical form but are still incorrect. Informal fallacies are related to the content of arguments rather than to form. There are many varieties of informal fallacies (see Chapters Five and Six). Arguments often contain unfounded or unproven premises. They may give the impression that they are valid arguments but because relevant facts have not been presented correctly (they may have been left out, evaded, or distorted), they are not valid. An example of the logical error of affirming the consequence is : (1) if he has measles, he should have red spots; (2) he has spots; (3) therefore, he has the measles. Denying the antecedent also involves a logical error: (1) if we don't conserve clinical resources, the supply will run out; (2) we will not waste clinical resources; (3) therefore, our supply should not run out.

In neither case above does the conclusion follow from the premises. These errors involve a confusion between one-way and bidirectional implication (Nickerson, 1986a, p. 82). Contradictions are a type of implication. For example, to say that X contradicts Z, is to say that if X is true, Z must be false. A premise implies another premise when the second premise must be true if the first is true. Contradictions involve a bidirectional relationship: if X contradicts Y, then Y contradicts X. However, this is not necessarily the case with implication; although X may imply Y, Y may not imply X. The premise conversion error occurs when the assertion "all X are Y" (all clinicians are human) is assumed to be the same as "all

**Figure 1. The Four Combinations of True or False Premises
and Conclusions in a Valid Logical Argument.**

	Conclusion True	Conclusion False
Premises True	Necessary (Conclusion must be true if premises are true)	Impossible (Conclusion cannot be false if premises are true)
Premises False	Possible (Conclusion *may* be true even if premises are false)	Possible (Conclusion *may* be false if premises are false)

Note: Entries in the table indicate how the truth or falsity of the conclusion depends on the truth or falsity of the premises.

Source: From *Reflections on Reasoning* (p. 90) by R. S. Nickerson, 1986, Hillsdale, NJ: Erlbaum. Copyright 1986 by Lawrence Erlbaum Associates. Reprinted by permission.

Y are X" (all humans are clinicians). Examples of clinical errors that result from this fallacy are illustrated in Chapter Nine. (See other sources for a description of logical fallacies, for example, Copi, 1961.)

Both deductive and inductive reasoning play a critical role in clinical decision making. Deductive arguments involve a sequence of premises and a conclusion; if the reasoning is logically valid, the conclusion necessarily follows (although it may not be true because one or more of the premises may be false) (see Table 3). Deductive arguments can produce false conclusions either when one of the premises is false or when one of the rules of deductive inference is violated, as in the example above illustrating the logical fallacy of affirming the consequent. The conclusion may be true but it is invalid because it is arrived at by an illogical inference. Seldom are the major premises as well as the conclusion clearly stated in deductive arguments; more typically, at least one premise is missing.

Table 3. Distinguishing Deductive from Inductive Arguments.

Deductive Example	*Inductive Example*
• No animals are persons. • Only persons have rights. • Therefore, no animals have rights.	• Both psychiatrists and psychologists have professional training. • Psychiatrists have hospital privileges. • Therefore, psychologists should also have hospital privileges.
• If you see one client, you've seen them all. • I have seen one client. • Therefore, I have seen them all.	• All clients I have seen have been demoralized. • Therefore all clients are demoralized when they first seek help.
Although the premises may or may not be true, if they are true, the conclusion is true as well, because, in a deductive argument, the information in the conclusion is implicitly present in the premises. Thus, adding information does not change the probability that the conclusion is true. A good deductive argument is called valid.	Although the premises provide evidence for the conclusion, it is possible that the conclusion is false even when the premises are true, because in an inductive argument the conclusion contains information not present in the premises. In an inductive argument, the probability of the conclusion may change with the addition of further information. A good inductive argument is called strong (or plausible).

Source: Adapted from *Inductive Arguments: A Field Guide* (p. 4) by K. D. Moore, 1986, Dubuque, IA: Kendall/Hunt.

Logical (deductive) arguments use deductive inferences; there are objective criteria that can be used to evaluate such arguments. With plausible (inductive) arguments, there are no objective criteria; what is convincing may differ from person to person. Key assertions can be identified in plausible arguments as well as other assertions that are assumed to support the main one (see Table 3). Inductive reasoning involves generalizing from the particular to the general. It is assumed that what is true of the sample is true of all possible cases. For example, if a psychologist sees three young successful professional men who use cocaine and who complain of stress in their work life, he or she may conclude that all young

professional men who use cocaine experience stress. Thus, in inductive reasoning, clinicians go beyond the data at hand in drawing a
conclusion that they cannot affirm with certainty; conclusions
probably follow from the premises. (See other sources for further
discussion—for example, Holland, Holyoak, Nisbett and Thagard,
1986; Popper, 1983b).

Analyzing Arguments

Skill in analyzing arguments will increase the quality of clinical decisions whether one is considering arguments presented by
others or examining one's own—the latter is more challenging:
"Playing prosecutor, judge, and jury when one is oneself the defendant requires an unusual degree of objectivity and commitment
to the truth" (Nickerson, 1986a, p. 88). There are many excellent descriptions of how to analyze arguments (see, for example, Nickerson, 1986a; Scriven, 1976; Toulmin et al., 1979). Arguments are
often incomplete. Key premises or conclusions may be missing, and
a critical part of examining an argument is filling in these parts.
For example, consider the following statements. What are key premises? "Sexualization for purposes of stimulation of a dead self is
frequent and addictive. In general, so-called masochistic behaviors
of all types are probably more often the result of the desire and need
to stimulate, even through pain, affects which will counter deadness
and nothingness. They can be seen as the outgrowth of a motivation
to be alive (self-cohesion enhancing) rather than a desire to be dead
(self-destructive). Behaviors such as promiscuity, exhibitionism, or
voyeurism, seem to be sexualized attempts to fulfill nonsexual stim-
ulating and calming self-needs, that is, mirroring, twinship, and
idealization, which are necessary to help maintain a cohesive sense
of self" (Chelton & Bonney, 1987, p. 41).

The following steps are helpful in analzying incomplete logical arguments.

- "Identify the conclusion or key assertion.
- List all the other explicit assertions that make up the argument
  as given.
- Add any unstated assertions that are necessary to make the

argument complete. (Put them in parentheses to distinguish them from assertions that are explicit in the argument as given.)
- Order the premises (or supporting assertions) and conclusion (or key assertion) so as to show the structure of the argument" (Nickerson, 1986a, p. 87).

Since induction is based on facts, "all the principles and lines of arguments on facts apply to induction. Whenever we talk in terms of percentages, ratios, indices, the majority of cases, and the minority, we are referring to terms statistical in nature" (Huber, 1963, p. 123). These statistics are usually gathered by sampling processes (an inductive process). Helpful questions raised when evaluating inductive arguments include the following (Huber, 1963, p. 140):

- Are the facts accurate?
- Do the examples consist of isolated or universal instances?
- Do the examples used cover a significant time period?
- Are the examples given typical or atypical?
- Is the conclusion correctly stated?
- Is the argument really of concern—the "so what" and "what harm" questions?

The context should be considered in attempts to understand the intended meaning of a claim; however, words should be interpreted as they generally would be defined in the English language. Arguments should not be dismissed simply because they are presented emotionally or because a conclusion is disliked; the emotion with which a position is presented is not necessarily related to the soundness of an argument (Scriven, 1976). Since plausible (inductive) arguments do not have to fit any particular form, objective evaluation is more difficult than it is with deductive arguments. As with logical arguments, the truth of the premises is important to assess. However, even if these are assumed to be true, clinicians may disagree as to whether they provide evidence for a conclusion. Questions of concern in evaluating a logical argument include: Is it complete? Is its meaning clear? Is it valid (does the conclusion follow from the premises)? Do I believe the premises? (Nickerson,

1986a, p. 88). An argument may be worthy of consideration even though it has some defects.

Counterarguments should be considered. Are there arguments on the same issue that point to the opposite conclusion or to a somewhat different conclusion? For example, an analogy may be used to support the opposite conclusion. Are there other arguments that support the same conclusion? Consider the following claims made by astrologers to support their belief in astrology (Kelly et al., 1986). What are possible counterarguments? (1) Astrology has great antiquity and durability. (2) Astrology is found in many cultures. (3) Many great scholars have believed in it. (4) Astrology is based on observation. (5) Extraterrestrial influences exist. (6) Astrology has been proved by research. (7) Nonastrologers are not qualified to judge. (8) Astrology works.

Many statements, written or spoken, are opinions or points of view; "they frequently don't pass the test of providing reasons for a conclusion, reasons that can be separated from a conclusion" (Scriven, 1976, p. 67). The question is, Can the premises be established independently of the conclusion? Is the argument convincing?

Kinds of Arguments

Arguments occur in different contexts, including courts of law, case conferences, Joe's Bar, and the American Psychiatric Association annual convention. These different contexts influence the manner in which a topic is discussed in terms of different norms, values, procedures, and requirements for and types of evidence that are acceptable or unacceptable (Bromley, 1986, p. 223). The focus in this book is on reasoning processes that occur during clinical interviews, as well as in other contexts related to clinical practice (such as professional meetings and case conferences). This kind of reasoning tends to occur in a consensual (cooperative) framework. The most elaborate and detailed set of rules related to the presentation and rebuttal of arguments can be found in the field of law. For example, specific grounds are described for objecting to the introduction of certain kinds of questions. Courts of law favor an adversarial (competitive) format in which each party tries to settle a dispute in its favor. In clinical settings, a concern such as child abuse must be considered from many different perspectives (for example, medical, legal, psychological, and educational), each of which has a unique framework for viewing problems and resolutions. Aristotle distinguished three kinds of arguments: didactic, dialectical, and contentious. The hallmark of dialectical arguments is a spirit of inquiry. The aim of people involved in teaching and learning was considered to differ from the aim of those involved in competition. ". . . for a learner should always state what he thinks; for no one is even trying to teach him what is false; whereas in a competition the business of a questioner is to appear by all means to produce an effect upon the other, while that of the answerer is to appear unaffected by him" (Topics, 159a 25). Aims of the questioner in contentious arguments include (1) to refute the opponent—that is, to prove the point contradictory to his or her thesis; (2) to show that the opponent has committed a fallacy; (3) to lead the opponent into paradox; (4) to make the opponent use an ungrammatical expression; and (5) to reduce the opponent to babbling (Aristotle cited in Hamblin, 1970, p. 63).

Adversarial arguments are competitive in nature; that is, each party concentrates on defending one line of reasoning and attacking other lines presented. In arbitrational arguments, the focus is on arriving at a compromise resolution that is satisfactory to both parties. Neither party may be fully satisfied by the conclusion reached, but agree to abide by it. The kinds of arguments that typically occur in clinical contexts can be contrasted to arguments in scientific contexts by the time frame involved; that is, judgments in clinical contexts must be made under time pressures and without all needed sources of information. In both professional and scientific contexts, value is (or should be) placed on a "willingness and ability to be self-critical, to deal sensibly with justifiable objections and queries from others" (Bromley, 1986, p. 233); that is, there should be dialectical arguments displaying a spirit of inquiry. (That this is not always the case can be seen in Chapter Eleven.) Conflict is viewed as a critical process in the development of concepts by many investigators (see, for example, Inhelder, Sinclair, & Bovet, 1974; Sigel, 1979).

Misunderstandings and bad feelings may result when participants in a discussion do not recognize that different kinds of arguments are being used. Lawyers and social workers often have negative views of each other because of their different frameworks for argument analysis. Lawyers may view clinicians as fuzzy thinkers, and clinicians may view lawyers as inhumane and legalistic in their questioning of the credibility of evidence.

Explanations

Many different kinds of explanations are used in clinical practice, including biological, genetic, psychological, and sociological. Explaining is closely connected with judging—is something good or bad? William James (1975) suggested that temperamental differences (tender versus tough-minded) account for preference for different kinds of explanations (p. 13). Optimists are more likely to prefer explanations that allow appreciable room for change, whereas pessimists are more likely to be drawn to explanations that allow little room for change. People differ in the kinds of explanations that satisfy their curiosity. Explanations are often given by defining a word in terms of other words (for example, synonyms) as in dictionary definitions. Other kinds of explanations by definition include classifying (for example, social work is a profession), offering examples, or describing operations.

Some clinicians prefer empathic explanations. (These may or may not assume a causal connection.) Techniques of empathy building include telling a history; describing circumstances; labeling character; presuming drives, instincts, and needs; and describing intentions and feelings (motives) (see Table 4). "The heart of empathy is imagined possibility" (Nettler, 1970, p. 34). The empathizer thinks, "Under these circumstances I, too, might have behaved similarly." An example of an empathic explanation is: "The reason he did it is because he hated her." Empathic explanations often involve concepts that are only variant definitions of the behavior to be explained as shown in the following examples (Nettler, 1970, p. 71).

Table 4. Hallmarks of Different Kinds of Explanations.

A. *Ideological Explanations*

  1. Provide few answers for many questions (a few principles cover a wide territory)
  2. Seek to clarify true meaning of "scriptures"
  3. Contain a high proportion of nonfactual sentences included as declarations. ("nonfactual" means ambiguous and unprovable or without empirical warrant," p. 186). Values disguised as facts
  4. Contain "A high ratio of hortatory-presumptive to declarative" sentences
  5. Contain many failures of logic
  6. Deny the possibility of objectivity; that is, "all explanations of social behavior are considered to be distorted (cues for distortion include "stating one's own motives . . locating the 'social position' from which the competing thesis allegedly originates," p. 186)
  7. Favor ad hominem arguments, which are viewed as tools not as errors; identification of "who said it" as an important test of a statement's validity
  8. Resort to reliance on authority
  9. Seek converts; respond to criticism with emotional defenses; attack critic's motives and develop "cultus" (practices that a believing group develops as its distinctive mode of "meeting the world," p. 186); may seek to force theories on others
  10. Prescribe action; have an interest in persuading rather than explaining
  11. Are action oriented

B. *Scientific Explanations*

  1. Reject ad hominem arguments as persuasive
  2. Encourge dispute of key ideas
  3. Do not encourage unexamined commitment to one side
  4. Value objectivity and observation
  5. Question everything
  6. Seek to reduce influence of moral judgments on observation and inference
  7. Reflect an interest in improving accuracy of judgments

C. *Empathic Explanations*

  1. Do not require proof; consider the test of empathy to be empathy (p. 49); common sense is sufficient
  2. Use vague indicators; hard "to know when one has understanding"; do not use independent tests of interpretations
  3. Accept ad hominem arguments
  4. Entangle moral judgments with understanding
  5. Have a cognitive bias; an attempt to explain behavior "as if it

Table 4. Hallmarks of Different Kinds of Explanations, Cont'd.

arose from thought alone'' (p. 56); an equation of awareness with verbal reports; knowledge of others limited by excessive attention to what they say

6. Are vulnerable to tautology; infer inner states from behaviors, and explain behaviors by reference to inner states; prove motives from acts

7. Confuse understanding and predictive capability; consider propositions to be nonpredictive

8. Assume that understanding of individuals can offer knowledge of groups

Source: Adapted from *Explanations* (pp. 49, 56, 186) by G. Nettler, 1970, New York: McGraw-Hill.

Case One

Probation: Why, doctor, does our client continue to steal?

Psychiatry: He is suffering from antisocial reaction.

Probation: What are the marks of "antisocial reaction"?

Psychiatry: Persistent thievery is one symptom.

Case Two

Defense: Whether one calls him insane or psychotic, he's a sick man. That's obvious.

Psychiatry: I should think that's largely a matter of terminology.

Defense: Do you mean to suggest that a man could do what that boy has done and not be sick?

A preference for empathic explanations reflects a search for explanations in terms of underlying essences—essential properties. Explanations that offer less are considered useless. Popper (1983a) refers to this position as *essentialism*. Essentialists seek empathic explanations and argue about the meaning of words rather than exploring meaning through empirical inquiry.

Characteristics of scientific explanations can be seen in Table 4. Objectivity and observation are valued, and there is an active effort to seek out errors in explanation through empirical inquiry. Scientific explanations are not essentialist accounts—quite the opposite:

science offers a method to eliminate errors, not to claim final accounts. As many writers have pointed out, ultimate claims stifle inquiry. Nor do scientific explanations assume that objective accounts can be offered—that is, accounts that are not influenced by diverse meanings associated with how events are interpreted. To the contrary, in no approach is objectivity so suspect as in those illustrated by the methods that have been devised to attempt to weed out subjectivity (see prior discussion of falsifiability). This point is stressed since many people seem to misunderstand it (e.g., Thompson, 1987).

Ideological explanations are distinguished from scientific ones by their rejection of objectivity, their ready acceptance of unproved and unprovable premises, and their reliance on ethical judgments. "Ideological explanations, then, became operative as they are believed, rather than as they are verified" (Nettler, 1970, p. 179). It is difficult to find a term that has a more speckled history than does *ideology*. Depending on who is talking and what they are talking about, ideology is a virtue or a sin. Criticisms of "let's drop the ideology" are used often in attempts to quiet critics. "The term 'ideology' is someone else's thought, seldom our own" (McLellan, 1986, p. 1). On the other hand, "ideology tells the point of it all. Life is no longer absurd. It describes the forces of light and darkness and names the innocent to be saved" (Nettler, 1970, p. 179).

Thompson (1987) distinguishes between two uses of the term *ideology*. One is use as a purely descriptive term. For example, the beliefs of a particular clinical approach, such as psychoanalysis, can be described. In the second use, the term is "linked to the process of sustaining asymmetrical relations of power—that is, to maintaining domination" (p. 518). It is this use of ideology that has negative connotations, and it is in this sense that language is used as a medium of influence. "The difference between the scientific orientation and the empathetic and ideological outlooks, however, lies in the criteria of conceptual utility. In the latter explain ways, terms are maintained as they serve the explicators' purposes of building empathy or justifying ethico-political causes. In the scientific schema, any concept or construct is, in principle, dispensable regardless of these empathetic or ideological effects" (Nettler, 1970, p. 136).

Ideological explanations are used to account for "collective behavior as empathetic ones do in the clarification of individual actions—they fill the needs of curiosity left by the gaps in knowledge" (Nettler, 1970, p. 187). In professional contexts, scientific explanations may be preferred over ideological ones—but not always, as the most casual perusal of professional writing demonstrates.

Explanations do not necessarily involve arguments. For example, empathic and ideological explanations may not involve arguments. A client may say, "I hit her because I was annoyed," or a person with a drinking problem may say, "I saw the bar and couldn't stop myself from going in and having a drink." Offering an explanation for taking some action (indicating a cause) does not necessarily offer a justification (reason) for the action taken. If, for example, a clinician claims that he or she did not obtain assessment data that is generally considered desirable to gather and, as a result, selected an ineffective intervention method, the excuse that he or she did not have time does not provide a moral justification for inaction. The latter refers to offering reasons that "are morally adequate to support a certain conclusion or action" (Scriven, 1976, p. 219). People tend to feel that they should be able to justify (have sound reasons for) their beliefs. An inability to explain why a certain view is held may create feelings of anger or embarrassment. It's not odd that cogent reasons for a belief may not be at hand since many beliefs result from processes that lie outside of awareness. Most beliefs are not examined in terms of providing explanations or justifications for these.

Prediction refers to forecasting what will happen in the future. An example is "attending Alcoholics Anonymous will help this client to remain abstinent." Explanations involve offering alleged reasons for certain behaviors or events. Thus, the explanation here may be that if this client attains peer support, she or he will be able to use self-management skills to avoid alcoholic beverages. Practice theories offer both alleged explanations and predictions. The question is "How much *real* understanding, as opposed to *feeling* of understanding, do these approaches provide? How much better are the predictions that they yield than those of an intelligent observer not using these theories but using all the other background knowledge that we have about psychological or socioeconomic events?" (Scriven, 1976, p. 219). Explanations may be psychologically compelling but be quite weak from an evidentiary standpoint.

For example, astrological explanations may give many people the feeling of understanding; this does not mean that these explanations are credible.

The Influence of Gender and Class on Reasoning

Thinking styles and skills are related to educational and socialization experiences. Some authors argue that it is socialization differences, not gender differences, that account for the differences in cognitive behavior of men and women (Conner, 1985). Thinking occurs in a particular context involving an interaction between an individual and a particular physical and social situation (Greeno, 1989). Women compared with men, as well as poor people compared to economically privileged individuals, often receive less training in the skills of rationality and objectivity and less cultivation of related beliefs, such as the belief that "knowledge is a product of individual and social intellectual construction" (Greeno, 1989, p. 139) (See Chapter Two.) The results of differences in educational and socialization opportunities are often attributed inaccurately to an inherent style difference—that women are naturally more subjective and intuitive in their approach to problems in contrast to men who are more objective. The superordinate position of class to gender is typically overlooked; that is, what is attributed to gender differences is really a matter of class differences in access to educational opportunities that nourish effective problem-solving skills. Feminist scholars argue that women are often socialized to be silent and receptive rather than to take an active role in critiquing and creating knowledge (see, for example, Belenky, Clinchy, Goldberger, & Tarule, 1986; Keller, 1982). This is true of poor people, too. Thus, a preference for subjectivity that is attributed to personal choice may, in fact, be the result of socialization experiences that discourage clear thinking and reflective thought.

The question is, what is gained and lost by such a preference? Encouraging intuitivism, depriving people of critical thinking skills helps to maintain current power imbalances. It is to the advantage of those with economic resources to encourage individuals in less advantaged positions to embrace an intuitive approach to the exclusion of an objective rational approach. As some have argued, it is the intellectuals who benefit most from the anti-intellectual bias in the general population in terms of the protection of privilege. Extreme subjectivism as a reaction against disliked "male styles of thinking" neglects the role of class differences (mistakenly attributing these to gender differences) and forgoes the option of reaping the benefits of both approaches. Clinicians can be clear thinkers as well as caring professionals. Effective decision making requires both creativity and reflective evaluative skills.

Summary

Clinical decision making involves reasoning, forming hypotheses about presenting concerns, offering arguments for conceptualizations and evaluating these assumptions. Reasons may be hot or cold—that is, developed by emotive associations or by reasoned argument. Reasoning does not necessarily yield the truth nor does the accuracy of a conclusion necessarily indicate that the reasoning used to reach it was sound. Plausible reasons are more likely to be offered if distinctions are made between facts (beliefs that are well supported by evidence), beliefs (confidence that a particular idea is true), and opinions (preferences that cannot be shown to be true or false).

Effective reasoning requires much more than logic in developing and evaluating arguments to arrive at those that are plausible. Being familiar with the steps in argument analysis is useful in examining the quality of arguments. Different criteria are used to assess the quality of arguments in different settings. Domain specific knowledge is also needed. Effective reasoning requires a certain kind of attitude toward the truth—a questioning attitude and an openness to altering beliefs in light of evidence offered. Creativity and reasoning are closely related, especially in areas such as clinical decision making in which needed information is often missing.

Clinicians differ in the kinds of explanations they prefer, which influences the plausibility of arguments offered. Many clinicians prefer empathic and ideological explanations rather than scientific ones.

5

❖━◇━◇━◇━◇━◇━

The Influence of Language
and Persuasion Strategies

◆━◇━◇━◇━◇━◇━◇━◇━◇━◇━◇━◇━◇━◇━◇━◇━◇━◇━◇━

Two of the most common sources of error involve use of language and the influence of social-psychological persuasion strategies. Clinicians use words to describe people and events, to describe relationships between behavior and events, and to express evaluations. Language is used in "thinking" about clinical questions and in processing material read in professional books and articles. Although considerable attention has been devoted to problematic use of language on the part of clients, less attention has been devoted to exploration of how common sources of error influence clinicians in their daily practice. The words clinicians use not only shape their own experience and actions but those of their clients as well. The tendency of clinicians to say "Yes, I know this" without really becoming knowledgeable about the specific ways language and persuasive strategies influence clinical decisions is the greatest obstacle to becoming informed about and avoiding these sources of error. Here, too, as with other sources of error described in this book, having a name for a fallacy is helpful: giving it a name helps highlight its uniqueness, recognize it, and plan how to avoid it.

The Influence of Language

Many clear thinking skills involve recognition of the ways in which language may affect decisions (Johnson, 1946). Language

116

plays an especially important role in clinical practice. Discussions between clients and practitioners serve as a major therapeutic component in most practice frameworks. Use of language is also integral to decisions made during case conferences and in court presentations, as well as in interpretations of clinical records. All writing in the professions and the social sciences can be viewed as rhetorical in that a position is advanced and a point of view is presented that is then reviewed for its soundness (Edmondson, 1984). The term *rhetoric* has varied definitions: (1) "the art of using words effectively in speaking or writing; now, the art of prose composition (2) artificial eloquence; language that is showy and elaborate but largely empty of clear ideas or sincere emotion" (*Webster's New World Dictionary*, 1988). It is in the latter sense that the term is in ill-repute. It is not unusual, for example, to hear someone say "we need less rhetoric and more straight facts." When rhetoric is defined in its broader sense, as in the first definition above, it is an important area of study and skill, especially in fields such as clinical practice that rely heavily on the spoken and written word.

There are three basic reasons that language may compromise the quality of decisions: carelessness, lack of skill in writing and thinking, and deliberate intent on the part of a speaker or writer. The many functions that language serves complicate understanding of spoken or written statements. One function is description. Description of clients, procedures used, and progress achieved is an integral part of clinical records. The aim of descriptive statements is to inform (for example, "Mr. Larkin has been hospitalized three times."). We can find out whether they are true or false. Another function is to persuade others to believe or act differently. Clinicians attempt to persuade clients to act, think, or feel differently in problem-related situations by talking to them. Use of language is a critical influence when considering the pros and cons of different clinical assessment or intervention strategies whether talking to oneself or to colleagues. A third function of language is purely expressive—to express some emotion or feeling or to create such a feeling without trying to influence future behavior. Other statements direct us or guide, as in "Call the parental stress hotline." A given statement may serve several functions; not only may a speaker or writer have more than one purpose in mind when making a statement, but the listener or reader also may have more than one in mind, which may or may not match those of the speaker. The context is used to interpret the speaker's or writer's purpose. Language also has presymbolic functions, such as affirming social cohesion (as in "Isn't it a nice day?"). Lack of understanding of this function may result in naive assumptions about the triviality of conversation as Hayakawa (1978) notes in his "Advice to the Literal-Minded" (p. 85). A sentence cannot be understood correctly unless the motive behind it is translated correctly.

Words differ in their level of abstraction. At the lowest level are definitions in extensional terms. Extensional meaning of a word refers to what it points to in the physical world; it is what the word stands for. A psychiatrist could point to the disheveled clothes of a person admitted to an emergency psychiatry unit—or to the behavior of pushing a nurse. Many words have no extensional meaning—that is, there is nothing we can point to. In operational definitions, a rigorous attempt is made to exclude nonextensional meaning, as in the well-known example of the definition of *length* in terms of the operations by which it is measured. The intentional meaning of a word refers to what is connoted or suggested. Clinicians may act toward people, objectives, or events in accord with the intentional (affective) connotations associated with a name. For example, reactions to terms such as "sociopath" or "welfare recipient" may go far beyond the extensional meaning of these terms without recognizing that this is happening. Definitions describe our linguistic habits; they are statements about how language is used. The higher the level of abstraction, the less the utility of referring to a dictionary definition to capture meaning—especially intentional meaning.

Fallacies Related to Language

Problems related to use of language that influence the quality of clinical decisions are described below, together with suggested remedies. This list is by no means exhaustive, and readers are referred to other sources for greater detail (see, for example, Hayakawa, 1978; Thouless, 1974). Carelessness is the culprit most responsible for foggy writing and speaking—not taking the time and thought to clearly state inferences and reasons for them.

Predigested Thinking. This term refers to the tendency to oversimplify complex topics or issues into simple formulas that distort content, such as describing Freudian theory as reducing everything to sex or describing behaviorists as believing in mechanistic stimulus-response connections. Clinicians are sometimes guilty of reducing an answer to a simple formula, such as "rapists will rape again." A practitioner who does not believe that evaluation of client progress can be done in a way that is meaningful may say, "evaluation is mechanistic," or "it trivializes concerns" or "does not represent the true complexity of human problems." This view overlooks the fact that evaluation can be carried out in an irrelevant or relevant manner. The latter requires considerable assessment and evaluation skills in working together with clients to select relevant, feasible, sensitive progress indicators (see Chapter Ten). This assertion also overlooks the complexity of evaluating client progress in terms of identifying progress indicators that will indeed reflect progress (or its lack) in a meaningful way. Another example is the statement that "a scientific approach to clinical questions offers trivial answers." This statement assumes that all scientific approaches are the same, but they really are not (see Chapter Three).

Predigested thinking in the form of slogans may be used to encourage actions, such as "support community care." The history of the community mental health movement reveals that such slogans were used often despite the minimal available community care for patients (Sedgwick, 1982). Slogans are easy to remember and so are readily available to influence us at an emotional level. The use of predigested thinking obscures complexities and so may encourage inaccurate inferences. This kind of thinking is common, because of indifference, lack of information, and idleness, and the fact that it usually offers a practical guide for life. The tendency to simplify complex matters may help to account for ignoring the undistributed middle (substituting *all* for *some*) and the readiness to accept an extension of a position (see Chapter Six).

The way to guard against predigested thinking is to avoid mental idleness, which encourages us "to accept mental food well below the limits of our digestion" (Thouless, 1974, p. 164). The remedy is to consider the actual complexity of the issue at hand. Recognition of the complexities related to a question increases tolerance for other positions. The emotional appeal of predigested thinking and the fact that it often provides a practical guide for daily life make it difficult to challenge such thinking. For example, a clinician may object to the oversimplistic presentation of Freudian theory that "everything is related to sex." The other person may protest that the objections raised are too "learned," that "nothing will convince him that art, romantic love, and religion are just sex, which is generally agreed by everybody to be the teaching of Freud" (Thouless, 1974, p. 161). Note the reaffirmation of the original position (begging the question) and the appeal to consensus. As Thouless points out, if this is a discussion with other people, the user of predigested thinking can usually rely on "having their sympathy, for his opponent will seem to be a person trying to make himself out to be too clever and who makes serious argument impossible by throwing doubt on what everyone knows to be true" (pp. 161–162). The only recourse here may be to state an argument so clearly that the inadequacies of a position are quite obvious. So, challengers of predigested thinking, who wish to take a more careful look at a point under discussion, should be prepared that some people may not like this; negative reactions can be avoided by posing inquiries in a tactful manner and by emphasizing common interests.

Pseudotechnical Jargon/Bafflegarb. Jargon can be useful in communicating in an efficient manner if listeners (or readers) share the same meaning of technical terms. However, jargon may be used to conceal ignorance and "impress the innocent" (Rycroft, 1973, p. xi). An economic incentive may perpetuate obscure writing; for example, highly specialized jargon in the legal profession increases the need to hire lawyers who can understand it. We tend to be impressed with things we cannot understand. Professors tend to rate journals that are hard to read as more prestigious than journals that are easier to read (Armstrong, 1980). Of course, it is possible that the more prestigious journals discuss more complex subjects that require more difficult language. This possibility was tested by Armstrong. Portions of management journals were rewritten to increase readability without changing the content; unnecessary words were eliminated, easy words were substituted for difficult ones, and sentences were broken into shorter ones. A sample of 32 management professors were asked to rate as easy or difficult versions of four such passages and rate them on a scale of "competence" ranging from 1 to 7. They knew neither the name of the journal nor the name of the author. Versions that were easier to read were considered to reflect less competent research than were the more difficult passages.

There are circumstances in which obscurity may be desirable, such as when exploring new possibilities. However, in most situations that arise in clinical practice, obscurity is not an advantage; it is often a cloak for vagueness. Examples of pseudotechnical jargon include *psychic deficiencies, structural frame of reference,* and *generational dysfunctions.* The proliferation of terms adds to pseudojargon in psychotherapy. Consider for example the terms that Firestone and Seiden (1987) present as similar to "microsuicide."

- indirect suicide
- masked suicide
- partial suicide
- hidden suicide
- installment plan suicide

- parasuicide
- slow suicide
- chronic suicide
- embryonic suicide

Who has not suffered from "bureaucratese"—turgid unnecessarily complex descriptions that yield only to the most persistent of readers (or listeners)? Examples include "mumblistic" (planned mumbling) and "profundicating" (translating simple concepts into obscure jargon) (Boren, 1972). The remedy is to simplify and clarify. Examples of rules suggested by Orwell (1958) include

"1.   Never use a metaphor, simile or other figure of speech which you are used to seeing in print.
2.   Never use a long word when a short one will do.
3.   If it is possible to cut a word out, always cut it out.
4.   Never use the passive when you can use the active.
5.   Never use a foreign phrase, a scientific word or a jargon word if you can think of an everyday English equivalent.

6. Break any of these rules sooner than say anything outright barbarous" (p. 143).

The potential for obscure terms to become clear can be explored by asking questions such as "What do you mean by that?" "Can you give me an example?" Asking such questions when reading case records and practice-related literature is a valuable rule of thumb.

Obscure language often remains unquestioned because of worries that the questioner will look ignorant or stupid. The risks of lack of clarification should be considered, as well as the risks of revealing a lack of knowlege. Writers and speakers should clarify their terms, bearing in mind appropriate levels of abstraction. If they don't, it may be because they cannot. They should be thankful that someone cares enough to want to understand their position and that lack of clarity is discovered. Not all people will be open to questions, especially those who use vague language to hide aims they would rather not reveal. "The great enemy of clear language is insincerity. When there is a gap between one's real and one's declared aims, one turns as it were instinctively to long words and exhausted idioms like a cuttlefish squirting out ink" (Orwell, 1958, p. 142). Some people will become defensive and try to put others down for asking simple-minded questions, perhaps using their prestige to do so. They may share Humpty Dumpty's attitude. "'When I use a word,' Humpty Dumpty said in a rather scornful tone, 'it means just what I choose it to mean neither more nor less.' 'The question is,' said Alice, 'whether you *can* make words mean so many different things.' 'The question is,' said Humpty Dumpty, 'who is to be master, that's all.'" (Lewis Carroll, *Through the Looking Glass*, p. 229). A question could then be asked in such a straightforward manner that if the person still cannot understand it, his own lack of astuteness is revealed (Thouless, 1974).

Use of Emotional or Buzz Words or Images. Professionals, as well as advertisers and politicians, make use of emotional words and images as illustrated in the letter to the editor, NASW News:

Example	*Comments*
The conspiracy of silence continues to state implicitly that social workers, because of their training and clinical expertise, cannot possibly be impaired by alcohol and drug abuse. As long as this conspiracy exists, impaired social workers will be afraid to seek help and to come out into the open about their addiction, just as I am ("Letter to the Editor," 1986, p. 15).	The term "conspiracy" is highly pejorative, as is "impaired." No evidence is offered that there is a "conspiracy of silence," or for the assumption that the "conspiracy" stops social workers from disclosing their "addiction." No evidence is offered for the assumption that people assume that social workers "cannot have a substance abuse problem because of their training and expertise." It is assumed that substance abuse is "an addiction."

Emotional terms are rife in the turf battles between psychologists and psychiatrists: "The latest in the barrage of inflammatory articles in *The Psychiatric Times* appears in the November issue. The article opens with this provocative statement: 'Clinical psychology is in a war for survival against American psychiatry'" (Buie, 1987, p. 25).

Proverbs, similes, or metaphors that have emotional effects may be used to describe or support a position. Often these are vague in their application to a topic obscuring rather than clarifying what is being discussed; they often create a feeling of understanding without an accompanying increase in real understanding. Points against a disliked (and perhaps misunderstood) position may be referred to as ammunition and points in favor of a preferred position referred to as reasoned and humanistic considerations. Clinicians who do not believe that clinical practice can be evaluated often refer to such efforts as mechanical and may appeal to an inappropriate analogy geared to demonstrate just how inappropriate it is to evaluate practice, such as saying that evaluation of practice entails treating people like cars—mechanistically, simplistically. Examples of the use of emotionally toned words can be seen in the excerpt from a case conference presented in Chapter Eleven.

The use of emotionally toned words is not always dysfunctional; however, in the context of trying to make correct inferences, such words may interfere with clear thinking (for example, they may interfere with identifying useful options). A vigilance about possible effects of emotional words will encourage use of terms that are more neutral, less value laden. Biases that may influence clinical decisions can be coaxed out by exploring reactions to terms such as *nursing home resident* and *developmentally disabled youth.* Noting the possible biasing effects of emotional terms and using more neutral ones will increase the quality of decisions in case conferences, in discussions about clinical questions, and in discussions with oneself!

Labeling. Labels often are applied incorrectly. A label such as *behavior modification* may be used inaccurately to describe a program that is just the opposite of what a behavioral program would be like (see discussion of faulty classification in Chapter Seven). Pseudoexplanations are one result of unexamined use of labels (see Chapter Seven). Stigmatizing labels often are applied to clients which have few if any implications for selection of treatment methods (see Chapter Seven for a discussion of labeling).

The Assumption of One Word, One Meaning. Words have different meanings in different contexts. As Hayakawa (1978) has bluntly put it, "Ignoring of contexts in any act of interpretation is at best a stupid practice. At its worst, it can be a vicious practice" (p. 56) as when for example a sentence is taken out of context. Differences that exist in the world may not be reflected in different use of words, or, differences in language may not correspond to variations in the world. Misunderstandings arise when different use of a word is mistaken for different opinions about a topic of discussion. "Unless people mean the same thing when they talk to each other, accurate communication is impossible" (Feinstein, 1967, p. 313). Two people discussing addiction may not have the same definition of this term, and a muddled discussion may result. One way to avoid this is to define key terms. The dialogue below illustrates how the same word may have different meanings.

Counselor: I think you have an addiction to alcohol.

Client: I don't think so.

Counselor: You drink every day.

Client: But it doesn't interfere with my life. I'm happily married and like my job. Just because I drink every day doesn't mean I'm addicted.

Counselor: I think it does.

Results of assessment are often presented in vague terms such as *probable* or *cannot be excluded,* which have a wide range of meaning among different clinicians (Bryant & Norman, 1980). Definition of terms such as *panic reaction* or *dementia* may be shared initially but diverge as a discussion proceeds. Clinicians differ in how they define behavioral and psychodynamic intervention methods (Ellis, 1987). Confusions can be avoided by checking definitions of key concepts.

Use of Vague Terms. Vague terms are common in clinical contexts. Examples of vague words are *uncommunicative, aggressive, immature, drug dependency, dependent patient, normal culture, dysfunction, family therapy, social work intervention, family oriented modality, psychic deficiencies, dysfunctional alignments,* and *proper boundary lines.* If terms are not clarified, different meanings may be used, none of which may reflect the real world. Fashionable phrases or terms often become vague phrases in time. Examples include *supportive therapy* and *case management.* Cliches and "unoriginal remarks do have their uses in terms of highlighting similarity between people; that those present are on the 'right-side' so to speak" (Hayakawa, 1978). It is when hackneyed phrases and cliches are used carelessly to communicate new ideas and perspectives that they become problematic.

Reification/Word Magic. Here it is mistakenly assumed that a word corresponds to something real; in fact, "the existence of a

word does not guarantee the existence of any corresponding entity"
(Fearnside & Holther, 1959, p. 68). The term *aggressive,* used as a
summary term for specific actions, may also be used to refer to an
aggressive disposition, which is believed to be responsible for these
actions. This disposition then comes to be thought of as an attribute
of the person (Bromley, 1977; Stuart, 1970). Staats and Staats (1963)
refer to this as the use of pseudoexplanations. Noting the circularity
of such terms reveals that no new information is offered and that
no evidence other than the behavioral referents described support
the influence of this higher order concept.

The influence of semantic linkages and cuing effects range
from the subtle to the obvious. A familiar example is the tendency
to think in terms of opposites such as good/bad or addicted/non-
addictive. Such thinking obscures the situational variability of behavior as well as the individual differences in behavior, feelings, or
thoughts that may occur in a given context. For example, consider
the term *addiction.* Patterns of substance use and abuse vary widely;
the description of a client as addicted really is not very informative.
This does not indicate what substances are used with what frequency, in what situations, nor offer any information about the
function served by ingestion of such substances (although within
some practice perspectives all clients who are "addicted" are assumed to have similar personality dynamics, which purport to account for the addiction, and a description of the exact nature of the
addiction may not be considered important).

Decisions concerning degree of responsibility for an action
differ depending on whether a person is the subject of the sentence
as in: "Ellen's car hit the fireplug" compared to "The fireplug was
hit by Ellen's car" (Loftus, 1979, 1980). We tend to offer extrinsically
motivated reasons for our own behavior (such as "I liked the material in the course" if given the lead-in, "I [engaged in the behavior]
because I . . .") and to give intrinsic reasons in other cases ("to do
well in the course" if given the lead-in "I [engaged in the behavior]
in order to . . .") (Salancik & Conway, 1975). Familiarity with the
influence of semantic linkages and cuing effects increases the likelihood that errors will be avoided. Statements can be rearranged to
see if this yields different causal assumptions.

Confusing Verbal and Factual Propositions. Questions (such as "What is a borderline personality?") often involve disputes about use of words as if they were questions of facts. Discussions of the meaning of mental illness are often conducted as if there were an independent objective reality to be discovered rather than with the realization that what will be accepted as referents for this term is at issue—a constructed reality, not a discovered reality. Questions of fact cannot be settled by arguments over the use of words. The problem of how to use a word is different from a problem of what is a fact. Pointing out the lack of objective criteria is helpful when there is a confusion between verbal and factual propositions.

Misuse of Verbal Speculations. This refers to the use of "speculative thinking to solve problems which can only be solved by the observation and interpretation of facts" (Thouless, 1974, p. 78). Speculation is valuable in discovering new possibilities, but it does not offer information about whether these insights are correct; that is, what is cannot be deduced from what ought to be, nor can vague terms referring to client behavior or situational contexts of interest be clarified simply by thinking about them. For example, if a client is described as a drug abuser and no information is provided about what this means, speculation will not be helpful. Facts gathered from some reliable and valid source are needed. Misuse of speculation occurs often in clinical practice and is not without its effects, since assumptions influence what clinicians attend to. Thus, a little speculation can be a dangerous thing.

Conviction Through Repetition. Simply hearing, seeing, or thinking about a statement many times may increase belief in the statement. As Thouless (1974) notes, we tend to think that what goes through our mind must be important. A willingness to challenge even cherished beliefs helps to combat this source of error. Valid inferences cannot be made on the basis of repeated affirmation, conviction, or the manner in which something is said. "If our examination of the facts leads to a conclusion which we find to be inconceivable, this need not be regarded as telling us anything about the facts, but only about the limits of our powers of conceiving" (Thouless, 1974, p. 80). Simply repeating a position increases the likelihood of its acceptance, especially if the statement is offered in a confident manner by a person of prestige and has a slogan quality that plays on our emotions. Repetitions of a statement are more effective if they are varied; we are less likely to discover that no reasons are provided as to why we should believe or act in a certain manner (Thouless, 1974). Conviction through repetition may be attempted in case conferences to influence group members. For example, a client may be continually referred to as mentally incompetent, when in fact no evidence has been offered. Pointing out the danger of repeating unsupported assertions may be helpful in discouraging such descriptions.

Bold Assertions. People often act as if they have a conclusive argument when they do not. They may simply assert a position with no attempt to provide any evidence for it. A clinician may protest, "Mr. Greenwood is obviously a psychopath who is untreatable." A confident manner and bold assertions often accomplish what should be achieved only by offering sound reasons for a position. Words that are cues for this tactic include: *unquestionable, indisputably, the fact is, the truth is.* Bold assertions are a form of *begging the question;* the truth or falsity of the point is assumed (see Chapter Six). This informal fallacy, like many others, takes advantage of our tendency to be lulled into accepting a position because of the confidence with which it is described. Evidence should be requested for the position asserted. An example of a bold assertion is "We know that social work is effective. More than any other single profession, we see the youth in the settings where we work. We know what is needed and what works" ("From the President," 1986, p. 2). In fact, there is considerable debate about this, and some research suggests the opposite (Blenkner, Bloom, & Nielson, 1971).

Primacy Effects. Clinicians are influenced by what they hear first. This is referred to as the primacy or anchoring effect (Nisbett & Ross, 1980). What we hear first influences what we attend to and thus influences our causal attributions. It narrows the range of data that is attended to. The influence of initial suggestions is shown by an experiment in which four groups of clinicians diagnosed a client under different conditions (Temerlin, 1968). One group was informed that the person was sane, one group was told that they were selecting scientists to work in research, one group (the control group) received no suggestions, and one group (the experimental group) was informed that the interviewees were mentally ill. Diagnoses were made by psychiatrists and clinical psychologists who then listened to a tape recorded interview, and the diagnoses differed greatly. All 25 psychiatrists and most of the clinical psychologists (22 of 25) in the experimental group made a diagnosis of mental illness. The majority of clinicians in the control group stated that the interviewee was mentally healthy. These results illustrate not only the influence of primacy effects on presumptions of illness but also the unreliability of psychiatric diagnoses.

Newsspeak. Newsspeak refers to "language that distorts, confuses, or hides reality" (MacLean, 1981, p. 43). Examples from the media include *neutralized* (meaning, killed), *misspoke* (meaning, lied), and *air support* (meaning, bombing and strafing). Newsspeak refers to the intentional abuse of language to obscure the truth. Orwell (1958) wrote, "In our time, political speech and writing are largely in defense of the indefensible. . . . political language has to consist of euphemisms, question begging, and sheer cloudy vagueness" (p. 136). Newsspeak occurs in the mental health industry as well, as illustrated in the following examples:

Statement or Term	*Translation*
Fiscal constraints call for retrenchment.	Some people are going to be fired; clinics will be closed.
New policies have been put in place to ensure better services for clients.	All services will be provided by psychiatrists.
Improve your practice tenfold.	Attend Dr. X's workshop.
Pregnancy crisis center	Prolife centers which are anti-abortion (5,500 currently exist in the United States [Jowett & O'Donnell, 1986])

Community care in place of warehousing	Patients will be discharged from mental hospitals even though no adequate community care is available.

The goal of protecting professional interests requires presenting one's own profession in a uniquely favorable light in comparison with other professions (Friedson, 1973). Political aims increase the likelihood that strategems will be used that distort material presented. Misleading or unfair headlines may be used; editors and publishers are aware that many more people read the headlines than read the material under the headlines. Thus, even if the small print presents an accurate view, the headlines may be misleading. Readers rarely are aware of what is not discussed in professional newsletters (see discussion of suppressed evidence in Chapter Six). Too seldom are the pros and cons concerning an issue presented, even though readers would benefit from this. Other sources of hidden bias include (Cirino, 1971) bias in the source of material, through selection or omission of material, in placement, in words, in selection of photographs, and hidden editorials (content presented as disinterested descriptions that present a biased account advocating one particular position). Use of these devices may or may not be deliberate. Whether deliberate or accidental, they may have biasing effects. Familiarity with commonly used strategies and ways to avoid or counter these will be helpful in avoiding distorting influences (see also Chapter Six).

Other Sources of Fallacy Related to Language. *Insisting on a specific definition* of a term is inappropriate if this obscures the complexity of a situation. Vagueness of terms may be an advantage in the early stages of thinking about a topic to discover approaches that otherwise may not be considered. Not recognizing that *words differ in level of abstraction* may create confusion and needless arguments. Both the one word–one meaning fallacy and the assumption that definitions are things reflect a confusion among (or ignorance of) different levels of abstraction. Metaphors may lead to faulty attributions and thus contribute to incorrect selection of intervention programs.

In the *fallacy of composition*, it is assumed that what is true of a part is also true of the whole. An example is the assumption that because each staff member in a psychiatric hospital is skilled, the hospital as a whole is an effective treatment center. A clinician may assume that because a young man has been caught stealing money at home he also engages in other criminal activities. The more vivid the particular behavior or person singled out for attention (that is, the more vivid the part), the more likely it is that generalizations will be made from the part to the entire person. In the *fallacy of division*, it is assumed that what is true of the whole is true of all the parts. A client may assume that because a clinic has a good reputation, every counselor on the staff is competent, but this is not necessarily true.

Ferreting out the nature of an argument is often difficult because of *excessive wordiness*. Consider the example given in Chapter 4 under the section on analyzing arguments. *Confusing factual and emotional uses of words* can result in errors. Offering descriptions is but one of the many functions of language. Persuading people to act is a common aim in many kinds of discourse including professional contexts and this is often accomplished through emotive use of language. Distinguishing between the emotive and informative uses of language will be helpful in avoiding influence by emotional terms.

The *eloquence* with which an argument is presented, whether in writing or in speech, is not necessarily related to its cogency. That is, words that move and charm may not inform. To the contrary, eloquence may lull our critical powers into abeyance. Some clinicians are excellent orators and engaging writers. However, efforts to use methods described may prove frustrating because of a lack of clarity. Appreciation of the nonrational aspects of a presentation (for example, facility with the English language) may decrease motivation to examine arguments because one tends to focus on the words alone. Eloquence may make it difficult to identify claims and premises. Given the scarcity of eloquence, it is hard to resist a desire for more. Best of all is the combination of eloquence and clarity. A summary of ways in which language may influence inferences is offered in Table 5.

The Influence of Persuasion Strategies

Persuasive attempts are common in clinical contexts. Clinicians try to persuade clients to carry out agreed-on tasks and try to convince other professionals to offer needed resources. Conversely, clinicians are the target of persuasive attempts by clients, colleagues, friends, family members, as well as by professional organizations and the mass media (see, for example, Cirino, 1971; Burnham, 1987). The essence of persuasion is influencing someone to think or act in a certain manner. Persuasion may occur intentionally or "unconsciously" as a part of the interpersonal context in which counseling occurs (see Chapters One and Two). Both beliefs and actions are influenced by persuasion efforts, which may be masked in terms of their intent to influence. Knowledge about social-psychological persuasion strategies is important for clinicians—both in resisting unwanted effects that dilute the quality of clinical decisions and in effectively using persuasive appeals toward clinically desired ends. Competence in the use of influence is a key component of "practical intelligence."

One route to persuasion is based on thoughtful consideration of arguments related to a topic. This review could of course be biased because of one or more of the information-processing errors described in other chapters. The other major route is through emotional associations or inferences based on peripheral cues in the persuasion context (Petty & Cacioppo, 1986, p. 191). In the first route, there is an elaboration process; people are motivated to think about arguments for and against a position. Persuasion by affect comes into play when we do not engage in elaboration and are influenced not so much by what people say, but by extraneous variables such as how attractive they are or how confidently they present their views. Persuasion strategies based on liking and authority attain their impact largely because of affective associations.

Becoming familiar with persuasion strategies and decreasing automatic compliance to these tactics will upgrade the quality of clinical decisions. Compliance induction strategies will be more

Table 5. Sources of Errors Related to Use of Language.

1. Assumption of one word, one meaning
2. The fallacy of composition
3. The fallacy of division
4. Use of vague terms
5. Shifting definitions of terms
6. Reification (acting as if an abstract concept actually exists)
7. Influence by semantic linkages and cuing effects
8. Predigested thinking
9. Confusing verbal and factual propositions
10. Use of pseudotechnical jargon
11. Misuse of speculation (assuming that what is can be discovered by merely thinking about a topic)
12. Conviction through repetition
13. Insistence on a specific definition that oversimplifies a situation
14. Influence through emotional words
15. Use of a confident manner and bold assertions
16. Judgments based on primacy effects
17. Newsspeak
18. Excessive verbiage
19. Misuse of labels
20. Confusion of different levels of abstraction
21. Confusion between descriptive and emotive uses of words
22. Careless use of language
23. Eloquence without clarity

readily identified and thus clinicians will be in a better position to decide if going along with the strategies will diminish or enhance the quality of decisions. (An entertaining, well-written, and empirically based presentation of such strategies is offered by Cialdini in his book *Influence,* 1984.) In everyday life, the principles on which these strategies are based provide convenient shortcuts that often work for us. Clinicians don't have time to fully consider the merits of each action they take or "pitch" they hear—they take shortcuts that usually work for them. These compliance-induction strategies thus take advantage of our natural human tendencies. However, people can exploit them for their own purposes; our automatic reactions work in their favor. "All the exploiters need do is to trigger the great stores of influence that already exist in the situation and direct them toward the intended target . . . Even the victims themselves tend to see their compliance as due to the actions of natural forces rather than to the designs of the person who profits from that compliance" (Cialdini, 1984, p. 24). Thus, these strategies offer others the ability to manipulate without the appearance of manipulation.

The principle of liking is one of the most frequently used persuasive strategies. We like to please people we know and like—that is, we like to comply with their requests. Clinicians prefer clients who are likeable (see discussion in Chapter Two). The liking rule is often used by people we do not know to gain our compliance. Factors that encourage liking include physical attractiveness, similarity, compliments, familiarity, and cooperation (see discussion of influences of client characteristics in Chapter Two). "Compliance professionals are forever attempting to establish that we and they are working for the same goals, that we must 'pull together' for mutual benefit, that they are, in essence, teammates" (p. 182). The "good guy/bad guy" routine takes advantage of the liking rule—we like the good guy (in contrast to the bad guy), so we comply with what he wants. The rule of liking also works through conditioning and association. Workshops that advertisers wish clinicians to attend are associated with positive qualities such as "big names" (for example, Carl Rogers). Clinicians will be more receptive to new material if they like the person presenting it. Associating "pitches" with food as in the "luncheon technique" is a well-known strategy (Razran, described in Cialdini, 1984, p. 189). Concerns about disapproval are often responsible for a reluctance to offer counterarguments to preferred views during case conferences.

Another persuasion strategy is based on a desire to be (and appear) consistent with what we have already done. (This is *not* a trait of creative people.) A colleague may argue that because insight therapy was used to help a client with her depression, it should also be used to help her with her substance-abuse problem. A clinician may be reluctant to alter a course of intervention even though such a change will help achieve client-desired outcomes because of a fear of appearing inconsistent to a client. Being consistent usually works for us. "But because it is so typically in our best interests to be consistent, we easily fall into the habit of being automatically so, even in situations where it is not the sensible way to be" (Cialdini, 1984, pp. 68–69). Consistency can protect us from troubling realizations we would rather not think about. Since automatic consistency "functions as a shield against thought" (p. 72), it can be exploited by people who want us to comply with their requests. Gaining commitment sets the consistency rule into effect. "Commitment strategies are . . . intended to get us to take some action or make some statement that will trap us into later compliance through consistency pressures" (p. 75). An advertisement for a clinical workshop on a new intervention method may urge readers to reserve a space now to ensure a place (scarcity principle) and send a refundable deposit of $10.00 (commitment). A clinician may encourage a reluctant spouse to come in for "just one interview" hoping to persuade him to enter a course of relationship counseling.

Obtaining an initial concession or offering a favor may be used to gain compliance through the influence of the reciprocity rule; we feel obliged to return favors. A colleague who is eager to receive referrals may refer some clients to other clinicians. Offering concrete help at an early point may be used to encourage clients to participate in a counseling program. It may be difficult to counter or neutralize the influence of reciprocation since we often do not know whether an offer is an honest one or the first step in an exploitation attempt. The rule of reciprocity "entitles a person who has acted in a certain way to a dose of the same thing" (Cialdini, 1984, p. 65). Thus, if an action is viewed as a compliance device instead of a favor, this rule will not work as an ally. The reciprocity rule lies behind the success of the "rejection-then-retreat technique," in which a small request follows a large request—the small request is viewed as a "concession" and is likely to be reciprocated by a concession from the other person. For example, when college students were asked to serve as a chaperone for a group of juvenile delinquents on a day trip to the zoo, 83 percent of those requested refused. However, when this was first preceded by a larger request (to spend two hours a week for two years as a counselor to the delinquent), three times as many students agreed (Cialdini, 1984, pp. 50–51). The contrast effect is also at work here (see later discussion).

Informal fallacies appealing to pseudoauthority take advantage of our tendency to go along with authorities (see examples in Chapter Seven). Many appeals to authority are symbolic, such as certain kinds of titles; they connote rather than offer any content supporting the credibility of the authority. Some appeals to authority attempt to influence through fear, as in the advertisement for professional liability insurance below (Exhibit 1). The test format is designed to convey a sense of "authority." Notice that no facts and figures are presented in relation to what percent of social workers are sued for what reasons. At the right are given the names of the types of strategies being used. Understanding the basis for the effectiveness of informal fallacies based on pseudoauthority is helpful in resisting inappropriate appeals (see Chapter Seven).

The scarcity principle rests on the fact that opportunities seem more valuable when their availability is limited (Cialdini, 1984, p. 230). A prospective client who is informed that a clinician has no time to take on any new clients for two months may value the chance to work with this clinician even more. A nursing home intake worker may say, "If you don't decide now, space may not be available" (which may not be true). Here too, as with the impulse to use other shortcuts, it is an "enlightened" one in its basic thrust; things that are scarce are usually more valuable; also, freedom is lost as opportunities become less available. Cialdini (1984) provided a good example of the influence of the scarcity principle.

> One set of customers heard a standard sales presentation before being asked for their orders. Another set of customers heard the standard sales presentation plus information that the supply of imported beef was likely to be scarce in the upcoming months. A third group received the standard sales presentation and the information about a scarce supply of beef, too; however, they also learned that the scarce supply news was not generally available information—it had come, they were told, from certain exclusive contacts that the company had. Thus the customers who received this last sales presentation learned that not only was the availability of the product limited, so also was the news concerning it—the scarcity double whammy. . . . Compared to customers who got only the standard sales appeal, those who were told about the future scarcity of beef bought more than twice as much. But

Exhibit 1. Self-Test Advertisement for Professional Liability Insurance.

Test Yourself

Answer the following questions to find out whether you need malpractice coverage.

	Yes	No		Type of Strategy
1.	___	___	I am a practicing social worker.	(setting the stage)
2.	___	___	I don't have my own coverage if I'm sued for malpractice.	(fear induction)
3.	___	___	I let my malpractice coverage drop.	(fear induction)
4.	___	___	I've heard about other social workers being sued.	(fear induction)
5.	___	___	I know I need my own liability insurance, even though my employer provides it.	(neutralization of counterarguments)
6.	___	___	I'm aware that malpractice suits against social workers have considerably increased over the past few years.	(fear induction)
7.	___	___	I don't want to worry about being sued.	(fear induction)

Source: NASW News, 1987, 32(4), p. 17. Copyright 1987 by National Association of Social Workers. Reprinted by permission.

the real boost in sales occurred among the customers who heard of the impending scarcity via "exclusive" information. They purchased six times the amount that the customers who received only the standard sales pitch did [Cialdini, 1984, p. 239; based on Knishinsky, 1982].

Actions are often guided by the principle of social proof— that is, finding out what other people think is correct. (Creative people are not as likely to follow this principle.) This principle also provides a convenient shortcut that often works well; however, if it is accepted automatically, it can result in errors. A clinician may decide that since most clinicians refer clients to Alcoholics Anonymous, he or she will do so as well. The danger in appealing to the principle of social proof is the "pluralistic ignorance phenomenon" (Cialdini, 1984, p. 129): the majority view may be (and often is) incorrect. As with other social-psychological sources of influence, this one is more effective under some conditions than under others. Uncertainty increases the effects of this principle; we are more likely to go along with what other people do in ambiguous situations. Similarity also influences the impact of social proof; this principle operates most powerfully when we observe the behavior of people who are similar to ourselves. Observation of the behavior of people who are similar offers "the greatest insight into what constitutes correct behavior for ourselves" (Cialdini, 1984, p. 140). False evidence may be provided to influence people through the principle of social proof, such as claiming (without evidence) that hundreds have benefited from use of a new therapy.

Clinicians are also influenced by the contrast effect. A client who is fairly cooperative could be viewed as extremely cooperative following an interview with a very resistant person. Men assign more negative ratings of pictures of potential blind dates when they are watching "Charlie's Angels" on TV than when they are watching some other program (Kenrick & Gutierres, 1980).

Summary

Misuse of language contributes to inaccurate clinical decisions. Careless use of language is perhaps the greatest source of error. Confusion about the different functions of language may result in muddled discussions, as may confusion among different levels of abstraction. If terms are not clarified, confused discussions (or thinking) may result due to the assumption of one word, one meaning. Reification of terms (using a descriptive term as an explanatory term) offers an illusion of understanding without providing any real understanding. Technical terms may be carelessly used, resulting in "bafflegarb" or "psychobabble"—words that sound informative but are empty in terms of being helpful for making sound decisions. We are often unaware of the influence of emotional terms. Labels, for example, have emotional connotations that influence clinicians in ways that do not necessarily enhance the accuracy of decisions. Clinicians are influenced by primacy effects (by what they hear first) and are often guilty of the misuse of verbal speculation (assuming that what is can be discovered by merely thinking about it). Knowledge of fallacies related to use of language and care in using language can help a great deal in improving the quality of clinical decisions whether thinking, listening, writing, or reading.

Clinicians both use and are influenced by social-psychological persuasion appeals in their everyday practice. A thorough knowledge of these strategies will be useful in enhancing client participation and in avoiding sources of influence that decrease the accuracy of decisions. Learning how to recognize and counter persuasion strategies (such as attempted influence based on liking and appeals to consistency, authority, or scarcity) will increase the extent to which clinicians make their own decisions.

6

Formal and Informal Fallacies: Mistakes in Thinking and How to Avoid Them

Fallacies that frequently occur in clinical (as well as other) contexts are described in this chapter as well as in Chapter Five. The term *fallacy* refers to an error or mistake in thinking. Becoming familiar with these and acquiring effective ways to avoid them will enhance the quality of clinical decisions. Familiarity with the names of fallacies can be helpful in identifying them and in pointing them out to others. The focus of attention concerning fallacies typically has been on clients: assessment of their thinking patterns and the identification of how distortions in their thinking are related to personal problems they experience (see, for example, Ellis & Grieger, 1977; Beck, 1976). The focus here is on clinicians—on how formal and informal fallacies may compromise the quality of decisions they make. Errors that may result include assuming that pathology exists when it does not, missing pathology that is there, and selection of ineffective intervention methods. Helpful data in the practice literature may be ignored because it is associated with a disliked practice perspective resulting in errors in assessment.

There have been many attempts to classify the different kinds of fallacies and a variety of systems have been suggested (Hamblin, 1970). "Not the least of the merits of a really good classification of fallacies would be that it could be used in the formulation of appropriate points of order . . . It should be made possible in princi-

140

ple, as Bentham wished, that the perpetrator of fallacy be greeted with voices in scores crying aloud 'Stale! Stale! Fallacy of Authority! Fallacy of Distrust!' and so on" (p. 284). (For helpful descriptions of fallacies, see Engel, 1982; Kahane, 1971; Michalos, 1971; Thouless, 1974.) The term *trick* or *stratagem* refers to informal fallacies that are often used deliberately as persuasion strategies, although they also may occur because of sloppy thinking or lack of clear thinking skills. Fallacies may be intentional or unintentional. Intentional fallacies could be called deceptions. Does it make a difference? It may in terms of what must be done to avoid their influence.

False Even Though Valid

Some arguments are false even though they are valid. A valid argument is one whose premises if true offers good or sufficient grounds for accepting a conclusion.

Doubtful Evidence. One kind of the "false even though valid" arguments are those in which a conclusion is accepted even though the premises are questionable and inadequately supported. That is, people may insist that the form of an argument is valid while ignoring the possible (or probable) inaccuracy of the premises. Clinicians often refer clients to other practitioners; they make decisions about the competence of colleagues. It may be assumed that "All psychologists are competent. Max is a psychologist. Therefore, Max is competent." If the premises are true, the conclusion is true. However, the truth of the first premise is debatable, and because one of the premises is doubtful, the argument is unsound and a client may be referred to a clinician who is not competent to offer needed services. (An argument must be both valid and have true premises for it to be sound.) Because the argument stands or falls on whether a false premise is accepted, those who use doubtful evidence often try to distract readers or listeners from examining the premises; they may even try to use a "below the belt" technique such as ridicule (see Chapter Eleven).

Many facts are unknowable by anyone (for example, the exact number of gay/lesbian people who live in the United States). Other facts are potentially knowable or are known by someone, but are not known by the person who is using doubtful evidence. Doubtful evaluation refers to the insertion of an "unsupported controversial value judgment into an argument as a premise" (Kahane, 1971, p. 9). This may be confused with simple opinion statements, which are not really arguments (see Chapter Four). Examples of such statements are, "behavioral methods are superficial" and "psychoanalytic methods are overly complex in their view of causative factors." Some arguments contain premises that are contradictory—so even if the form of the argument is accurate, the conclusions cannot be true. The contradictory nature of the premises may not be obvious because of vagueness.

Suppressed Evidence. The suppression of evidence is one of the most widely and successfully used strategies. These "errors of omission" allow people to create false impressions and mislead others without actually lying. One kind of evidence that is often withheld from clients is information about the effectiveness of alternative treatment methods. That is, a clinician may suggest to the client that "x" intervention is best without informing the client that other intervention options are available that may have greater empirical support concerning their effectiveness. This may, of course, influence decisions of clients to go along with the method proposed. Clients, since they are typically unaware of what is not offered to them, are in a disadvantaged position to request alternative methods. Information concerning the false-positive rate and false-negative rate yielded by a clinical instrument may not be reported in a description of a clinical measure. Without these data, clinicians may make incorrect decisions because of overestimating the accuracy of a measure.

Presenting just the facts that will serve one's own purpose while intentionally ignoring other significant data is especially insidious, because readers or listeners are often unaware of facts that are left out (MacLean, 1981, p. 37). Often there is a conscious effort to suppress evidence. That is, someone does not just have a point of view that he is ready to examine; actually, he is interested in persuading us of the truth of his conclusion by appealing to our emotions. However, not considering important evidence is often unintentional; it often occurs because of implicit biases and preconceptions (see discussion of partiality and evidence in Chapter Nine). The more educated the readership (or listeners), the more likely is a tactic such as suppressed evidence to be used (rather than an obvious tactic such as use of emotional language).

Published sources contribute to use of suppressed evidence by failing to discuss both sides of issues and by failing to include corrections of inaccurate reports. A sophisticated campaign may be mounted to suppress data contradictory to a preferred position, as described below in excerpts from an article describing court proceedings concerning death of a smoker (Janson, 1988, p. A13).

> "Evidence presented by the plaintiff," Judge Sarokin said, "particularly that contained in documents of the defendants themselves, indicates the development of a public relations strategy aimed at combating the mounting adverse scientific reports regarding the dangers of smoking.
>
> "The evidence indicates further that the industry of which these defendants were and are a part entered into a sophisticated conspiracy. The conspiracy was organized to refute, undermine and neutralize information coming from the scientific and medical community and, at the same time, to confuse and mislead the consuming public in an effort to encourage existing smokers to continue and new persons to commence smoking.
>
> Judge Sarokin noted that evidence had been introduced showing that results of industry-sponsored research adverse to the industry's goals had been 'suppressed and concealed.'
>
> "At least one scientist testified as to threats made to him if he published his findings, and there was other evidence of attempts to suppress or coerce others," he said.

The remedy to use of suppressed evidence depends partly on whether the suppression is intentional or unintentional. The main goal is to identify critical unmentioned information that bears on the accuracy of a conclusion. Possible options include (1) talking to people holding other views; (2) exploring all possible effects of a certain decision; and (3) asking speakers if there are any important consequences of a proposed view that have not been mentioned (they may not be willing to lie and so reveal the suppressed evidence or may be unwilling to appear uninformed at a later date by having failed to recognize other important effects under direct questioning).

Irrelevant Appeals

There are an infinite number of types of irrelevant appeals. Some common ones are described in the sections that follow. Irrelevant appeals include fallacies in which the wrong point is supported or when a conclusion established by premises is not relevant to the issues being discussed. These are informal fallacies, that is, none involve a formal mistake. Many of these fallacies achieve their effect through taking advantage of one or more of our natural tendencies, such as wanting to please people or going along with what others think (the principle of social proof).

Ad Hominem Arguments. Here, the background, habits, associates, or personality of an individual are attacked or appealed to rather than his or her argument. The appeal or attack may be subtle or obvious. Consider, for example, the ad hominen attacks made about Jeffrey S. Masson (1988), author of the controversial book *Against Therapy;* rather than addressing the arguments made in the book, some writers chose to make negative statements about the author. The theories of Jung may be rejected because of his alleged racism and anti-Semitism; this rejection is made on an ad hominem basis: these alleged characteristics do not necessarily bear on the cogency of his theory. Improper appeals to authority to support a position are a kind of ad hominem argument. The effectiveness of ad hominem arguments depend partially on the principle of liking (disliking), as well as the principle of authority (see Chapter Five).

Is an ad hominem attack or appeal ever relevant? If an attack on the presenter of the argument is related to the issue at hand, then in some cases it may be relevant. For example, someone could be shown to offer unreliable accounts on most occasions. However, this person may be offering a correct account this time. Thus, the credibility of the person presenting an argument is certainly important to consider. Ad hominem arguments are surprisingly effective for a variety of reasons, only one of which is failure to identify the fallacious nature of the argument. Others include the following

- Implicit agreement with the implications about the individual
- Agreement with the point of the argument with little concern for its correctness
- Unwillingness to raise questions, cause a fuss, or challenge authorities who may counterattack
- Social pressures in group settings—not wanting to embarrass others

The remedy in relation to ad hominem arguments is to point out that the appeal made provides no evidence for or against a claim.

Guilt (or credit) by association is a variation of an ad hominem argument—judging people by the company they keep. A youth accused of theft may associate with a gang known to engage in a variety of criminal activities. Such association offers indirect and circumstantial evidence—it does not offer direct support for the argument that he is guilty. The best use of circumstantial or indirect evidence is as a cue for further exploration. There may be a grain of truth in assessing credibility of an argument by considering the associates of the person proposing a position. However, not all of an individual's friends may be disreputable or uninformed (or reputable or informed in the case of assumptions of credit). And, even if they all are (either one or the other), the individual may still speak the truth. An attempt to discredit a position may be made by associating it with a disliked institution, value, or philosophy, as in the statement that behavioral methods are antihumanistic or psychoanalytic methods are antifeminist. "Imposter terms" or "euphemisms" may be used to make an unpopular view or method acceptable. For example, use of long-term lockups in a prison may be referred to as a behavior modification. Dumping patients into the community from mental hospitals may be called "community care" (see Chapter Five). As Nickerson (1986a) points out, we are indeed more likely to agree with institutions and philosophies we favor—however, it is unlikely that we will agree with every facet, and similarly, it is unlikely that we would disagree with every facet of a disliked view. So, "Credit or discredit by association becomes a fallacy when it is applied in a blind and uncritical way. Whether or not a particular view is one that is held by a specific individual, institution, or philosophy that we generally support (or oppose) is very meager evidence as to the tenability of that view" (Nickerson, 1986a, p. 116).

In the bad seed fallacy, it is assumed that a person's character or habits are passed on to his descendants (Michalos, 1971, p. 54); that because a client's parents acted in a certain way, that is why the client acts in this manner. The bad seed fallacy is quite common in clinical contexts. A striking example of guilt by association is shown in the excerpts from a case conference given in Chapter Eleven. Genetic factors do play a role in influencing behavior; however, the correlations presented are typically far from perfect and, in any case, may not securely imply a causal connection.

An argument may be made that a position is not acceptable because the person's motives for supporting the issue are questionable. For example, a proposal that a new suicide prevention center be created may be denied on the grounds that those who propose this are "interested parties"—that they will profit from such a center by gaining needed jobs. In fact, the accuracy or inaccuracy of the view proposed cannot be determined from an examination of the motives of those who proposed it, but only from an examination of the evidence presented in its favor. It may be argued that because one's intentions or motives are good, a claim is true. A psychologist may wish to place a child on Ritalin even though there is little behavioral evidence that this is indicated. He may protest that his intent is to help this child. Appeals to good intentions are the opposite of the assumption of suspect motives. In both cases, evidence is needed that the claim is correct; motives, whether altruistic or otherwise, are not evidence.

The fallacy of special pleading involves favoring our own interests by using different standards for different people as in "I am firm, thou art obstinate, he is pigheaded" (Thouless, 1974, p. 11).

A clinician may claim that she does not have to evaluate her work as carefully as other clinicians because of her lengthy experience.

A discrepancy between a person's behavior and his principles may be invalidly used against him. For example, an argument may be dismissed on the grounds that the person's behavior is not consistent with his argument. A clinician who is not sympathetic to behavioral methods may say to his behavioral friend, "If behaviorists knew so much about how to change behavior, why are you still smoking when you want to stop?"

Another kind of false claim of inconsistency is when a charge is made that a person's behavior is not consistent with his principles when his principles have changed. It may be argued that because a clinician held a certain view many years ago, he holds the same view today. Altering a position does not necessarily entail inconsistency. It depends on whether a person states that his position has changed and explains the reasons for these changes. Not recognizing that people often have rational grounds for changing their opinions results in a false charge of inconsistency. This fallacy takes advantage of our desire to be consistent and to expect others to be consistent as well. (See discussion of persuasion in Chapter Five.)

Objections to a position or action may be countered with "You'd do it too if you had an opportunity," as in "you would refer difficult clients to someone else if you could." This argument does not provide evidence for (or against) a position.

Vacuous Guarantees. A warrant may be offered for a claim that is without substance. Self-help books are often criticized for offering unsupported vacuous guarantees of effectiveness (Rosen, 1982). For example, an advertisement in a professional journal directed to mental health facilities and substance abuse centers assures potential customers interested in consultation, training, and supervision that "it works," that they "custom-design safe programs," that "I can, you can, together we can." No criteria are described as to what is meant by "it works" or what a "safe program" consists of. No evidence is offered in support of claims made. The costs in time and money of holding people responsible for vacuous claims may far outweigh any benefits.

The fallacy of ignorance involves the assumption "that the

absence of evidence for (against) a claim must be counted as evidence for (against) it" (Michalos, 1971, p. 52). A clinician may argue that because there is no evidence showing that "directed aggression" (hitting objects such as pillows) does not work, that it should be used. The fact that no one can think of a course of action that is better than one proposed may be used as an argument that the proposed course is a good one. In fact, they could all be bad. It is hard to believe that this fallacy would ever work (that is, influence people), but it does, as do some other weak appeals—such as simply asserting that a position is true.

An example of the fallacy of appeals to will is to say that "if he really wanted to . . . he would." It would be hoped that clinicians with their more sophisticated conceptualizations of motivation (compared with laymen) would not use appeals to will. However, I have often heard clinicians say, "If she really was interested in getting better, she'd come in for counseling." Appeals to "will power" offer no information about how to actually create the changes that are desired. Wishful thinking involves the assumption that because some condition ought to be, it is the case without providing any support for the position. This fallacy could also be included under the category of begging the question. Statements made concerning declassification (hiring staff without advanced clinical degrees) are often of this variety. It is assumed that declassification is bad; no evidence is presented to support the position by showing, for example, that hiring staff without graduate degrees results in lower quality services being offered to clients. "We continue to hear about professional caregivers coming into conflict with case managers who lack the requisite training to perform the complicated tasks involved in assessment and evaluation" (From the President, 1987, p. 2). No evidence is provided that case managers without professional training lack the requisite training to perform the tasks described and the conflict alluded to is assumed to reflect negatively on the case managers rather than on "professional caregivers."

Attacking the example is a relatively transparent strategy—the example given of a position is attacked rather than the position itself. The example offered might not be an apt one. A remedy here is to point out that a successful attack on the example does not take away from the possible soundness of a position and to offer a better example. This fallacy is the opposite of the use of a suspect particular case as proof for a generalization (see later discussion). It may be argued that two wrongs make a right—that because other people do something, it is all right to do the same. Common practice is a variety of this fallacy. It may be argued that it is all right not to keep up with practice-related empirical literature because other clinicians do not do so.

Evading the Facts

Fallacies that evade the facts such as "begging the question" appear to address the facts but do not: "Such arguments deceive by inviting us to presume that the facts are as they have been stated in the argument, when the facts are quite otherwise" (Engel, 1982, p. 114).

Begging the Question. This refers to assuming the truth or falsity of what is at issue; that is, trying to settle a question by simply reasserting a position. This tactic is surprisingly effective often because it is accompanied by appeals to authority. Such appeals take advantage of persuasive bases such as liking (we are less likely to question poor arguments of people we like), authority (we accept what experts say), and social proof (being influenced by what other people do) (see Chapter Five). Consider, for example, the statement, "The inappropriate releasing of mentally ill patients must be ended." The speaker assumes that releasing mentally ill patients is inappropriate, instead of offering evidence to show that it is. Presenting opinions as facts is a common variant of this fallacy. Michalos (1971) has identified seven ways to beg the question, some of which overlap with improper appeals to authority (see Chapter Seven).

One method is to use alleged certainty to encourage readers or listeners to accept a claim without providing any evidence that the claim is accurate. The claim is presented as if it were obvious, in the hope that our critical senses will be neutralized. Examples are (1) "No one doubts the number of alcoholics in the U.S. today." (2) "It is well accepted that therapy works."

Appeals to consensus may be made with no evidence provided that there is a consensus concerning a position. A clinician may say that "use of play therapy with autistic children is the accepted method of choice." Even if evidence for a consensus is offered, that does not mean that the position is correct. This appeal, as well as the appeal of alleged certainty, takes advantage of the principle of social proof (our tendency to believe that what most other people think or do is correct).

Speakers or writers are guilty of using question-begging epithets when they add evaluative terms to neutral descriptive terms—the aim is to influence through emotional reactions. For example, "Fairview Hospital opened today" is a simple declarative statement. "The long-needed Fairview Hospital opened its door today" includes evaluative epithets. Examples of question-begging epithets can be seen in the descriptions of Mary Walsh in Chapter Eleven. Other names for this fallacy include the use of emotive language (see Chapter Five), loaded words, and verbal suggestion. Emotional terms may be used to attempt to prejudice the facts by using evaluative language that supports what we want to prove but have not proved. "By overstatement, ridicule, flattery, abuse and the like, they seek to evade the facts" (Engel, 1982, p. 120). Question-begging descriptions can be used as a clue that relevant facts are being evaded.

Circular arguments are a form of question-begging as in the following example (Engel, 1982, p. 142).

People can't help what they do.
Why not?
Because they always follow the strongest motive.
But what is the strongest motive?
It is, of course, the one that people follow.

This argument is circular in saying that A is so because of B and B is true because of A. The conclusion that a speaker or writer is trying to establish is used as a premise or presupposed as a premise. Such circular arguments may seem so transparent that they would never be a problem in clinical practice. However, they are a common occurrence and profoundly affect clinical decisions. Consider the following dialogue.

> Mr. Levine can't control his outbursts.
> Why is that?
> Because he is developmentally disabled.
> Why do you say that he is developmentally disabled?
> Well, for one reason, he has outbursts when he is frustrated.

Attributing the cause of outbursts to the developmental disability offers no information about how to alter the frequency of the outbursts.

A clinician may alter a definition or question a diagnosis, rather than admit that a counter example to a position has been identified. Believers in the disease view of alcoholism contend that drinkers who can return to limited nonproblem drinking were never "true alcoholics." "In its extreme, this argument maintains that even individuals who have suffered distinct alcohol withdrawal symptoms must have been misclassified as alcoholics" (Sobell & Sobell, 1982, p. 156). As Michalos (1971) points out, "facts cannot shake the generalization because the truth is guaranteed by definitions."

A priorism is a form of question-begging in which a position is claimed as true (prior to any investigation) because it is necessary according to a particular view of the world (or of clinical practice). For example, consider the assertion of psychiatrists that they should supervise treatment of patients (implying that psychologists and other kinds of mental health professionals such as social workers would work under their supervision) and that to arrange services otherwise (to allow other kinds of professionals to work autonomously) would lower the quality of service offered to clients. The view of practice that is assumed is that training as a psychiatrist is superior to other kinds of professional training. This, of course, is not necessarily true. What is needed is evidence to support the position advanced.

Unfounded generalizations may be used to support a conclusion. For example, someone may assume, "Offering positive incentives for desired behaviors is dehumanizing because it is behavioral." The unstated assumptions are that behavioral methods are dehumanizing and that offering positive incentives for desired behaviors is behavioral. Since the truth of the wider generalizations is questionable (especially the first one), the particular example is questionable. In another example, a clinical supervisor could beg the question of whether practice should be evaluated on the grounds that this violates client confidentiality. When a more general claim is assumed, the accuracy of this claim should be examined.

Complex, leading, or trick questions with indirect assumptions may be used. A question may be asked in such a way that any answer will incriminate the speaker (for example, "Do you still beat your wife?" or "Where do you keep your cocaine?"). This is the interrogative form of the fallacy of begging the question; the conclusion at issue is assumed rather than supported. "Complex questions accomplish this by leading one to believe that a particular answer to a prior question has been answered in a certain way when this may not be the case" (Engel, 1982, p. 122). These questions bring with them assumptions that influence the ways they will be answered. The remedy is to question the question. Because of their leading nature, some questions would be ruled out in a court of law, given that lawyers were on their toes. Such questions are also fallacious "because they assume that one and the same answer must apply to both the unasked and the asked question as in the example of 'Isn't Dr. Green an unthinking feminist' " (p. 124). If the question is divided into its parts, different answers may apply: Is Dr. Green a feminist? Is she unthinking? Thus, the remedy is to divide the original question into its implied components and answer each one at a time.

Complex questions are often used to encourage clients to comply with a request as in the example of a staff member who is having trouble getting a patient to take a bath. Rather than asking him if he wants to take a bath tonight, she might say, "Do you want to take a bath now or at 7?" Another variation of complex questions is requesting explanations for supposed facts that have not been supported as in "How do you account for ESP (extra sensory perception)"? Since there is controversy about whether such effects exist and many people believe that research exploring such phenomena has yielded negative results (see, for example, Blackmore, 1987), there may be no extraordinary effects to explain, perhaps just fallacies or questionable experimental designs to be uncovered.

One way to respond to a criticism is to ignore it—that is, to simply proceed as if the statements had never been made. This tactic can be successful if no one is present who will object, perhaps because the point introduced is not critical or because everyone agrees with the original position. One form of ignoring the issue is to claim there is no issue. The question may be swept aside as irrelevant, trivial, or offensive.

Overlooking the Facts

Relevant facts are often neglected, as in the fallacy of the sweeping generalization in which a rule or assumption that is valid in general is applied to a specific example to which it is not valid (Engel, 1982). It might be argued that since expressing feelings is healthy, Susan should do it more because it will help increase her self-esteem and make her happier. However, if expressing feelings will result in negative consequences from significant others (such as work supervisors and her husband), the general rule may not apply here. This kind of fallacy can be exposed by identifying the rule involved and showing that it cannot be applied accurately to the case at hand. (Another name for this fallacy is the fallacy of accident, Toulmin et al., 1979, p. 161.)

The fallacy of hasty generalization is the opposite of the one above; here, an example is used as the basis for a general conclusion that is not warranted. For example, if a psychologist has an unpleasant conversation with a social worker and says "Social workers are difficult to work with," the generalization to all social workers might be inaccurate. This fallacy is also known as the fallacy of the hasty conclusion (Kahane, 1971), and it has many variants. All have in common making unwarranted generalizations from small or biased samples. This fallacy entails a disregard for the law of large numbers (see Chapter Eight). (See also discussions of suppressed evidence below and of either/or thinking in Chapter Seven.)

Distorting Facts/Positions

A number of informal fallacies distort positions. In straw person arguments, a position similar to but different from the one presented is attacked; an argument is distorted and the distorted version is then attacked. Such arguments are often seen in the discussion of disliked practice theories. For example, it is not unusual to read or hear distorted views of a behavioral approach presented, such as the incorrect view that Skinner believes in stimulus-response Watsonian behaviorism. This incorrect assertion may then be criticized. Inaccurate adjectives may be used to give a misleading view of what indeed occurred as in the statement that "there is an epidemic of drug use" when in fact there has been a modest increase. Clinicians more readily believe extreme but inaccurate statements that support their biases.

Forcing an extension may be intentionally used by someone aware of the fact that it is usually impossible to defend extreme positions; that is, most positions have some degree of probability attached to them, like the statement that insight therapy is useful with many (not all) clients. The original position may be misstated in an extreme version (insight therapy is effective with all clients) and this extreme version then criticized. The original, less extreme position should be reaffirmed.

The fallacy of false cause involves arguments that suggest that two events are casually associated when in fact no such connection has been established. It may be argued that because one event followed another, the latter caused the former. For example, a client may state that, because she had a bad dream the night before, she made a number of mistakes the following day (see Chapter Nine).

An argument may be made for a conclusion that is not the one under discussion. While seeming to counter an argument, statements of irrelevant thesis advance a conclusion that is different from the one at issue. Other names for this fallacy include *red herring*, *irrelevant conclusion, ignoring the issue*, and *diversion*. This fallacy can be quite deceptive because the irrelevant argument advanced often does support a conclusion and so gives an impression of credibility to the person offering it and the illusion of a lack of credibility for the original argument—but, the argument does not address the conclusion at issue (Engel, 1982). An example is, "the advocates of reality therapy contend that if we adopt their practice methods, clients will be better off. They are mistaken, for it is easy to show that reality therapy will not cure the ills of the world."

There are two different points here: (1) whether reality therapy is effective and (2) whether it will "cure the ills of the world." Showing that the latter is not true may persuade people that the first point has also been shown to be untrue. The fallacy of irrelevant thesis is a version of forcing an extension. Notice that distortion of a position can make it look ridiculous and so easily overthrown. If the presenter of the original, more modest view is duped into defending an extreme version, he or she will likely fail.

Inappropriate Use of Analogies. Analogies can be helpful in understanding clinical problems and in selecting effective treatment methods. Analogies often are used in daily life to decide what to do in novel situations; that is, we try to identify a familiar experience and use it to make decisions in new contexts. Analogies often are used to clarify meanings. For example, the Freudian theory of motivation is sometimes likened to a hydraulic system in which repressed forces are kept in check by defenses, and if these are removed, repressed content will emerge. Analogies can be helpful if they compare two phenomena that are indeed similar in significant ways; the more familiar event can be helpful in highlighting aspects of the less familiar event that should be considered. However, if the two events differ in important ways, then the analogy can interfere with understanding. Two things may bear a superficial resemblance to each other but be quite unlike in important ways. Consider the question "Should couples have sex before marriage?" A response might be "You wouldn't buy a car without taking it out for a test drive, would you?" (Bransford and Stein, 1984, p. 88). Some people who hear this argument simply say, "Oh, yes, you have a point there." Others will see that the analogy is inappropriate; marriage is significantly different from buying a car. The soundness of the analogy must always be explored. It is only a guide; it becomes dangerous "when the conclusions to which it points are regarded as certain and not merely as probable" (Thouless, 1974, p. 171). There are two main ways analogies can be misused.

Argument by mere analogy refers to the use of an analogy "to create conviction of the truth of whatever it illustrates, or when it implies that truth in order to deduce some new conclusion" (Thouless, 1974, p. 169). When an argument from analogy is reduced to its bare outline, it "has the form that because some thing or event N has the properties a and b which belong to M, it must have the property c which also belongs to M" (p. 171). Arguments from analogy may sometimes be difficult to recognize; that is, the analogy may be implied rather than clearly stated. The mind of a child may be likened to a container that must be filled with information. This analogy carries some implications that may be untrue, such as that containers have limited capacities. So "the use of analogy becomes crooked argumentation when an analogy is used not as a guide to expectations, but as proof of a conclusion" (Thouless, 1974, p. 176). Analogies create vivid images that are then readily available. Their vividness may crowd out less vivid but more accurate analogies and discourage a review of possible limitations of an analogy. There is thus an emotional impact; analogies play upon our emotions. We forget that, although they may be a useful guide as to what to look for, "They are never final evidence as to what the facts are" (Thouless, 1974, p. 175). They are one of many devices for creating conviction even though there are no rational grounds for the convictions. Arguments from mere analogy can be dealt with by noting at what point the analogy breaks down.

In argument from forced analogy, an analogy is used to advance an argument when there is so little resemblance between the things compared to ever expect that they would resemble each other in relation to the main point under discussion. One example is "delusional processes are like a machine run amok." Those who use such analogies are often aware of their influence in creating beliefs despite the absence of rational grounds for such beliefs. Forced analogies tend to be used in public speeches where their deficiencies cannot be pointed out readily. The remedy consists of examining just how closely the analogy really fits the matter at hand. Thouless (1974) recommends trying out other analogies and noting that these carry as much force as the original one.

Distortions may occur because of misquotes or false identifications of individuals or procedures (see discussion of incorrect classification of procedures in Chapter Seven).

Diversions

Many informal fallacies succeed by diverting attention away from the main points of an argument. Some of the informal fallacies already discussed could be so classified, such as ad hominem arguments in which attention is focused on the person making the argument rather than the argument itself. Trivial points or irrelevant objections may be focused on. "If you find that you are being worsted, you can make a diversion—that is, you can suddenly begin to talk of something else, as though it had a bearing on the matter in dispute" (Schopenhauer, n.d., p. 29). Here the diversion is not to a new question (as in the fallacy of irrelevant thesis), but to a question related to the prime question under consideration. In any discussion, a number of points may be raised, one or more of which may not be true. In this fallacy, some trivial point is addressed and shown to be incorrect and it is assumed that the main question has been disposed of. Showing the inaccuracy of a fact that is actually not relevant to a position can create the impression that the entire argument is incorrect. Certainly all points related to an argument should be examined; however, this is just the beginning of an evaluation of a position. Witty comments and jokes can be used to divert attention from the main point of an argument or from the fact that little evidence is provided for a position. A joke can be made that makes a valid position appear ridiculous or poorly conceived. Attempts to defend a position in the face of such a response may seem pedantic. The remedy is to point out that, although what has been said may be true (or humorous), it is irrelevant.

In an appeal to ignorance, a "why" is met with a "why not?" (Michalos, 1971, p. 81). In the fallacy of answering questions with questions, hypothetical questions are introduced that provide a distraction from important points. Questions cannot be true or false so continued questioning is not informative. Certainly, some questions are vital to evaluation of arguments. However, in arguments, they are never an end in themselves. In other contexts, such as an exchange between Buddhist monks, another end may be sought (see Engel, 1982, p. 82).

Creating anger is another way to distract people. Emotional

language can be used to create anger, anxiety, or blind adherence to a position and to distract us from noticing flaws in an argument. Anger may be created by inflammatory statements about a position or by ad hominem attacks. The focus may shift to insults, rather than the issues under discussion. Anger may be distracting also if others become very angry.

Appeals to anxiety and fear are widely used to distract listeners and readers from the main issues. Arguments based on emotions result in compliance rather than conviction. In an article entitled "Marketing: A Lifeline For Private Practice," readers are told that "as more social workers go into private practice, and as competition between them and other mental health professionals heats up, marketing becomes a necessary survival tool" *NASW News*, Oct. 1987, 32(9), p. 5. Notice the term *survival* appealing to the scarcity principle (see Chapter Five). The principle of social proof is one of the bases of appeals to anxiety—"You will be out of step with 'everyone else' if you don't agree with an accepted position." Thus, appeals to anxiety and fear may draw on any one of the sources of persuasion as illustrated in Table 6 (see also Chapter Five). Appeals to fear are often used by psychiatrists in their battle against psychologists to retain and expand their turf. For example, they may predict that the quality of services will decrease if psychologists receive hospital admission privileges (Buie, 1989). Appeals to pity or friendship may also direct attention away from careful examination of the evidence (see Chapter Eleven).

The Use of Confusion

Some fallacies work by confusion: "If you can't convince them (or if you don't know what you're talking about), confuse them." People may attempt to create confusion by citing a counter example to a position saying that "the exception proves the rule." It does no such thing. Finding an example that does not fit a rule may be informative about the boundaries within which a rule is applicable, but may say nothing about the truth or falsity of the rule in question. (See discussion of the fallacy of the sweeping generalization earlier in this chapter.) Excessive verbiage is a common means of creating confusion—talking about many different things

Table 6. Use of Persuasion Tactics to Create Fear and Anxiety.

Social-psychological principle	Anxiety-arousing appeal
Liking	You don't like me if you don't go along with my position (and therefore I won't like you as much).
Consistency	You're inconsistent with your beliefs if you don't agree with me.
Reciprocity	I helped you out in the past, now you're not fulfilling your obligation to return the favor if you don't support my position.
Authority	Other people (namely me) really know what is best.
Scarcity	We won't have this opportunity very long—it's now or never.
Social proof	Everyone (but you) accepts this position—what's the matter with you?

and then stating a conclusion that supposedly stems from all of them. Excessive words used in the presentation of arguments, whether written or spoken, make the task of argument analysis difficult. Irrelevancies, unstated premises, and implicit assumptions must be culled out in order to reveal the actual premises and conclusions.

Use of pseudoarguments takes advantage of our tendency to assume that if someone is talking (or writing), he or she must be making sense. That is, we tend to think that we have missed the point and that we are limited in our lack of understanding; we "tend to put the burden of comprehension on ourselves" (Michalos, 1971, p. 79). If excessive verbiage is complemented by prestige, the use of pseudoarguments is even more likely to confuse and mislead. We are misled by our tendency to go along with what authorities say. Another persuasive influence at work here may include liking—if we like someone, we are more prone to agree with what they say and to think they are saying something of value.

Equivocation involves playing on the double meaning of a word in a misleading or inaccurate manner (see Hamblin, 1970). "If someone informs you that Simon Butcher is independent, exactly what has he told you? Is he politically, religiously, economically, or socially independent? Is he a free thinker or a free lover? Is he a lover of free thinking or does he just think about loving freely? The fallacy of *equivocation* would be committed if someone began with a premise attributing independence in one sense to Butcher and concluded from that that Butcher possessed independence in an entirely different sense (Michalos, 1971, p. 71)."

People may claim a lack of understanding to avoid coming to grips with an issue or try to confuse issues by repeatedly asking for alternative statements of a position (Michalos, 1971, p. 75). This tactic, like some others such as arousing anger, may be used to gain time to consider a position better in terms of what to do next in order to prevail. Feigned lack of understanding is often combined with use of power, as when a clinical instructor tells a student that he does not understand the point being made. Often there is an implication that the other person's point of view is irrelevant or silly anyway.

Summary

Both formal and informal fallacies may occur when making clinical decisions that dilute the quality of clinical decisions. Some arguments are false even though they are valid. A valid argument is one whose premises if true, offers good or sufficient grounds for accepting a conclusion. The incorrectness of premises is often over-looked in clinical practice resulting in inaccurate clinical decisions. Most fallacies are informal ones; that is, they do not involve a formal mistake. There are many different kinds of informal fallacies. Ad hominem arguments may be used in which the background, habits, associates, or personality of the person (rather than the arguments) are criticized or appealed to. Variants of ad hominem arguments include guilt (or credit) by association, the bad seed fallacy, appeals to faulty motives or good intentions, special pleading, and false claims of inconsistency. Vacuous guarantees may be offered, as when someone assumes that because a condition ought to be, it *is* the case without providing support for the position.

Fallacies that evade the facts (such as begging the question) appear to address the facts, but do not. Variants of question begging include use of alleged certainty; circular reasoning; use of un-founded generalizations to support a conclusion; complex, trick, or leading questions; and ignoring the issue. Some informal fallacies overlook the facts, as in the fallacy of the sweeping generalization, in which a rule or assumption that is valid in general is applied to a specific example for which it is not valid. Other informal fallacies distort facts or positions; in straw person arguments, a position similar to (but significantly different from) the one presented is described and attacked. The informal fallacies of false cause and forcing an extension and the inappropriate use of analogies also involve the distortion of facts or positions. Diversions may be used to direct attention away from a main point of an argument. Trivial points, irrelevant objections, or emotional appeals may be made. Some fallacies work by creating confusion, such as feigned lack of understanding and excessive talk that obscures arguments. Knowl-edge of formal and informal fallacies decreases the likelihood that clinical decisions will be influenced by these sources of error.

7

Classification, Pseudoauthority, and Focusing on Pathology: Additional Sources of Error

Additional sources of fallacy that have special relevance to clinical decision making are discussed in this chapter. These include fallacies related to classification; appeals to pseudoauthority; a pathological set; and the rule of optimism.

Fallacies Related to Classification

Classification (sorting objects, events, or people into different categories and giving different names to these categories) is necessary in everyday life as well as in clinical practice. Among the potential benefits of classification are selection of effective treatment methods and standard usage of terms. Mennerick (1974) suggests that the creation and use of client typologies is influenced by facilitation of work tasks, control over performance, gain from exchanges with clients, danger in the client-counselor relationship, and the moral acceptability of clients. Predictions of new discoveries may result from classification. For example, Mendeleef's classification of the elements according to their atomic weights and chemical properties enabled the prediction of the discovery of unknown elements (Masson, 1988). Causal relationships may not necessarily be implied by classification. A belief that classification systems accurately reflect the world can lead clinicians astray. "Science and com-

162

mon sense inquiry alike do not discover the ways in which events are grouped in the world; they invent ways of grouping" (Abercrombie, 1960, p. 113). Faulty classification may occur when the classification is not exhaustive or exclusive, is not adequate to the purpose for which it was created, or does not permit precise divisions resulting in serious marginal cases.

Labels that point to effective interventions are helpful. In fact, not applying the correct label may prevent clients from receiving appropriate intervention (Meehl, 1973). Labels can normalize client concerns (Grunebaum & Chasin, 1978). For example, parents who have been struggling to understand why their child is developmentally slow may view themselves as failures. Recognition that this "slowness" is a result of a specific kind of disability can be a great relief. Too often, however, labels, although they may sound sophisticated, offer little or no information about what to do to help a client and often have iatrogenic effects; they often medicalize, stigmatize, and pathologize clients (Morgan, 1983).

Classification requires overlooking differences among objects, people, or events and focusing on similarities. At lower levels of abstraction, difficulties may not be great in correctly classifying people, events, or objects. It is at the higher levels of abstraction that problems often occur and cause such errors as inappropriate stereotyping. Even at lower levels, sloppy thinking may lead to inaccurate generalizations, such as "a rose is a rose" (in the context of a competition among rose growers for the most beautiful rose of the year, a rose is certainly not a rose. Even the same rose may differ from day to day). The context influences the features attended to in categorizing an event, object, or behavior; these may differ from person to person and time to time. For example, Rosenhan's (1973) research suggests that once a "normal" person enters a psychiatric hospital, he or she will continue to be viewed as mentally ill. Overlooking cultural differences may result in misdiagnosis, neglect of problems, or overestimation or underestimation of pathology (Gibbs & Huang, 1989; Sue & Sue, 1987; Westermeyer, 1987).

Classification is of great interest in psychology and related fields. An enormous literature is devoted to the development of measures that will permit the reliable and valid classification of clients into different categories. For example, hundreds of reports have appeared on the MMPI. A wide array of disorders appears in the *Diagnostic and Statistical Manual* (DSM-III, 1980), and spirited discussions have taken place about adding or removing some disorders. (See also DSM-III-R, 1987.) Diagnostic labels must be applied to clients as a requirement for third-party payments. Clinical labels are used in two main ways. First, they are used as shorthand terms to refer to specific behaviors. The term *hyperactive* may refer to the fact that a student often gets out of his seat at school and talks out of turn in class. The teacher may use *hyperactive* as a summary term to refer to these behaviors. Second, and more commonly, labels are used for diagnostic categories that are supposed to have implications for resolving clients' problems. Where a label such as *hyperactive* connotes more than a cluster of behaviors, it involves additional assumptions about the person labeled which supposedly will be of value in altering the situation. For example, a counselor after verifying that a student does engage in these behaviors, may say that he is hyperactive, meaning that he has a psychological disturbance and therefore should be placed on medication. That is, inferences are based on observed behavior that a condition of hyperactivity exists, and intervention recommendations are based on these inferences. In fact, the label is based simply on the two observed behaviors. This is an example of the use of a descriptive term as a pseudoexplanatory term (see Chapter Five).

The consensual nature of diagnostic categories is reflected in the recent controversy about adding the terms *self-defeating personality disorder, sadistic personality disorder,* and *premenstrual syndrome* (later changed to late luteal phase dysphoric disorder). Opponents argued that a diagnosis of sadistic personality disorder would offer a legal defense to child abusers and wife beaters and that women would be stigmatized by the addition of late luteal phase dysphoric disorder. Recent debates concerning other labels also illustrate the consensual nature of diagnosis. Consider the definition of the term *learning disability.* A new definition proposed includes social skills, for the first time, on the list of skills a learning-disabled person may have difficulty acquiring. Former definitions included listening, speaking, reading, writing, reasoning, and mathematics. The U.S. Education Department, concerned with the increase in the number of students identified as learning disabled (120,000 in 1919

and 1,872,399 in 1987), warned that inclusion of social skills deficiencies would increase the number of children classified as
learning disabled and eligible for special education services (Landers, 1987, p. 35). Cantor (1982) argues that psychiatric diagnostic
knowledge conforms better to a fuzzy prototype description in
which categories are described by a set of correlated features than it
does to a small set of necessary and sufficient defining features as
in the normative descriptions in the DSM-III. "According to the
classical model, categorization is simply a matter of presence or
absence of all of the defining features of a category. By contrast, the
prototype model characterizes categorization as a probabilistic process of assessing degree of similarity of a particular target to each
of the prototypes for a set of relevant categories—categorization is
a matter of degree" (Cantor, 1982, p. 33).

Labeling theorists stress the relativity with which labels are
used in accord with changing societal views about what is proper
and improper behavior (Lemert, 1951; Scheff, 1984a, 1984b). That
is, labels reflect moral judgments based on societal definitions of
what is normal and abnormal. The relation between judgments of
moral character and ascriptions of deviance is emphasized by sociologists as well as by some clinicians who have been quite critical
of accepted psychiatric practices (see, for example, Basaglia in
Scheper-Hughes & Lovell, 1987) and is often neglected by clinicians.
In the labeling theory of mental illness, "symptoms of mental illness" are conceptualized as a kind of "nonconformity: the violation
of residual rules" (Scheff, 1984b, p. 188). The term *residual rules*
refers to all of those situations in which a conventional label of
deviance such as drunkenness cannot readily be found. Scheff
(1984b) argues that it is here, in this residual category, that the label
"mental illness" is applied. Rule breaking may occur for a variety
of different reasons, only some of which (a small percentage according to labeling theorists) are a true result of disease. The key question of concern to labeling theorists is "from whatever cause, why
are some [symptoms] short-lived or self-limited and others stable?"
(Scheff, 1984b, p. 189). They believe that societal reactions to residual rule breaking stabilize the symptoms and result in a career of
deviance. Thus, within labeling theory, the label itself is considered

to be partially responsible for the continuation of and increase in deviant acts.

Labeling is viewed as a behavior that varies from culture to culture, from person to person, and from time to time and which has social functions in relation to regulating the boundaries between accepted and unaccepted behavior. This stance is very different from a psychiatric one, in which there is a search for some objective diagnostic label for a client that justifies use of certain intervention methods (see DSM-III, 1980). In the former instance there is a concern that labeling stigmatizes clients and encourages deviant behavior, and diverts attention from client strengths and related environmental factors; also that it results in "blaming the victim" and deflects attention away from social and political conditions that encourage deviant behavior. In the psychiatric enterprise, an effort is made to label clients correctly so that appropriate intervention methods can be selected. What is considered appropriate may differ for clients and clinicians. That is, services then offered may not be for the benefit of clients, but, to the contrary, may result in loss of freedom and independence (Scheper-Hughes & Lovell, 1987). Critics of the mental health industry argue that, rather than fulfilling new promises of alleviating human suffering, helping professions such as psychiatry, psychology, and the social sciences have helped create cultural institutions and practices that classify and define behavior and that ignore primary needs but fulfill the interest of dominant groups (Basaglia in Scheper-Hughes & Lovell, 1987, p. 151).

Incorrect Classification of People. Incorrect classification of people may result in inappropriate selection of intervention methods. Classification may result in false-positives or false-negatives. The consequences of a false-positive (for example, saying someone is a danger to society when he or she is not) or a false-negative (that is, deciding someone is not a danger to others when he or she is) depend on the situation. Physicians are trained to be conservative in their judgments of pathology—that is, when in doubt, to err in the direction of a false-positive judgment. They are trained to accept the norm that judging a sick person to be well is worse than judging a well person to be sick (Scheff, 1963). (See later discussion of fallacies related to a pathological set.) The accuracy of classification is related to the reliability and validity of measures used to make these. Concerns about the reliability and validity of DSM-III categories have been discussed by many critics (see, for example, Jampata, Sierles & Taylor, 1988; Kirk & Kutchins, 1988; Kutchins & Kirk, 1987; McReynolds, 1989). The less reliable and valid a measure, the greater the likelihood of incorrect classification. Overestimating the accuracy of measures and ignoring base rate data (the frequency with which a sign or symptom occurs in a population) increase the likelihood of inaccurate classification (see Chapter Nine).

Diagnostic labels are typically imprecise. They say too little about positive attributes, potential for change, and change that does occur, and they say too much about presumed negative characteristics and limits to change. Someone who carries a negative label such as *schizophrenic* often is regarded as if he possesses only the characteristics of this category (Rosenhan, 1973). Negative labels may result in the neglect of other conditions that need attention, and they do not reflect rapid changes that often take place; that is, even though changes occur, the same label (such as *retarded*) may be retained. Acceptance of a label may prematurely close off consideration of options. The tendency to use a binary classification system, in which people are labeled as either having or not having something (for example, as being an alcoholic or not), obscures the many patterns to which vague terms may refer and further isolates those labeled from normal people. Classification efforts often have resulted in little success (Mischel, 1968) although some recent efforts appear to be more promising (McReynolds, 1989). Labels that limit exploration do not have to be fancy ones like *hyperactive* or *paranoid;* they can be everyday terms like *old lady*. Lack of agreement among professionals in their use of labels has already been noted. In some contexts, such as criminal justice settings and child welfare agencies, overattention to pathology may be replaced by the "well-well fallacy" to protect the service system from being overwhelmed (see later discussion of the "rule of optimism").

Psychiatric classification systems have been criticized for blaming the victim for his plight rather than examining the social circumstances responsible for problems (Ryan, 1976). In his recent review of the DSM-III and DSM-III-R, McReynolds (1989) raises concerns about the extent to which this system of classification assumes that mental disorder is an inner condition of the individual and ignores environmental causes of personal problems. The very notion of psychiatric classification implies the existence of objective criteria. The history of psychiatry shows that objectivity is difficult. Even when empirical data are available, such information may not be used in the definition of diagnostic categories and criteria used are often quite judgmental (McReynolds, 1989). Many have argued that psychiatric classification serves the interests of the ruling majority (Scheper-Hughes & Lovell, 1987; Sedgwick, 1982). The fact that assignment of a deviant status and subsequent actions partially depend on social class supports the social control function of labels (Ennis & Litwak, 1974). "Categories and labels are powerful instruments for social regulation and control, and they are often employed for obscure, covert, or hurtful purposes: to degrade people, to deny them access to opportunity, to exclude 'undesirables' whose presence in some way offends, disturbs familiar custom, or demands extraordinary effort" (Hobbs, 1975, p. 11). There is a need to control what we cannot understand. Placing labels on people with the presumption of scientific credibility fulfills this need.

Although labeling theory emphasizes the relativity of labels and their effects on stigmatizing clients, no methods to alter basic structural conditions have been offered. Both psychiatry and sociology impose labels on deviants and neither offer a framework for altering the structural conditions that create deviants. Writers and clinicians such as Sedgwick (1982) and Basaglia (in Scheper-Hughes & Lovell, 1987) have noted this limitation and move beyond it in offering a broader perspective related to the economic structure of society. Those who receive psychiatric (or criminal) labels are those who are observed in deviant acts because they are poor and so have little access to privacy. Consider, for example, who is usually imprisoned for possession of controlled substances (Nadelmann, 1988). Those labeled "are forced as deviants into an ideological category that defines them, continues to create them, and controls them" (Basaglia in Scheper-Hughes & Lovell, 1987, p. 105). New labels are created to stigmatize any behavior that deviates from the norm and from the descriptions of traditional psychiatric syndromes (p. 110).

"Whoever is exuberant is labeled overly emotional. Whoever shows excessive altruism causes serious concern. Whoever stands up for himself suffers from a combativeness that could turn into protest and contentiousness" (p. 112). "Confronted with new forms of deviance and abusive behavior, which might be symptoms of an unbearable, abnormal life, lists and technical terms are found to categorize them. This may be brought up to date with a vague reference to a hypothetical 'social' factor, which supposedly guarantees that the problem will be confronted in contemporary modern terms. In the meantime, prisons and asylums continue to preserve their marginal, class character" (p. 218). Classification magnifies and strengthens differences between people, thus perpetuating the isolation of deviants from others. If this isolation enhanced well-being for consumers, that would be one thing. But some argue that it does not. Many critics of the DSM raise concerns about the growing number of behaviors classified as mental disorders and suggest removing some difficulties now included. For example, McReynolds (1989) notes that it seems inappropriate to view children's problems in reading, spelling, and arithmetic as psychiatric disorders.

Use of Vague Terms. Refutation of a claim may be impossible because the nature of the claim is vague. A distinction can be made between vague and ambiguous terms in that ambiguous terms can be clarified by describing the context in which the term is used. In contrast, vague terms remain imprecise even when the context is clear (Michalos, 1971, p. 89). Examples of clinical terms that are vague include *supportive therapy, family systems theory, resistance, neurotic,* and *sociopath.* Although some terms may have more precise meanings, this does not mean they are used precisely; that is, they may mean different things to different people, resulting in different classifications and decisions (see discussion of the one word, one meaning fallacy in Chapter Five).

False Dilemma. It may be proposed that there are just two possibilities in relation to a question when, in fact, there are many. A clinician may argue that either a client is mentally disturbed or he is not. Such accounts get in the way of discovering individual variations. This fallacy often occurs in conjunction with other fallacies, such as the straw person argument, which sets up a false black-and-white account (Kahane, 1971). A continuum may be involved rather than a polar representation, as in family versus individual therapy, drug dependent versus drug independent, dysfunctional versus functional, and sick versus well. Contrary statements may be presented as if they were contradictory statements (Engel, 1982, p. 111) Contrary statements are two statements that cannot both be true but may both be false. Contradictory statements are those that cannot both be true nor can they both be false (for example, "either today is New Year's Day or it is not"). The fallacy of the false dilemma presents two contraries as two contradictory statements. Engel (1982) classified this under fallacies of presumption since facts are overlooked—namely, the fact that choices are not limited to only two alternatives. This fallacy is known also as the either/or fallacy and black-and-white fallacy. A remedy is to point out other possibilities that have been ignored.

Incorrect Classification of Procedures. Errors in classification may be due to incorrect use of terms. For example, consider the following statements that appeared under the title "Human Subjects at Risk of Torture, U.S. Style," in the *California NASW News* (Montenegro, 1988, p. 5), which is distributed to 10,000 social workers in California: "Information provided by the Prisoners Rights Union reveals that the Bureau of Prisons has built a high security unit (HSU) for women in Lexington, Kentucky, based on guidelines provided by experts in brainwashing and behavior modification techniques. HSU is designed to isolate inmates from the outside world. No personal clothing is allowed. Nothing can be placed on the walls. One hour per day is allowed in an opaque fenced yard with no view of the outside world. . . . A recent sleep deprivation experiment involved waking the women every half hour throughout the night. Rules are changed arbitrarily at random time intervals. This tactic was used by Hitler's SS" (Montenegro, 1988, p. 5). The conditions described are quite the opposite of conditions characteristic of a behavioral approach. Hallmarks of the latter include an emphasis on the use of positive reinforcement, arranging environments that are as similar as possible to real-life settings, and offering multiple opportunities for the reinforcement of desired behaviors. Thus, prolonged isolation would not be a part of a behavioral program; sleep deprivation would not be used. I wrote to the editor requesting further information and received a brochure titled "Buried Alive in the Lexington Women's Control Unit" (n.d.) published by the National Campaign to Abolish the Lexington Women's Control Unit (294 Atlantic Ave., Brooklyn, NY 11201). This source described the Lexington Unit as "a behavior modification unit characterized by systematic use of sensory deprivation, extreme isolation and degradation." According to the brochure, the Bureau of Prisons learned about "new techniques of behavior modification . . . in part, from Professor Edgar Schein of MIT, who spent five years doing research for the CIA on the brainwashing techniques used by North Korea and China against American POWs in the Korean war" (Dillinger, 1988, p. 18). However, the procedures described are the complete opposite of a behavior modification approach (see, for example, Meyer & Evans, 1989).

What are the effects of incorrect classification of procedures? If this practice results in people being deprived of helpful methods, those effects are worrisome. Korzybski (1980) was so concerned with the effects of spreading false information that he recommended licensing of public workers and speakers. "Even at present no professor, teacher, lawyer, physician or chemist, is allowed to operate publicly without passing an examination to show that he knows his subject . . . At present public writers or speakers can hide behind ignorance . . . They may 'mean well'; yet, by playing upon the pathological reactions of their own and those of the mob, they may 'put over' some very vicious propaganda and bring about very serious sufferings to all concerned. But once they would have to pass an examination to get their license as public speakers or writers, they could not hide any longer behind ignorance. If found to have misused the linguistic mechanism, such an abuse on their part would be clearly a willful act, and 'well meaning' would cease to be an alibi" (Korzybski 1980, p. 486).

The history of psychiatry is replete with euphemisms for cruel and unusual punishment of psychiatric patients. The pleasant-sounding term *community care* often means that the patient is released from an institution to fend for himself. Sources of social control are often called revolutionary new views or innovative methods. New but distrusted methods may receive the "kiss of death" by being inordinately praised as marvelous when the intention is to "cool them out."

Fallacy of Stereotyping. Clinicians often represent people as examples of categories and, on the basis of this classification, entertain certain feelings toward and expectations about them that influence how they respond to these individuals. The clinical literature offers a rich source of stereotypes such as the *schizophrenagenic mother* (now dismissed by most clinicians), *co-dependent partner, sociopath,* and *personality disorder.* The fallacy of stereotyping refers to treating a description as if it represents all the individuals in a group of which it may (or may not) be a fairly typical example (Scriven, 1976, p. 209). One example that comes to mind is that of the homeless. There really are many different kinds of homeless people requiring many different kinds of intervention. Similarly, there are many different patterns of substance abuse ranging from once a week cocaine use by a middle-class white-collar worker to daily use by a teenager. Possible classifications can be illustrated by diagrams (see Figure 2).

Stereotypes may be cultural—that is, shared by many people in a society. Other stereotypes are unique to certain individuals based on their past experiences. Stereotypes are often inaccurate in that they reflect only one of many aspects of an individual. Nevertheless, stereotypes affect what we see since we tend to seek information that supports our stereotypes. The influence of stereotypes can be seen in a study by Duncan (1976). Subjects watched a videotape of a discussion between two men during which one of the men shoved the other. The race of the actors was varied in different versions. Subjects were asked to classify a behavior whenever they received a signal from the experimenter. More subjects classified the black protagonist's behavior as violent than so classifed the white protagonist's behavior especially if the person shoved was white.

The influence of labels on stereotyping is illustrated by a study in which information about socioeconomic background was varied. One group of subjects was informed that a child was from a high socioeconomic background, and another group of subjects

Figure 2. Euler's Circle Diagrams Showing the Possible Relations Between A's and B's for Four Premise Types.

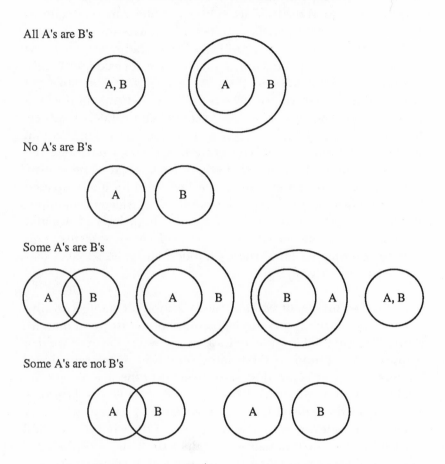

All A's are B's

No A's are B's

Some A's are B's

Some A's are not B's

Source: From *Cognition and Cognitive Psychology* (p. 360) by A. J. Sanford, 1985, Hove, East Sussex, Eng.: Erlbaum. Copyright 1985 by Lawrence Erlbaum. Reprinted by permission.

was informed that the child was from a low socioeconomic background (Darley & Gross, 1983). Both groups watched a videotaped performance of the child taking an academic test. Subjects who had received information that the child was from a high socioeconomic background rated her capabilities well above grade level; subjects in the other group rated the child's abilities as below grade level. In both groups, subjects indicated that the ability test was used as evidence to support their ratings. This study offers another example of the influence of stereotypes on judgments; hypotheses are tested in a biased manner. There is an extensive literature exploring the influence of stereotypes in clinical practice (see, for example, Franks & Rothblum, 1983; Kaplan, 1983; Sherman, 1980). The danger of stereotyping is that ways in which individual clients do not fit a stereotype may be overlooked and incorrect clinical decisions may be made as a result, such as selecting an ineffective intervention method or deciding to intervene when there is no good reason to do so. For example, a behavior, thought, or feeling may be normative. (This is not to say that intervention is not called for if a behavioral pattern is normative. Clearly this is not true. Consider, for example, the low level of positive feedback and the high level of negative feedback that secondary school teachers offer their students. This pattern is normative but certainly not desirable, and a school psychologist may strive to reverse it.)

Other Sources of Fallacy. Classification often offers an illusion of objectivity. For example, consider use of the term *normal*. The view of normal as the condition of the average man or woman acquires the meaning of the healthy condition. If the statistically normal condition is accepted as equivalent to the psychologically healthy condition (Trotter, 1916), the result may be inappropriate recommendations for clinical intervention (for people who vary from the statistical norm). The vagueness of the word *normal* and the tendency of professionals to link the term with healthy are discussed by Abercrombie (1960) in her work with medical students.

In the fallacy of the continuum, it is argued that because there is a continuous distribution of gradations between two extremes, there is no real difference. Staff members in a residential treatment center for adolescents may argue that hitting residents is really no different from yelling at them. A common argument attempting to justify the use of torture makes use of this fallacy; saying that all governments take steps to protect the integrity of their countries and sometimes encroach on the rights of its citizens. There is a refusal to recognize a shift from a quantitative to a qualitative difference. In the slippery-slope fallacy, a position is opposed on the grounds that, if it is acted on, it will result in a series of inevitable negative consequences. A clinician may argue (incorrectly) that if a client's overidentification with her father is focused on, a series of negative effects will follow such as increased anxiety and depression. A decision may be made not to offer services to one needy group of clients on the basis that this would require provision of services to all other needy groups. A familiar example is the domino theory: if Vietnam falls, all of Southeast Asia will fall into Communist hands.

Appeals to Pseudoauthority

Many weak appeals work by taking advantage of common human tendencies (Cialdini, 1984). One example is the use of pseudoauthority. We grow up learning to respect authority, and those who use appeals to illegitimate authority take advantage of this tendency. Appeals to pseudoauthority also take advantage of the principle of social proof. Decisions are based on what other people think is correct (as in appeals to traditional wisdom and to consensus). Proper appeals to authority should be distinguished from improper ones. The following rules of thumb can be used to distinguish proper from improper appeals.

- Remember that an authority in one area is not necessarily an authority in other areas.
- Do not accept the opinions of authorities when experts disagree or there is little known in a field. For example, experts often disagree about the sanity of a defendant; therefore, it would be unwise to accept the opinion offered by any one person.
- Examine the evidence, reasons, and arguments when experts disagree. If psychiatrists claim that a client is psychotic, find out why they believe this and evaluate the reasons given.
- Review the track record of the expert (Kahane, 1971).

Inappropriate appeals to authority can take quite subtle forms in the area of clinical decision making and occur during clinical interviews as well as in case conferences, in discussions among colleagues, and during moments of self-reflection. Data supporting a position may be described in detail, whereas data counter to it may be mentioned only in passing or not at all (see discussion of suppressed evidence in Chapter Six). The remedy to appeals to pseudoauthority is to point out that no evidence is offered in support of the appeal or to request or seek such evidence.

Appeals to pseudoauthority are another kind of informal fallacy—that is, they may occur without any formal error. Michalos (1971) identifies sixteen varieties of pseudoauthority. A number that are common to clinical situations are reviewed in the sections that follow. Some of the informal fallacies discussed under the influence of language in Chapter Five could be included here as well, such as the use of pseudotechnical jargon. Appeals to authority are often used to present preferred positions with a false aura of credibility.

Popular Sentiments. The feelings and attitudes of a group may be appealed to in order to gain acceptance for a position. In the statement "As members of the American Psychological Association, we know that," the appeal is to a respected professional group. Stereotyped descriptions of an out-group (as in the statement "Sophisticated diagnostics are eschewed in narrow behavioristic approaches") appeal to the sentiments of an in-group. Although appeals to popular sentiment may make people feel better, superior, or complacent, they do little to advance the quality of arguments. Such appeals are particularly insidious in a clinical setting where they may bolster personal beliefs about what is normal and what is deviant without the clinician recognizing this connection (see later section on fallacies related to a pathological set). The remedy for appeals to popular sentiments is to point out that no evidence is offered for the position stated.

Misleading Aura of Authority. Most of the material printed in the media consists of secondary information: "Most news is given to reporters, not discovered by them" (Kahane, 1971, p. 153). However, the material is often presented in a way that makes it seem as if it were based on firsthand experiences. Opinions may be presented as facts, as in the statements "reality therapy works" or "codependents need help." Here one should ask questions like "What evidence is provided for the statement?" References cited in support of a comment in an article may in fact provide none. For example, a claim may be made that feminist counseling has been shown to be effective followed by a series of references which, in fact, contain no data supporting the claim (Huston, 1986). Reliance on secondary sources amplifies such errors. Other ways in which a misleading aura of authority may be given is by use of impressive-sounding but vague terms and by obtuse descriptions of data analysis methods or clinical procedures in place of straightforward clear accounts (which may reveal weak or incorrect methods that compromise claims made).

Popular People and Irrelevant Authority. The authority of popular people may be appealed to in order to support a claim. A writer may cite Freud far more often than is necessary in a manuscript submitted to a psychoanalytic journal, hoping that such name-dropping will lend an aura of credibility to the work. This tactic is often used in advertising. For example, a famous baseball player may be shown talking about the positive attributes of cereal. Gullible viewers may not realize that an outstanding baseball player is not necessarily an expert in evaluating cereal. This appeal (as well as the next one) is a type of ad hominem argument (see Chapter Six).

Titles and Supposed Experts. In some variants of this use of pseudoauthority ("Doctors report that," "Studies show that"), we may not even be informed which particular person is responsible for the statement (Michalos, 1971). The studies cited were supposedly conducted by scrupulous, well-trained researchers. The possession of a credential or degree in an area does indicate some level of expertise in the subject. The question is, does this background by itself substantiate the claim being made by the bearer of these credentials? Appeals to authority can be buttressed by use of pseudotechnical jargon that is geared to impress listeners with the speaker's erudition. The remedy is to ask the person to explain points more simply. Clearly presented ideas are often dismissed as simpleminded (see discussion of "apparent profundity" in Chapter Five).

Traditional Wisdom. It is often assumed that what is old is best, with no evidence offered in support of the view other than people used that method in the past. An example is "That's the way I've always done it." Reluctance to question such appeals in case conferences is related to not wishing to accept an unpopular view, or to appear contrary or difficult. Appeal to traditional wisdom may be combined with other kinds of appeals to authority, as in the statement "Historians have found that this has been the custom for many centuries" (reference to supposed experts). Or, it may be combined with question-begging definitions. A clinician may say, "The traditional role of women is the proper role because it is the traditional role" (Michalos, 1971, p. 40). One antidote to persuasion by appeals to traditional wisdom is a sound education in the history of science or medicine, which offers countless examples of times when the majority view or traditional wisdom was incorrect (see, for example, Broad & Wade, 1982; Gardner, 1957).

Appeals to Consensus and the Authority of the Many. This variant is also referred to as the appeal to large numbers (Michalos, 1971) and the fallacy of popularity (MacLean, 1981). It refers to attempted support of a claim by saying that many people agree with a position (see discussion of social proof in Chapter Five). "We view a behavior as more correct to the degree that we see others performing it" (Cialdini, 1984, p. 117). Alcoholics Anonymous may claim that their success is demonstrated by the thousands of people who have taken part in their program. Appeals to consensus and traditional wisdom may block the acceptance of new methods for years or decades. Consider, for example, the neglect of Semmelweiss's discovery that puerperal fever could be eliminated "by having doctors wash their hands in a chlorine solution before examining the mother" (Broad & Wade, 1982, p. 137). His work was ignored for years, resulting in thousands of unnecessary deaths. The authority of the psychiatric profession is often appealed to to bolster claims as in "Most psychiatrists believe that psychotropic medication is of benefit for clients."

Provincialism. Provincialism is a variety of the use of traditional wisdom and popular sentiment. It appeals to the tendency to identify with an in-group and to assume that the familiar is better or more important. The source of error here is failure to recognize the importance of other people or ideas and the values that they reflect. A feminist counselor may assume that all women clients want to be liberated and fail to consider the preference of some clients who want to maintain a traditional female role. Imposition of Western views of psychological problems and proposed remedies on non-Western clients is perhaps the most common form of provincialism in clinical practice (see Chapter Two). Provincialism is carried to an extreme in cases in which beliefs are based more on loyalty to a position than on evidence. This appeal, as well as plain folks and bandwagon appeals that are variants on it (see below), exerts influence through the principle of social proof (see Chapter Five). The plain folks appeal is at the opposite end of the spectrum from snob appeal and the appeal of pseudo-jargon (MacLean, 1981, p. 39). This tactic works (if it works) by associating the appearance of simplicity and straightforwardness with a particular view of reality. In fact, there may be little relation between reality and this appearance.

Bandwagon Appeal. In the *bandwagon appeal,* it is assumed that everybody is behind something: What is implied is that everybody who "knows what's best" supports a position. An article about a topic that is controversial may start with "We all know that." This tactic takes advantage of our tendency to be influenced by what other people do: if other people do it it must be good or right (the principle of social proof). This kind of pitch partly accounts for the fads and fashions in psychotherapy. There are a number of questions that should be raised such as *"Is* everybody doing it?" Probably not. Even if many people do act in a certain way or accept a certain belief, that does not mean they are correct. History is replete with infamous examples of the acceptance by many of incorrect ideas. Take, for example, the hundreds of papers by scientists and doctors in the early twentieth century concerning "N-rays"—these were "discovered" in many places, including the human brain (Nye, 1980). Popular clinical approaches are not necessarily those that really help clients achieve valued outcomes.

Imaginary Authority. Reference may be made to imaginary evidence; that is, a speaker or writer may refer to evidence that does not exist. A psychologist may report that he has seen many clients with anorexia and so he can speak with authority about this disorder, when in fact he has seen one such client. An infamous example of the use of imaginary authority is the extraordinary case of Sir Cyril Burt. This is perhaps the most well-known and flagrant example of "the failure of psychologists to spot dogma masquerading as objective truth" (Broad & Wade, 1982, p. 203). Burt invented data to support his views. "He used his mastery of statistics and gift of lucid exposition to bamboozle alike his bitterest detractors and those who claimed his greatness as a psychologist" (p. 204). He submitted articles in favor of his views under an assumed name and published them in the *British Journal of Statistical Psychology,* of which he was editor for sixteen years. He not only made up data, he invented coauthors "from the vasty deep of his tormented imagination and clothed them so well in the semblance of scientific argument that the illusion fooled all his fellow scientists for as much as thirty years" (p. 204). Some people believe that the fabrication of data is becoming more common as pressures mount to publish and competition for funding becomes keener. (For a recent discussion of fraud and error in science see Kohn, 1988.)

The claims of an authority may be changed or completely misrepresented; a sentence may be taken out of context or minor parts of a sentence may be presented as major parts. It is not unusual, for example, to find grossly inaccurate accounts of a behavioral approach to practice (see Todd & Morris, 1983). As an extreme, a claim can be attributed to a famous person who never said or wrote such a thing. How many people have read all of a person's writings to check such claims? How many readers check sources cited in support of statements made in the professional journals and books? Research findings are often misrepresented (see, for example, Lipton & Hershaft, 1985).

Other Kinds of Appeals to Pseudoauthority. Some writers and speakers refer to the authority of a proverb, maxim, cliche, or aphorism (a concise statement of a principle, truth, or sentiment), instead of offering evidence that supports their position. These sayings have a ring of truth that encourages their acceptance (see discussion of empathic explanations in Chapter Four). They can usually be interpreted in a variety of ways and thus may seem "psychologically compelling." When asked why he does not carefully evaluate his work with clients, a clinician may say that "capturing human experience is like trying to describe a beautiful smell; it is not possible." Metaphors and similes can be helpful in suggesting solutions to clinical problems, as well as in offering clients a view of concerns that maximizes maintenance of gains—as in the metaphor of a journey used by Marlatt and Gordon (1985) in their relapse prevention program (see also *Metaphors We Live By*, Lakoff & Johnson, 1980).

Views may be presented as those of a vague or mysterious and generally respected group or ideal (Michalos, 1971). For example, a clinical supervisor may argue that to challenge her views is to challenge the very authority required to maintain high-quality training programs—that is, to challenge idols. A clinician may support his use of an unfocused approach to therapy by saying that this reflects a humanistic approach to counseling in which client values are respected and nourished. Snob appeal (authority of a select few) takes advantage of our feeling that we are special—one of a select few. Only recently have psychologists been permitted entry into psychoanalytic training programs: previously, acceptance required a medical degree, a restriction that ensured privileged entry to psychiatrists. Historians of social work have noted the tendency of social workers to identify with psychiatrists in order to bolster their image. People can sometimes be seduced into going along with a position in an uncritical way (without examining the soundness of the position) by the promise of association with an elite group. Persuasive strategies based on elitism may be combined with strategies based on the principle of liking—for example, friendly overtures may be made toward typically ignored or disliked colleagues to win their support.

In an appeal to faith, we are asked to accept a position based on faith alone—when evidence for or against the claim could be produced. A counselor may tell a client who questions her selection of intervention, "Trust me, I have your interests at heart." This may be combined with an appeal to expertise or longevity: "I've been a psychiatrist for twenty years."

Fallacies Related to a Pathological Set

Clinicians tend to emphasize client pathology. Lack of cooperation on the part of clients is often attributed to their deficiencies. This search for personal causes of resistance discourages recognition of environmental obstacles and reflects a lack of appreciation for the difficulty of achieving change. Resistance is a natural part of any effort to change. Many writers have noted the recycling of sickness ideology under new euphemisms (such as *clinical population,* which is considered to be qualitatively different from nonclinical populations, Bandura, 1978). Such terms continue to select out as unique those people with a given behavioral pattern who seek or are sent for help from the much larger group of people with the same behavioral pattern (such as excessive use of alcohol) who do *not* seek help. Meehl (1973) referred to the tendency to focus on pathology as the "sick-sick" fallacy. Professional training increases this tendency (Wills, 1978). Certainly it is important to accurately identify pathology, especially if treatment implications follow. However, this should be balanced by a search for client assets and potential for change. Undue attention to pathology results in a neglect of client assets, creates undue pessimism about the possibility of positive outcomes, and may stigmatize clients if negative views are conveyed to clients, significant others, and authorities. For example, a negative label such as *sociopath* may make it more likely that a client will be involuntarily hospitalized (or imprisoned) and less likely that services will be offered that are designed to be beneficial. Another disadvantage of a pathological emphasis is that negative impressions are more difficult to alter (Hodges, 1974). Studies show that negative information carries more weight than does positive information (see, for example, Wills, Weiss & Patterson, 1974).

Factors That Encourage an Overemphasis on Pathology. Factors that encourage an overemphasis on pathology include the practice theories emphasized during graduate education, an interest in protecting oneself from failure, personal ideologies in relation to adjustment and mental health, lack of awareness of structural influences on what is defined as a problem, lack of (or ignoring) empirical information about base rates and individual differences, and an interest in appearing erudite.

Professional training often biases students toward pathology, not only by what it includes but also by what it excludes (for example, political functions of varying definitions of deviance, as well as information regarding base rates and individual differences). Often, practice theories are emphasized that focus on pathology; the focus is on discovering sources of pathology in both the client's history and current functioning. Students are introduced to the DSM, which describes a myriad of different ways in which behaviors, thoughts, and feelings may be pathological. Labels for describing behavior at the opposite pole are usually tepid (such as *well adjusted, normal*). Some more lively labels are suggested in Table 7. An emphasis on dispositional attributions for problems and a tendency to ignore environmental causes encourages a pathological view of clients; people rather than their environments are blamed for problems of living (see discussion of dispositional bias in Chapter Nine). The common occurrences of negative experiences in the history of both individuals who do not seek counseling and those who do make it quite easy to discover pathogenic experiences that are assumed to be responsible for presenting complaints of clients and render the causative character of these symptoms questionable. Renaud and Estess (1961) interviewed 100 men who were selected because there was no indication that they had any problems. They had no history of either mental or psychological conflict and did not complain of any problems. The men were functioning as normal or superior on all objective indices. They were in good health, had attained superior educational and occupational status, and had positive relationships with others both in their personal and work lives. The interviews held with these 100 men were similar to clinical intake interviews. These interviews revealed all kinds of traumatic events and experiences that could well be considered pathogenic and were at least as serious as experiences in the histories of psychiatric patients.

Clinicians are influenced by the moral values of the society in which they live. Some clinicians have not been exposed to a

Table 7. Negative Labels and Positive Counterparts.

Negative Label	Positive Counterparts
Paranoia	Perspicacity (acute sensitivity to the motives and feelings of others); perceptive identification and neutralization of hostile intentions
Depression	Élan vital
Substance abuse	Creative drug use
Obsessive compulsive disorder	Creative attention to detail; good attention span
Exhibitionism	Freedom from undue modesty
Multiple personality	A creative mixture of personas

political and social perspective on deviance—to the fact that what is considered to be a social or personal problem is consensual and relative (that is, ascribed), rather than inherent (fixed). What is considered *pathological* changes with the times and differs in different cultures. Only in 1975 did the American Psychiatric Association decide that homosexuality was not a sickness. Without exposure to material describing the social and political functions of all forms of deviance, including psychiatric problems (Sedgwick, 1982; Scheper-Hughes & Lovell, 1987; Scheff, 1984a, 1984b; Szasz, 1961, 1970) as well as ethnic and cultural differences in the expression of problems and the acceptability of different kinds of interventions, clinicians are likely to be overly acceptant of current popular conceptions of pathology and health (see Chapter Two).

Without effective skills for handling the inevitable uncertainty and lack of success involved in clinical practice, it is easy to fall into acceptance of a pathological focus as a protection against failure. Negative pronouncements offer a reason for lack of success in remedying or preventing problems.

Personal beliefs about what is normal may encourage a focus on pathology. For example, some psychiatrists continue to believe that homosexuality is an illness despite the decision of the American Psychiatric Association that it is not. The fact that a professional organization decides what is and what is not a mental illness illustrates the consensual basis of psychiatric labels. How many practitioners carefully review their personal biases in relation to given kinds of behavior? How many accept a view of deviance as ascribed rather than inherent? Many biases are implicit, and it is thus easy for clinicians to unknowingly impose their beliefs about what is normal, what is good on clients. Since their beliefs usually mirror commonly accepted norms of proper and improper behavior, little in the way of contradiction may challenge personal beliefs. For example, a heterosexual counselor may be consulted by a lesbian couple who want to have a child by artificial insemination. A counselor with a traditional view of family life may respond differently to this request than may a counselor with a broader view of healthy family life. As Meehl (1973) points out, "Many family psychiatrists have a stereotype of what the healthy family ought to be; and if anybody's family life does not meet this criteria, this is taken as a sign of pathology" (p. 237). This tendency is increased by the fact that practitioners tend to be from the middle class and many of their clients are from the "working class." Meehl notes that clinicians will say, "Yes, we know about that." Knowing about something is not enough—effective steps must be taken to put this knowledge to use.

Inferences of pathology often occur because of lack of familiarity with normative data concerning behaviors, thoughts, or feelings—that is, from a lack of knowledge regarding base rates and the range of individual variability of a behavior. Imposition of a clinical label on clients further removes them from individuals considered normal. Clinical case studies reported in the professional literature typically focus on pathology and neglect positive attributes of individuals and families (see, for example, Kazak & Marvin, 1984). Information about people who do well despite difficult challenges, such as caring for a developmentally disabled child, is often absent (see also Anthony & Cohler, 1987). A clinician may be familiar with normative data but ignore this in making decisions. Ignoring information about base rates, consensus, and individual variations increases the likelihood of pathologizing clients; that is, making inaccurate clinical judgments. Normative data may be ignored because of one or more of the other reasons discussed in this section. In our increasingly diverse society, ethnic and cultural differences may result in the imposition of biased views of health on clients. To the extent to which clinicians are unaware of such differences or ignore them, clients may suffer from imposed arbitrary views of health. Another reason clinicians may be inclined to overemphasize pathology is the biased sample of people they are exposed to during training and in practice; rare conditions (such as schizophrenia or severe depression) are overrepresented in the clinical population.

Vague metaphorical descriptions of exotic pathology may appear profound; clear descriptions of presenting problems and related factors may appear simpleminded. Describing exotic inferences about the presumed causes of a presenting problem not only offers an illusion of astuteness, it also gains the attention of listeners due to the vividness of accounts offered. Whether it is accurate and helpful in alleviating presenting problems is another question.

The Rule of Optimism

This is the opposite of the "sick-sick fallacy" and might be called the "well-well fallacy." It refers to the tendency not to see pathology or behavior that harms others when it is actually there. Dingwall et al. (1983) argue that this rule is used in child protection agencies because the resources of the system would be depleted if all families that needed state intervention were taken into the system. This rule states that the least discrediting interpretations of observed conduct will be used (p. 218). These authors identify cultural relativism as one vehicle through which the rule of optimism is carried out—the view that "any style of child rearing may be justified as a valid cultural statement which should not be illiberally suppressed" (p. 218). The dialogue below illustrates cultural relativism (Dingwall et al., 1983, p. 84).

Social Worker: Her father was very annoyed and beat her with a strap.

Senior SW: With a strap?

Social Worker: Oh, this sort of thing happens in this community.

Senior SW: This violence is very difficult to prove and we have to accept that it is just part of the West Indian culture.

Dingwall and his colleagues found that the more familiar a professional was with a particular area in which a family lived, the more likely such reactions were. A second vehicle consists of appeals to natural love; the parent/child relationship is viewed as a natural rather than as a social phenomenon with the implication that a charge of mistreatment is equivalent to an allegation that the parents involved do not share in our common humanity. As with cultural relativism, behaviors are recognized as deviant but there is no allegation of moral liability. These two views "combine to produce an attitude of acceptance towards parental accounts and a sense that an accusation of parental failure is a matter of almost inconceivable gravity" (p. 218). They combine to eliminate the majority of potential cases by "allowing front-line workers to prefer an optimistic reading of client behavior" (p. 82). (They also save the taxpayer a great deal of money by not addressing the social conditions related to questionable parenting practices.) These authors offer an example in which a child was clearly made a scapegoat. Because her parents demonstrated a capacity for loving relationships with their other children, the agency did not intervene (p. 87). The following excerpt describes a health visitor overlooking a quite prominent black eye on a baby. The researcher who accompanied the health visitor to the home wrote this:

> This baby had a fairly large and extremely obvious black eye. From what I could gather the health visitor made no comment to the mother about it nor did the nursing auxiliary (who was helping with a routine domiciliary hearing test) . . . HV went off to speak to another mother (in the same house) . . . While HV was doing this, the nursing auxiliary was talking to the other mum and saying things like, "Amy's at a very difficult age." The mother said to her, "I nearly strangled her last night." I pricked up my ears rather and then the mother said to the nursing auxiliary, "I

expect you are wondering how she got her black eye."
The nursing auxiliary didn't really take much notice
and the mother says, "It was my fault." The nursing
auxiliary continued to sort of coo and chuckle at the
baby. . . . The mother went on to talk about something else. Once we were in the car I asked HV if she
had said anything about the black eye to the mother.
She said not. She thought some explanation would be
given and she didn't think that this was a bashed baby.
The nursing auxiliary made no reference to the fact
that the mother had tried to speak to her about it and
we let the subject drop. HV, however, referred to this
later and again the next day. (next day) HV once again
brought up the child with the black eye. It seems to
be preying on her mind that she didn't ask this mother
about it and she tried to explain to me again why she
didn't think that this mother would batter her child
[Dingwall et al., 1983, p. 100].

Just as clinicians may misinterpret the significance of signs
that are there, they may misinterpret the importance of signs that
are absent (see discussion of nonoccurrences in Chapter Nine).

Dingwall and his colleagues discuss the elasticity of the rules
of cultural relativism and natural love. "What may seem like eccen-
tricities or perversions are elevated into valid cultural statements"
(p. 88). Reliance on these rules encourages acceptance of clients'
accounts or conclusions "that the fault lies within them, for failing
to sufficiently empathize with the alleged deviant." These authors
point out that use of these principles helps to solve the problems
faced by helpers. That is, cultural relativism and natural love can
be invoked to bridge the gap between ideals and the realities of
practice. At a higher level, they serve to maintain current imbalances in resources between those who are poor and those who are
not.

Summary

One activity in which clinicians engage is classification. Factors that may compromise the accuracy of classification, such as

lack of reliability of measures, are sometimes forgotten in the rush of everyday practice resulting in errors such as inappropriate stereotyping and false dilemmas. Pathological labels are often, if not typically, accepted as describing reality with little understanding of the ascribed nature of these labels and the political and social functions that they serve—for example, to control and regulate undesired behaviors. Clinicians base their selection of practice knowledge on various kinds of authority, some of which are legitimate (evidence is offered for the claim) and many of which appeal to pseudoauthority (such as popular sentiment, traditional wisdom, and appeals to consensus). Clinicians often have a pathological set; they search for deficiencies and neglect client assets. This creates undue pessimism about the possibility of change and may stigmatize clients. Factors that contribute to this tendency include practice theories that emphasize pathology, lack of familiarity with the political functions of psychiatric labels, ignorance of norms and the range of individual differences, and protection against failure. An opposite rule, the rule of optimism, may come into play when resources would be overwhelmed by recognizing all the problems that are present. This also serves a function in saving the considerable funds that would be required to address the social and economic conditions related to many kinds of client problems, such as child maltreatment, depression, and substance abuse.

8

Collecting Data: Factors Affecting What People See and Report

Decisions are made about what data to collect, how to gather this data, and when to stop. Individuals, situations, and their interactions can be described in innumerable ways; requiring attention to some characteristics and ignoring others. The way problems are defined influences what data is gathered. For example, consider a presenting problem of depression. A practice theory with an emphasis on dispositional characteristics would encourage collection of data concerning personal factors, such as repressed anger based on past experiences of loss. A theory that emphasizes external causes would encourage collection of data concerning environmental influences, such as a decrease in pleasant events and an increase in negative ones. Thus, preferred theories influence what clinicians look for and what they notice as well as how they process and organize data. Theories differ along a number of dimensions, including the attention devoted to the past and present; the unit of concern (individual, family, or community); the attention devoted to environmental and personal characteristics; and the degree of optimism concerning how much change is possible (Briar & Miller, 1971). Studies of clinical decision making indicate that decisions are made on the basis of quite limited data (for example, Kendell, 1973); even though a great deal of data are gathered, only a small subset is used. Clinicians tend to gather more data than are needed; and as the amount of data gathered increases, so does confidence in its usefulness, even though, in fact, accuracy is not increased (Oskamp, 1965). The collection of data appears to have a "self-reinforcing" function since it is often unclear how additional data will be useful in making more accurate decisions (Corbin, 1980). Uncertainty may be decreased subjectively even though the additional time involved in collection of new data may not objectively decrease uncertainty. Irrelevant as well as relevant data may be influential. This chapter offers an overview of sources of bias in different kinds of "evidence" in the spirit that being forewarned is being prepared to avoid errors.

Selection of assessment methods may be based on sound reasons, such as feasibility (what is possible) and empirical research concerning the accuracy of a source and constraints imposed. On the other hand, selection may be based on questionable grounds, such as personal preferences contradicted by empirical data about the accuracy of given sources or inaccurate assumptions from a practice theory. Some objections to a procedure based on a theoretical perspective may not follow from the theory. For example, a clinician may prefer an ego psychology perspective, but nothing inherent in this approach supports the clinician's complete reliance on self-report data and neglect of other methods such as observation. Mistaken beliefs about given sources of data may limit selections. For example, some clinicians may believe that observation of interaction in real-life contexts is useless since such observation drastically alters natural interaction patterns, but this is not necessarily true (Foster, Bell-Dolan, & Burge, 1988). Some data may be collected from existing sources such as case records; other material is produced through observation and questions. Regardless of the source, the process of data collection and evaluation is influenced by both procedural and content knowledge as well as by beliefs. Clinicians differ in how much information they seek before the search process is stopped. Flexibility in approach increases the likelihood that helpful as opposed to misleading or irrelevant data will be obtained. "Flexibility affects the criteria used to decide if an idea, piece of information, or alternative is relevant to the problem at hand. A very narrow view of the situation or problem can produce very narrow criteria and thus limit the generation and production of potentially useful information" (Yinger, 1980, p. 21).

Factors That Influence What Clinicians See and Report

Perception is selective. Clinicians, like any other group of individuals, are affected by limited information-processing capacities and motivational factors (Nisbet & Ross, 1980). As a consequence, clinicians don't see all there is to see. Because of preconceptions and biases, things that are not actually present may be reported and objects that are present may be overlooked.

Availability and Vividness. Information is sought that is consistent with preferred theories and preconceptions, and contradictory information tends to be disregarded. Preferred practice theories and preconceptions are readily available. People who are informed that an instructor is warm, perceive him quite differently than people who are told that the same instructor is cold (Kelley, 1950). The more ambiguous a situation, the more preconceptions and biases affect what is seen. Abercrombie (1960) describes a radiologist who examined an X-ray of a child with a persistent cough. The radiologist discounted a button observed on the X-ray, assuming that the button was on the boy's vest—in fact, the button was inside of the boy and was causing his cough.

Availability is affected by the vividness of material. It is easy to recall bizarre behavior and pay excessive attention to this, ignoring less vivid appropriate behavior. The frequency of data that is available is overestimated. Many factors that are not correlated with the true frequency of an event influence estimates of its frequency and how important it seems (such as how visible it is, how vivid it is, and how easily it can be imagined—that is, how available it is). The prevalence of diseases that receive attention in the media is overestimated and the prevalence of illnesses that receive little media attention is underestimated (Lichtenstein, Slovic, Fischhoff, Layman, & Coombs, 1978). People tend to exaggerate their own contributions to tasks; information about our own contributions is more available to us (Nisbett & Ross, 1980). Chance availability may affect clinical decisions—that is, certain events may just happen to be available when thinking about a clinical problem, and these have an impact on what clinicians attend to (Hogarth, 1987). Clinicians in given settings are exposed to particular kinds of clients, which may make them predisposed to make certain assumptions. For example, a clinician who sees many severely depressed individuals may be primed to attend to signs of depression in their clients.

Base rate data which is abstract tend to be ignored, which increases the probability of inaccurate clinical inferences (see Chapters Nine and Ten). The abstract data presented in reports of empirical research are often uninteresting compared with concrete case examples that we see with our own eyes. The influence of vividness is illustrated by the finding that college students who spoke to four people were more swayed by the reports of these four individuals concerning the desirability of different psychology courses than were students who read a printout describing the course evaluations of 500 students (Borgida & Nisbett, 1977). The influence of vividness accounts for the reliance by clinicians on the credibility of their own experience. The more distinctive the client, the more vivid and the more memorable. A vivid case history, unless it is known to be typical, ought to be given little weight in making decisions. A single example certainly should be given less weight than accurate relevant statistical information that contradicts the example.

Motivation. Whether data are used affects what is perceived. For example, people are often incorrect in their answers about which way Lincoln's profile faces on a penny because they do not normally use this information. This example illustrates the difference between perceiving and noticing; perceiving is prior to noticing. Noticed information can be verbally reported, whereas perceived data that are not noticed cannot be reported. We may perceive without noticing; that is, just because something is perceived does not mean that it is noticed and something can be noted without appreciating its significance in terms of how it affects behavior. Information that is unnoticed is not likely to be processed in long-term memory and is thus not available for recall.

Insensitivity to Sample Size. Clinicians must often make generalizations from single instances to larger populations. For example, a psychologist may make generalizations about a person on the basis of one meeting. Generalizations about a mother's parenting skills may be made on the basis of her self-report during one interview. A lack of appreciation for sample size and sample bias can lead to incorrect judgments (Nisbett & Ross, 1980). The larger the sample, the more likely it actually reflects the characteristics of the population from which it is drawn. People have little appreciation of the importance of the law of large numbers. They are willing to make strong inferences based on few data. This tendency offers one explanation for disagreements about how to describe certain events—each person may be using a different sample to generalize from, and each sample may be small (as well as biased). Some clinicians use verbal report in the interviews as their only data source, neglecting other sources such as role play and observation in real-life settings. They have but a tiny sample of behavior and a tiny sample in just one situation—the interview—which is not a real-life setting. Yet they may remain confident in their ability to make accurate generalizations about clients on the basis of small, biased samples. The empirical literature does not support this belief. The size of the sample on which decisions are based can often be substantially increased by referring to samples collected by others that are described in professional journals and books. For example, consider a clinician who is working with a client who is having trouble finding a job, but the clinician has only worked with a handful of such clients previously. Familiarity with the development and evaluation of the Job Finding Club offers a sample of hundreds of individuals who have participated in a helpful program (Azrin, Philip, Thienes-Hontos & Besalel, 1980).

Sample Bias. The samples to which clinicians have access are usually biased. Few samples are random, in which each element of the population has an equal chance of being selected. Only a small percentage of people who experience distress or who engage in deviant behavior may seek help from a clinician. Those with such problems who do seek help or are referred to clinicians thus represent a biased sample of the total population of individuals who evidence certain behaviors. If a sample is randomly selected, there is less likelihood that it will be biased. Thus, it is important to know whether a sample was randomly drawn. The general failure to understand this is illustrated by the cabinet officer who did not accept the results of a poll that he did not like because people were chosen at random (Tversky & Kahneman, 1971).

Agency Policy/Social Pressures. Agencies have preferred practice beliefs that influence the kind of staff they hire and, consequently, the kind of data gathered. These preferences are revealed in steps that are taken to facilitate (or hamper) collection of certain kinds of data. For example, some agencies discourage home visits and observation of family members at home. Peers and supervisors may exert pressures to gather certain kinds of data and to ignore other sources.

The Quality of Feedback. The timing and relevance of feedback obtained about the accuracy of observations influence descriptions offered. Helpful feedback provides opportunities to correct initial assumptions (see Chapter Ten).

Ignoring Nonoccurrences. Events that do not occur tend to be ignored, even though these events may be highly relevant. A clinician may fail to note that a certain bizarre behavior does not occur in 95% of situational contexts, attending instead to the small percentage of situations in which it does occur. Certainly, such unusual behavior is a concern. However, overlooking situations in which it does not occur deprives clinicians of valuable information about environmental influences on behavior.

Temporary Biases. Assumptions made in specific situations influence perception sometimes with tragic results as illustrated by hunters who shoot people instead of deer. Temporary moods, either positive or negative, affect decisions made as illustrated in Chapter Two. Different decisions may be made about a client who is seen at the end of a hectic day than may be made if the same client had been interviewed at the beginning of that day.

Not Distinguishing Between Description and Inference. A basic distinction in collecting data is between inference and description. A descriptive statement can be confirmed by reference to the real world. For example, if a counselor states "the teenager sat between his parents," she could point to evidence for this. An inference involves extrapolation; it cannot be confirmed or rejected without other information that is not present via observation. If this counselor said, "The youth purposely sat between his parents in order to separate them as a team" or "because of his unresolved Oedipal complex," she would be making inferences. Although distinguishing between descriptions and inferences sounds easy, in fact some clinicians lack this skill; that is, they cannot distinguish between descriptions and inferences that may cloud their thinking in a number of ways, including confusion between what actually happened in a situation and interpretations of what happened. For example, a clinician might say that a husband is hostile toward his wife. When asked to give examples, he may say that "He does not like her." A further question may yield "He is aggressive and punishing toward his wife." Note that we still do not have any clear example of the referents for the term *hostile*.

The difficulty of distinguishing between descriptions and inferences is shown by Abercrombie's (1960) efforts to enhance the clear thinking skills of medical students. (Her description of the diplomatic skills required to succeed in this task is fascinating.) She showed the students X-rays of two hands and asked them to list the differences between them. The students typically reported that one X-ray showed an older hand than did the other. This inference was made swiftly on the basis of certain preconceptions related to the fact that one X-ray was smaller than the other. "During the discussion it became clear that the apparently 'factual' statement that 'B is an older hand than A' is an inference which had been arrived at as a result of picking up a number of clues, calling on past experience and information which was more or less relevant, ignoring the limitations of their knowledge, and inadequately testing hypotheses to estimate the probability of their being correct. The inferences the students had made were not arrived at as a result of a series of logical steps, but swiftly and almost unconsciously. The validity of the inferences was usually not inquired into, indeed the process was usually accompanied by a feeling of certainty of being right, and consequently the discussion of incompatible views sometimes became very heated" (Abercrombie, 1960, p. 105).

Different Kinds of Evidence

Clinicians draw on various kinds of evidence in making clinical decisions. Each type of evidence has strengths and weaknesses in relation to accuracy.

Real Evidence. Actual objects may be "offered to prove their own existence or to allow an inference to be drawn from their existence" (Smith & Hunsaker, 1972, p. 112), as in circumstantial evidence described below. Staff may show an attending psychiatrist broken objects in a patient's room to support their statement that the patient is "out of control."

Hearsay Evidence. This refers to reports that are based on what someone heard someone else say; the presenter of the information did not see the event himself, he is merely reporting what someone else told him. There are elaborate rules concerning acceptance of hearsay evidence in courts of law. Hearsay evidence is relied on extensively in clinical practice. Sources of inaccuracy include limitations in the perception of the original witness and bias on the part of the "reporter." A major problem with hearsay evidence is that the original witnesses cannot be interviewed to probe the credibility of their perceptions. Clinicians often discount sources of error in accepting hearsay evidence.

Expert Witnesses. An expert witness has special knowledge concerning a particular matter and can therefore offer authoritative opinions (conclusions based on facts). Clinicians are often called in to testify in court hearings as expert witnesses. How expert such individuals really are has been the subject of many spirited discussions. The rules of hearsay evidence are less stringent in expert testimony, in which a clinician may rely on data gathered from significant others as well as archival records (Blau, 1984). Of course, lawyers and judges may raise questions about the reliability and validity of such evidence. Whether these questions will be profitable depends partly on whether an expert has insider knowledge that cannot be checked. For example, only a psychiatrist may have access to a patient's behavior in the hospital, or other witnesses may be present who also have insider knowledge and who may confirm or contradict the psychiatrist's testimony. The excerpts below illustrate the importance of access to insider knowledge. This hearing involved a patient who was committed for assault with intent to commit murder and for breaking and entering into an automobile (Decker, 1987). The patient was characterized as a model patient during the psychiatrist's introductory testimony. The psychiatrist's argument for recommitment was based on the patient's criminal record and his "refusal to talk about his past troubles to gain insight and emotional control" (p. 167). The public defender raised the question as to whether there was any recent history of violent behavior.

> Then the public defender asked if there was "any recent history . . . of violent behavior." Again, the psychiatrist did not answer the question but shifted to the patient's reluctance to discuss the past, stating in part that . . . the fact that he (the patient) is "touchy" on any discussion of the past, you know, and sort of pushes it aside is not, you know, that favorable symptom. People that try to gain insight do not feel vulnerable to discuss, you know, the past.
>
> The psychiatrist's responses framed the public defender's concerns as irrelevant to the patient's disposition. At this point in the hearing, the psychiatrist was not confronted by "new facts" or an alternative construction of biography. However, the psychiatrist eventually lost these advantages of "insider" knowledge over the remainder of the hearing.
>
> Following the psychiatrist's response to his question about recent violence, the public defender asked the patient if he would like to ask the psychiatrist any questions. The patient began by explaining why he is "very lazy about speaking about something of the past," stating in part, "I'm more concerned about my future and how to get it structured so that I can live and cope with it. I can't cope with it constantly antagonizing myself and think that I have

done something wrong and I must always remember it and discuss it with anyone very freely at hand."

Then the patient stated that the statements in the clinical summary about past charges were wrong. The clinical summary indicated he was arrested for carrying a concealed weapon, but the patient said he actually "was shooting birds with a BB pistol. The weapon was not concealed. The charges were all thrown out." He also pointed out that the history of incarceration depicted in the clinical summary was inaccurate. This led to the following exchange between the psychiatrist and the patient:

Psychiatrist: I'm not a lawyer.

Patient: I realize that.

Psychiatrist: I'm really stating what's behind. It looks very bad when you say well, "He had concealed weapons." Everyone's first thought in mind was well, "He had a .38 or a Saturday Night Special or something." This is not so. It was a BB pistol.

Here the psychiatrist was not asked about the substance of the criminal record but was told. She could not gloss over the patient's revelations as irrelevant without reopening the earlier dialogue over the criminal record. Also, since the psychiatrist had already characterized the patient's hospital behavior in favorable terms—as a "model patient"—she could not readily refer to other hospital behavior to support a theme of violence or delusional thinking without contradicting her earlier testimony. Faced with this situation, the psychiatrist apparently tried to maintain—but qualify—her professional authority by placing responsibility for the accuracy of the criminal record with the legal profession.

Before terminating the hearing, the hearing officer asked the psychiatrist if she had any additional testimony to offer. The psychiatrist stated that even though she said favorable things about the patient's hospital behavior, the patient's hearing behavior (i.e., his rebuttal of the psychiatrist's testimony) demonstrated how the patient is vulnerable to sudden changes, "emotional upheaval," and the "same trigger reaction" when discussing past troubles. The hearing officer then asked if this would lead the psychiatrist to a conclusion that the patient "would be likely to injure other persons if released."—adding that "it seems that would be a long step." This led to the following exchange between the psychiatrist, hearing officer, and public defender:

Psychiatrist: I mean, we witnessed it. It happened before your very eyes, and with these certain situations—well, whatever they might be—he can be triggered very suddenly and unexpectedly. I cannot predict what other circumstances might produce this kind of reaction.

Hearing Officer: Well certainly—let's let the record be clear on this, that Mr. [patient's name] did seem agitated when talking about the previous charges, uh, which he maintains are untrue. Let me say further that by agitated, I don't think anyone in the room thought that he was going to explode and cause damage to any of us.

Psychiatrist: True, but nevertheless, it was such an abrupt change from the previous, very smooth general tone.

Public Defender: If I could comment. Uh, Mr. [patient's name] is the center of attention here. Uh, he is the subject matter and in his defense, I don't find it that irregular that he might speak a little forceful in defending himself and trying to correct, uh, what he feels are inaccuracies or untruths in a current record that concerns himself.

At that point, the hearing officer stated his agreement with the public defender and stated his [intention] to order the patient returned to court for a new disposition.

Although the psychiatrist attempted to document her earlier biographical theme of "dangerousness" by referring to the patient's hearing behavior, she could no longer rely on her privileged organizational location as a resource for this interpretative work. In this instance, other hearing participants shared direct observational knowledge of the referenced patient behavior [Decker, 1987, pp. 167–168].

Circumstantial Evidence. Here, the existence of an object or the occurrence of certain circumstances provides a basis for inferring that certain facts are true. Only one person may have had an opportunity to start a fire on a certain occasion. Thus, although no one witnessed a youth starting a fire, opportunity may be used as circumstantial evidence that he is guilty.

Reluctant Evidence. Information may be provided under duress; that is, respondents may be reluctant participants in offering information. Intentional misrepresentation or denials may be offered. The circumstances under which data are collected should be considered when weighing the accuracy of data. This sounds like, and is, a truism; however, in the everyday world of clinical practice, the demand characteristics of settings in which data are collected are often overlooked.

Factual Evidence. This refers to potentially verifiable statements that describe people or objects. Factual evidence is descriptive rather than evaluative or explanatory. Statistics may be used to support a claim, or observational data describing interaction may be offered.

Firsthand Reports (Testimonials). Clinicians have to evaluate the accuracy of reports provided by eyewitnesses. These reports may include descriptions of facts directly witnessed by a client, as well as descriptions of opinions. The possibility of inaccurate accounts is of major concern in courts of law, in which special procedures such as cross-examination and use of multiple witnesses have been developed to reveal inaccurate accounts. Consider the following example concerning a young freelance photographer:

> Dillen's initial arrest was little more than a misunderstanding. What is significant is the fact that the arrest resulted in a mug-shot photograph of Robert Dillen in the files of the Dormont police. By chance, one investigating officer thought he noticed an uncanny resemblance between Dillen and a composite sketch made by holdup victim, Diane Jones. Several weeks after the holdup, Diane Jones was asked to look at a set of ten mug-shot photographs, one of which was Dillen's. It was Dillen's that she identified.
>
> Copies of Dillen's photographs were then sent to other police departments, where they were identified by the witnesses and victims of 13 different crimes, leading subsequently to the identification of Dillen in a live lineup by several witnesses and finally to an identification in court by a 16-year-old victim of rape and abduction. Dillen was eventually proved innocent. (Hall, Loftus & Tousignant, 1984, pp. 124–125).

Errors in observation can be revealed by staging an interaction and asking witnesses to describe what they saw. This kind of demonstration is often used in law schools to illustrate the limitations of eyewitness testimony—a kind of testimony that is considered superior to other kinds of evidence. Stages that influence perception of an event include (1) an acquisition stage in which information is encoded in the memory system, (2) a retention stage (the time between when the event occurred and our recollection of the data), and (3) a retrieval stage when we recall information (Loftus, 1980). Failures may occur at any of these three points.

There has been great interest in why witness reports often differ (see, for example, Lloyd-Bostock & Clifford, 1983). Both characteristics of the event itself (such as exposure) and characteristics of the witness (such as amount of stress or fear) influence accuracy. As Loftus (1980) points out, someone who is thinking "How can I get myself out of this situation?" (p. 32) will be less attentive to characteristics of faces than will someone who observes people carefully. Prior knowledge and the expectations of the witness influence what is perceived. Testimony may be discounted on faulty grounds. For example, if a person cannot recall peripheral details of an incident, his testimony regarding identification of a suspect in a lineup may be discredited, even though memory for such details is not correlated with accurate identification (Wells & Lindsay, 1983). The confidence with which memories are reported is a predictor of whether the report will be believed (but not of how accurate the report is). This confidence in turn is influenced by response biases when reporting memories. Some people have a conservative bias; they are reluctant to identify someone unless they are very sure of the identification. Other people have the opposite tendency—they act more certain than they actually are. Greater credibility is accorded to an account if a person has previously freely admitted a memory failure on another item (Wells & Lindsay, 1983, p. 51). Verbal qualifiers (such as "I think" or "I guess") increase skepticism on the part of listeners concerning accuracy of reports. These qualifiers are cues that a "reporter is in a state of reconstructive memory" (Wells & Lindsay, 1983, p. 32).

The research on eyewitness testimony is relevant to the concerns of clinicians in evaluating the accuracy of reports. As we have seen, there are many paradoxes in this area—all is not what it seems. Confidence does not necessarily reflect accuracy and hesitancy does not necessarily reflect a lack of accuracy. Memory changes and the very review of its contents may create changes in our memories (see following discussion of self-report data).

Sources of Data

Sources of data include self-report by clients and significant others, self-monitoring, observation in analogue or real-life situations, physiological indicators, and case records. Some clinicians depend on self-report as their main source of information. Clinicians who supplement self-report data with observation and who are trained how to maximize the likelihood of obtaining accurate data through observation are less likely compared to clinicians who rely solely on self-report to fall prey to inaccurate self-reports. Inaccurate assumptions about helpful assessment methods may discourage their use. For example, some clinicians reject self-monitoring as a potential source of information on the grounds that clients will not do it. True, some will not, but others will. As with any source of data, self-monitoring will not be suitable for all clients and has disadvantages as well as advantages. Another source of data that is often neglected is the observation of interaction between a client and his or her significant others. One objection is that observation changes interaction, steps can be taken to increase the fidelity of what is observed, and, in any case, complete accuracy is not necessary (see other sources for further detail, for example, Ciminero, Calhoun, & Adams, 1986; Foster et al., 1988; Barlow, Hayes & Nelson, 1984). Learning how to structure situations so that relevant interactions can be observed will be useful (see, for example, Forehand & McMahon, 1981). Another objection to observation is that it is too time consuming. Use of hand-held computers allows coding and analysis of interaction patterns in a time-efficient manner; these can be used in a variety of settings, including the home and school.

Self-Report. Self-report gathered during interviews is the most widely used assessment procedure. Computerized interviewing programs have been developed for a variety of presenting problems (Greist, Carroll, Erdman & Wurster 1987). Reports may, of course, not be accurate (Greenwald, 1980; Linton, 1982). For example, when parents' reports were compared with observational data, non-treated children actually became worse during a four-week period, but most of the parents said their children had improved (Walter & Gilmore, 1973) (see also Schnelle, 1974). The more specific the question is, the more likely the answer is to be correct if the respondent has no reason to hide the truth (Mischel, 1968). Familiarity with sources of bias and error will be helpful in reducing distortions in self-reports of events that may be obtainable no other way. Disadvantages of self-report include the possibility that clients cannot provide the requested information, are not willing to provide it, or present inaccurate views. Information may not be accessible to clients. Perhaps they forgot some sequence of events or never noted a sequence of events accurately. Clients may not understand a question and so report incorrect information. Inaccurate accounts may be offered because of embarrassment over a lack of information or fear about the consequences of providing accurate accounts. Reports are influenced by clients' perception of how they are expected to behave.

Often, people do not accurately observe the relationship between behavior and environmental events and instead offer reports based on biased assumptions. Self-reports tell us more about what people think they have perceived rather than about what actually happened. Weiss and Brown (1977) investigated the accuracy with which women identified factors that influenced their mood. For a two-month period, subjects recorded their mood twice a day and also kept track of several factors that might affect mood (for example, amount of sleep, the weather, health, sexual activity, and day of the week). The subjects reported their views about the relative influence of these factors on their mood at the end of the two-month period. Multiple regression analyses were performed on the mood score of each subject to derive objective weights for each factor. Analysis of the results indicated that there were large discrepancies between these objective weights and the average subjective weights. In fact, the overall correlation between objective and subjective weights was slightly negative. Weiss and Brown (1977) also examined data for individual subjects. This analysis revealed a similar pattern; subjects were not accurate in assessing the relative effects of certain factors on their mood; they mistook strong influences for weak ones, and weak influences for strong ones. In some cases, they failed to distinguish between positive and negative influences. This study was followed by another one in which undergraduate students were asked to estimate the impact of the same factors on a person's mood. The relative weights obtained were identical to those reported by the women in the original study. "Participants daily experience of emotional ups and downs and their concomitants, even the daily recording of these events—gave them no advantage in estimating the correlates of their moods . . . These data seem inevitable given people's covariation detecting capacities. That is, weak objective covariations are difficult, if not impossible, to detect in the absence of a previous theory, and illusory correlations reflecting one's theoretical biases are quite apt to be falsely 'detected' " (Nisbett & Ross, 1980, pp. 222–223).

A great deal of information is available on some subjects, such as parents' reports about the behavior of their children. It is known for example that "Social desirability influences parental reports in terms of placing the information in a positive light, showing precocity of development, or tending to be in line with socially accepted childrearing practices" (Evans & Nelson, 1977, p. 616). Parents give different reports at different times (Brekstad, 1966), and their perceptions may shift over time in line with cultural stereotypes and popular books. Parents cited problems with "sibling rivalry" more often after Dr. Spock's (1945) book appeared (Robbins, 1963). Reports by clients may describe events accurately or inaccurately. Certainly, people have unique knowledge about themselves; what they have done in the past, and their future hopes and fears. That is, "the actor enjoys privileged access to many 'clues' " (Nisbett & Ross, 1980, p. 224), which, depending on the situation, may or may not be shared with clinicians. However, actors, like observers, are influenced by availability and representativeness of data that may or may not be related to causal importance.

Research on memory offers some intriguing explanations of why clients often find it difficult to offer specific examples. One way large amounts of information can be handled is to summarize inconsistencies in experiences. A wife who has had difficulty with her husband for months or years will focus on certain regularities in her experience and relate them to a theme that represents these ("He is bad tempered"), rather than offering specific examples. There is a transition from episodic to semantic memory (Linton, 1982; see also Barclay, 1986). However, "there is a fundamental integrity to one's autobiographical recollections" (Barclay, 1986, p. 97)—"not just any 'memory' is acceptable as one's own" (p. 97).

The importance of the questions asked. Questions are used to clarify client statements and to refine and confirm clinical assumptions. Preferred practice models influence choice of questions as do other factors such as biases and expectations about which clinicians may or may not be aware. Which questions are asked, how they are asked, and when they are asked all have an effect on the response received. Questions asked reflect preconceptions about clients. Snyder and Swann (1978) asked college students to explore the hypothesis that someone was either an extrovert or an introvert. The questions selected differed depending on whether the students considered the person extroverted or introverted. Students who thought that the person was introverted selected questions that probed for examples of introversion. Students who believed that the person was an extrovert probed for examples of extroversion. This study was replicated with counselors with similar results (Dallas & Baron, 1985). That is, therapists selected questions that offered confirming evidence for their assumptions. How questions are asked (for example, wording, order, concreteness) influences both the expression and formulation of values by affecting the definition of problems, the encouragement and organization of perspectives, and the degree of confidence in the judgmental process (Fischhoff, Slovic, & Lichtenstein, 1980) (see Table 8). Selection of values and goals to emphasize represents a critical choice in counseling. Given the influence of subtle social psychological processes in therapy, it could be argued that nondirective methods are the most manipulative of all methods; predispositions and preconceptions of the inquirer are unanalyzed and unshared without even a courtesy warning of this to the respondents (p. 124). One way to overcome subtle priming effects on clients is to ask about values and goals in a variety of ways to coax out inconsistencies that can then be clarified. This method of proceeding will be helpful in preventing an imposition of values on clients.

Maguire and Rutter (1976) found that medical students often avoided personal issues; accepted jargon; were imprecise in relation to dates and other key events; needlessly repeated topics; overlooked clues; failed to confront patients with inconsistencies or gaps in accounts; allowed patients to talk about irrelevant matters; often buried their heads in their notes; gave little encouragement to patients to continue talking; asked leading questions, and assumed there was only one illness. Only 10% of the students ended their

Table 8. Ways an Elicitor May Affect a Respondent's Judgments of Value.

Defining the issue
  Is there a problem?
  What options and consequences are relevant?
  How should options and consequences be labeled?
  How should values be measured?
  Should the problem be decomposed?
Controlling the respondent's perspectives
  Altering the salience of perspectives
  Altering the importance of perspectives
  Choosing the time of inquiry
Changing confidence in expressed values
  Misattributing the source
  Changing the apparent degree of coherence
Changing the respondent
  Destroying existing perspectives
  Creating perspective
  Deepening perspectives

Source: From *Cognitive Processes in Choice and Decision Behavior* (p. 123) by B. Fischhoff, P. Slovic, & S. Lichtenstein (Eds.), 1980, Hillsdale, NJ: Erlbaum. Copyright 1980 by Lawrence Erlbaum Associates. Reprinted by permission.

interviews on time, and only 8% checked to determine if the history they had gathered was correct. Inconsistent reports on the part of clients may be due to differences among interviewers. "When two different examiners get variations in a history from the same patient, they often assume that the patient is unreliable or perverse. In many instances, however, the fault lies with the examiners, not with the patient. The differences in history may arise from many aspects of the examining procedure. Among the major sources of variability is the specificity with which details of symptoms are noted" (Feinstein, 1967, p. 318). Research concerning witness testimony indicates that allowing people to offer an open narrative account results in greater accuracy than does asking many questions. The demand characteristics of the situation (what clients think others want to hear) will influence reports.

Memories may be modified during the process of an interview. Question comprehension and information retrieval through memory search are related. Alteration of memories is an integral part of comprehension because it is necessary to correct erroneous inferences and change unfulfilled expectations created during the process of understanding (Robertson, Black & Lehnert, 1985, p.191). (This assumes that a client is indeed trying to comprehend a question.) An example of the influence of questions on memory change is provided by a study of Loftus and Palmer (1974). Subjects watched a film of a traffic accident at an intersection; they were later asked "How fast was [the car] going when it ran the stop sign?" For some subjects, no stop sign appeared in the film. However, many of these subjects reported that they had seen a stop sign in the pictures viewed. This misleading question introduced information that was not initially available into reconstructed memory. Memories are not permanent—they are altered as new information is introduced and motivations change. Each time a memory is retrieved, the potential is there for substitution or alteration; "the contents of the interview may not reflect a person's earlier experience and attitudes so much as their current picture of the past" (Loftus, 1980, p. 50).

Checklists and Personality Inventories. Checklists and personality inventories are forms of self-report and are susceptible to sources of error and bias similar to those described in the discussion of verbal reports (see Corcoran & Fischer, 1987, for examples). The use of self-report inventories typically involves the assumption that the client's report provides accurate accounts of feelings, attitudes, behaviors, and related events. In fact, they may not reflect experiences either in the past or present. Concerns about personality tests are similar to those used in educational settings. That is, tests may be used for both predictive as well as prescriptive purposes; however, they may not offer correct predictions concerning future behavior, nor may they offer guidelines about how to achieve desired outcomes (Campione, 1989). For example, test results may offer no information about the reasons for a given score, whether correct or incorrect, "healthy" or "pathological." There may be no available normative data that allow comparison of a client with other people. Another disadvantage of checklists is their tendency to emphasize problems rather than resources (see, for example, Eyberg & Ross, 1978). Overall scores are often used to describe a client encouraging trait conceptions that obscure the situational variability of behavior

(Mischel, 1968). Personality tests, as well as intelligence tests, may be used in a "static" manner to pigeonhole the client at a given time rather than in a "process" manner to reflect where the client can go. Tests are subject to faking of responses (see, for example, Albert, Fox, & Kahn, 1980; Faust, Hart & Guilmette, 1988). Problems of reliability and validity are often overlooked in everyday practice, and personal experiences in using tests are given far greater weight than empirical data concerning tests (Wade & Baker, 1977).

Computer programs are available for administering and scoring many personality tests including the Beck Depression Inventory and the Michigan Alcohol Screening Test. Options for enhancing the accuracy and utility of computerized testing include item branching, speech analyzers, and physiological monitoring during testing.

Self-Monitoring. Self-monitoring, in which clients keep track of behaviors, thoughts, feelings, and the conditions related to them in real-life settings offers another potential source of information. Depressed clients may keep track of negative thoughts as well as the situations in which they occur; clients who complain about anxiety may note the circumstances related to changes in anxiety level and rate their subjective anxiety level. Benjamin Franklin used self-monitoring to keep track of various virtues he wanted to increase, such as temperance (that is, eat not to dullness) and tranquility (that is, be not disturbed by trifles) (Silverman, 1986). Advantages of self-monitoring include lack of expense, lack of intrusion by outside observers, and helping clients to see the relationship of behaviors, thoughts, and feelings to significant events such as the reactions of other people. Whether clients will gather information and how representative this information will be depends partly on whether a feasible data-gathering method is designed that matches client skills and opportunities and whether the client understands the procedures involved in and the purpose of monitoring.

Variables that influence the reactivity of self-recording (that is, the degree to which recording a behavior alters how often it occurs) include the motivation the client has to change a behavior and the nature of the behavior monitored. The timing of self-recording (whether it occurs before or after a behavior of concern, such as smoking) and the kind of recording device used also influence reactivity. Setting performance goals and offering reinforcement for attaining these increase the reactive effects of self-monitoring. Many steps can be taken to increase the accuracy of self-monitoring (see, for example, Barlow et al., 1984; Ciminero, Calhoun, & Adams, 1986).

Monitoring the Behavior of Significant Others. Another way in which assessment information may be gathered is by asking a client to observe and record behaviors of significant others. The same factors that may affect accuracy of self-monitoring may affect the accuracy of information noted about the behavior of others. If people know their behavior is being observed, there may be reactive effects as there are in self-monitoring. Another effect that may occur is a change in the observer's behavior as a result of observing someone else.

The Use of Analogues. Analogues include those in which clients interact together but do so in an artificial setting (such as the office) as well as contexts in which clients participate in role-playing with someone other than a real-life participant (such as with a psychologist rather than a parent). Advantages of the use of analogues include convenience and efficiency. Information can be gathered without going into the natural environment. Drawbacks include the possibility that behavior seen may not be representative of what occurs in real life (Nay, 1986). The more similar the artificial situation is to real-life conditions, the more likely behavior will be representative of that in real life.

Observation in the Natural Environment. Advantages of observation in real-life settings include the opportunity to view clients in their natural environments. Disadvantages include cost and inconvenience, restriction of observed data to overt behavior, intrusiveness, and reactive effects of observation (that is, being observed may alter interaction). For example, when parents were aware they were being observed, they played more, were more positive in their verbal behaviors and structured their children's activities more than when they were unaware of being observed (Zegiob, Arnold, & Forehand, 1975). Such effects are usually temporary, and many steps can be taken to increase the likelihood of gaining representative data (Kent & Foster, 1986). The same objective situation may create different emotional reactions. Because of different past experiences two people may see an event quite differently. People are often unaware of the ambiguity of a situation (various ways in which it could be viewed) but simply view it as they have done in the past (DeRivera, 1985, p. 385). Thus, gathering data by observation in the natural environment usually requires training. Decisions must be made about what, when, where, how long, and whom to observe, as well as how to remain unobtrusive. Structured situations may be used to increase the likelihood of gaining access to relevant interactions. (See, for example, use of the parent's game and the child's game described by Forehand and McMahon, 1981.) The more vague the categories used to describe behaviors, the lower the reliability in coding behaviors; vague terms make it difficult or impossible for observers to agree on referents.

Case Records. Case records are often consulted to gather assessment information. Deficiencies of case records include missing or vague information, a focus on pathology, and neglect of client assets. Written reports are based on one or more sources of information already discussed and so may reflect errors associated with these. Often, the source of information is not noted. If a case record states "Mrs. M. is an alcoholic," does it give the source of this information? Did the author of this report directly witness related behavior? If so, where? How often did he or she witness it? What does alcoholic mean? Clinicians are often willing to accept vague statements in case records without asking such questions.

Tallent (1988) has written an engaging and valuable book on psychological report writing in which pitfalls in recording are described. As he notes, these are remarkably persistent over time. His research is based on a survey of psychologists, psychiatrists, and social workers concerning problems with psychological reports. Pitfalls in recording are divided into five categories, as described below in the hope that being forewarned will be helpful in avoiding these limitations. After all, records take time to write and to read and have important purposes—such as facilitating clinical decision making.

1. Problems of content include omission of essential information, inclusion of irrelevant data, and unnecessary duplication.
2. Problems of interpretation. This category refers to irresponsible interpretation, overspeculation, unlabeled speculation, and inadequate differentiation. Examples of unlabeled speculation include drawing conclusions from insufficient data, expressing theory as fact, and not relating inferences to the tests they presumably are derived from. Overspeculation is a kind of irresponsible interpretation and seemed to irritate readers. "Facts, inferences, speculations are often mixed and not labeled" (Tallent, 1988, p. 31). "The distinctions between reasonable deduction from the data, speculative extrapolations from the data, and the psychologist's clinical impression are not clear" (p. 31). Inadequate differentiation refers to reports that deal in generalities: "They tend to present generalizations that might apply to anyone rather than to the particular individual" (p. 32): "They tend to rely on vague, psychoanalytically oriented phrases that fail to convey an individualized picture of the client" (p. 32).
3. Problems of attitude and orientation include complaints about lack of practical use, exhibitionism, excessive authoritativeness, test oriented rather than client oriented and overly theoretical. Complaints included the following: "A lack of humility. I never cease to be amazed by the confidence some psychologists have in their tests and in their own abilities to interpret them. To accept such reports the psychiatrist would have to lose what little intelligence he or she is supposed to have" (1988, pp. 33–34). "They often are too theoretical or academic in language to be comprehensible or meaningful in terms of future treatment goals for the client. They occasionally give us the feeling that no client was present at the time" (1988, p. 34).
4. Problems of communication included vagueness, unnecessary length (wordiness), too technical and complex, style problems, poor organization, and hedging. Complaints included the following: "Often padded with meaningless multi-syllable words

to lengthen report" (1988, p. 36). "They are too often written in a horrible psychologese—so that clients 'manifest overt aggressive hostility in an impulsive manner'—when, in fact—they punch you on the nose" (p.36). "They suffer mainly from vagueness, double-talk and universality without enough of an attempt being made to specify more precisely what sets this person off from other people (and what does not)" (p. 37). "Too often they are so poorly organized that the reader has a difficult time to get a clear psychological picture of the client" (p. 39). "When several tests have been administered, many psychologists cannot integrate the findings without giving separate results for each test" (p. 39). "They too often are riddled with qualification—'it appears that' 'it may well be,' 'the test reports indicate.' This is fine when speculation is being introduced, but many reports merely convey the inadequacy and timidity of the writer" (p. 39).

5. Problems of science and profession refer to criticism based on characteristics of research and professions rather than of individuals. Examples include lack of agreement as to how reports should be written, inadequate theories of behavior, and unreliability of diagnostic categories. Problems of role conduct were also mentioned: "They frequently do not mind their own business and go beyond their ken—invading territory properly allocated to the MD" (1988, p. 41). Many social workers reported that psychologists invaded the realm of the psychiatrist.

These various pitfalls become downfalls, as Tallent suggests (1988, p. 233), in the courtroom when lawyers critique a clinician's credibility and conclusions. Problems with validity and reliability that are overlooked by clinicians are often the focus in court. Errors that are especially common include overinterpretation, omission of needed information, and hedging. Ziskin (1981) states, "I have almost invariably found the clinician's report to be a goldmine of material with which to challenge his conclusions" (quoted by Tallent, 1976, p. 233).

Physiological Measures. Physiological measures are often used for assessment and evaluation of progress, especially in behavioral medicine. Measures include pulse rate, blood pressure, muscle tension, respiration rates, Palmer sweat index, and urine analysis. Here, too, questions of reliability and validity are important. For example, accuracy of urine analysis in relation to drug use varies widely over different laboratories.

Archival Data. Police reports, school records, and other sources of archival data may be used. Sources of error here include missing information and changes in procedures that may result in spurious increases or decreases in reported frequency.

Evaluating Statistics

Statistics may be misleading in a number of ways that relate to the size and representativeness of the samples on which they are based. There are many different meanings of the term *representative sample* (Kruskal & Mosteller, 1981). The most common one refers to an absence of selective factors that would render the sample unrepresentative of the population from which it is drawn. The importance of asking for precise figures is illustrated by the varied meanings given to words referring to frequency expressions, such as *sometimes, often,* or *rarely.* For example, the meaning of the term *sometimes* has been found to range from 20 to 46 percent (Pepper, 1981).

Figures may be used to mislead rather than inform. Proponents of a new suicide prevention center may say that there has been a 200 percent increase in the number of suicides over the past year. The total increase may be two additional cases. Thus misleading percentages may be offered. The total number of occurrences of a given event may be cited when a percentage would be more informative. A drug company may claim that more people have improved using drug X than any other drug. However, the best drug on the market may only be effective 5 percent of the time. Drug X may be effective 6 percent of the time—usually not much to write home about. Groups with a special interest in a problem may deliberately inflate the number of people affected by a problem.

Visual Distortions (Biases)

Our tendency to be influenced by vivid material makes us vulnerable to distortions created by visual material such as photographs, charts, and graphs (Huff, 1954; Tufte, 1983). Consider, for example, the chart of the shrinking family doctor in Figure 3. Graphic displays often lie by omission—by what is left out—leaving unanswered the question "compared with what?" Only a portion of a graph may be shown, resulting in a distorted version of data. Visual representation should be consistent with numerical representation. Often it is not as shown in Figure 4. Principles of graphical excellence suggested by Tufte (1983) include the following: (1) Complex ideas are communicated with clarity, precision, and efficiency; (2) the viewer receives the greatest number of ideas in the shortest time with the least ink in the smallest space; and (3) the truth about the data is depicted (p. 51).

Weighing the Value of Data

Decisions are made about the value of data collected. Variables that influence judgments about the credibility of data include recency (how recent was the observation), credibility of the source, and the capability of the source to offer the data presented. The source of data is a key consideration in evaluating accuracy. Other criteria are shown below.

Judging the credibility of a source

- Expertise
- Lack of conflict of interest
- Agreement among sources
- Reputation
- Use of established procedures
- Known risk to reputation
- Ability to give reasons
- Careful habits

Figure 3. The Shrinking Family Doctor in California.

THE SHRINKING FAMILY DOCTOR
In California

Percentage of Doctors Devoted Solely to Family Practice

1964	1975	1990
27%	16.0%	12.0%

1: 4,232
6,212

1: 3,167
6,694

1: 2,247 RATIO TO POPULATION
8,023 Doctors

Source: *Los Angeles Times*, August 5, 1979, p. 3. Reprinted by permission.

Criteria for observing and judging observation report

- Minimal inferring involved
- Short time interval between observation and report
- Report by observer, rather than someone else (that is, not hearsay)
- If report is based on a record, it is generally best that:
  The record was close in time to the observation

The record was made by the observer

The record was made by the reporter

The statement was believed by the reporter, either because of a prior belief in its correctness or because of a belief that the observer was habitually correct

- Corroboration
- Possibility of corroboration
- Conditions of good access
- Competent use of technology, if technology is useful
- Satisfaction by observer (and reporter, if a different person) of credibility criteria (Ennis, 1987, p. 13)

Reliability. One meaning of the term *reliability* is the consistency of reports or judgments by the same person at two or more different times. For example, the reliability of the Automatic Thoughts Questionnaire (Hollon & Kendall, 1980) could be evaluated by asking people to complete this at two different times. A second meaning of the term is the degree of agreement between observers of the same situation. As noted in the discussion of eyewitness testimony, this is often low. Sources of error include changes in ratings due to fatigue, lack of sufficient training, and different preconceptions. A third meaning of the term refers to degree of correlation among test items on a measure (known as homogeneity).

The degree to which different sources provide similar or identical reports is typically used as a sign that a description is accurate. Both a husband and a wife may offer identical reports concerning the husband's drinking pattern. Both staff members in a retirement home, as well as other residents, may offer similar reports about a resident's behavior. Inconsistent reports call for further investigation; they may indicate that one or more of the sources is inaccurate. Agreement between two or more witnesses of an event is often considered indicative of accuracy; however, all these witnesses may have been influenced by a similar biasing effect that distorted the accuracy of all descriptions. For example, the appearance of a suspect in a particular lineup may influence all observers' reactions similarly (Wells, Lindsay, & Ferguson, 1979). Talking together about an event may increase agreement but not accuracy—thus the admonishment that jury members not talk to each other about the trial before their final deliberations. A major concern in relation to the consistency of data is that it results in overestimation of the informativeness of material. Reliability of measures used and of psychiatric diagnosis is often quite low (Kutchins & Kirk, 1987). Agreement between different clinicians and agreement between different ratings of the same person at different times also may be modest in other fields, such as medicine.

Relevance: "So What?" Are the data relevant? Do they help to define presenting problems in a way that points to a feasible way of resolving concerns? Clinical decisions are influenced by irrelevant as well as by relevant data. Thus, collection of additional material is not necessarily helpful and in fact may decrease accuracy as well as take time to gather and record (Sisson, Schoomaker, & Ross, 1976). Consider, for example, the influence of irrelevant data on social workers' decisions about the guilt of a father in apparent child abuse (see Chapter Nine). Asking "so what?" when thinking about collecting data will keep irrelevant data to a minimum.

What's Missing? Another helpful rule of thumb is to ask "What is missing?" For example, data for all four cells in a contingency table are often missing (see Chapter Nine). Data are collected that support preconceptions and favored practice theories, unless rules of thumb are used to encourage exploration of alternative views.

Validity. The value assigned to data should be moderated by concerns about validity. A measure is valid to the extent to which it reflects the concept or object it is supposed to measure. Consider, for example, the Beck Depression Inventory (see Beck, Rush, Shaw, & Emery, 1979). To what extent does a client's score reflect his or her depression? What is the likelihood that a client who scores high on a suicide potential scale will attempt suicide in the next six weeks? (See discussion of the predictive value of tests in Chapter Ten.) There are many different kinds of validity and it is helpful to be familiar with these (Campbell & Stanley, 1963).

Recording Information

Clinicians are required to keep records, and, depending on where they work, may spend considerable time "recording." Deficiencies in memory highlight the value of records. The importance of case records is affirmed by court rulings that inadequate records hinder the development of treatment plans (for example, *Whitree v. New York State,* 1968). Records are helpful to the extent to which they fulfill the purposes of recording; these include administrative, case planning, and supervisory functions. Information should be easy to locate. Well-designed forms permit ready location of material as well as reminders to include helpful data. Use of a loose-leaf binder permits easy reordering of pages as needed; when cases are no longer active, records can be stored in another format. Problems with case records were discussed in a previous section; guidelines for recording are offered in Exhibit 2 (see also, Kagle, 1984).

Summary

Gathering data is the first step in clinical decision making. Decisions are made about what data to collect, how to gather data, and when to stop. Sources of information include self-report, self-monitoring, observation (in interviews, analogue situations or in real life), personality inventories, physiological measures, and case records. Each source has advantages and disadvantages. Familiarity with the strengths and weaknesses of each will be helpful in selecting those which offer helpful data. Some clinicians confine their attention to self-report, forgoing other valuable sources such as self-monitoring and observation in real-life settings that may correct biases in self-report data.

Clinicians cannot seek data with complete objectivity. Practice theories influence how presenting problems are defined, which in turn influences what data are gathered. Clinicians are influenced by their preconceptions and by the vividness of data; they pay undue attention to data that are vivid and ignore material that does not have this quality yet nevertheless may be helpful. Broad generalizations may be based on small samples, reflecting an insensitivity to the size of the samples on which inferences are based. Many studies high-

Exhibit 2. Quality Check of the Psychological Report.

	Yes	No
Does the report meet all responsibilities, ethical and legal, to the client, and to the community, and, as applicable, to other professionals and agencies?	☐	☐
Is the completion of the report timely?	☐	☐
Is the report properly focused in terms of the reason for assessment, data on the client, and a frame of reference?	☐	☐
Does the content unnecessarily duplicate that of others? (Is there encroachment on the established role of other professions?)	☐	☐
If raw data are presented, is the material also interpreted or used for illustration?	☐	☐
Is all appropriate illustrative material presented?	☐	☐
Is all of the content relevant and significant?	☐	☐
Is content presented with appropriate emphasis?	☐	☐
Are diagnoses, prognoses, and recommendations given as necessary?	☐	☐
Is all other essential material included?	☐	☐
Is interpretation sufficiently focused (not too general, differentiating among clients)?	☐	☐
Are conclusions adequately supported by data?	☐	☐
Is speculation within reason?	☐	☐
Is speculation properly labeled as such?	☐	☐
Are all interpretations within acceptable levels of responsibility?	☐	☐
Is the report written so as to be meaningful and useful?	☐	☐
Are exhibitionistic, authoritative, or similarly offensive statements avoided?	☐	☐
Is the report client-oriented rather than test-oriented?	☐	☐
Are concepts that are too theoretical or too abstract avoided?	☐	☐
Is word usage appropriate (absence of jargon, stereotyped, esoteric, overly technical, or complex language)?	☐	☐
Is the language used clear and unambiguous?	☐	☐
Is the report too long (padded, redundant, rambling, unfocused, offering useless content, or in the manner of a "shotgun approach")?	☐	☐
Is the style appropriate for the mission, for the setting, and for those who may read it?	☐	☐
Is the report logically and effectively organized?	☐	☐

Exhibit 2. Quality Check of the Psychological Report, Cont'd.

	Yes	No
Are the conclusions of the report set forth without hedging?	☐	☐
Is the report adequately persuasive in terms of needs and forcefulness of the data?	☐	☐
Is the report self-contradictory?	☐	☐

Source: From Psychological Report Writing (3rd ed.) (p. 244) by N. Tallent, 1988, Englewood Cliffs, NJ: Prentice-Hall. Copyright 1988 by Prentice-Hall. Reprinted by permission.

light the difficulty of distinguishing between inferences and descriptions; when descriptions are asked for, inferences are often offered. Too much data tends to be gathered, and clinicians tend to be overly confident of the accuracy of the data gathered and assumptions made.

Familiarity with sources of error associated with different kinds of data will be helpful in avoiding errors. The value of data is associated with its reliability, validity, and completeness. As in other problem-solving situations, "what's missing" may not be obvious but may be critical in arriving at helpful conceptualizations.

9

Causes of Clients' Problems: Making Accurate Assumptions

Clinical practice requires making judgments about the cause of presenting problems. The history of public health, medicine, psychiatry, and psychology is strewn with fascinating examples of skilled (and not so skilled) detective work in the identification of causes. Consider the assumption that dyslexia was a medical problem. "In all likelihood, nothing has done more to hinder the scientific study of reading disability than unwarranted popularization of medical explanations for the condition. It has taken this field decades to rid itself of the many incorrect physiological explanations that sprouted from the few uncontrolled case studies that were at one time introduced into the medical literature" (Stanovich, 1986, p. 169). The time lag between identification of a causative factor and acceptance of this information is often discouragingly long. Causes are often difficult to identify because of the gradual introduction of a causative factor (such as gradually failing health) or because of a considerable lag in effect (as between smoking and the development of lung cancer). Assumptions about the causes associated with presenting problems are influenced by practice theories; these theories guide selection and organization of material. If a practice theory stresses the importance of personal characteristics, environmental variables may be neglected. Theories that are ecological in focus will encourage a broader search for causative factors, including at-

223

tention to the role of significant others (those individuals who influence clients) as well as community characteristics. For example, Wahler (1980) found that the nature of a mother's social contacts outside the home influenced the quality of her interaction with her children at home. An ecological view of excessive alcohol use would entail far more than a description of individual characteristics that may encourage this pattern of behavior. A given theory or approach to problems may be applied to an increasingly wide range of presenting problems over time, even though this theory may not be the most appropriate one in these many instances. Informative feedback concerning the accuracy of approaches can decrease this tendency.

Research on clinical decision making indicates that, even though a great deal of data are collected, decisions are based on only a few items (see, for example, Kendall, 1973). Elstein and his colleagues (1978) found that physicians generated hypotheses early in the process of thinking about a problem and that only a few hypotheses were considered. Expert physicians use only factors considered particularly relevant about a case; they restrict their attention to a relatively small model (Kuipers & Kassirer, 1984). This research raises questions about programs that recommend a long search in order to locate helpful strategies. Two problems with long searches are (1) that standards in reviewing ideas may be lowered and (2) that the best option is not necessarily selected from the longer list of alternatives (Perkins, 1985). Expert chess players do not search any more elaborately than do merely competent players (Simon & Chase, 1973). The implications of such findings is not that long searches are bad per se, but that they do not account for expertise in an area and may not improve performance (Perkins, 1985). This should be reassuring to clinicians who must make decisions in a timely manner without all the evidence that might be desirable. Assessment requires the integration of diverse sources of data, which is difficult. (The comparative effectiveness of actuarial and clinical judgments in integrating data is discussed in Chapter Ten.)

Causal rules derived from practice knowledge are used to describe the relationship between variables. These rules may not be readily accessible to awareness or correctly derived from a theory. Clinicians differ in their knowledge base, which influences the accuracy of the "if-then" rules they use. For example, Patel and Groen

(1986) presented a case to seven specialists in cardiology and asked them to describe the underlying pathophysiology and to provide a diagnosis. The four physicians who arrived at the correct diagnosis used a different set of production rules than did the three physicians who did not find the correct diagnosis.

Sources of error in assessing covariations and causal relationships are described in the sections that follow, together with rules of thumb that can be used to avoid such errors.

Assessing Covariations

Clinical assessment involves the description of covariations among behaviors, environmental events, or personality traits (depending on preferred practice model). A clinician may note that only when a client fails to state her preferences in a number of social exchanges do angry outbursts occur. People have beliefs (which may or may not be correct) about what kind of personality traits go together. A clinician may believe that dependent people often have a high need for social approval. Beliefs about covariations (what events tend to go together) influence selection of presumed causes, and beliefs about causes influence judgment of covariations. Assumptions about the strength of association between variables is influenced by their correlation as well as by the causal clues implied in how variables are labeled (Einhorn & Hogarth, 1985). For example, when people were asked to assess the relationship between two variables on a scatterplot, the correlation had to be high to enable a relationship to be perceived (Jennings, Amabile, & Ross, 1982). However, when variables were given labels, the degree of correlation required to see a relationship was much lower.

Confusions between covariation and causation are often easy to spot. That both swimming and ice cream consumption increase in the summer does not mean that one leads to the other. Mistaken assumptions of covariations may not be so easy to spot, however, if they complement beliefs about what events go together (as in the assumption that parental substance abuse will result in similar behavior on the part of their children). In the first example, there is no cultural or professional belief to support a causal relationship between ice cream consumption and swimming. In the second example, however, representativeness (the tendency to make judgments based on similarity) may influence judgment and result in an overestimate of the correlation between two similar events and the assumption of a causal connection. The history of science is a fascinating compendium of faulty assumptions of causal effects based on correlations. Even the great British statistician Pearson assumed that a correlation of .50 between a parent's tendency to develop tuberculosis and his or her children's tendency to contract tuberculosis reflected evidence for a hereditary cause of this disease (Blum, 1978). Another example of confusion between covariations and causation can be seen in superstitious behavior. A client may be convinced, for example, that, because she had a dream that her mother would die, she is in some way responsible for the death of her mother, which happened shortly after the dream. Thus, mistaken assumptions about covariations may result in incorrect causal assumptions.

Terms that describe personality traits, such as *dependent* and *aggressive,* supposedly convey information about the relative frequency of joint occurrences of behavioral dispositions of individuals. As mentioned previously, the search for cross-situational behavioral dispositions has been disappointing. Hypothesized traits often account for very small proportions of the individual differences that occur in real life (Mischel, 1968, 1973), and method variance is often larger than person variance. That is, greater differences are found as a result of different methods for describing events (for example, self-report versus observation) than as a result of differences between individuals.

The Influence of Preconceptions. Assumed covariations are influenced by preconceptions about the origins of given behaviors that may have no relation to the true level of covariation of two events. Practice theories are one important source of preconceptions. Clinicians selectively attend to factors that are compatible with their own practice preconceptions. A cognitive-behavioral practitioner who interviews a depressed woman will attend to her thoughts—what she says to herself to identify irrational assumptions and expectations. A clinician who emphasizes the role of environmental contingencies will gather information about what the client does; what events she enjoys; what recent change has occurred in the frequency of these events; and what recent factors in her life are related to this decrease or increase. A psychiatrist who favors a biochemical basis may emphasize the client's medication regime— what medication is she taking (if any), and what changes should be made. A psychoanalytic clinician might concentrate on exploring her past, searching for material that may relate to current complaints. Knowledge about the empirical literature related to a presenting problem will influence what questions are asked, what is noticed, and therefore what data are at hand when assessing covariations and making causal analyses. Thus, clinicians are influenced by the availability of material as well as by representativeness—beliefs about what goes together.

Lack of knowledge about the relationship between certain signs and underlying causes may result in incorrect clinical decisions. Consider, for example, the incorrect assumption that psychological and physical changes (such as trembling) are due to psychological causes, when in fact they may occur because the client has Wilson's disease (an illness related to copper absorption, which can be diagnosed by a blood test as well as by certain other physical characteristics such as changes around the pupils of the eyes). Failure on the part of clinicians to accurately diagnose Wilson's disease has resulted in the death of clients.

Illusory Correlations. The influence of preconceptions is highlighted by research on illusory correlations. Clinicians tend to overestimate the degree of covariation between variables, resulting in illusions of validity and reliability. Studies by Chapman and Chapman (1967, 1969) illustrate that expectations based on theories and semantic associations overwhelm the influence of data that does not match these expectations or even refutes them. They started with the question of how clinicians can persist in reporting associations between certain responses on projective tests and specific clinical symptoms, when research has shown that there is little or no association between these signs and symptoms. In one study, the reports of 32 practicing clinicians who analyzed the Rorschach protocols of homosexual men were reviewed (Chapman & Chapman, 1969). These clinicians listed signs that had face validity but were empirically invalid as responses characteristic of homosexual men. That is, they selected signs based on "what seemed to go together," on what ought to exist, rather than on empirically determined associations between signs and the criteria. Clinicians were more likely to report illusory correlations than were lay observers.

Illusory correlations are influenced by assumptions about what goes together: "Everyone possesses what might be called 'data' on the degree of covariation between various socially relevant dimensions and behavior dimensions, but the data are usually skimpy, hit-or-miss, vague, and subject to bias and distortion in both encoding and recall" (Nisbett & Ross, 1980, p. 98). We tend to overestimate the size of correlations between factors we believe go together and to underestimate the degree of covariation when we do not have any preconceptions about the relationship between two or more factors (Jennings and others, 1982). Incorrect estimates often persist in spite of firsthand experience with data that do not confirm these. For example, a clinician may insist that a woman is schizophrenic because she was once labeled a schizophrenic, even though no evidence obtained for the past three years supports this diagnosis. This tendency is increased by the confirmation bias (not attending to data that do not support a position and ignoring negative instances) and by lack of appreciation of the importance of attending to all four cells of a contingency table (see later discussion). Clinicians who believe that behavior is determined mostly by personal characteristics will be less likely to attend to possible correlations between environmental factors and behavior. Some researchers have been so struck with our limited ability to use correlation appropriately in making decisions that they believe that we lack an intuitive concept of correlation (Shweder, 1977) and that we tend to blur the distinction between likeness and co-occurrence. This blurring is at the heart of the representative heuristic—the tendency to be influenced by the similarity of events. Consider, for example, that, when people were asked to make estimates of the relative frequency of tense and tolerant people (Shweder, 1977), one person estimated that of 100 people, seventy individuals would be tense and seventy-five would be tolerant. When asked about co-occurrence, the subject estimated that 10 percent (seven) of the people who are tense would be tolerant. "Given the earlier estimate of the judge that 75 persons out of 100 are tolerant, it follows that 68 (75 minus 7) must be both tolerant and *not tense*. This is a glaring contradiction. The judge first claims that only 30 persons out of 100 are *not tense*. Then she makes a conditional-probability estimate that requires that there actually be at least 68 (out of 100) who are *not tense*" (p. 643).

Expectations of consistency encourage illusory correlations. That is, clinicians tend to assume that people behave in trait-consistent ways when, in fact, correlations between personality traits and behavior are relatively low (for example, see Mischel, 1968). One reason for this is that "we tend to see most people in a limited number of roles and situations and thus are exposed to a more consistent sample of behavior than we would obtain from a true random sample of a person's behavioral repertoire" (Nisbett & Ross, 1980, p. 107). Apparent discrepancy is readily explained away. Subjective feelings of control are enhanced by the belief that other people are consistent in their traits and thus predictable.

So, we are not very good at detecting covariations based on experience. This weakness highlights the importance of helpful theories. How do we get through a day if our power to deduct covariations is so poor? As Nisbett and Ross (1980) note, the ability to detect covariations in more specific domains may be much greater, possibly because we have more opportunities to observe such covariation. Take, for example, the relation between making certain changes in steering when driving a car. In this situation, we benefit from immediate feedback about the effects of our actions. Experience offers an opportunity to observe covariations and thus may help to correct the influence of inaccurate preconceptions in relation to what "ought" to go together. However, if preconceptions are rigid and feedback is vague or irrelevant, experience may do little to change incorrect notions, especially in areas such as clinical practice, in which indicators of progress are often vague and not agreed upon and practice often is not systematically monitored (see discussion of experience in Chapter 3).

Misunderstanding Probabilities. People tend to focus on "hits" when estimating covariation; negative instances tend to be disregarded. Consider, for example, the belief that there is a relationship between worry about an event and the event occurring. For example, parents often worry about their teenage children arriving home safely, without getting into a car accident. So, if mother worries and then her daughter is involved in an accident, the mother (as well as the press) may attribute this coincidence to clairvoyance or some other mystical power. Headlines may read: "Mother Worries—Daughter Injured." As Jensen (1989) notes, only the "hits" (worry followed by accident) receive attention; false alarms, misses, and correct rejections are ignored. In fact, no judgment of association can legitimately be made without considering all four of the possibilities illustrated in Table 9. The risk of an accident if the mother worried would have to be compared to the risk in the absence of worry. In assessing covariations, pointing only to particular cases is misleading. The tendency to discount negative instances is responsible for beliefs in suspect causes such as prayer and worry. People who say that their prayers are answered may not pay attention to times when their prayers were not answered. That is, they may not keep track of *all* the times they prayed, noting the outcome of each. "Answered prayers" are more vivid—they may say, "What a coincidence." The confirmation bias (the tendency to selectively search for evidence that supports preconceptions) encourages a focus on hits.

In clinical practice, covariations (and thus causal relationships) often are assumed between certain personal and environmental characteristics (for example, personality traits or recent life changes) and problems, and also between certain symptoms and diagnostic categories (for example, between vigilance and scanning and generalized anxiety disorder). Decisions about the association between variables often are made without considering the necessary probabilities. The result is overestimation of pathology. The use of the terms *symptom* and *disease* in this section does not imply acceptance of a medical model of personal problems. In fact, the bias of this book is quite the opposite (see Chapter One). These terms are used here because many clinicians do accept an illness metaphor (a disease model) of psychological problems. The DSM-III-R (*Diagnostic and Statistical Manual of Mental Disorders,* 1987) is based on the assumption that the problems described are a result of a "mental

Table 9. Contingency Table.

		Mother Worries	
		Yes	No
Accident	Yes	Hit (Correct Positive) (a)	Miss (Incorrect Negative) (b)
	No	False Alarm (Incorrect Positive) (c)	Correct Rejection (Correct Negative) (d)

Source: From Jensen (1989), p. 158.

disturbance" (McReynolds, 1989). Examples from the field of medicine, as well as examples from clinical practice by psychologists and other professionals in interpersonal helping, are used to clarify the discussion of probabilities. Considerable data on the diagnostic value of some medical tests are available, unlike data on the value of many psychological tests. Even when such data are available, this is often overlooked by clinicians, resulting in incorrect clinical decisions.

Smedslund (1963) found that nurses tended to focus on joint occurrences of symptom and disease when they were asked to determine whether there was a relationship between symptoms and the disease. Each nurse received a pack of 100 cards, which supposedly depicted excerpts from the files of 100 patients. The presence or absence of the symptom and the presence or absence of the disease were noted on each card in the ratios shown in Table 10. Eighty-five percent of the nurses said that there was a relationship between the symptoms and the disease, and most justified their claims by noting the number of cards in which both the symptom and the disease were present (thirty-seven); that is, they tended to focus on joint occurrences of symptom and disease and to ignore other combinations.

The probability of A given B is usually not equal to the probability of B given A. The probability of being a male if a person is a head of state is quite different than the probability of being a head of state if a person is a female (Bar-Hillel, 1983). The prob-

**Table 10. Correlation-Relevant Frequency Information on the
Relationship Between a Hypothetical Symptom and a Hypothetical
Disease in 100 Hypothetical Patients.**

		Disease		
		Present	Absent	Total
	Present	37	33	70
Symptoms				
	Absent	17	13	30
	TOTAL	54	46	

Source: Based on Smedslund (1963).

ability of being a chronic smoker if a person develops lung cancer
is about .99; the probability of developing lung cancer if a person
is a chronic smoker is .10 (people probably die of something else
first) (Dawes, 1982, p. 42). Not distinguishing between two such
probabilities is known as "the confusion of the inverse."

Another source of incorrect estimates is not distinguishing
between compound probabilities (the probability of this and that)
and conditional probabilities (the probability of this given that). A
second principle is as follows: $P(A|B) = P(A,B)/P(B)$. "Simple, and
hence conditional, probabilities can be inferred from compound
probabilities, but not vice versa. But compound probabilities can be
inferred—via principle 2 only when both conditional and simple
probabilities are known. If just simple or just conditional probabilities are known, however, no other type of probability can be inferred" (Dawes, 1982, pp. 43–44). Consider, for example, the
probability of being addicted to heroin (A) if a person smokes marijuana (B). This equals the probability of being addicted both to
heroin and smoking marijuana (A,B) divided by the probability of
smoking marijuana (B). "It is decidedly not *equal* to $P(A,B)/P(A)$—
the probability of both smoking pot and being addicted divided by
the probability of being addicted; hence the fact that most heroin
addicts (A) also smoke pot (A,B) is an irrational justification for
draconian marijuana laws" (Dawes, 1982, p. 43).

A third principle is that "the probability of a symptom is
equal to the compound probability of the symptom and the disease

plus the compound probability of the symptom without the disease: $P(S) = P(S,D) + P(S,\bar{D})$." Dawes uses the example that "the probability of seeing dragonflies on the Rorschach (S) is equal to the probability of seeing dragonflies and being schizophrenic (S,D) plus the probability of seeing dragonflies and not being schizophrenic $(S,\bar{D})$" (p. 43). If the probability of the sign without the problem— $P(S,\bar{D})$—is quite high, the probability of the problem given the sign—$P(D|S)$—may be very low even though $P(S|D)$ is high. This can be presented in a contingency table (see Table 9). Determining the probability of a sign given the problem and the probability of the sign without the problem involves comparisons between the columns, whereas the probability of the problem given the sign and probability of the problem without the sign involve row comparisons. Thus, as Dawes notes, if it were known that all schizophrenic patients in a clinic saw dragonflies on the Rorschach and only 10 percent of nonschizophrenic clients did, but the proportion of clients who were schizophrenics were *not* known, then there would be no way to assess the likelihood that someone who saw dragonflies was schizophrenic.

The probability of a sign or symptom is greater than the probability of a disease or problem because signs are common to many problems; that is, $P(S|D) > P(D|S)$. Dawes (1982) points out that it is only because so many women have neither cancer nor a positive reading that there is such high agreement between mammogram results and the occurrence of breast cancer. Agreement often is confused with accuracy. Many people "believe the .20 probability of cancer given a positive reading to be the .80 probability of a positive reading given cancer" (Dawes, 1982, p. 46). Diagnosis is confused with prognosis (Einhorn, 1988). So a positive mammogram is much less diagnostic than is presented by physicians. The upshot is that "too many biopsies are carried out" (p. 48) (See also discussion of using test results in Chapter Ten). Research results that clinicians draw on in their practice may be problematic either in incorrectly overestimating the degree of correlation between two or more variables (spurious correlations) or in falsely underestimating the correlation between two or more variables (causalation) (Einhorn & Hogarth, 1985, p. 320).

Causal Analysis

Clinical practice requires making inferences about the causal relationship between variables. The purpose of assessment is to understand the client and his or her situation so that appropriate help can be offered. Focusing on incorrect causes of a presenting problem will result in cutting off a search for alternative explanations. Assessment should be integrally related to intervention; that is, how problems are structured and what causal factors are assumed to be important should influence selection of intervention methods. It could even be argued that if intervention fails, assessment was incorrect. Assessment is an ongoing feature of clinical practice; additional information concerning causal factors usually is gained as counseling proceeds. Additional data may or may not require changes in intervention decisions. Incorrect identification of the cause of a problem may result in no improvement or even a worsening of the situation. Consider, for example, the client who complained about abdominal pains at bedtime (Valins & Nisbett, 1972). The therapist interpreted these as pains related to sexual anxiety. As a result, the client became concerned about her emotional stability. Her anxiety and her negative image of herself increased. Later, a relative suggested that her pain might be caused by an allergic reaction to tomatoes; the client stopped eating tomatoes, and the pains disappeared.

Intervention methods are selected on the basis of the presumed causes of problems. Cues to causality include temporal order, contiguity in time and space, similarity of cause and effect, covariation, and availability of alternative possibilities (Einhorn & Hogarth, 1986). Conditions that must be met in order to presume a causal relationship between two variables include the following: (1) the presumed cause must occur before the presumed effect; (2) the correlation must be consistent; and (3) it must be shown that a third variable is not responsible for the relationship between the two variables. Attention to only one of the three conditions can result in post hoc reasoning—the assumption that because one event follows another, it is caused by it. Different cues to causality draw "attention to different aspects of causal strength" (Einhorn & Hogarth, 1985, p. 323). Constant conjunction is represented by cells a and d in Table 9; cells b and c represent instances that disconfirm constant conjunction or support alternative accounts (Einhorn & Hogarth, 1985). Temporal order is reflected in which variable is selected as causative.

Inaccurate assumptions may occur because of a failure to consider alternative explanations or because of false assumptions based on contiguity in time and space. The fallacy of false cause is committed when an event is inaccurately assumed to be the cause of some other event. Consider, for example, the case of Clever Hans, the wonder horse (reported by Stanovich, 1986). Clever Hans supposedly could solve mathematical problems. When presented with a problem by his trainer, he would tap out the answers with his hoof. Many testimonials were offered in support of his amazing ability. A psychologist, Oskar Pfungst, decided to study the horse's ability. He systematically altered conditions to search for alternative explanations. This exploration revealed that Clever Hans was an astute observer of human behavior. He watched the head of his trainer as he tapped out his answer. His trainer would tilt his head slightly as Hans approached the correct answer, and Clever Hans would then stop. What are in fact the results of self-selection are often mistakenly attributed to other factors, as in the assumption that since student achievement is superior in private school, private schools are better than public schools. Conflicts between degree of statistical correlation and cues to causality (such as similarity between two variables) may result in either spurious correlation or causalation (incorrect assumption that variables are not related based on low or no correlation). Although much attention is often devoted during graduate training to sources of and warnings about spurious correlations, too little attention may be given to causalation. Quite different causes may be identified by changing which "causal field" is emphasized (Mackie, 1974). For example, clinicians who emphasize dispositional causes focus on a different causal field than do systems-oriented clinicians, who attend to environmental as well as personal causes.

Identification of causes is not necessarily explanatory; that is, the cause of an illness (such as cancer) may be known, and the symptoms and associated pathology may be identifiable but the etiology may not be understood. Thus, causes differ in the level of explanatory completeness they offer. Beliefs about which events are causally related to each other influence the data selection, as well as data processing and organization. If a clinician believes that childhood experiences account for a client's feelings of loneliness, insight therapy may be selected to increase awareness of how past experiences relate to this concern. Owing to this causal analysis, recent environmental changes (such as loss of friends) may be overlooked. A focus on one cause alone may result in inaccurate judgments. This is one reason for holding interdisciplinary case conferences in which the biases of one kind of professional may be neutralized by the biases of other kinds of professionals. For example, recent investigations indicate that many factors are related to relapse in depression: age, gender, history of depression, current stresses, and availability of a social support (Krantz & Moos, 1988). A focus on only one or two factors may result in incorrect assumptions. Clinicians, like other people, are adept at creating explanations. Once an account is offered, it may bias subsequent search for data.

When asked to explain which factors affect their behavior in a situation, people often overlook correct sources of influence and identify irrelevant ones (Nisbett & Ross, 1980). The particular causes identified depend partly on how advanced knowledge is in an area. For example, causes proposed for explaining variations in behavior change over time; few, if any, clinicians now rely on examination of bumps on the head (see discussion of phrenology in Leahey & Leahey, 1983). Widespread belief in the occult (Schultz, 1989) and the popularity of a variety of other beliefs illustrate the readiness with which suspect causes are accepted (Blackmore, 1987; see also Gardner, 1988). Rules of thumb (heuristics) may increase or decrease the likelihood of identifying accurate causal assumptions.

There is nothing odd or negative about weighing data in relation to causal theories. "The problem arises only when flimsy, ad hoc theories are invented for the purpose at hand, and causal mechanisms that would have predicted other events or relationships are both initially overlooked and never reconsidered when the individual's initial presumptions are discredited or challenged by new data" (Einhorn, 1980a, p. 28). This tendency may be heightened in an eclectic approach to practice, which increases the likelihood of holding many ad hoc theories or notions. The more tenuous a theory is, the less it should be relied on when assessing data and the more attention should be focused on data—that is, we "should become less theory-driven and more data-driven" in making judgments (Einhorn, 1980a, p. 32).

Just as a causal model may not be used in situations in which it is appropriate, it may be applied in situations in which it is inappropriate (Nisbett & Ross, 1980, p. 135). For example, transactional analysis may not have much to offer in dealing with a homeless young single parent addicted to crack cocaine. Being influenced by initial impressions of a client (anchoring effects), as well as overlooking the unreliability of sources of data about clients and their situations, may result in errors. A deterministic causal relationship may be assumed in situations in which the relations are probabilistic (statistical), as in the Gambler's fallacy (see Chapter Ten).

Lack of knowledge of cause-effect relationships comprises the quality of judgments. For example, many clinicians are unaware of the ways in which schedules of reinforcement influence behavior and misattribute the cause of presenting problems to personal characteristics—overlooking the role of scheduling effects in the environment. In another example, lack of knowledge about the effects of drugs may result in incorrect assumptions about the cause of an elderly client's depression.

Sources of Error

Sources of error that interfere with clear thinking about the causes of presenting problems are discussed in the sections that follow. The errors described result from and in missing or ignored causal assumptions. They may influence diagnosis of the client (for the many clinicians who use the *Diagnostic and Statistical Manual of Mental Disorders*, 1987) as well as influence assessment for those clinicians who do not use this classification system.

Misuse of Resemblance Criteria. One source of error in inferring causal relationships is the assumption that factors related to an event resemble that event. We have strong beliefs about what types of causal factors are associated with certain effects and "are far

more confident than is warranted in [our] ability to judge the plausibility of a specific cause-effect relationship based on superficial
resemblance of features" (Nisbett & Ross, 1980, p. 117). Beliefs about
how events are related stem from many sources. Some originate
from summaries of empirical data; some rest on informed expert
opinion or systematic observation; others are based on myths, fables, metaphors, and maxims that may or may not reflect reality. In
reality, "causes and effects may bear little or no resemblance to one
another" (p. 117). Everyday explanations of deviant reactions often
rely on causal assumptions based on resemblance, as in bad seed
arguments (see Chapter Six). Nisbett and Ross (1980) note that
many causal assumptions within psychoanalytic theory rely on
crude forms of the representative heuristic, as in the assumption
that symptoms may have identical or opposite characteristics to
their psychic causes. Timidity may be presumed to reflect underlying aggressive or hostile tendencies. In actuality, the form of a behavior may not reveal its function.

Preconceptions. Preconceptions and practice theories influence selection of causes. For example, many clinicians believe in the
disease model of substance abuse, as well as in the addictive personality. Other perspectives focus more on identifying environmental
as well as personal factors that may be related to substance abuse
and do not view it as a disease. A counselor who accepts the disease
model will focus on dispositional causes (see later section on dispositional bias). Theories that are appropriate in some situations
may be inappropriately applied in other contexts. Theories that are
familiar are more available and are therefore more likely to be influenced than are unfamiliar theories. The tendency to be more
confident than there is good reason to be about theories compounds
the distorting effects of preconceptions. The following quote from
Popper (1959) is apt:

> I found that those of my friends who were admirers of
> Marx, Freud, and Adler, were impressed by a number
> of points common to these theories, and especially by
> their apparent explanatory power. These theories ap-
> peared to be able to explain practically everything that

happened within the fields to which they referred. The study of any of them seemed to have the effect of an intellectual conversion or revelation, opening your eyes to a new truth hidden from those not yet initiated. Once your eyes were thus opened, you saw confirming instances everywhere: the world was full of verifications of the theory. Whatever happened always confirmed it. Thus its truth appeared manifest; and unbelievers were clearly people who did not want to see the manifest truth; who refused to see it, either because it was against their class interest, or because of their repressions which were still "un-analyzed" and crying aloud for treatment.

The most characteristic element in this situation seemed to me the incessant stream of confirmations, of observations which "verified" the theories in question; and this point was constantly emphasized by their adherents. A Marxist could not open a newspaper without finding on every page confirming evidence for his interpretation of history; not only in the news, but also in its presentation—which revealed the class bias of the paper—and especially of course in what the paper did not say. The Freudian analysts emphasized that their theories were constantly verified by their "clinical observations."

The influence of preferred practice theories is illustrated by a study (Plous & Zimbardo, 1986) in which clinicians were asked to list the most likely explanations for three different problems—a sleep disturbance involving nightmares, severe headaches, and depression—variously portrayed by actors in a series of vignettes. Some referred to the therapist, some to the client, and some to the therapist's closest friend of the same sex. Psychoanalysts made more dispositional attributions and fewer situational or mixed attributions than did behavioral therapists. Nontherapists (college students) made the highest number of both dispositional and situational or mixed attributions. Psychoanalysts made significantly more dispositional attributions in relation to their friends and clients than they did for their own behavior. Medical training was associated with the attributional bias of psychoanalysts; that is, those with medical training gave more dispositional attributions than did clinicians without medical training. Using only one method of approaching client problems over a long period increases the likelihood of using this method with all clients, whether or not it is appropriate.

Metaphors and similes influence the conceptualization of experiences (Lakoff & Johnson, 1980). If we think of arguments as war, we may respond to arguments by trying to win and we may view others as opponents. The tendency to personify objects is one type of metaphor, such as in "Her past finally caught up with her." The sickness metaphor is very prevalent in clinical practice, in such statements as "They have a sick relationship," and "She is an alcoholic." Metaphors may be helpful in revealing factors related to clinical problems and how best to attain desired outcomes (as many have argued in relation to the metaphor of comparing psychological problems to physical illnesses) or they may result in negative outcomes both for society and for clients (Sarbin, 1967; Schur, 1971; Szasz, 1961, 1970). For example, because of the use of the illness metaphor, dispositional attributions for problems may be made ("alcoholism as disease" metaphor) or people who have committed violent crimes may be excused on the grounds that they are mentally ill and thus not responsible for their behavior.

Preconceptions influence what clinicians recall as well as what data they note and how they organize that data. For example, consider the study in which subjects read a description of some events in the life of a woman (Gahagan, 1984, p. 93). Some subjects were told later that the woman had met a lesbian and had started a homosexual relationship with her. Other subjects were told that she met a man and initiated a relationship with him. A third group of subjects received no information about sexual relationships. A week later, all subjects were asked to recall details of the woman's earlier life. Subjects who were told that she had initiated a homosexual relationship showed strong distortion effects in their recall, which were in accord with stereotypes about "typical characteristics of lesbians" (p. 93).

The Fundamental Attribution Error. The fundamental attribution error (the tendency to attribute behavior to enduring qualities of people rather than to situational events) results in blaming people for problems and overlooking relevant environmental events. "Everyday, people make harmful and damaging judgments about themselves, or harmful judgments about their spouses even to the point of severing marriages, because they wrongly attribute current crisis to stable personal dispositions instead of transient pressures (Nisbett & Ross, 1980, p. 252). An example of the willingness to ascribe behavior to stable dispositions is offered by a study conducted by Jones and Harris (1967). People who read an essay advocating or opposing Castro's leadership of Cuba inferred that the author of the essay believed in the view described even when they were told that the theme of the essay was dictated by someone else (Jones & Harris, 1967). One effect of preconceptions is the tendency to perceive greater consistency in behavior than exists.

Research has shown that behavior is quite inconsistent across situations and that "slight differences in situations often produce large differences in the behavior of most people in those situations" (Nisbett & Ross, 1980, p. 120). In one study that highlights our tendency to seek internal causes and data to justify these causes and to ignore or underestimate situational influences, subjects were recruited for a game involving tests of general knowledge (Ross, Amabile, & Steinmetz, 1977). They took part either as participants or as observers and were randomly assigned to these roles. Subjects were aware of this random distribution. Questioners could ask any questions as long as they knew the answer themselves. After completing the game, observers, contestants, and questioners were all asked to rate contestants and questioners on their general knowledge and other competence-related items. The contestants received lower ratings by all parties despite the fact that they had little opportunity to display their knowledge because of the situational factor of random distribution. The influence of the context in which exchanges occur is often overlooked by clinicians who blame lack of honesty on the part of clients on personal characteristics. For example, it is to the advantage of clients who seek eligibility for social security payments on the grounds of mental handicap, to conceal information that may weaken their request and to exaggerate information that may strengthen it.

Both availability and resemblance encourage the fundamental attribution error. When clinicians observe clients, their behavior is often more vivid than are environmental variables and thus behavior is more available when clinicians think about causes. The situation is the reverse from the actor's point of view; that is, to the actor, it is the situation that is more vivid. This probably explains why actors attribute a greater role to environmental variables when offering reasons for their own behavior than do people who observe the actors (Jones & Nisbett, 1972).

The Readiness to Explain Coincidences. Many events simply happen by chance; chance and randomness are natural aspects of our everyday world and are much more likely to occur than people think (Falk, 1981). Most people, however, do not appreciate the prevalence of randomness and readily offer explanations for events that are actually a result of chance. "Subjects appear to underestimate the ease with which virtually *any* outcomes, even mutually contradictory ones, can adequately be explained. They underestimate their own fecundity as causal theorists, and hence are overly convinced of the veridicality of their beliefs by the ease with which they were able to postulate relevant causal linkages" (Einhorn, 1980a, p. 28). Our need for control encourages a search for explanations for events that offer an illusion of control (Langer, 1975). One of the problems with offering explanations is that they influence what we see and assume on subsequent occasions, even when they are incorrect.

Outcomes that are really the result of chance tend to be attributed to personal characteristics such as skill or its lack. For example, Langer (1975) found that subjects who selected a lottery ticket insisted on more money to buy back their tickets ($8.67) than did subjects who had been handed a ticket ($1.96). This illustrates a basic confusion about chance, skill, and responsibility.

Vividness. Clinicians are influenced by the vividness of events in ways that produce inaccurate inferences. People who are unusually prominent in some way are more likely to be considered to have a causal role. Someone who is visually prominent in a discussion is viewed as having an influential role in the outcome of the discussion (Taylor & Fiske, 1975). We tend to seek causes (attributions for events), especially when our expectations are not confirmed (Weiner, 1985). The proximity of one event to another may lead us to believe that a causal relationship exists. The effects of repeated affirmation of a point and the use of emotional terms on judgments offer additional examples of the role of vividness (see Chapter Five). If a suspected murderer is called a "vicious killer," we may more readily believe that he was responsible for the alleged crimes. Clinicians tend to select their most vivid case examples when discussing causal attribution. Such biased selection (attempted proof by selected instances) may result in incorrect inferences. Events that have only a small probability (that is, they occur rarely) tend to be overestimated (Tversky & Kahneman, 1981). If a rare event is associated with a particularly negative outcome, it may receive undue attention. As Elstein (1988) points out, it is often difficult to separate probability and utility.

Ignoring Consensus Information. Information about how many people act a certain way is often disregarded when trying to determine why a particular person acts in a certain manner. For example, in Milgram's study of obedience (1963), data on the percentage of subjects who delivered high shocks to people had little impact on judgments made by individual subjects; even though they knew that delivering high shocks was the modal response, they still made strong negative dispositional inferences about people who delivered high shocks (Miller, Gillen, Schenker, & Radlove, 1973). Information about normative behavior may be dismissed even though such information would be helpful. Consensus information is also underutilized in self-perception. Subjects who were informed that feelings of depression such as the "Sunday blues" were the rule not the exception were no less inclined to inaccurately attribute their mood to personal inadequacy and weakness (Nisbett, Borgida, Crandall, & Reed, 1976). Nisbett and Ross (1980) suggest that consensus information is ignored because it is less vivid than information about events or people.

In a false consensus effect, we make the assumption that the percentage of people who would act and believe as we would is higher than it actually is. The more other people's behavior differs from our own, the more likely we are to regard their behavior as unusual and as revealing of personal dispositions (Ross, Greene, & House, 1977). The tendency to associate with people who are similar and the greater ease of recalling our own beliefs and actions encourage this false consensus. Since the practice of many clinicians involves individuals who are quite different from themselves, such effects are likely to encourage incorrect inferences of pathology.

The Self-Fulfilling Prophecy. There is a self-fulfilling prophecy—our expectations influence what befalls us. Clinicians often have advance descriptions of a client, perhaps from a referral source or case record. These descriptions may create expectations about a client, which then influence the exchange that occurs. For example, consider the study by Snyder, Tanke, and Berscheid (1977) in which men were asked to speak to an unknown woman over the phone. Men in one group were told that the woman was very attractive; the men in the other group were told that she was unattractive. After speaking to the woman, they rated the woman on a number of traits. The conversations were recorded, and the interactions were rated by observers who could hear only the man or only the woman and knew nothing about the attractiveness manipulation. The observers rated the "attractive woman" as being more confident and more animated, enjoying the conversation, and liking the partner. The "unattractive woman" was rated as more sensitive, trusting, kind, genuine, and modest. Men who were told they were speaking to an "attractive woman" were rated as more sociable, sexually warm, interesting, independent, permissive, bold, outgoing, humorous, socially adept, and pleased with the conversation. These results indicated that the men behaved differently in the two different conditions.

Snyder and Thomsen (1988) suggest that self-fulfilling prophecies are especially likely to occur in situations of unequal power, such as therapist-client relationships. That is, many clients can readily be persuaded that the therapist's impressions are accurate (Keisner, 1985). Some clients may even fall in love with their therapists or develop a dependence on them, which increases the probability of accepting views presented by therapists.

Overconfidence. Clinicians are usually overconfident of their causal assumptions; this overconfidence discourages a search for disconfirming data. Einhorn (1980a) believes that overconfidence "is a result of the way in which feedback is used to evaluate and learn from judgmental accuracy" (p. 2). This raises questions about what is learned from experience. The main effect of experience may be to support inaccurate assumptions due to the nature of the feedback provided—it could be irrelevant or inaccurate (see Chapter Ten). For example, clinicians often rely on their experience in judging the value of intervention methods. Feedback available is often limited or irrelevant, allowing no opportunity to check the accuracy of decisions. Personnel managers, for example, do not see how applicants they reject would have performed. Customs inspectors do not know about "false negatives"—travelers who had illegal or declarable goods and who passed through customs unnoticed—and are thus overconfident of their skills in spotting contraband. Clinicians usually do not find out how effective other intervention methods would have been with a client.

Confusing Naming and Explaining. Naming (offering a diagnosis for an observed pattern of behavior) is often confused with explaining. That is, it is assumed that because something has been named, it has also been explained (see discussion of empathic "explanations" in Chapter Two). This is rarely the case in the field of psychology, although it may be so in the field of medicine (such as when a physician determines that a patient has tuberculosis). Pseudoexplanations involve a confusion of naming and explaining and can result in frustration because, although helpful data now seem to be on hand about how to resolve a clinical question, in fact, none has been added.

Partiality in the Use of Evidence—The Confirmation Bias. Attending to only some important data and overlooking other data is perhaps the most common source of error in clinical decision making. Studies of decision making in medicine show that physicians who are not accurate tend to discount evidence that contradicts a favored hypothesis (Elstein and others, 1978). New information is assigned to a favored hypothesis rather than offering a new causal account that could more effectively account for this data (Elstein et al., 1978). This tendency is referred to as conservatism or overinterpretation. Diagnoses based on the DSM-III-R (*Diagnostic and Statistical Manual of Mental Disorders,* 1987) are usually made as a result of attending to two or three prototypic characteristics (Horowitz, French, Lapid, & Weckler, 1982). Other characteristics that may not be in accord with decisions may be ignored. Vested interest in a view compromises the ability to weight evidence and sample data objectively. For example, research that offers mixed evidence in relation to a favored hypothesis increases belief in initial views (Lord, Ross, and Lepper, 1979). Decisions made by journal reviewers of manuscripts are in the direction of preferred practice theories (Mahoney, 1977). Nor are researchers immune to the influence of their assumptions and elaborate precautions are taken to avoid this influence. The study of experimenter effects has yielded a great deal of information about such influences (Rosenthal, 1988).

The belief that there is only one cause of behavior when there are many may result in faulty causal assumptions. The best-guess strategy, in which complex situations are simplified by ignoring or discounting uncertainties, encourages this source of error. Consider, for example, depression. Often both personal and environmental factors are related to depression, and recent research indicates that the probability of relapse can be predicted by five factors (Krantz & Moos, 1988). Ignoring important causative factors decreases the likelihood of successful intervention. The use of predigested thinking (see Chapter Five) and the tendency to think in either/or terms (see Chapter Seven) involve misguided parsimony.

Confusing Content and Structure. Errors may occur because of confusion between content and structure. Content may differ while structure remains the same; research indicates that this is difficult to appreciate (Einhorn, 1980a). The distinction between form (the typology of a behavior) and function (what maintains the behavior, why it occurs) is a basic one in some practice theories, such as applied behavior analysis (Martin & Pear, 1988). This error is less likely to occur when practice theories that emphasize this distinction are used.

The design of clinical training programs may encourage the

confusion of content and structure Many courses are organized around problems—problems of aging, anxiety, depression, family violence, and so on. This curricular arrangement may discourage recognition of similar structures underlying diverse problems. For example, many graduate programs do not require students to take a course in basic behavioral principles, in terms of potential application, that cuts across all problem areas. This is not to say, for example, that specialized content about developmental tasks at different ages is unimportant. There are no courses in the physics department on the physics of refrigerators, the physics of air conditioners, and so forth, because there is agreement on a certain core of structural relationships (Blalock, 1984).

Other Sources of Error. Subtle differences in how problems are framed (for example, to avoid negative events or to achieve positive benefits), how questions are posed, and how responses are gathered (such as either by closed or open questions) can influence judgments (Fischhoff, Slovic, & Lichtenstein, 1980). This highlights the difficulty in clarifying client preferences. The particular scale that is used to assess a client may influence decisions. For example, scales allowing only bipolar answers (yes or no) may yield different decisions from those that allow a wider range of answers; open interviews yield different answers from interviews using multiple-choice questions (Slovic, Fischhoff, & Lichtenstein, 1982a). Gains or losses that are certain are weighed more heavily than those that are uncertain. Linguistic factors, such as different surface wordings of identical problems, influence judgments. An event is more likely to be selected as a cause if it is presented as the subject of a sentence than as the object (Pryor & Kriss, 1977). "Thus, Sue is more likely to be identified as the causal agent in her preference for a restaurant if subjects are told that she likes the restaurant than if they are told that the restaurant is liked by Sue" (Nisbett & Ross, 1980, p. 127). The influence of surface wordings on clinical judgments has not been investigated. However, there is every reason to suppose that such influences occur in clinical practice as they do in other settings.

Inconsistent use of rules may result in errors. A rule may be used appropriately in some instances but be overlooked in other situations in which it would be helpful. This tendency towards inconsistency offers an advantage to actuarial methods of prediction compared with clinical inference (see Chapter Ten). Errors may occur because areas of uncertainty are overlooked or ignored. Sources of uncertainty in clinical practice include potential effectiveness of intervention methods, validity of measures, and longevity of gains. Causal inferences may be incorrect because premises are untrue or because the form of the argument is incorrect. The factual soundness of an argument (its plausibility) as well as its logical soundness must be considered (see Chapter Six).

It is easy to ignore nonoccurrences (events that do not occur); they are not vivid (Nisbett & Ross, 1980). Such information tends to be overlooked when it can be of crucial importance. Consider, for example, the case in which Sherlock Holmes noted the importance of the fact that a dog did not bark at an intruder because this indicated that the dog knew the intruder. Attention may be focused on situations in which excessive drinking occurs; situations in which it does not occur may be ignored. This biased focus encourages an overemphasis on problems and limits understanding of situations in which problematic drinking does not occur. Both clinicians and researchers tend to ignore areas in which parents of developmentally disabled children cope well (Jacobson & Humphrey, 1979; Kazak & Marvin, 1984). Yet another source of error is primacy effects; we tend to be influenced by what is first heard or read.

A Dispositional Bias

Clinicians make decisions about what the problem is, where it lies, and what causes it. Although some writers make a distinction between causal attributions (what caused a problem) and locus attributions (where the problem lies), these two kinds of attributions could also be viewed as causes at different points in time. Dispositional bias refers to the tendency to attribute the cause and locus of problems to the client rather than to environmental events or to the interaction of personal and environmental factors (see earlier discussion of the fundamental attribution error). The dispositional bias of clinicians has received a great deal of attention. The following discussion of factors related to this source of error is based on Batson, O'Quin, and Pych (1982). Four factors involve characteristics of the observer (the clinician) and three result from being in a helper role.

1. *In their role as an observer, clinicians tend to focus on the client.* It is the client who is interviewed; the client is salient in the interview context, and such focus encourages dispositional attributions. Many studies support this. For example, Storms (1973) found that when observers of an interaction were shown a replay of the situation from a participant's point of view, they made more situational attributions. In another study, undergraduates listened to an audiotape of a peer-counseling session (Snyder, Shenkel, & Schmidt, 1976). The client depicted on the tape presented her problem as being related to her situation. Her problem was viewed as more situational by observers asked to take the client's role and was viewed in more dispositional terms by subjects instructed to take the role of a peer counselor. "These results are quite consistent with the suggestion that people who identify with the helper role are prone to adopt an observer set and, as a result, to make more dispositional attributions" (Batson, O'Quin, and Pych, 1982, p. 65).

2. *Information gathered is selective, or the "office bound helper."* Many counselors see their clients only in the office, which may result in incorrect assumptions about the consistency of behavior. They do not see clients in other situations in which behavior may differ considerably from that seen in the interview. Behavior that is the direct result of the unusual situation of being in a client role may be inaccurately assumed to reflect behavior in other situations. It is still common for agency policy to prohibit home visits. Reasons offered for this policy include the views that (1) clients should be motivated for treatment (that is, motivation is shown by their willingness to come to the agency) and (2) observation in the home does not offer helpful information because of reactive effects caused by the presence of the observer. Even when home visits do occur, the sample of behavior gathered may be small, and little care

may be exercised to ensure that a representative sample is gathered. This is not to say that real-life observation is always relevant or ethical. It is to say that, even though it might be both relevant and ethical, it is often not used as a source of assessment information (see Chapter Eight). For example, in some agencies, one clinician may see a child and another clinician may see the child's parents. This is still common practice—one that discounts the mutual influence processes between children and their parents.

3. *Practice theories influence attributions.* The preferred practice theories of many clinicians encourage dispositional attributions. Many clinicians favor a sign approach to assessment, in which behaviors are viewed as signs of hypothetical internal dispositions. This contrasts with a sample approach to assessment in which behaviors are viewed as important in their own right as a sample of a broader class of actions. Compared to behaviorally oriented clinicians, psychodynamically oriented clinicians viewed a person as significantly more maladjusted and viewed his problems in more dispositional terms when the person was labeled a patient than when he was referred to as a job applicant (Langer & Abelson, 1974). The label "patient" created a dispositional bias on the part of psychodynamically oriented counselors.

4. *Situational information provided by the client is discounted.* Information that clients provide about situations related to their problems may be discounted. In fact, Batson and his colleagues (1982) believe that counselors are especially likely to discount information that suggests the problem is situational. They identify three factors that contribute to this tendency. First, clinicians are aware of people's tendency to make situational attributions for their behaviors, and there may be an attempt to correct for this bias by emphasizing dispositional causes. Second, labels and diagnoses applied to clients encourage dispositional attributions by compromising the client's credibility as a provider of accurate information. A clinician may have read in a case record that a client has a history of being hospitalized for schizophrenia and subsequently emphasize personal limitations as causal factors. Many studies illus-

trate the influence of third-party information on clinical decisions. In a study that Batson (1975) conducted, counselors who
received information that a client had low scores on self-
awareness and high scores on manipulation made fewer situational attributions, even though this client presented evidence
that the problem was situational. Third, offering a situational
attribution for a problem is usually less damaging to one's self-
esteem. Thus, a client who blames a problem on the situation
may be assumed to be acting in his own best interest and, for
this reason, his statements may be discounted.

5. *Professional training encourages dispositional attributions.*
   Trained helpers are more likely to make dispositional attributions concerning clients' problems than are untrained helpers.
   Batson and his colleagues (1982) found this true of different
   types of helpers, for example, clinicial psychologists as well as
   social workers. They conclude that there is "a pervasive tendency for trained helpers, however trained, to perceive clients'
   problems as more dispositional than do people without training" (p. 69). As the authors note, such differences in attribution
   may be due to selection effects (people who are prone to make
   such attributions choose helper roles) rather than to socialization effects of training.

6. *Calling a healthy person sick is less serious than calling a sick
   person healthy.* Clinicians are supposed to protect society from
   people who may be dangerous. Physicians are trained to be
   conservative; they are trained that it is better to call a healthy
   person sick than to call a sick person healthy. If a social worker
   attributes child abuse to dispositional characteristics of a
   mother and removes a child, at least the child will not be
   harmed by the parent (although harm may result from the foster parents and/or from the trauma of separation). On the other
   hand, if a situational cause is assumed (such as stress, which
   could be relieved) and the child is left in the home and abused,
   there may be an uproar in the press. In this kind of situation,
   possible problems with other living situations such as the foster
   home are much less vivid at the point of making a decision
   about whether to remove a child, since the foster home situation is often unknown. On the other hand, the injuries to the

child, the child's reactions to these injuries, and a parent who may be uncooperative and angry are all very vivid.

7. *Resources available relate mostly to changing the client.* Batson and his colleagues (1982) argue that helpers want to succeed but are aware that success is more likely if they change the client's situation. However, they realize that often this will not be possible. This is especially true in social work, in which many problems are related to environmental problems over which social workers have little control, such as poor housing, poor education, lack of day care, and unemployment. So helpers concentrate instead on dispositional accounts; accounts that may enable them to help. Batson, O'Quin, and Pych (1982) base their views on the assumption that clinicians believe that they are better able to help with dispositional than with situational problems. They cite three reasons for their beliefs. One is that helpers have more immediate access to clients than to their clients' environments. A second reason is that changing the environment is more difficult: "to change a sick situation may involve legal or political action affecting many people and costing much money and time" (p. 71). The third reason is that the helping resources that are available are geared toward personal rather than situational problems. "The majority of our societal resources are directed toward helping individuals adapt to their social environments; far fewer are directed toward changing the social environments that breed poverty, crime, depression, and despair" (p. 71).

Research exploring the influence of attributions for client's problems indicates that available resources do influence attributions for problems. For example, in a study carried out by Batson, Jones, and Cochran (1979), some of the subjects received a list of referral sources that emphasized the dispositional nature of problems, such as a mental hospital, a residential treatment center, a mental health clinic, group therapy, and a family counseling service. Other subjects received a list of resources emphasizing environmental contributors, such as a career information center, an ombudsman, and a community coalition. Subjects who received the former list were more likely to view the client's problems in dispositional terms. Again, vividness is an influential factor: the client's presence compared with an unseen environment. This tendency is compounded by the fact that many clinicians are not trained how to carry out contingency analyses in order to identify environmental factors that contribute to problems (Martin & Pear, 1988). Not having such skills, the influence of environmental contingencies may be overlooked. The long-term effects of decisions made based on resources available produces a vicious cycle; the more problems are viewed in dispositional terms, the more services compatible with this view will be requested.

Use and Misuse of Intuition

One definition of intuition is "the direct knowing or learning of something without the conscious use of reasoning; immediate apprehension or understanding" (*Websters New World Dictionary*, 1988). Investigation of creative insights shows that these occur in the context of immersion in a task, although they may be attributed to other causes (Weisberg, 1986). That is, a particular problem has been the focus of attention for some time, and there is an active restructuring of understanding (Greeno, 1989). Intuition refers to reliance on insight as well as on appeals to immediate apprehension. When asked, for instance, "How do you know that?" or "What made you decide to use X rather than Y?" one's answer may be "I based it on intuition." Intuition involves a "responsiveness to information that is not consciously represented, but which nevertheless guides inquiry toward productive and often profound insights" (Bowers, 1987, p. 73; see also Polanyi, 1958; Pollio, 1979). This view is compatible with the differences Dreyfus and Dreyfus (1986) found between experts and novices. That is, experts have internalized rules and cues that they may no longer be able to describe. It is this lack of awareness of knowledge used that encourages attributions for productive solutions to intuition.

One of the ways in which clinicians sell themselves short is to attribute wise judgments to their intuition. When clinicians are asked how they knew that a certain intervention would work, they might answer, "intuition." Pressed by requests for further explanation, they may describe reasons that reflect knowledge of content and appropriate inference rules. That is, far more than intuition in the form of uninformed hunches was involved; practice-related knowledge of content and procedures was used. Attributing sound judgments to intuition may undermine confidence and decrease opportunities to teach clinical skills.

When intuition is used in place of reliance on empirical information, what "feels right" is relied on, rather than what has been shown to be true. This error is the reverse of one described above. There is no doubt that knowledge related to clinical practice is fragmentary, forcing clinicians to rely on practice theories and creative application of these theories to fill in the gaps. However, the sole reliance on intuition is questionable, especially when material that has empirical support is available (see discussion of actuarial versus clinical prediction in Chapter Ten).

Problems with Memory

Clinicians rely on their memory when processing and organizing data. Familiarity with the limitations of memory will be helpful in avoiding errors. One reason memory may be imperfect is that events are not accurately noted in the first place. Many clinicians are not trained how to carefully observe interaction; to identify specific behaviors, as well as related cues and consequences. Lack of training increases the likelihood of biased observation.

Just because a sequence of events is accurately observed does not mean that the memory of these events will remain accurate. Distortions may creep in over time. "With the passage of time, with proper motivation, with the introduction of special kinds of interfering facts, the memory traces may change or seem sometimes to change or become transformed" (Loftus, 1980, p. 37). This can result in memories of things that never happened. Errors of construction occur; some details about an experience are accurately recalled, but we use inferences that may not be correct to fill in gaps in our memory and to create what seem to be logical sequences of action. We then imagine that we really saw these events. We thus have artificial memories. The illusion of having a memory of an event can be created by including inaccurate descriptive data in a question. For example, studies in which subjects viewed a film of an event such as a car accident and later received new information about the accident changed their description of the event (Loftus, 1980, p. 46).

Events may be forgotten because of interference from other similar memories or because information cannot be retrieved. Thus, effective retrieval skills are important. Another possibility is motivated forgetting, in which negative events are forgotten and positive events remembered. For example, happy times from a vacation tend to be recalled and sad times tend to be forgotten (Loftus, 1980, p. 71). Gamblers tend to remember instances when they have won and to forget about the times when they lost. Clinicians tend to recall their successes and to forget their failures. Moreover, sometimes memory is not stored in the first place. High anxiety interferes with remembering events; high arousal decreases attention to detail so that events may not be noticed. Drugs and alcohol also affect memory. Considerable attention has been devoted to the discovery of strategies to jog memory. Methods used to detect weak memories include multiple probes, use of different question forms, hypnosis, and monetary incentives (Hall, Loftus, & Tousignant, 1984) (see Chapter 3 for guidelines for improving memory).

Improving the Accuracy of Causal Assumptions

There are differences as well as overlaps in recommendations made in the many different programs that have been designed to increase problem-solving skills (Nickerson, Perkins, & Smith, 1985). Guidelines often suggested include the following (Fischhoff, 1982; Greeno, 1989; Rubenstein, 1975):

- Get the total picture
- Withhold judgment
- Use models
- Change representation; restructure situations
- Ask helpful questions
- Develop facilitating beliefs about knowledge, thinking, and learning (see Chapter Three)
- Be willing to doubt

Tools and rules of thumb that can be used to improve the accuracy of causal assumptions are described in the sections that follow. These share a focus of becoming self-conscious about the nature of the reasoning process used; they help to make implicit processes explicit so that assumptions can be examined. The suggestions described often involve self-regulatory metacognitive questions (such as, "What's missing?" or "Do I need more information?") and prompts (such as, "Stop and think") (see, for example, Brown & Campione, 1981). Many decision aids help to simplify problems; others encourage identification of alternative explanations.

Take Advantage of Helpful Tools. Tools that can be helpful in understanding problems and highlighting important content include diagrams, models, and graphs. All involve writing down some representation of a problem. Depiction of a problem is a good indication of how well it is comprehended (Greeno, 1978). Some problems that are quite difficult may be easily solved with the aid of diagrams (see, for example, Hayes, 1981). Drawing a graph of the presumed relationship between two events or making a contingency table can help identify assumptions and alternative possibilities. Tree structures can be used to describe the relationships among different variables as shown in Figure 4. Statistical tools are of value (see, for example, Wolf, Gruppen, and Bills, 1985), as are computer programs (see, for example, Hand, 1985).

Flow charts and algorithms can be used to aid decision making. These illustrate the sequence of steps involved in making a decision and highlight the data needed at each point. Venn diagrams provide a helpful aid for analysis of arguments (Bransford and Stein, 1984, p. 80). Consider two arguments. Argument 1 is (1) some theories that have been criticized have turned out to be valid; (2) my theory is being criticized; (3) therefore, it could turn out to be valid. Argument 2 is (1) some theories that have been criticized have turned out to be valid; (2) my theory is being criticized; (3) therefore, it is valid. The Venn diagram in Figure 5 indicates that argument 2 is not logically sound.

Statistical methods can be used to increase accuracy. Once it is mastered (which can be a rapid process in effective training pro-

Figure 4. Nine Psychiatric Categories from DSM-II.

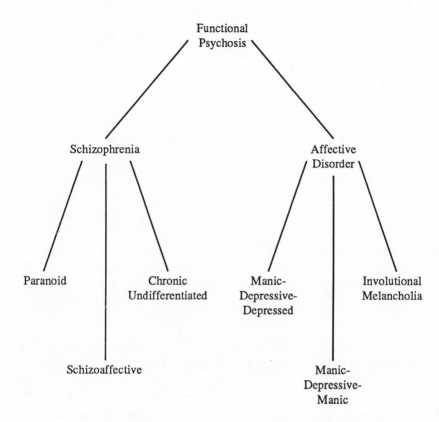

Source: "'Everyday' Versus Normative Models of Clinical and Social Judgment," by N. Cantor. From *Integration of Clinical and Social Psychology* (p. 31) by G. Weary and H. L. Mirels (Eds.). (1982). New York: Oxford University Press. Copyright 1982 by Oxford University Press. Reprinted by permission.

grams), statistical reasoning can be more efficient and more accurate than intuitive reasoning (Nisbett, Krantz, Jepson, & Kunda, 1983).

Make Assumptions Explicit. Clinicians often do not make their assumptions explicit, and so they cannot examine them to determine their plausibility. Drawing cognitive maps of perceived

Figure 5. Examples of the Use of Venn Diagrams to Analyze Arguments.

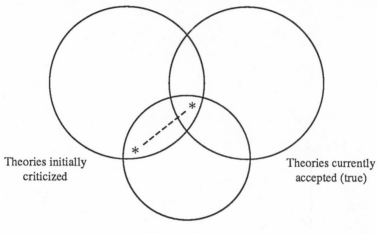

Theories initially
criticized

Theories currently
accepted (true)

Theories like mine

Source: From *The IDEAL Problem Solver* (p. 80) by J. D. Bransford and B. S. Stein, 1984, New York: Freeman. Copyright 1984 by W. H. Freeman and Company. Reprinted by permission.

interrelationships among concepts may be helpful in clarifying implicit conceptual structures that influence clinical practice (Novak & Gowin, 1984).

Clearly Define Relevant Events. Clinical decisions often involve estimating probabilities, for example, the likelihood that a client's depression is related to recent environmental changes. Probabilities cannot be determined—even off the cuff, unless relevant events are clearly defined. It is important to clearly describe the factors involved, such as the exact nature of recent environmental changes. Clear description of presenting problems and related factors is critical in accurately identifying the factors related to vague presenting problems such as depression, anxiety, and poor communication (Wolpe, 1986).

Inquire About Values and Goals in Different Ways. In view of tendencies of many clients to match the goals and values of their therapists and other sources of behavioral confirmations in the counseling process and in view of the influence of subtle differences such as question wording and order on the expression of preferences, a variety of methods of inquiry should be used, rather than only one method of inquiry that may result in inaccurate accounts (see, for example, Osborn, 1963).

Restate (Redefine) the Problem. Redefining problems is especially useful with ill-defined goals. For example, if a clinician has accepted a client's goal of "being happier" but feels stymied as to how to pursue this goal, realization that this goal is the outcome of a number of different behaviors and situations encourages a focus on arranging these changes rather than on the desired consequence of being happier.

Use Multiple Metaphors and Analogies. Different kinds of metaphors and analogies can be used to simplify problems and to avoid a fixedness on one kind of problem structure or view that hinders solution of a problem.

Decrease Compartmentalization. Practice in clinical problem solving with a focus on the process as well as the product encourages generalization of helpful skills. Questions that encourage generalization of content and procedural knowledge from one domain to another include "How could I apply that to this?" and "Could I use that to understand this problem?"

Use Effective Troubleshooting Skills. Skill in troubleshooting is one of the competency clusters that distinguishes effective from ineffective problem solvers. Setbacks and mistakes are responded to as opportunities to use task-focused skills, such as asking questions that will be helpful in getting unstuck (for example, "How can I break this down into smaller steps?" "What is it I need to know here?" "How can information be rearranged here?").

Cultivate Positive Moods. Salovey and Turk (1988) review research that suggests the mood of the therapist influences the decisions made. Negative moods tend to encourage a focus on negative events and may thus encourage clinicians to pathologize clients. They also note possible biasing effects of positive moods, such as underplaying the severity of concerns and encouraging clients to take risks they are not ready for. However, given the research which suggests that many clinicians err in seeing too much pathology and given that positive support and belief in client's options for achieving desired outcomes facilitates progress, if one has to err, a positive bias is better—it would result in the fewest, least damaging errors (see Chapter Two). Turk and Salovey (1986) suggest the use of a bias innoculation procedure in which clinicians receive experience in how their moods influence their memories. Clinicians could briefly reflect on their mood before each interview as a check on possible bias and as a cue to alter their mood or at least be aware of it. Mood could be noted in a log to identify mood-generated influences on work with clients.

Use Helpful Rules of Thumb. Rules of thumb that can be useful in avoiding errors in causal assumptions are described below.

1. *Look for alternative explanations.* Causal assumptions may be retained even though they do not fit the data, as illustrated in the failure of debriefing described in Chapter Three (see also Ross and Lepper, 1980). The rule to "never rely on one way of asking" (Edwards & Von Winterfeldt, 1986, p. 657) can be used in counteracting this tendency. Incomplete or inaccurate causal assumptions may be discovered by the search for alternative explanations; this search will help to counteract tendencies to (1) focus on cues that direct attention to the obvious (cues to causality) and (2) look only for evidence that confirms favored assumptions. Bromley (1977) recommends inclusion of a heading *Alternative Accounts* in case records to encourage this kind of search.

2. *Pay attention to sources of uncertainty.* Clinical decisions are made in a context of uncertainty. Overlooking uncertainty does not make it go away. Decisions are more likely to be accurate if sources of uncertainty are recognized. Often, steps can be taken to decrease this (see Chapter Eight) such as attending to the error rate of tests.

3. *Attend to negative information.* Clinicians often discount
    contradictory information. This tendency highlights the value
    of attending to disconfirming or negative information. Let's
    say that a psychologist believes that problems with children are
    always related to marital difficulties and is confronted with a
    family in which no evidence of marital difficulties can be
    found. Reasons to discount this lack of evidence may be readily
    created. It may be said, "They *seem* happy, but there really are
    problems—I just haven't found them," rather than using neg-
    ative data to question initial assumptions. The assumption
    that some effect always occurs usually oversimplifies a prob-
    lem. Although in many cases marital problems may accom-
    pany child problems, in other instances this may not be so.
4. *Attend to environmental causes.* The influence of environmen-
    tal variables often is overlooked, resulting in incorrect selection
    of treatment methods (see earlier discussion of the dispositional
    bias). Using a rule of thumb to explore the possible role of
    environmental variables related to presenting problems reduces
    this tendency. Inclusion of a title *Environmental Causes* on
    case record forms can be a useful reminder. Since environmen-
    tal causes tend to be noted more frequently from the actor's per-
    spective than from the observer's perspective, making it a habit
    to view clinically relevant events from the client's point of view
    may help the clinician discover environmental contributions to
    presenting problems (Jordan, Harvey, & Weary, 1988; Regan &
    Totten, 1975). Using different sources of assessment data also
    helps counteract the fundamental attribution error, especially
    if observation in real-life settings is used. Reliance on self-
    report alone encourages a dispositional bias (see Chapter
    Eight).
5. *Examine all four cells of contingency tables.* Errors in assump-
    tions about causes often occur because attention is focused on
    one cell (usually the positive-positive cell) of a four-cell contin-
    gency table.
6. *Ask "what if."* Asking "what if" questions should help the
    clinician avoid errors due to premature closure about causes.
    Questions that could be asked include: "What if X caused Y,
    rather than Y caused X?" or "What if X had never happened,

would Y still have occurred?" If alternative explanations can readily be offered, the original account given is questionable.

Summary

A key aspect of clinical practice is identification of the cause of presenting problems. Effective searches for the causes of client concerns require clear thinking skills as well as creativity and imagination. Practice theories guide both the collection and the processing of data in this search. Causal analysis in clinical contexts involves the integration of different kinds of data, a task we are not very good at. Clinicians can take advantage of a variety of heuristics (rules of thumb) to decrease the mental effort involved. Research on clinical decision making indicates that hypotheses about presenting problems are arrived at quite early and that, although a great deal of data is collected, decisions are based on a modest amount of data; that is, we do not use all the data gathered. Decisions are influenced by irrelevant as well as by relevant data.

Assumptions about covariations—what events go together and how strongly they are associated—affect causal assumptions. Errors that are common in assessing how closely two or more events are related include failing to attend to nonoccurrences, preconceptions about which events are related, and attempted proof by selected instances (attending to observed rather than relative frequency). Here, too, in assessing covariations and making causal assumptions, clinicians are influenced by availability and representativeness. The fundamental attribution error in which causes are mistakenly attributed to the client rather than to situational variables is especially common in clinical practice. Clinicians often assume that behavior will be more consistent than it actually is; that is, the variability of behavior in different situations is overlooked. In searching for the relationship between personal characteristics and environmental variables and presenting problems, we tend to give undue attention to the present–present cell of contingency tables, the cell that represents having both the presumed important characteristic and the problem. This results in overestimates of pathology.

An interest in control over the environment encourages a

readiness to offer explanations for chance occurrences. Clinicians are influenced by vivid events, which gain undue attention in terms of their causative role and are often misled, by the consistency of data, into giving undue weight to sources of evidence that are actually related to each other. Clinicians tend to be overconfident of the assumptions they propose. They often underestimate their knowledge and attribute wise decisions to their intuition (one of the hallmarks of becoming expert in a field is difficulty in identifying exactly how one arrived at a decision). An important distinction here is between this kind of intuition and the kind that relies on "inspiration without perspiration"; that is, intuition that is *not* based on knowledge of content and procedure.

Research concerning sources of error in assessing covariations and making causal assumptions can be used to suggest guidelines for improving accuracy. Such guidelines include making assumptions explicit, searching for alternative explanations, and taking advantage of tools such as diagrams, algorithms, notes, and computer programs.

10

Predictions About Clients and Treatment Effectiveness: Improving the Odds

Making choices and predictions is a routine part of clinical practice. Choices are made between different constructions of presenting problems, different intervention methods, and different outcomes to pursue. These choices involve implicit or explicit predictions as to which alternatives are best.

Many kinds of predictions are made in clinical practice. Some concern what clients will do in the future, such as: Will this man rape again if released from jail? Will a client kill herself over the weekend? Will this father participate in treatment plans? Other predictions concern the potential effectiveness of intervention methods: Will play therapy work here? Will symbolic or in vivo desensitization be most effective? How long will positive gains be maintained?

Decisions about which type of intervention to use should be based on (1) predictions about a client's likely future in response to different procedures or without any intervention and (2) an evaluation of the desirability of each alternative (Runyan, 1977). Often, there is no access to the former two kinds of data. Different kinds of effects that are important to consider include short-term versus long-term consequences and effects on clients, as well as on their significant others. A program may help an individual but do nothing to alter societal conditions that contribute to a problem. For clinicians who work in agencies, vague policies allow a wide range of individual discretion in making choices in accord with each clinician's unique view of justice and value. Predictions are intimately connected with causal assumptions and typically involve the prediction of some clinical variable of interest, such as prognosis or recidivism based on a number of predictors, such as history, age, and quality of social support available. "Other things being equal, the greater the predictive validity of some variable, the greater its causal relevance" (Einhorn & Hogarth, 1985, p. 320). The correlation coefficient often is used as a measure of predictive validity. Possible misinterpretations of correlations were discussed in Chapter Nine. Predictions differ in complexity and the nature of feedback to check their accuracy. The more complex they are, the more likely it is they can be made only with aids such as Bayes's Theorem (see later discussion). The more vague and delayed the feedback is, the less help it offers in improving future predictions. Unlike medical practice in which the outcome of a decision often can be checked against a pathologist's report, there is often no agreed upon criterion in psychological prediction. Clinicians disagree about the criteria that should be used to assess the effectiveness of therapy.

Measures used to make predictions include self-reports, test scores, ratings based on observation, and impressions gathered in interviews. Problems of reliability may be overlooked when evaluating the usefulness of data. For instance, one might assume that a small difference in scores reflects a true difference when, in fact, the difference is a result of an unreliable measure. This might result in inaccurate classification of clients (such as assuming that clients are clinically depressed when they are not) or faulty selection of an intervention method (for example, deciding to intervene because a measure indicates a pathological condition when, in fact, no such condition exists). The predictive accuracy of a measure, such as a suicide potential scale, is often unknown. Judgments are made under considerable uncertainty in attempts to maximize some values while minimizing associated costs. How much we value an outcome is often confused with the probability that it will occur (Elstein, 1988). It is not surprising, given the high degree of uncertainty in making predictions and choices, that clinicians often protest that they really do not make any predictions or that they avoid them through delay, inattention, or refusal (Corbin, 1980). The tendency to put off difficult decisions was one of the major reasons for the development of permanency planning procedures in child welfare—procedures designed to encourage social workers to arrive at a case plan for children in a timely manner (Stein & Gambrill, 1985).

Explanations do not necessarily yield predictions, and predictions may not yield accurate explanations even when the predictions are accurate. Some treatment procedures in medicine are effective but the process through which success is achieved is unknown. An explanation may be implemented in a variety of ways. For example, a prediction about whether an individual will pursue a given course of action may not be possible even though considerable information is available about a person's developmental history. Consider, for example, the following case report (based on Pilpel, 1976; Morgan, 1984).

Caseworker's Report

SUBJECT: The "C" Family

1. R. C., male, age forty-three. Unstable personality. Irregular employment during last eight years; frequently makes unreasonable demands of employer and threatens to resign. Very bitter toward former co-workers. Easily irritated. Has minimal contact with his children, but evinces marked hostility toward eldest son. Appears to be in poor health. (CONFIDENTIAL: medical records reveal condition of advanced tertiary syphilis, date of infection unknown.)

2. J. C., female, age thirty-eight. Unemployed. Known to have had many extramarital affairs. Estranged from R. C. for a number of years. (CONFIDENTIAL: medical records reveal no sign of venereal infection.) Shows only an erratic interest in her children. Has difficulty handling money matters.

3. W. C., male, age eighteen. Weak constitution; bouts of respiratory illness. Disciplinary problem in schools. Poor student. Frequently fails examinations despite special tutoring. Evinces self-destructive tendencies.

4. J. S. C., male, age twelve. May be son of J. C. and one of her

lovers. Submissive and indecisive. Appears intimidated by rest of family. Does well in school, however. Appears to hero-worship his brother.

ANALYSIS

1. The Cs present clear symptoms of family disintegration. R. C. and J. C. married despite initial strong opposition from the former's parents who did not attend the wedding; latter's parents seem to have been unenthusiastic about the union even though they acquiesced to it. The birth of W.C. seven-and-a-half months after the marriage ceremony did nothing to ameliorate the situation, and his "premature" arrival may be partly responsible, along with Oedipal factors, for R. C.'s obvious hostility to him.

2. Both J. C. and R. C. move in a subculture of sexual promiscuity not at all conducive to family stability. Extramarital adventures appear probable for the period between births of W. C. and J. S. C. and certain for the years following. Cohabitation within the marriage seems to have ceased at least nine or ten years ago.

3. Parental neglect of the children in terms of psychological and emotional nurture has been fairly chronic throughout. It has been aggravated by blatant favoritism toward the younger child on the part of both J. C. and R. C. W. C. shows clear signs of maladjustment. His misbehavior at his first school is said to have become "legendary." In his secondary school he was usually at the bottom of his class. He appears to have repressed his anger (understandable) toward his parents and turned it against himself. Seems prone to depression. Recently he jumped off a thirty-foot high bridge while playing with his brother and a cousin, on the theory, as he explained it, that he would grab onto the top of a nearby fir tree and thereby break his fall. Instead, he fell thirty feet to the bottom of the ravine, rupturing a kidney which caused him to be laid up for six weeks.

4. J. S. C. suffers from a marked lack of self-direction. He tries very hard to please and be agreeable, sensing himself inade-

quate to deal with the three high-powered personalities around him. His autonomy seems seriously impaired.

Prognoses

Poor. R. C.'s health will continue to deteriorate. J. C.'s indiscrete sexual dalliance seems likely to continue also. In any case, the neglect of the children will not abate. J. C. and R. C. essentially lead separate lives now, observing only the formalities of a marriage relationship. Neither has a compelling interest in their sons, and neither seems competent to handle family finances. W. C. seems certain to have further severe problems of adjustment ahead of him, and he is ill-equipped to cope with them. J. S. C. seems to have a chance for healthy development, but he must overcome his timidity and avoid mimicking his bother's dubious exploits.

Summary

For all practical purposes this family has ceased to exist as a viable social unit.
26 September 1893

Updates

R. C. died in 1895.
J. C. died in 1921.
J. S. C. became a stockbroker in 1900.
W. C. became Prime Minister of Great Britain in 1940.

Actuarial Versus Clinical Judgment

Diagnosis and prediction are highly interrelated. That is, predictions concerning the client (such as degree of dangerousness, likelihood of relapse, likelihood that a given intervention method will be successful) are related to how problems and desired outcomes are structured and assumptions about causal factors. For example, responses on the MMPI (as well as other sources of data) may be used to decide whether a client is schizophrenic. This decision may result in selection of a certain intervention option. To be sure, many clinicians do not use test results in their work with clients. Still, whether tests are used or not, different sources of data are considered in thinking about problems and related factors, and clinicians arrive at assessments of their clients in attempting to understand them and they make predictions (implicit or explicit) about the clients' future behavior. Both assessment and prediction require the integration of diverse sources of data and the selection of relevant rather than irrelevant variables. Here many sources of inaccuracy creep in. Prediction involves forward inference (reasoning from present causes to future outcomes), whereas assessment (or diagnostic inference) often involves backward inference (reasoning from symptoms, signs, and so on to prior causes). Assessment and prediction are closely related in that "success in predicting the future depends to a considerable degree on making sense of the past" (Einhorn & Hogarth, 1985, p. 313). Errors in assessment may result in incorrect predictions as a result of a confusion between "diagnostic and prognostic probabilities" (Einhorn, 1988) (see later section on use of test results).

One of the oldest controversies in the field of psychology concerns clinical versus statistical judgment. Meehl's classic book appeared in 1954, and this has been an active area of inquiry since that time. Statistical or actuarial judgment involves the systematic combination of data from a variety of sources, including life history data, test scores, ratings of behavior, and subjective judgments based on information gained during interviews. Judgments are based on empirically determined relationships between sources of data and an outcome such as job success. Clinical judgment also draws on a variety of data sources including impressions gained during interviews; however, judgments are intuitively arrived at on the basis of assumptions that often (if not typically) remain implicit rather than explicit. Meehl (1954) made a persuasive case for the superiority of actuarial methods over intuition, and an even more persuasive case can be made today in relation to many different kinds of judgments. Dawes, Faust, and Meehl (1989) note that there are now over 100 comparative studies in the social sciences and in almost every one, "the actuarial method has equated or surpassed the clinical method" (p. 1669). Areas investigated include diagnosis of medical versus psychiatric disorders; description of personality; and prediction of treatment outcome, violent behavior, and length of hospitalization. Actuarial judgments have been found to be superior to clinical judgments in many areas, even though they rely on linear models for what may be nonlinear relationships among variables. Research to date indicates that in many instances there is no evidence that clinicians can take advantage of additional knowledge that is not captured in linear models, when making predictions that are superior to those based on actuarial methods (Fischhoff, Goitein, & Shapira, 1983).

Clinicians are better at selecting and coding information than they are at integrating it, and this may be one of the reasons why decisions made by actuarial methods are often more accurate than decisions based on clinical inference. It is particularly difficult to combine different sources of information as must be done in clinical contexts in which environmental, medical, psychological, and biological factors all may have to be considered. Fortunately, there are some helpful statistical tools that can be used to integrate different kinds of data (see, for example, later discussion of Bayes's Theorem). The prediction paradigm used in clinical practice assumes a set of predictor variables, which are combined in some way, resulting in a predicted criterion score that is then compared with a criterion score (see Figure 6). This model highlights the complexity of clinical decision making.

Several methods have been used to try to find out how clinicians combine data and which data they use. One method is to ask them to describe what they are doing and why they are doing it as they make decisions. Kleinmuntz (1984) attempted to find out how experts make judgments based on responses on the MMPI. An expert was asked to describe what he was doing and thinking as he evaluated the adjustment of college students from MMPI profiles. A flow chart of rules was derived based on these descriptions, and a computer program was developed. The programs developed following such procedures rely on interpretations made by clinicians: they are "not based on known empirical relationships between predictor and criterion scores" (Wiggins, 1981, pp. 8-9). So these kinds of systems are not actuarial or statistical; they are automated clinical-prediction systems. One problem with this approach is that experts

Figure 6. The Prediction Paradigm.

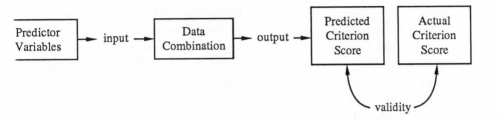

Source: From "Clinical and Statistical Prediction: Where Are We and Where Do We Go from Here?" by J. Wiggins, 1984, *Clinical Psychology Review*, *1*, pp. 4. Copyright 1984 by Pergamon Press. Reprinted by permission.

may not be able to describe how they arrived at decisions (see discussion of experts and novices in Chapter One) or may identify incorrect decision rules and models. That is, expert systems may "incorporate biases and ineffectiveness as well as true expertise" (Elstein, 1988, p. 22).

Another approach is to ask clinicians to review a set of profiles that include a set number of input variables and to predict the criterion status (for example, psychotic) of the individuals who produced these profiles. The values of the data used are reviewed over a series of profiles, and regression weights are determined by correlations. A "bootstrapping" approach can be used to generate programs that make more accurate decisions than the clinicians whose data were used to develop the program. For example, Goldberg (1970) asked clinicians to predict known criterion scores based on a set of profiles. These judgments were then regressed on the input variables to determine a rating system, and the resulting equation was then used as a prediction model to forecast scores on a new sample. This model outperformed the clinicians whose responses were used to create it, probably because it was applied more consistently than were the predictions made by clinicians in the simulated model. Some studies have found that models based on randomly determined regression weights and unit weighting (using coefficients with equal weights) outperform clinical predictions and models based on these (Dawes & Corrigan, 1974; Wainer, 1976). So what has research in this area told us? The summary offered by Wiggins (1981) is sobering: "(a) Is there something special about clinical judgmemt as manifested in *performance*? That is, are clinicians any better or worse than ordinary folk at forecasting uncertain outcomes? (Answer: probably not.) (b) Is there something special about clinicians' judgmental *processes*? That is, are clinicians more or less configural in combining information or do they weight cues differently than do nonprofessionals? (Answer: probably not.) (c) Are the judgmental shortcomings and biases of clinicians distinctively different from those of other professional decision makers? That is, have these *same* shortcomings been demonstrated in groups of stockbrokers, physicians, intelligence analysts, electrical engineers, etc.? (Answer: definitely yes). (d) Given that all of us—laypersons, clinicians and other professionals—are in the same boat, how would you evaluate our characteristic judgmental and inferential strategies with reference to the formal canons of scientific inference? (Answer: C-)" (p. 14).

Certainly there are many areas in which actuarial methods are not available. Still, the question must be asked, what are the implications for clinicians in relation to areas in which actuarial methods are available and have been shown to be superior in accuracy to clinical judgments? The implication in terms of benefits to clients is that they should be used when they are superior to clinical judgments. That is, clinicians can improve the accuracy of their judgments in relation to some decisions by taking advantage of known empirical relationships in combining diverse sources of data. The topic of actuarial versus clinical judgment is a hot one, and those who advocate use of actuarial methods when they are superior in accuracy to clinical inference often are attacked as advocating complete reliance on such methods. This is not what is being argued here nor is this the position of those who have reviewed the literature in this area (for example, Dawes, Faust, & Meehl, 1989).

In the actuarial approach, error is accepted which decreases the likelihood that it will be ignored. Acceptance of error decreases possibilities of lost opportunities for control (assuming there is no way to predict an outcome when there is) and the illusion of control (assuming that predictions can be made when they cannot be made). Consistency is enhanced by use of actuarial methods.

Prediction, Choice, and Probability

Making predictions and choices requires the assessment of probabilities. Probability can be viewed as a quantified opinion. The probability assigned to an event represents a clinician's subjective degree of belief that it will occur and can be expressed on a continuous scale ranging from 0 to 1. Only the end points of the scale are certain; degrees of uncertainty are represented by the points in between. A psychiatrist may predict that there is a 70 percent probability that a patient admitted to a psychiatric emergency service is a danger to others if released. In some cases, information is available about past relative frequencies that can be used to make estimates. More often it is not; probabilities based on reliable statistical data are rarely known in clinical practice. Clinicians must rely on *subjective* probabilities—their estimates of the likelihood of given outcomes that reflect their personal beliefs about the degree of uncertainty related to a decision, such as whether a depressed client will make another suicide attempt in the near future. Typically, they can only guess at the relative importance of different "predictors." Subjectivists would argue that assigning probabilities always requires an interpretation; that there is no such thing as an objective probability (Fischhoff, Goitein, & Shapira, 1983).

Even in areas in which extensive research has been carried out to determine criteria used to make predictions, results are often fragmentary and conflicting and do not offer a great deal of help to decision makers. Research does show that clinicians usually differ in the kinds of data used and in the weighting of these data. One clinician may base predictions on perusal of genograms, whereas another may base them on a contingency analysis of family interactions. Staff who make parole decisions consider different types of data important and view information in different ways (Wilkins, Gottfriedson, Robison, & Sadowsky, 1973). Research suggests that predictions concerning dangerousness are not very accurate (see, for example, Hinton, 1983; Steadman & Cocozza, 1974). Decisions may be influenced by irrelevant factors. For example, decisions made by judges are influenced by race and gender. Non-whites receive heavier sentences than do whites for crimes such as rape (Zatz, 1984); women receive fewer charge or sentence reductions than do men, regardless of the pleas they offer (Sarri, 1987).

Clinicians must also assign value or worth *(subjective utilities)* to outcomes. These represent the relative desirability of different outcomes. How much weight should be given to protecting potential rape victims and how much to maximizing freedom of those who have a history of rape? Helping clients to clarify their values is often one of the main goals of psychotherapy, especially in relation to clients who seek therapy to give meaning to their lives; for self-actualization (Beit-Hallahmi, 1987). Helping clients to clarify their values is a key aspect of Rogerian approaches. Research shows that accurate descriptions of personal values is a difficult process that is influenced by many variables, including the kind of questions asked, their sequence, and how responses are obtained (Slovic, Fischhoff, & Lichtenstein, 1982a). Such efforts are further complicated by behavioral confirmation influences in clinical exchanges (see Chapter Two) and by the fact that clients often do not know what they want. Ideally, gains would be maximized and costs minimized as well as efficiency maintained in terms of time, money, and effort devoted to making a decision. Often, there is a direct conflict between minimizing costs and maximizing gains.

Clinicians differ in the outcomes pursued, as well as in the probabilities and values placed on different outcomes. The assessment of probabilities and subjective utilities are interdependent. For example, certain outcomes are assessed as more valuable than uncertain outcomes. Optimists tend to exaggerate the likelihood of positive outcomes (Weinstein, 1980). People often believe that they are more likely than other people are to have good things befall them and are less likely to experience maladies. Attitudes toward risk differ; potential losses are more influential than are potential gains. That is, people usually worry more about what they will lose than consider what they will gain. An illustration of this tendency can be seen in a study by McNeil, Pauker, Sox, and Tversky (1982) concerning preference for surgery or radiation therapy for lung cancer. One group of subjects received statistics that showed the percentage of patients that survived for different lengths of time after treatment. The other group received mortality statistics (percentage of patients who died). When the choice was posed in terms of mortality, 42 percent selected radiation therapy; only 25 percent of patients who received survival statistics selected radiation therapy. The advantages of surgery relative to radiation therapy loomed larger in the minds of respondents when framed in terms of the probability of survival than they did when stated in terms of the probability of death. The observed effect occurred with physicians as well as patients.

Selection of an intervention plan is influenced by degree of perceived risk associated with different options. Research concerning physicians' decisions about whether to recommend estrogen replacement therapy for menopausal women suggests that physicians feel more responsible for negative outcomes that are a result of their direct actions (for example, cancers that result from the treatment) than they do for negative outcomes that just happen (for example, bone fractures due to osteoporosis) (see Elstein, 1988). This difference may account for their failure to recommend estrogen replacement therapy even though physicians know that the combination of estrogen and progesteron reduces the risk of cancer to the level found with no treatment. Preferences for intervention methods that have the smallest maximum loss may decrease attention to methods that would result in maximum gains.

Clinicians often have to consider results from different sources when making decisions. A variety of models have been developed for making choices. In the compensatory model, weights are assigned to each variable and the weighted values are summed. Another model is the conjunctive model, in which cutoff points are set in relation to each dimension, and any alternative that falls below these points is dropped. The placement of the cutoff point will influence the relative number of successes and failures that occur; the higher the cutoff point is, the greater is the proportion of successes to failures. The lower the criteria of success is, the more successes will be observed, regardless of predictive ability and the location of the cutoff point. In the disjunctive model, a high score on one or several dimensions compensates for a low score on a variable. Past decisions can be used to create a model for current decisions, as in the program designed to increase equity in assigning homemaker chore time (Clark, Miller, & Pruger, 1980).

Using Test Results

Many clinicians use tests to decrease uncertainty. Tests may be used to predict future behavior. For example, a cutoff score on the Beck Hopelessness Scale of 9 or above successfully predicted 90.9 percent of the eventual suicides in a sample of 165 hospitalized "suicide ideators" who were followed from five to ten years (Beck, Steer, Kovacs, & Garrison, 1985). In a survey of 551 psychologists, it was found that most respondents used psychological tests (Wade & Baker, 1977). Psychological tests may be used in the course of assessment to attempt to understand clients (see Chapter Eight), or they may be used to predict how clients are likely to respond in the future. Clinical rather that actuarial judgments are typically used in combining test results with other sources of data to arrive at clinical judgments. That is, most clinicians do not use predictive equations in combining different sources of information (see discussion of clinical versus actuarial judgment).

Tests should be used to revise subjective estimates concerning a client—that is, to change a decision about how a client should be treated (Eddy, 1982; Einhorn, 1988). If, for example, a clinician suspects, based on an interview, that an elderly client has Alzheimer's disease and obtains psychological test results as well, the test results should be used to choose among different intervention options in light of the new estimate based on the test results. That is, estimates of the probability that the client has Alzheimer's disease will be revised. Test sensitivity (the test's accuracy in correctly identifying people who have a disorder) may be confused with test specificity (accuracy of a test in correctly identifying people who do *not* have a disorder), resulting in incorrect predictions; that is, test sensitivity is often incorrectly equated with the predictive value of a positive test result and test specificity is incorrectly equated with the predictive value of a negative test result (Beck, Byyny, & Adams, 1981; Elstein, 1988). Use of Bayes's Theorem helps present such errors.

Clinicians tend to overestimate the predictive accuracy of test results. One cause of this error is ignoring base-rate data. The predictive accuracy of a test depends on the initial risk of a condition in the person receiving the test. The probability that a client with a positive (or negative) test result for dementia actually has dementia depends on the prevalance of dementia in the population from which the patient was selected—that is, on the pretest probability that a client has dementia. Because there is little appreciation of this point, predictive accuracy often is overestimated. What percentage of applicants would succeed on the job anyway—without any testing procedure? If 90 percent would, then testing does not add much information.

The example of mammograms is drawn on in the discussion of the predictive accuracy of tests because of the extensive data available about this test, including base rate data concerning the prevalence of breast cancer in the general population. Use of this example from the field of medicine illustrates that, even when relevant information is available, it is often ignored in interpreting test results. As highlighted often in this book, the availability of information (data that decrease uncertainty) is no guarantee that it will be used for the benefit of clients. Consider the following example described by Eddy (1982), in which a physician thinks that there is a 99 percent probability that a breast mass is not cancerous. The subjective probability at this point is 1 percent that this woman has cancer. What should the new estimate be if a positive mammogram is obtained? The accuracy of mammogram results must be considered in answering this question. In a study reported in 1966, it was found that 79.2 percent of 475 malignant lesions were correctly diagnosed and 90.4 percent of 1,105 benign lesions were accurately diagnosed, for an overall accuracy of 87 percent (Snyder, 1966). (See Table 11).

Bayes's formula, as applied to this example, is as follows:

$$P(\text{ca} \mid \text{pos}) = \frac{P(\text{pos} \mid \text{ca}) \, P(\text{ca})}{P(\text{pos} \mid \text{ca}) \, P(\text{ca}) + P(\text{pos} \mid \text{benign}) \, P(\text{benign})}$$

where

$P(\text{ca} \mid \text{pos})$ is the probability that the patient has cancer, given that she has a positive X-ray report (the posterior probability)

Table 11. Accuracy of Mammography in Diagnosing Benign and Malignant Lesions.

Results of X-ray	Malignant lesion (cancer)	Benign lesion (no cancer)
Positive	.792	.096
Negative	.208	.904

Source: Data are from "Mammography: Contributions and Limitations in the Management of Cancer of the Breast" by R. Snyder, 1966, *Clinical Obstetrics and Gynecology, 9.* Copyright 1966 by Lippincott/ Harper & Row. Reprinted by permission.

$P(\text{pos} \mid \text{ca})$ is the probability that, if the patient has cancer, the radiologist will correctly diagnose it (the true-positive rate, or sensitivity)

$P(\text{ca})$ is the probability that the patient has cancer (prior probability)

$P(\text{benign})$ is the prior probability that the patient has benign disease [$P(\text{benign}) = 1 - P(\text{ca})$]

$P(\text{pos} \mid \text{benign})$ is the probability that, if the patient has a benign lesion, the radiologist will incorrectly diagnose it as cancer (the false-positive rate) (Eddy, 1982, p. 253)

The results are as follows, using the new information and the 1 percent estimate of the prior probability that the mass is malignant.

$$P(\text{ca} \mid \text{pos}) = \frac{(0.792)\,(0.01)}{(0.792)\,(0.01) + (0.096)\,(0.99)} = 0.077$$

Thus, clinicians may either fail to revise or incorrectly revise their probability estimates when thinking about additional data.

These kinds of problems are harder than clinicians realize. They are also typical of the problems clinicians confront, although in fields such as psychiatry, social work, and psychology, less information is available concerning base rates and test accuracy. Two kinds of odds should be considered (Arkes, 1981). One kind consists of prior odds—odds before additional information about a client is available. Obtaining more information (data that are useful in decreasing uncertainty) should change these prior odds. Bayes's Theorem can help clinicians to improve the accuracy of judgments in situations in which base rate data (that is, prior odds) tend to be ignored. It can help clinicians to appropriately consider the effect of case-related data, such as the results of a diagnostic test, on assessment of a client in determining the posterior odds. This does not mean to say that use of Bayes's Theorem in making predictions will always result in more accurate decisions; it may not (Cohen, 1979). Both astute clinical judgments and use of this aid may be needed in many instances.

Errors concerning the predictive accuracy of tests are also a result of confusion between two different conditional probabilities, as discussed in Chapter Nine. That is, clinicians tend to confuse retrospective accuracy, the probability of a positive test given that the person has a condition, and predictive accuracy, the probability of a condition given a positive test result. Retrospective accuracy is determined by reviewing test results after the true condition is known. Predictive accuracy refers to the probability of having a condition given a positive test result and the probability of not having a condition given a negative test. It is predictive accuracy that is important to the clinician confronted with a test result on an individual (see Chapter Nine for further discussion).

Another source of error in making predictions is the assumption that the accuracy of a test can be represented by one number. In fact, test accuracy will vary greatly, depending on whether a test is used as a screening device in which there are large numbers of people who do not have some condition of interest or whether it is used for clients with known signs or symptoms. In the latter case, the true positive and true negative rates are much higher than in the broad screening situation, and so there will be fewer false-positives and false-negatives. Overlooking this difference results in gross overestimations of test accuracy in screening situations resulting in a high percentage of false-positives. Consider an example described by Elstein and Bordage (1979). Assume that school officials want to use a screening test to identify children who will be abused by their parents and that about 3 percent of school-age children are abused. Officials claim that 95 percent of abused children will be detected and that 10 percent of nonabused children will be false positives. What is the probability that a child is abused if the screening test is positive? The following information is available: (1) the proba-

bility of a child who is abused being identified by the test is P(Test
+ Child Abuse) = .95; (2) the probability of a false positive, P(Test
+ Normal Child) = .10; and (3) the prior probability of a randomly
selected child being abused is the population base rate, .03. According to Bayes's Theorem (p. 359):

P(Child Abuse/Test +) =

$$\frac{\text{P(Test + Child Abuse) P(Child Abuse)}}{\text{P(Test + Child Abuse) P(Child Abuse) + P(Test + Normal Child) P(Normal Child)}}$$

$$\frac{.95 \times .03}{(.95 \times .03) + (.10 \times .97)} = \frac{.0285}{.1255} = .227$$

So the probability that a child who is positively identified by the
test is actually an abused child is .0285/.1255 = .227. If 10,000 children are screened, the resulting data can be represented in a 2 x 2
contingency table (see Table 12). Note the large number of false-
positives. The moral is, consider base-rate information in evaluating test accuracy.

Sources of Error

Predictions are made in relation to concepts and data that are
available; here again clinicians are influenced by practice theories
and preconceptions. Availability is a useful guide if it encourages
clinicians to think of cues that are helpful in making predictions
or if an accurate estimate of the frequency of an event is provided.
Behaviors that have occurred with a high frequency in a certain
situation in the past are likely to do so again (other factors being
equal). It is when available cues do not reflect the true frequency
of an event or result in ignoring the importance of other events
(such as nonoccurrence) that these result in errors. An illustration
is reliance on the number of times an event occurs (absolute frequency) rather than the relative number of occurrences (the relative
frequency) (see Chapter Nine).

The earlier discussion highlighted the importance of considering base rate data (the general prevalence of a behavior or event

Table 12. Accuracy of Test in Identifying Abuse.

		True State		
		Abused	Not Abused	
Test	Abused	285	970	1,255
	Not Abused	15	8,730	8,745
		300	9,700	10,000

Source: From "Psychology of Clinical Reasoning" by A. S. Elstein and G. Bordage. In G. C. Stone, F. Cohen, N. E. Adler, and Associates, *Health Psychology*, p. 359. San Francisco: Jossey-Bass. Copyright 1979 by Jossey-Bass Inc., Publishers. Reprinted by permission.

in the population) in making predictions. Because of preconceptions about what things go together, clinicians often overlook base rate data, assuming that they have nothing to do with case data. Often, clinicians do not have access to base rate information; such information may be difficult or impossible to acquire. Ignoring base rate data when they are available can result in self-delusion, as in overestimating clinical success; the question of how many cases would be successful anyhow is overlooked (see later section on feedback). Estimates of the prevalence of events are influenced by the attention topics receive in the media. For example, the relative frequencies of cancer and homicides are overestimated, whereas the relative frequencies of asthma and diabetes, which receive less media attention, are underestimated (Lichtenstein and others, 1978). Currently, there is a great deal of interest in children of alcoholics. This subject gets a lot of attention in the media, workshops are held, and so on. This probably leads clinicans to overestimate the prevalence of this concern. Consider also the attention given to stranger-abduction of children. A review article in *Public Interest* indicated that the prevalence of abductions by strangers has been grossly overestimated by special-interest groups and, that once correct figures become available, later correction of inflated figures may do little or nothing to correct initial inaccurate estimates (Best, 1988). Overestimating the prevalence of a problem is not without effects. The result may be redistribution of clinical and other resources away from areas where need is greater. People tend to worry about what has recently happened and to let events slip from their minds as the events recede into the past. Clinicians may worry more about whether they should report a threat by a client against a significant other right after a lurid description of a crime committed by another client when the clinician did not warn the involved party. The purchase of earthquake insurance increases right after an earthquake (Slovic, Kunreuther, & White, 1974).

Clinicians are influenced by the degree of similarity between the characteristics of an event, object, person, and the class to which it belongs. Psychologists who work in personnel departments have images, for example, of what successful people are like in certain jobs. These images are used as a guide in evaluating the qualities of applicants. This sterotyping effect is shown in a study by Kahneman and Tversky (1973). Subjects received the following description written by a psychologist. "Tom W. is of high intelligence, although lacking in true creativity. He has a need for order and clarity and for neat and tidy systems in which every detail finds its appropriate place. His writing is rather dull and mechanical, occasionally enlivened by somewhat corny puns and by flashes of imagination of the sci-fi type. He has a strong drive for competence. He seems to have little feel and little sympathy for other people and does not enjoy interacting with others. Self-centered, he nonetheless has a deep moral sense." They were informed that Tom was a graduate student and were asked to indicate in what area he would probably specialize in graduate school.

- Business administration
- Computer science
- Engineering
- Humanities and education
- Law
- Library Science
- Medicine
- Physical and life sciences
- Social science and social work

Subjects selected computer science and engineering as most likely and education, social science, social work, and the humanities as least likely. These choices were influenced by the consistency of data offered, which supposedly favored this selection (see later discussion of the conjunction fallacy). Representativeness is a valid indicator only to the extent that data sources are not redundant or that it does not result in ignoring other information (Hogarth, 1980, p. 31).

Information that is inconsistent with stereotypes of what characteristics are predictive of a given event is often ignored. Reviews of the literature on the effects on family life of a child with a disability emphasize how both professionals as well as researchers ignore positive coping skills of families (Kazak & Marvin, 1984). Professionals who work in special-education programs (including social workers, psychologists, and teachers) overestimate problems that families have and overestimate parents' use of negative parenting methods. Parents' use of positive approaches is underestimated (Blackard & Barsh, 1982). The views of these professionals reflect their stereotypes about what it is like to raise a child with a disability. Their views are encouraged by the biased selection of case examples presented in the professional literature (see Chapter Seven).

Evidence should be weighed in relation to its predictive value—how informative is it? Is it helpful in making accurate causal attributions and predictions? Research shows that we do not weigh evidence that way. Rather, information is weighed in terms of whether we think it is causally related to a criterion. Questions such as "Is it meaningful to us?" are asked rather than "Is it diagnostic?" Clinicians choose intervention methods on the basis of what they believe will work. But what does that mean? It depends on what is meant by the term *work* (Eysenck & Nias, 1982, p. 211). Does it mean that it is helpful to the people who believe in it? If this criterion is used, then we would have to say that many causes, including astrology, are effective. The popularity of astrology would leave no doubt that it does work: "to most people astrological ideas have undeniable beauty and appeal, the birth chart is nonjudgemental, the interpretation is unfalsifiable, and astrologers tend to be nice people. In a society that denies ego support to most people, astrology provides it at a very low price. Where else can you get this sort of thing these days?" (Dean, 1986–1987, p. 178).

Another meaning of "what works" concerns validity—Is it true? The distinction between utility and validity explains the conflict between astrologers and critics of astrology. "Critics see a lack of factual evidence and conclude it doesn't work, whereas astrologers see that it helps people and conclude that it does work" (Dean,

1986–1987, p. 178). Both are right and both are guilty of not wanting to know what the other is talking about.

Reliability places an upward boundary on the predictive validity of measures (the extent to which a measure corresponds to the real position of a client on whatever dimension is being measured). It does this by increasing the variability of the data source; that is, scores will be different from time to time. A clinician could, for example, ask about the test-retest reliability of the Beck Depression Inventory: What is the likelihood that a client's score will be the same over a six-week period? Validity refers to whether a measure reflects what it is supposed to measure. For example, does the Beck Depression Inventory really measure depression? Inattention to unreliability and lack of validity of measures often result in false attributions of assumed causal effects which, in turn, result in inaccurate predictions.

Clinical practice often requires the assessment of joint probabilities. Let's say that a psychologist in a student counseling center wants to determine the probability that a student (a) will select journalism as a college major, (b) become unhappy with his choice, and (c) change to engineering. This involves estimating the probability of conjunctive events. Such events are usually overestimated. For example, when different groups of subjects were asked to estimate the probabilities of (a), both (a) and (b), and the probability of all three, they gave the following average estimates: .21 for (a); .39 for (a) and (b); and .42 for all three (a, b, and c) (Slovic, Fischhoff, & Lichtenstein, 1976). The key condition that was not attended to is that, in most cases, the joint probability of two events cannot be greater than the smaller of the probabilities that are associated with the events (see section on overlooking important probabilities in Chapter Nine).

Consensus information tends to be ignored in making predictions, not only in relation to other people but in relation to self-perception as well. If people are informed that most other individuals act in a certain way in a situation and are then asked what a particular person will do in that context, they tend to ignore normative data in arriving at a judgment. A helpful rule of thumb is to find out what is known about the most frequent outcome in a situation and to attend to these data when making predictions.

Overlooking regression effects can result in clinical errors. Extreme effects will usually not be so extreme when they are reassessed. If a client does unusually well on a test, she is likely to do less well the next time around; or conversely if she does very poorly, she is likely to do better the next time around. "The implication of the regression phenomenon is that when prediction is based on sources with imperfect predictive ability, predictions should be less extreme than the information generated by the sources. The term 'regression phenomenon' simply means that in the presence of imperfect predictive sources, predictions should be regressed toward the mean" (Hogarth, 1980, p. 35). Both reliability and validity problems add to the regression effect. For example, lack of reliability may lead to predictions that are too extreme. This is a special problem in clinical contexts in which clinicians are heavily influenced by cues that have an extreme value; extremes stand out, they are vivid. Essentially, "a failure to understand chance fluctuations leads to judgmental errors" (Hogarth, 1980, p. 35). Expecting extreme values to be less marked on repeated assessment helps avoid this source of error.

Superstitious beliefs may result from overlooking regression effects. Superstitions are beliefs about the causal relation between two or more events (for example, carrying a lucky rabbit's foot, and avoiding bad luck) that are not true. An interesting example described by Kahneman and Tversky (1973) concerns Israeli flight instructors who were encourged to use positive reinforcement and to avoid punishment to help pilots learn to fly. After doing so, they argued that these methods were not effective since it was their experience that praise of superior performance resulted in less effective outcomes on the next efforts, while criticism of poor performance produced improved performance on subsequent attempts. They concluded that punishment was more effective than positive reinforcement in increasing desired behaviors.

Irrelevant data increase the probability of incorrect predictions; a few worthless items can dilute the effect of one helpful item. The influence of irrelevant data is illustrated in a study in which social work graduate students were asked to estimate the likelihood that some people were child abusers. Inclusion of information that the person "fixes up cars in his spare time" and "once ran away from home as a boy" decreased the effects of data that he has "sadomasochistic sexual fantasies" (see Nisbett & Ross, 1980, p. 155). Irrelevant material about this person tended to make him less similar to someone who might abuse his child. A rule of thumb here is to ask whether data have any real predictive value.

Anchoring effects are influential in all stages of decision making, including making predictions. Since initial judgments are often wrong, actions taken based on these may be incorrect. Initial judgments can be remarkably resistant to change. For example, even though subjects were told that initial estimates they received were based on random information such as the throw of dice, they did not alter their estimates (Tversky & Kahneman, 1974). Progress may be influenced by knowledge of prior relapses. Adjustments in predictions are often made on the basis of information that is initially available, thus compounding possible biasing effects of initial judgment (Hogarth, 1980, p. 47).

Sources of assessment data are not necessarily independent. Take, for example, the prediction of intelligence. Data concerning grade-point average, intelligence test scores, recommendations, and past employment are not independent sources of information; they are related, which decreases the amount of information each source offers. Clinicians often overlook the consistency of redundant data in making predictions; that is, the more data sources they have available, even though these are not independent, the more confident they feel in their predictions. Consider the study of Oskamp (1965) in which the judgments of clinical psychologists were studied as a function of the amount of data they received. These clinicians were asked to make a prediction based on a case study and to indicate their degree of confidence in these judgments under different conditions in relation to the amount of data they received. As the data they received increased, so did confidence in their judgments. There was, however, no increase in predictive accuracy. Kahneman and Tversky (1973) refer to the influence by the consistency of redundant data and the influences of extreme values of predictive cues as the illusion of validity—both increase confidence in judgments even though both are inversely related to the predictive accuracy of data sources. Our tendency to overestimate the degree of covariation between variables adds to the illusion of validity.

Hearing a persuasive causal explanation of an event increases a belief that an outcome associated with that event will occur. For example, Tversky and Kahneman (1983) asked a group of professional forecasters to indicate the probability of a complete suspension of diplomatic relations between the United States and the Soviet Union in 1983. Another group was asked to estimate this same outcome occurring simultaneously with another event, "a Russian invasion of Poland and a complete suspension of diplomatic relations between the U.S.A. and the Soviet Union." The probability of the second description was evaluated as more likely than the first. The causal coherence of a scenario is used to assess the likelihood of its occurrence; that is, causal persuasiveness is confused with outcome (Hogarth, 1987, p. 49).

Errors may occur because of vague and shifting criteria for judging alternatives. Being overloaded with information reduces the consistency of judgments; one form of presentation (such as charts) is usually selected and others (such as the text) are ignored. This lack of consistency is one of the reasons that actuarial judgments are often superior to clinical judgments.

Errors in prediction often occur because of misperception of chance fluctuations. People believe that the immediate future will compensate for unusual outcomes by reversing these patterns, and they base predictions on such beliefs (Nisbett & Ross, 1980). This source of error is known as the gambler's fallacy, because gamblers often make this error. The gambler's fallacy refers to the belief that the next event in a sequence that is probabilistic in nature, such as flipping a coin, will redress prior imbalances. It is assumed, for example, that the outcome of tossing a coin on one occasion influences the outcome on the next occasions; that if three heads in a row appear, the next flip will yield tails. This belief is exploited by gambling casinos as well as by those who claim to have paranormal power. Clinicians are also subject to this source of error. Making predictions can lead to an illusion of control; a feeling that there is control over a future that is indeed uncertain (see later discussion of feedback).

The confusion between a conditional probability and its inverse is likely to result in inaccurate predictions of pathology. The probability of a sign given a disorder is not necessarily equal to the probability of the disorder given the sign; the probability of the sign is usually higher than the probability of the disorder. If P (S|D) and P (D|S) are confused, many more clients will be falsely diagnosed as having a disorder that they do not have (Eddy, 1982) (see Chapter Nine).

The manner in which data are presented influences predictions. In addition to primacy effects (items early in a series gain our attention), recency effects (items last in a series gain our attention) also occur; information in the middle tends to be ignored. Data presented in the form of "no" (negativism) is more difficult to comprehend than data presented in positive terms. Clinical predictions are also influenced by preferences for certain outcomes; the probability of desired outcomes is judged to be higher than is justified by information available. This has been called wishful thinking (Hogarth, 1980). Predictions as well as causal analyses differ depending on question format. Thus, the response mode influences the judgment (Slovic, Fischhoff, & Lichtenstein, 1982a). Clinicians tend to overestimate their ability to make accurate predictions. For example, they often fail to appreciate the random variability in behavior that may be beyond any current models of explanation.

Increasing the Accuracy of Predictions

One step that can be taken to enhance the accuracy of predictions is to be explicit concerning possible risks and gains of considered alternatives and to make explicit predictions. Few clinicians offer specific probabilities in making predictions, even though research shows that predictions become more accurate if this is done (Einhorn & Hogarth, 1978). Rather than offering vague predictions (such as "I think insight therapy will be effective"), a psychologist could predict that there is an 80 percent chance that a certain intervention will be successful in increasing positive exchanges in a family. Comparison of outcomes with specific predictions offers more fine-grained feedback about accuracy than do vague predictions such as, "There will be improvement." Considering maximum possible gains from a given method may help counteract undue attention to minimizing risks associated with different options.

Visual representations can be helpful. Some writers recommend the use of decision trees (Figure 7). Attending to base rate data

**Figure 7. Subjective Probabilities Associated with Various Outcomes
Following a Pre-Retirement Decision.**

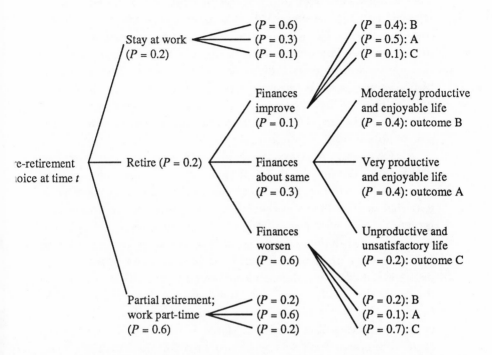

Source: From *The Case-Study Method in Psychology and Related Disciplines* (p. 284) by D. B. Bromley, 1986, New York: Wiley. Copyright 1986 by John Wiley & Sons. Reprinted by permission.

when these are available, as well as to reliability and validity of measures, will enhance accuracy.

Taking advantage of statistical tools will increase the accuracy of clinical predictions. Many of the problems clinicians confront are quite complex, requiring tools such as Bayes's Theorem to overcome cognitive limitations and to counter tendencies to make certain kinds of errors (such as ignoring base rates). Use of actuarial methods will increase the consistency with which known relationships between predictors and an outcome, such as the effectiveness of a given intervention method, are considered and will help to make up for cognitive limitations in combining data from many sources. Although some clinicians believe that reliance on a predictive equation dehumanizes clients, this view ignores the human costs of increased error that may result from not using these tools (Dawes, Faust, & Meehl, 1989). The compelling vividness of personal experience in "what works" will continue to discourage clinicians from using actuarial methods that may be more accurate than clinical-judgments. The tendency to focus on the conjunction of two events (such as certain kinds of dreams and negative events) will be checked by attention to disconfirming combinations (see Table 9 in Chapter Nine). Asking about all four cells of a contingency table should help to counter the focus on "hits."

Decreasing reliance on memory will increase the accuracy of predictions. Because of the confirmation bias, clinicians tend to remember data that support their assumptions and may even recall data that were not present that support assumptions, and they may forget data that were present that do not support their views. These tendencies encourage excessive confidence in our judgments (Arkes, 1981). Keeping good records will help decrease errors due to memory lapses. Collecting data about degree of progress will improve the quality of feedback and therefore improve the accuracy of predictions. Checklists can be useful in increasing clinicians' adherence to intervention programs (see, for example, DeDombal, Leaper, & Horrocks, 1974), which in turn should enhance the accuracy of prediction outcome since treatment fidelity will be enhanced. Being aware of subtle influences on clients' expressed preferences of the types of questions asked and types of responses requested, and posing a variety of questions in attempting to clarify client values so that inconsistencies may be revealed, may be helpful in identifying preferences.

Feedback

Feedback is essential to the learning of expertise (Hogarth, 1981). One of the many choices clinicians make is how to determine the accuracy of their decisions. They have a choice between strategies that will be helpful in improving future accuracy and strategies that will prevent the "de-bugging" of clinical practice (Bransford & Stein, 1984). Judgments in clinical work typically involve continuous rather than discrete evaluation, and thus many opportunities for correcting decisions are available. The more rapid and continuous are the feedback, the more sensitive and valid are the measures of progress; the more outcomes are clearly related to decisions made, the more opportunities clinicians have to learn how to make better decisions in the future.

What and how to measure outcome is a hotly debated issue in the field of psychotherapy. Choices are influenced by practice perspectives. Measures used include therapist opinions, self-report of clients, self-monitoring, role playing, observation of behavior in real-life settings, and archival records such as hospital admissions. These sources differ in their accuracy. Should interpretations be considered correct if clients accept them? Not necessarily; research shows that insecure people tend to accept both positive and negative feedback more readily than do more secure individuals (Snyder & Clair, 1977). People who seek treatment may be especially insecure and tend to accept any interpretations offered, accurate or not. Concerns about pleasing therapists may encourage clients to offer inaccurate reports of degree of progress. The interactive nature of actions taken and predictions made often obscures the true relationships between effects of actions and outcomes (Einhorn, 1988). That is, actions taken as a result of predictions influence outcomes. Consider the old example of a prediction that the banks will fail, which is followed by a "run on the banks" and their subsequent failure. A therapist who believes that a client can be helped may extend greater effort because of this belief, which in turn increases the likelihood of the predicted positive outcome. If an applicant is accepted for a job, opportunities available on the job may help to ensure success.

Testimonials are often offered in support of the effectiveness of intervention methods. They are vivid—usually consisting of a detailed case presentation or clients speaking for themselves. They are usually presented with a confident demeanor. There is typically no doubt about the good intent of the speaker, which adds to the aura of credibility. But what do they tell us? They tell us about only one or a few cases that may not represent the population of concern. Reliance on testimonials as evidence for effectiveness of a particular method is a version of the fallacy of the small sample and of the use of absolute rather than relative frequencies (see Chapter Nine). Testimonials usually describe positive results; rarely do they describe failures (for an exception, see Foa & Emmelkamp, 1983). Possible biases toward favored kinds of practice approaches make it especially important to include relevant comparative and control groups in assessing the benefits of different methods. Clinicians often overlook the possible role of other changes in a client's life circumstance when attributing positive gains to therapy. Thus, reasons given for success or failure may be self-surviving (Jordan, Harvey, & Weary, 1988).

One way the quality of feedback can be improved is to take advantage of subjective and objective measures of progress. Some clinicians rely on self-report alone; clients are asked whether they feel better, are less depressed, have a happier social life. Certainly this kind of feedback is needed. However, is this the only information that should be obtained? Research in psychotherapy indicates that there is often a lack of correlation between self-report and observed changes (Lang, 1977). Clients tend to report satisfaction with counseling even though little change in the presenting problem has taken place (Zilbergeld, 1983). For example, mothers who complained that their children were not attending school reported that attendance had improved following intervention when there had actually been no change in attendance (Schnelle, 1974). The tendency to report a situation as worse than it is at the beginning of therapy and as better than it is at the end, is known as the hello-goodbye effect. This occurs because of situational demand characteristics—clients report themselves as worse than they are when seeking treatment and, to please the therapist, report more improvement than is true at the end. If self-report of clients is relied on, the hello-goodbye effect is likely to suggest overly positive accounts of progress. Use of both objective and subjective measures will offer a more accurate picture of outcome than will reliance on either alone.

Another way to enhance the quality of feedback is to select specific progress indicators that are also relevant and feasible. Only if specific progress indicators are tracked on an ongoing basis can case-planning decisions be made in a timely manner and results reviewed on an ongoing basis. Feedback that is vague, irrelevant, or delayed gets in the way of discovering relationships between predictions made and outcome. Selection of sensitive, relevant progress indicators often requires creativity, as well as a knowledge of practice-related literature about possible options. Identification of progress indicators may be especially challenging with clients who participate in therapy not to address a particular problem but to address a more general concern such as self-actualization or self-understanding. Feedback may be irrelevant to learning; that is, outcomes observed may offer inaccurate or incomplete data about predictions, which may result in overconfidence in judgments. Vague feedback is more likely to be irrelevant than is specific feedback. Clearly describing objectives and keeping track of progress on an ongoing basis will be helpful in assessing the accuracy of clinical judgments (S. C. Hayes, 1981; Hawkins, 1989). Clear indicators of progress may enhance client motivation to continue their participation in intervention programs.

Feedback concerning outcome is often unknown in clinical work. Even if progress is assessed in relation to a specific outcome that results from using a particular method, this offers no information about the effectiveness of other methods that deal with the same problem. Although immediate feedback may be available in many cases (for example, does a depressed client report improved mood and increased activities at home and work?), in other cases it may be quite delayed (for example, will a rapist rape again when released from prison?). In some cases current indicators of the probability of a later behavior, such as daily urges, can be monitored.

Selection of specific progress indicators requires identification of specific objectives. Setting vague objectives makes it difficult or impossible to distinguish among those that are probable, possible, or impossible to achieve, thus increasing the likelihood of pursuing impossible goals with the resulting discouragement this creates for both clients and clinicians. Incorrect beliefs about selecting *specific* objectives and tracking these on an ongoing basis may pose an obstacle. Examples include the belief that specificity requires selection of trivial outcomes, that it interferes with the therapeutic relationship, and that it requires the use of behavioral methods (Gambrill, 1988).

Knowledge of an outcome encourages the view that it was inevitable, that we should have known what the outcome would be even though, at the time, it was uncertain. We tend to assume that outcomes are consistent with our preconceptions—"I knew it all along." Another characteristic of hindsight bias is a tendency to assume a direct relationship between an outcome and certain causes when in fact, no evidence is offered for or against such an assumptions (Fischhoff, 1975). Since explanations are readily created, possible accounts are usually always at hand. Hindsight bias often results in blaming people for what appear to be errors that could have been avoided; looking back, knowing the outcome that occurred, it is assumed that "he should have known." Hindsight bias also results in praising people for what were just lucky guesses (Hogarth, 1980). There are benefits from hindsight bias; it helps one to remember associations that work as well as ones that do not work. Awareness of the effects of hindsight bias will be helpful in making effective use of feedback.

The tendency to be overconfident about the accuracy of our predictions is as common among experts as it is among other people (Slovic, Fischhoff, & Lichtenstein, 1982b). Use of vague or irrelevant feedback obscures the true relationship (or lack thereof) between predictions and outcomes. Success tends to be attributed to personal skill, and failure tends to be attributed to chance. Faulty memory influenced by preconceptions may result in errors in recall about factors related to an outcome. These errors will obscure the relationship between predictor variables and outcomes. Trying to recall events is an active process in which accounts are often reconstructed. Feedback may be ignored, especially if this contradicts predictions and favored value systems on which these predictions are based.

Summary

Predictions are one of the products of clinical decisions. The predictions made are related to causal assumptions and typically involve the prediction of a criterion variable, such as likelihood of relapse, based on a number of factors. For example, a psychiatrist may have to predict whether a homeless, mentally ill person will make another suicide attempt in the near future.

Clinical prediction involves the integration of different kinds of data—a task that is difficult. Comparison of statistical versus clinical prediction shows that actuarial methods usually are more accurate than clinical inference. The nature of clinical decisions makes it difficult to learn predictive relationships. Predictions must be made under considerable uncertainty in terms of the relationship between predictor variables and a criterion such as the likelihood that an intervention method will be successful. There is controversy over what criteria to use (for example, client self-report, opinion of the clinician, changes in real-life behavior). Competing values must be considered, for example, to protect potential victims from assault and maximize individual freedom of the potentially assaultive individual. Given the importance and uncertainties of the predictions that clinicians make, it is not surprising that they often say they do not make predictions or that they delay or avoid making them.

Making predictions and choices requires the assessment of probabilities. There are certain kinds of errors that clinicians are prone to make such as the "confusion of the inverse" (assuming that the probability of a sign given a disorder is the same as the probability of the disorder given the sign). Other sources of error include overlooking the unreliability of data, being influenced by the consistency of redundant data, and using vague and shifting criteria for evaluating options. Ignoring consensus information and base rate data are common sources of error. Relevant data are often ignored because of our limitations in considering many different sources. Clinicians are prone to hindsight bias; that is, knowledge of an outcome encourages a view that it was inevitable. Undue weight often is given to observed outcome rather than to examining all four cells of a contingency table; in addition, error may arise from irrelevant, delayed, or vague feedback concerning the accuracy of decisions.

Here, too, being forewarned is being prepared; that is, if clinicians are aware of common sources of errors, they are more likely to avoid them. Statistical aids such as Bayes's Theorem can be used to combine subjective beliefs with objective data to arrive at subjective probabilities. In addition, it is helpful to use visual representations and to attend to sources of uncertainty. The quality of feedback about the accuracy of clinical predictions can be increased by making precise estimates of the probable success of intervention methods, by identifying clear objectives, and by monitoring progress in an ongoing fashion. Selection of valid, reliable progress indicators will enhance the quality of feedback.

11

Enhancing the Quality of Case Conferences and Discussions

Making clinical decisions often involves discussions with other professionals, as well as with clients and their significant others. Sources of error that have been discussed in previous chapters may occur during such conversations. Many clinical decisions are made in case conferences, a setting that does not necessarily enhance the accuracy of decisions. The classic article by Paul Meehl, "Why I Do Not Attend Case Conferences" (1973), describes many reasons why this occurs. Meehl believes that "many intelligent, educated, sane, rational persons seem to undergo a kind of intellectual deterioration when they gather around a table in one room" (p. 227); that "the group situation brings out the worst in many people" in terms of intellectual functioning. The impressions that Meehl offered in 1973 have been supported by in-depth studies of dialogue in case conferences. For example, a study of decisions made in case conferences concerning child abuse found that, rather than a balanced search for the truth, these involved premature closure in assignment of responsibility for the abuse (Dingwall, Eekelaar, and Murray, 1983).

Case conferences represent a complex social situation in which participants have different goals, skills, values, styles of interaction, practice theories, prejudices, and biases. The setting in which they take place influences what occurs, as do the tasks addressed, the physical environment (for example, comfortable or uncomfortable, noisy or quiet), and the particular pressures (for example, to contain costs). Conferences are an ideal setting for the use of persuasion strategies that are not likely to further the quality of discussion. Emotional language may be used to create positive or negative views of clients. Opinions may be changed and actions taken on the basis of appeals to emotion rather than in response to sound arguments. Meehl (1973) suggests that clinicians take on questions to which they would never consider offering blithe answers in other contexts (for example, suggesting complex psychodiagnostic accounts even though they have had only a brief exposure to a client and little evidence has been offered to support their accounts).

Characteristics of Case Conferences That Decrease the Quality of Decisions

Questionable practices that occur in conferences are discussed in the sections that follow. Other tendencies that encourage inaccurate decisions, such as the sick-sick fallacy and use of pseudoauthority, which are also common in case conferences, are discussed in Chapter Seven.

Attributing Value to All Contributions. There is a reluctance to criticize anyone's views, even though these may be uninformative or inaccurate. The value of high-quality data is often disregarded: "the prestigious thing to do is to contribute ideas to the conference . . . whether or not the quality of evidence available is adequate to support the view offered" (Meehl, 1973, p. 235). The tendency to be impressed by plausible-sounding but uninformative explanations is encouraged by not asking such questions as "What evidence is there for this view?" or "How does this help us understand and know what to do about this problem?" "In order to maintain the fiction that everybody's ideas are worthwhile, it is necessary to lower the standards for what is evidential. As a result, a causal anecdote about one senile uncle remembered from childhood is given the same group interest and intellectual respect that is accorded to the citation of a high quality experimental or field actuarial study" (p. 228).

Participants tend to forget ordinary rules of scientific inference and principles of human development. Meehl offers an example of a nurse equating a childhood imaginary companion with an adult's visual hallucination. Trivial statements that are uninformative may be made because they are true of all people (Kadushin, 1963). This has been called the Barnum effect. Examples are: "She has intrapsychic conflicts," or "He has problems with object relations." Along the same lines, the vagueness of astrological descriptions allows readers to see themselves in such accounts and so consider them accurate and meaningful. Tolerance for feeble statements will occur if these statements, even though flawed, succeed in persuading others to accept a favored position. Fallacies may be recognized but not pointed out because their acceptance will bolster a favored position.

Asking pointless questions slows down the process of decision making. Questions can be divided into three categories in terms of encouraging helpful answers: (1) irrelevant, (2) of possible relevance; and (3) highly relevant. So, the question should be asked "Will the answer make any difference in handling a case?" Asking "and therefore?" following irrelevant questions may, as Meehl suggests, encourage participants to think more carefully before asking questions. Questions sometimes are posed not to advance toward an informed decision based on sound arguments and evidence, but to do quite the opposite (for example, to sidetrack a discussion or create biasing emotional reactions). Such questions, indeed, have a point, but it is not to encourage informed decisions.

Confusing Inclusion and Exclusion Tests. One kind of decision clinicians make is to assign diagnoses to clients. Some characteristics may indicate that a client is not an X (an exclusion test) whereas others indicate that if the client has certain characteristics he is an X (an inclusion test). These two kinds of criteria are confused when it is incorrectly argued that because Mr. A does not have a certain characteristic, he is not an X when, in fact, this characteristic may not be associated with a particular diagnosis (that is, it is not *critical* to the diagnosis). Meehl (1973) uses the example of a trainee who argues that a patient is not schizophrenic because he does not have "delusions or hallucinations with clear sensorium" (p. 230). Meehl argues that not all schizophrenics have these accessory symptoms.

Confusing the Consistency of and Differential Weight of a Sign. Another kind of statement that does not advance discussion in an informed manner is pointing out that a certain diagnosis is consistent with a characteristic when it is also consistent with other possibilities among which the group is trying to distinguish. For example, if a group is trying to decide which of two parents abused a child and each of the parents has a history of abuse as a child, pointing out that the mother has a past history of abuse is not informative since the father also has such a history. This sign has no diagnostic relevancy at this point. This error "illustrates one of the generic features of case conferences in psychiatry, namely, the tendency to mention things that don't make any difference one way or the other" (Meehl, 1973, p. 231).

Neglect of Statistical Logic. Unreliability of measures may be neglected when interpreting score changes or difference scores. Relatively small differences (for example, in before and after measures) may reflect unreliable measures rather than a true difference. (Whether the measures are valid is another question.) If the reliability of a measure is questionable, then small differences should be interpreted with caution or ignored. Ignoring the size and representatives of samples used to infer traits or tendencies is one of the most common errors made in arriving at clinical decisions. Inferences are often based on small, unrepresentative samples of behavior. For example, a judgment about a resident of a nursing home may be based on a fifteen-minute observation period in an interview (see the discussion of the law of large numbers in Chapter Eight). There are many ways in which samples may be unrepresentative. Behavior may have been sampled in a context that differs considerably from the one in which the presenting problem occurs. Aggressiveness of a child at home may be the problem, but perhaps the only observational data available may have been gathered at school. Behavior in this situation may not reflect behavior at home. Furthermore, since no information is offered about the antecedents and consequences of behavior labeled *aggressive,* little is known about the circumstances in which such behavior may occur. Errors may occur because of a lack of understanding about how probability logic applies to individual cases. Estimates of prior probability (for example, the base rate for a diagnosis of schizophrenia in a particular population) and the degree of leverage added by a given characteristic (such as history of hospitalization) often are neglected (see Chapters Nine and Ten). Actuarial data often are ignored, and clinical decisions are based on clinical intuition even though research supports the superiority of actuarial methods. A clinician may decide to rely on clinical intuition even though no other outstanding factors offer sound reasons for overriding actuarial data. When a decision must be made about whether to accept an applicant who has a low college grade point average for clinical training, it is not rare for someone to say, "Let's interview him." Clearly, there are instances in which other factors should be considered. However, disregard for empirical data results in more misclassifications than correct classifications.

Inappropriately Minimizing Signs or Symptoms. This fallacy occurs when a behavior is excused on the grounds that anyone would do it. The question is would anyone do it? Thinking about doing something and doing it are two different things. Clinicians are influenced by personal biases when selecting characteristics viewed as normal, as well as when identifying what is pathological. This fallacy is the opposite of the sick-sick fallacy, and is illustrated by the nurse who attempted to belittle the importance of a patient's hallucinations by telling the group that she herself had an imaginary companion as a child (Meehl, 1973). Both tendencies result from the inappropriate imposition of personal biases in relation to what is healthy and what is sick. Both tendencies are encouraged by lack of knowledge about what is normative and a reluctance to seek such data (see also discussion of the rule of optimism in Chapter Seven).

Identifying the Softheaded with the Softhearted. A regard for rigorous examination of a topic may be viewed as cold, unemotional, unfeeling, whereas a disregard for vagueness, non sequiturs, and tolerance of fallacies may be considered a mark of caring and compassion. An actuarial basis for making decisions (see Chapter Ten) may be abandoned because of a concern that the client will not receive optimal treatment. Such a departure may not only increase the chances of making a mistake for an individual client, but increase inaccurate predictions for other clients as well (Meehl, 1973). Unless there is a sound method that allows clinicans to discriminate between cases in which clinical inference would be the optimal method for making a decision, and cases in which it would be more effective to rely on actuarial methods, neglect of actuarial methods that have a better success rate will decrease the accuracy of clinical decisions. Sympathy is not a sound reason to abandon actuarial methods of making predictions.

Other Problems. Different standards of evidence may be used to support a favored position than are used to critique opposing views; that is, more rigorous evidence may be requested when considering perspectives other than our own. For example, inferences based on projective tests may be offered with no corroborative evidence to support a preferred diagnosis. In contrast, data based on observation of behavior in real-life settings may be requested in support of alternative views of a client's problem. It may be assumed that a certain kind of mental health professional is only qualified to offer certain information. Psychiatrists may assume that the role of psychologists is mainly to offer assessment data based on psychological tests and that they have little else to contribute. Actually, the particular degree that a professional has does not necessarily indicate their areas of competence. A psychiatrist, for example, may not be able to offer much information about different kinds of psychotropic drugs—perhaps because of a lack of interest and a tendency to focus on other aspects of his or her work.

The "spun glass theory of the mind" refers to the belief that people are very fragile and should be treated as such; that relatively minor deprivations, rejections, or failure experiences play a causative role in major traumas (Meehl, 1973, p. 253). As Meehl (1973) notes, such a belief may have counter-therapeutic effects in protecting clients from reality or not offering them effective intervention methods. For example, one clinician objected to interviewing in a new setting a client about to be discharged on the grounds that this unusual situation might undo the successful effects of therapy.

The fallacy of uncertain consequences involves the argument that because the consequences related to an option (such as selection of a given kind of intervention) are uncertain, it should not be selected—it would be too risky. If no data are offered supporting such anticipated risks, the fallacy of uncertain consequences has been made (Michalos, 1971, p. 100). The crummy criterion fallacy occurs when the criteria used to assess the soundness of an argument are weak or inappropriate. Meehl (1973) offers the example of dismissing psychological test results on the basis that these do not agree with the assessment of a psychiatrist who has held a ten-minute interview with a client.

Cheap Shots

Some tactics can be called cheap shots because of their failure to advance high-quality decision making. Like other kinds of strategies, they may be subtle or obvious. Such cheap shots often are used by people in power positions. Negative labels (such as "nitpicker"), may be used to refer to someone in order to discredit a position. This unimaginative ploy often is made more effective by including actions that attempt to convince listeners that the person using the negative labels does so only because he or she has been forced to by the supposed "facts." A sad expression of inevitability may be assumed or a joking manner may be used so that the negative label will leave its mark but the name caller can deny that he meant it that way.

One possible remedy here is to ignore the cheap shot and reintroduce the real question at hand. This remedy is suitable unless the name calling has a negative effect on the decision-making process. There are two situations in which it may have such an effect. One is when the recipient of the name is a client or significant other who may be stigmatized in terms of decisions made about her or him. Another such situation is when the negative name is attached to one of the decision makers whose views are then ignored as a result, even though they are sound.

Ridicule may be communicated in how something is said as well as by what is said. A roll of the eyes may change the impact of a statement. A look of shared commiseration and strained long-suffering directed toward other participants (a raise of the eyebrows and a sigh) may accompany a statement. Remedies here include restating a position clearly, noting why it should be taken seriously. If the ridicule is offered by a person in authority, others in the group could ask for more appropriate criticism of the position. The success of these remedies depends on several factors, such as the cogency of a point, the views of others, and the status of the ridiculer. Those who use ridicule may attempt to make the target appear pedantic for continuing to uphold an ill-advised position. A more subtle but no more admirable tactic is to make negative innuendoes about a position without offering any evidence for this assumption—to imply, for example, that a certain action will have bad effects. Ad hominem arguments and innuendoes are two stratagems often used to encourage others to discount cogent points.

Force or intimidation is sometimes used to gain compliance in place of offering sound reasons to create conviction. Threats of removal of resources or punishing consequences such as loss of a job may be made. There is, of course, no assurance that decisions based on this foundation are sound.

Why Is the Quality of Discussion in Case Conferences Often Poor?

Reasons for the poor quality of many case conferences are related to the factors discussed at the beginning of this chapter, namely that case conferences represent complex social contexts in which people have different goals, values, styles and skills and in which they are influenced by the particular setting and the pressures within this setting. Reluctance to hurt or embarrass people encourages many of the characteristics described in the sections above. Meehl calls this the "buddy-buddy syndrome." It results from the false belief that high-quality discussions cannot occur unless harsh or discourteous methods are used. This is not so.

If it is argued that you can't prevent people who have nothing significant to contribute from talking without being cruel or discourteous, I submit that this is empirically false. I point to case conferences in other specialties like neurology and internal medicine, where, so far as I have observed, there is no social discourtesy or cruelty manifested by those in charge; but the general atmosphere is nevertheless one which says, in effect, "Unless you know what you are talking about and have reason to think that you are saying something really educational for the rest of us or beneficial to the patient, you would be well advised to remain silent. Mere yakking for yakking's sake is not valued in this club." I have rarely had to listen to trivia, confused mentation, plain ignorance, or irrelevancies when I have attended case conferences in internal medicine or neurology or the clinicopathological conference on the medical service. If an atmosphere of decent intellectual scholarly standards can be created and maintained on those services, I cannot think it is impossible to approximate the same thing in clinical psychology and psychiatry (p. 284).

Participants have different goals. These may be explicit or implicit and may be shared or competitive (if some goals are achieved, others may not be). The explicit goal of case conferences is to make clinical decisions, such as what treatment should be recommended for a client or whether to transfer a client to another facility. The manifest purpose of the group may not be the real one. Take "rubber stamp groups" for example. Here, the ostensible purpose is to arrive at a decision. In reality, the decision has already been made and the purpose of the meeting is to simply go through the motions of having a discussion about a matter that has already been decided. Strains and differences among goals account for some of the odd happenings at group meetings. Personal goals that often do not contribute to the process of decision making include the following: show how bright you are, avoid anyone knowing you don't know what you are doing, impress your superiors, be as invisible as possible (a chair potato), skewer your boss or most disliked colleague, and win your point. Common goals in most groups include maintaining positive relations, controlling intimacy and accessibility, appearing normal, maintaining claims to roles, and controlling information presented.

If participants have different values, misunderstandings may occur. For example, a psychologist may focus on harm done to a victim of rape whereas a lawyer may focus on protecting the rights of the accused. Fallacies that occur may not be recognized, even blatant ones. Case material is often presented in a disorganized fashion, which makes error detection difficult. An agreed upon format for case presentations can be helpful in encouraging descriptions that make it easier to catch errors. Participants may not realize that their biases encourage them to ignore contradictory information. Pfohl (1978) found that diagnostic team members usually passed over contradictory information and, when directly confronted with contradictory evidence, would ask the group "to look beyond this irrelevant 'fact,' to grasp the whole picture of a patient's problem" (p. 175). In many cases, evidence that is contradictory to a position may be transformed into additional evidence for a preferred diagnosis, for example, by interpreting a client's statements as denials that yield further evidence for a diagnosis. Errors are particularly likely when a practice theory is used that can account for anything—even contradictory claims. The high status of psychiatrists in case conferences increases the probability that errors they make will be accepted.

Even if defense lawyers are present at commitment hearings, reliance on knowledge about the patient's behavior in the hospital (to which lawyers do not have access unless they locate and use another insider) gives the upper hand to psychiatrists (Decker, 1987). Sometimes false biographical material is used to bolster a position and remains standing unless challenged.

At times, fallacies are recognized but not commented on because of past failures to improve the quality of discussions. The power structure in a group may be such that no matter how cogent a point, it will not be persuasive because of the apathy and fear of most participants. Or, diplomatic skills that are useful in countering or neutralizing fallacies may be lacking. A history of harsh criticism for speaking up in case conferences or fear of negative evaluation discourages participation. Participants may lack effective social skills, such as focusing on common interests. Strong ideological bias may interfere with balanced consideration of different perspectives. If there are no incentives to alter such biases, the level of discourse may remain at a low level.

Some discussions are not so much arguments but an exchange of opinions. That is, there may be so little clarification of claims and grounds for these, that no one knows what is being discussed. Topics discussed may be of little or no interest to participants. There may be little shared sense of working together toward common goals.

The fact that people sit around a table does not necessarily mean that they will be listened to if they speak. Whether others listen and whether an opportunity to speak is even given depends on factors such as status in a group. Studies of decision making in predicting the dangerousness of psychiatric patients suggest that the effective neutralizing of information contradictory to a preferred diagnosis is based largely on the authority and control of the psychiatrist over other team members (Pfohl, 1978). Psychiatrists used a variety of tactics to control interaction, including interruption of team members in the process of interviewing a patient and disrupting the timing of the presentation of information.

Participants often have different frames of reference and knowledge bases for viewing a concern. A psychiatrist may focus on intrapersonal causes; a social worker may emphasize environmental factors. An administrator may be concerned about the precedent a decision may set. Use of different frames of reference may result in misunderstandings.

Denunciations and Pitches

Some investigators who have made detailed examinations of case conferences conclude that these can most accurately be described as contexts in which someone is prematurely assumed to be responsible for an act such as child maltreatment, and then a denunciation effort is made to bolster this account. "A successful denunciation establishes the act as one typically committed by persons of a 'bad' character and constructs a biography of the actor that indicates such a character. A successful pitch normalizes the act and the biography" (Emerson, 1969, p. 156). Opinions may be changed and actions taken based on appeals to emotion rather than in response to well-thought-out arguments that offer sound reasons. The excerpts below show how participants who disagree with a position are ignored and illustrates the use of emotional language to encourage acceptance of a preferred position. It is based on a transcript of a case conference* held to determine whether a child's injuries resulted from maltreatment and, if so, who was responsible (Dingwall, Eekelaar, & Murray, 1983).

An Example of a Case Conference

The participants in this conference included a social worker (SW), her senior (SSW), a health visitor (HV), her nursing officer (NO), a medical social worker (MSW), two policemen (PC1 and PC2), two physicians (Cons1 and Cons2), a registrar (Reg), a medical student, and a secretary. The family involved in this case included the mother, Mrs. Hancock; her live-in boyfriend, Mr. Finnegin; Mary Walsh, who lived with the family and helped out with the children following the mother's recent accident; Lindy Oates, the eight-month-old baby brought to the hospital; and three other children (pp. 152–153). (All names used throughout this case are fictitious.)

"The child came to casualty at 5 p.m. . . . The boyfriend had come home and said that he had held the child up because it was crying and had discovered a lot of bruises. He didn't know how they had got there and he called the GP [general practitioner]. The GP had said that he had been called only because of a cough and a runny nose. The only prior admitted incident was that the child fell off the sofa and had a bruised cheek. The mother was living with a twenty-six-year-old boyfriend called Finnegan but the child was a child of her former boyfriend. The mother had had her hand in plaster because she had broken her wrist after falling on ice. They

*Source: From *The Protection of Children* (pp. 152–165) by R. Dingwall, J. Eekelaar, and T. Murray, 1983, Oxford, England: Basil Blackwell. Copyright 1983 by Basil Blackwell, R. Dingwall, J. Eekelaar, and T. Murray. Reprinted by permission.

were living with three other children in the house. There was some-
body else living in the house as a kind of help for them who was
known to the social services. On examination the baby was crying.
She had a torn upper frenulum . . . and was covered in bruises . . .
These were on the mouth, the chest and the upper abdomen and
they were usually circular. Some of them were recent, only a few
hours old but others had been there a few days. No other abnormal-
ity had been found and there was no bone injury. The child had
been admitted for observation . . . Everybody commented how wary
the child was when anyone approached the cot . . . She looked
suspicious and afraid . . . and sometimes she cried if anybody tried
to touch her" (pp. 153–154).

There was agreement based on the clinical evidence as well
as on the social context (that is, irregular cohabitation, previous
contact with social services) that the injuries resulted from maltreatment. The discussion then focused on identifying the person guilty
of this abuse.

"*MSW:*   This is complicated by the fact that there are three adults
in the house. No one knows very much about Finnegan. She (Mrs.
Hancock) claims that she wants to marry him and that he is won-
derful with children. Mary Walsh is a vulnerable person who has
been known to the social services and she has been the main caretaker of the child. It's a complicated situation.

SSW: Yes, she was known to us a long time ago but we have had
no contact since then.

CONS1:   Does the present cohabitee have a police record?

PC1:   We don't know.

HV: He is a divorcee with children aged six and four whom he
visits. He looks to be in his 20s. He's Irish, he comes from Belfast.

PC1:   Could the injuries have been due to a fall from a cot?

REG: No.

SW: I know the priest to whom Mary goes when she is in trouble.
I had a phone call on Monday from him saying that Mary has been

upset about the baby. Mary's version, and she is a person who tends to drift around with problem families, is that four weeks ago she was worried about the baby's chest but the parents would not call a doctor. She knows that she is under suspicion, and her explanation is that they didn't call the doctor because of the bruises and she thought that the boyfriend used to grip the baby too tightly. When asked who gets up when the baby cries at night, she says it is the boyfriend. She thinks the bruises come from the boyfriend's holding the baby too tightly" (p. 155).

The authors note that Mary Walsh is discredited by references to her vulnerability as well as by her previous contact with social services, which offer evidence of an uncertain mental state and impairment of responsibility. She is also presented as the person with the greatest opportunity to injure the children, given her role as their main caretaker. On the other hand, Finnegan and the mother are presented as considering marriage and Finnegan's skills with children are praised.

"This debate runs through the conference as the area team social workers attempt to make a pitch for Mary Walsh and the others denounce her. After the MSW's initial proposal, the senior from the area team makes a rather weak attempt to dispute the first two references: her contact with social services was a long time ago and it is therefore wrong to stigmatize her as a current client and as someone who is so vulnerable as to need frequent help. The following utterances generally contribute to the favorable view of the cohabitee: he has no known police record; he is of mature age; and although divorced, he visits his children . . . Mary Walsh's social worker than comes in with another challenge to the MSW's formulation of the household. She links Mary to her parish priest, as someone who might be thought to have a special competence as a receiver of true statements and might be a candidate for the status of 'reputable sponsor,' to assert that Finnegan and Mrs. Hancock are colluding to cover up Finnegan's rough handling of the child . . . The consultant pediatrician points to the limitations of this (second-hand) story in accounting for the clinical presentation" (pp. 156–157).

"CONS1: That doesn't account for the torn lip.

SW: No . . .

CONS1: It seems as if the torn lip was caused by a blow to the face but (Cons2) is more expert at this.

CONS2: There could have been no other way.

SW: Mary is rather dim but very fond of babies. She says that she has had too much put on her of late. She has always looked after other people's children" (p. 157).

Dingwall points out that the social worker "does not have a license to challenge the statement of the consultant." The MSW asks the senior social worker about previous contacts with the family. The senior social worker noted that the first contact with the family was in 1973 when Mrs. Hancock and her husband were homeless and that occasional contacts occurred at other times for financial difficulties and marital problems. "Her husband had left and came back with another woman and tried to turf her out" (p. 157). He was evicted by order of the County Court. The health visitor then spoke:

"HV: I saw Mrs. Hancock yesterday . . . She said she didn't know how the bruises had happened. She said that on Friday her boyfriend said that she should call a doctor and that he was cross when this was not done when he had come home. There was no mention of the bruises to the doctor but the doctor noticed it when he came. She said she didn't know how they had happened and said that Mary had baby sat the previous day and said that she hadn't broached the subject with Mary because Mary was upset due to the death of an aunt. About the lip she said she thought it was simply teething. She said that Mary had been looking after the child the day before. She also said that it was only occasionally that the children were left in a room with the baby but they were not left alone in the house with [the baby]. I asked Mary if she knew how the bruises came and she said no. I asked if she had seen them before and she said that she had seen them on Wednesday. I asked why she hadn't mentioned it and she said she didn't want to cause trouble. I had met them just before the baby was born. Mother/baby interactions

always seemed to be good. Mr. Oates wasn't living with them at the time. He was divorced and had custody of his own children. They originally had planned to get married when they got a four-bedroomed house. Mrs. Hancock came to the clinic in January and then I heard that she had not got a new boyfriend who was Mr. Finnegan—I visited her—Lindy looked well and went to both Mrs. Hancock and her boyfriend readily and cuddled with them and that was the last I saw of them" (pp. 157–158).

The authors comment: "This sequence continues the character work on the three adults. The senior social worker runs over Mrs. Hancock's record. She is known to the department but not as a persistent or highly dependent client. The most recent contacts with her have been as the victim of her husband's attempt to prise her out of the matrimonial home and as a self-referral for help with her children's behavior." The health visitor "depicts Mrs. Hancock as worried about the baby's health, as a reliable source of data on her boyfriend's concern and as a kindly woman who had not liked to ask Mary about the bruising on the child because of Mary's recent bereavement" (p. 158).

"*CONS1:* Has anybody else anything to say? (There is a long silence.) I think it appears to be a child who by persons unknown has been subject to repeated assaults over a period of time . . . I would feel that the child should not be allowed to return home when further damage might occur . . . Does anybody feel that they would like the child to go home?

SW: Whoever caused the injury, it's quite clear that the others have colluded with it. Because of the relationship, it is not possible to point the finger.

MSW: Mary might be being used as a scapegoat" (p. 159).

The authors note that nobody is yet firmly identified as the agent of the abuse. The consultant still holds out the possibility that Mrs. Hancock was responsible, but whoever has done it, as the social worker and her colleague point out, all the adults may be responsible. The "consultant shuts out the possibility of disagreement with his conclusion about returning the child. A view is stated and the obligation placed on the hearers to show why it should not prevail, an exercise which would involve breaching a strong interactional preference for agreement, an act which is capable of discrediting the speaker as a person of sound judgment. By her partial agreement, however, the social worker gets into a position where she can renew her attempts to defend her client" (p. 159). The discussion continues.

> "*SW:* Mary is leaving this weekend. She has known the baby since it was born and she has looked after the older children when Mrs. Hancock had her baby . . . What might happen is that if a child is miserable for four weeks with a cold this could be a trigger.
>
> *PC2:* Was Mary married?
>
> *SW:* Yes to Matt Walsh, an inadequate person who drank a lot.
>
> *PC2:* What's her age?
>
> *SW:* 28 and she is fairly dim.
>
> *PC1:* Could the children have been responsible? The eldest is seven.
>
> *HV:* I don't think that she would leave them alone with the baby. Maureen's a tearaway; she has set light to a bedroom.
>
> *REG:* But they are adult fingertips.
>
> *PC2:* Has anybody seen them separately?
>
> *SW:* Not really.
>
> *PC2:* Mary hasn't been seen about it?
>
> *HV:* No. She has gone to her GP this morning." (pp. 159–160)

Another possible cause of the injuries, the other children, is discussed. The discussion continues, and some additional evidence of the abuse is brought forward.

"CONS2: Is this Mrs. Walsh part of the famous Walsh family? There is a subculture, of which the Walshes are a part, who have been battering their children for 30 years.

SW: He is the brother of Bridget.

CONS2: That's right, she was a Walsh, she flung her baby across the room in front of me. The first time I actually saw classic baby-battering myself. They all belong to a subculture of batterers. My God, a bloody Walsh, God help us.

SW: But she is a Walsh by marriage only.

CONS2: Oh it doesn't matter. It isn't a question of the genes. Well I am very doubtful of taking them on with any hope for success. (There is some further muttering along these lines.)

PC1: Are there any signs of neglect, for example, nappy rash?

HV: No.

CONS2: All this is very recent. A very recent intrusion and we have now an intruder with an ominious name.

PC1: It is one for us?

CONS2: Yes, it is for you gentlemen. When the mother broke her wrist, someone intervened.

PC1: So long as we have a statement of complaint we can act. Is the baby being taken into care?" (pp. 161–162).

The authors comment that this passage is the key to the conference outcome; that it "opens up the possibility of . . . a 'total denunciation,' which overrides all possible defenses by declaring that the person's character is so irremediably damaged as to eliminate all chance of successful voluntary intervention. By linking Mary Walsh to a known child abuser, her sister-in-law, Bridget, she is tied into a group for whom child mistreatment is a natural way of life. As such, she must be the agent of these particular injuries. Moreover, the actions involved are so intrinsic to her moral nature as a member of this 'subculture of batterers' that there is little prospect of changing them without compulsion or punishment. Mary's social worker "still attempts to test the analysis."

"*CONS2:*   It doesn't seem as if the mother neglected her.

SW: But she colluded.

CONS2:   Yes, that is a matter for the police." (p. 162).

The authors note that the absence of neglect of the child is being tied to the children's mother rather than being used as evidence on Mary's behalf. "Again, we have the 'facts' being assembled to support a particular characterization. Debate on this is quickly shut down" (p. 162).

"*PC1:*   How long will the child stay here?

CONS1:   We could keep her a week

PC1:   That'll give us time to do our business.

SW: Has the mother visited the child? How does the baby react?

REG: She has . . .

MSW: So we should wait to hear from the police and then consult with you.

CONS2:   Yes, I will do some research.

SW: Yes, it is relevant. She has looked after children before.

CONS2:   I'm not accusing her. The link-up is a necessary piece of knowledge.

MSW: I could find out from the social workers where she looked after children before.

NO: What if the parent wanted to take the child home?

CONS2:   You should get a place of safety. . . .

CONS1:   Is there anything else?

PC2:   I need some personal details of Walsh.

SW: Is there any way of finding out a bit about Martin Finnegan?

PC1: We will (laughter)." (pp. 162–163).

The authors note that even though "the social worker asks about the child's reaction to her mother, points to Mary Walsh's record of satisfactory child caretaking and to their ignorance of Martin Finnegan's past . . . none of these challenges is picked up. The registrar attempts to deal with the first and is cut off, the second is ignored, and the third . . . is treated as a joke . . . By the end of the conference the police are already referring to 'Walsh' in the way they would characteristically talk of a suspect. Mary Walsh is to be prosecuted and the children left at home" (p. 163).

This case conference illustrates an effort to determine who is responsible for the maltreatment of a child—who is capable of such an action. The authors believe that the selection of Mary was the predictable outcome of a process that permeates the whole system for the identification and management of mistreatment. She seemed to be the person least responsible for her actions and therefore most likely to have been responsible for the abuse. Identification of Mary as the culprit allows the family to remain intact and minimizes the amount of coercion involved. Dingwall and his colleagues note how difficult it would be to challenge the preferred account "without calling one's own competence into question" (p. 164). When a "total denunciation is initiated, those who hold other views must be brought into line or discredited" (Emerson, 1969, pp. 140–141). Dingwall, Eekelaar, and Murray are also aware of the long-term effects of being discredited; these professionals will see each other again in the future.

And what was the outcome? Mary Walsh was arrested and was prosecuted on a charge of bodily harm. The case was dismissed. "About two weeks after this hearing, Lindy Oates was admitted to hospital with two skull fractures, a broken arm and three broken ribs. Her brother had bruising in nineteen separate places. It emerged that Martin Finnegan had, five years previously, been convicted of causing grievous bodily harm to his own daughter. He pleaded guilty to the assaults on Lindy and her brother and was jailed for four years. Mrs. Hancock continued to insist on his competence as a stepfather and announced her intention of standing by him" (p. 165).

The authors believe that the identification of Mary Walsh as the person responsible for the abuse was the expected outcome of the reasoning process that characterizes the system in which these kinds of cases are reviewed. "Once Lindy Oates had been adequately characterized as a victim, Mary seemed to be the person least responsible for her own actions and therefore most likely to have perpetrated the injuries. Moreover, her prosecution left Mrs. Hancock's household/family intact and the children out of state care. The decision gives effect to the liberal principles which child protection operates" (p. 165). (See Chapter Seven for a discussion of the rule of optimism.)

Enhancing Effectiveness in Case Conferences

Steps that can be taken to enhance effectiveness in case conferences are described below.

Use Effective Interpersonal Skills. Effective use of clear thinking skills in group contexts requires complementary social skills. This became clear shortly after I had introduced material on clear thinking in my classes for graduate students. For example, one student said that the chief psychiatrist became quite irritated when she questioned the clarity of a term he used during a conference. Rather than clarify the term, he asked the student "Don't they teach you that at Berkeley?" He attempted to use his prestige and authority in an ad hominem attack on the student's school. So, colleagues may not appreciate others who ferret out vagueness and identify fallacies even though this is helpful in avoiding clinical errors. Women should be prepared that they may be liked less and viewed as less competent and qualified than their male counterparts if they rely on power bases traditionally associated with men (Falbo, Hazen, & Linimon, 1982). Clear thinking skills can be used to identify and counter methods others may use to discourage active involvement. Gaining the attention of the group will require skill in identifying appropriate opportunities to enter a discussion. Holding the floor against interruption attempts is an important skill (see Gambrill and Richey, 1988).

Humor can be used for many different purposes including encouraging others to feel relaxed, defusing aggressive reactions, relieving embarrassment, reminding people of social rules, introducing risky topics, and unmasking pretentions (McGee & Goldstein, 1983; Chapman & Foote, 1977). A sense of humor helps to keep things in perspective.

Present Ideas Clearly and Persuasively. Guidelines offered by Rieke and Sillers (1984) for the use of evidence include using detailed persuasive examples that relate to the experience of the audience, noting exceptions to a position, and selecting representative examples. How ideas are presented as well as what is said influences the persuasiveness of a message. Practice helps in presenting views clearly and persuasively. Women may need special coaching because of their greater tendency to use brief words or phrases rather than elaborated opinion statements in expressing their views (Hall, 1972). An elaborated opinion statement starts with a pronoun and contains a compound sentence such as "Well, I think this because of . . ." Women sometimes have a tendency to smile or even giggle when talking and, if the matter being discussed is a serious one, such responses will dilute the impact of what is said. Seating position may influence persuasiveness at least for men. Porter and Geis (1981) found that even avowed feminists did not perceive women who sat at the head of a table as leaders. Eye contact with others will enhance the credibility of statements.

The "humble inquirer and doubter" approach that Benjamin Franklin found so useful in having others consider his views may be effective in some groups. Franklin "resolved never to advance any view as certainly correct, but rather to express himself in terms of 'modest diffidence' (Silverman, 1986, p. xix). In other groups, phrases that minimize the importance of what is said (such as, "I don't know if this is important, but" or "this may not be significant, but") may encourage others to tune out rather than tune in.

Present Ideas Positively. Presenting ideas in a positive manner involves avoiding unnecessary negative comments about other views, recognizing common interests, and praising other people's good ideas. Temptations to make hostile or sarcastic comments should be resisted. Points can be persuasively made without resorting to put-downs, which although they may temporarily impress people by their wit, will not win any friends or influence many people.

Do Not Take Things Personally. Assuming the best rather than the worst about other people's intentions helps one identify and move beyond fallacies and stratagems without becoming overly emotional. Certainly there are times when a direct request for a behavior change is called for. One of the reasons unconstructive behaviors persist is because no one does anything to discourage them.

Prepare for Meetings. The likelihood of offering sound arguments can be increased by practicing how to present views, anticipating counterarguments, and being prepared with responses. A search for accurate explanations requires an open exploration and critique of different alternatives. Consideration of different options or perspectives about a topic, such as what treatment regimen may be best for a depressed elderly woman, before case conferences will be helpful in weighing the credibility of evidence during meetings.

Those with privileged access to relevant data will have an advantage since their statements cannot be checked. During a commitment hearing, a psychiatrist may be the only one present with knowledge of a patient's behavior in the hospital (Decker, 1987). If the psychiatrist's report cannot be corroborated, there is no way of knowing whether it is accurate or not. Studies of periodic commitment hearings show that evidence offered is not always accurate (see, for example, Decker, 1987). Other staff members may have access to a patient's behavior, and their reports may be sought. Case records should be reviewed before case conferences to check statements based on these records for accuracy. Memories of what was contained in case records may be altered by confirmation biases. That is, malicious intent or deliberate misreporting is probably not the reason for false reports.

One purpose of group meetings may be to discuss a change

in procedure or policy. Decisions discussed in group meetings may really be made outside the group. For example, a small cohort may run things in a hospital by laying the groundwork for support of preferred positions prior to meetings. This may be done by meeting together and agreeing on a position and by seeking the support of others who are sympathetic to a position prior to the group meeting. It is much easier to distort positions if these do not appear in writing. People who are propagandists rather than "point-of-viewers" are aware of this and will try to discourage this—usually by claiming that putting things in writing is unnecessary, foolish, a waste of time, or dangerous. This is not to say that noting things in writing is always a good idea. Clearly it is not, for example, if a policy is to be flexibly implemented.

Clarify Vague Terms and Evaluations. General terms and vague evaluations often are heard in case conferences. Unless these are clarified, their relevance and validity cannot be judged. Metaphors should be clarified in terms of how they apply to a discussion. The same is true for fables and descriptions of personal experiences. Such descriptions may be psychologically moving but may not help in making accurate decisions. Vague statements such as "she's mentally ill," and vague labels such as "borderline personality" or "depressive syndrome" should be clarified. Abstractions sometimes hide a lack of supportive evidence.

Distinguish Between Strong Opinions and Bias. Strong opinions often are mistaken for bias (Scriven, 1976). People can accurately be called biased only if their reasons for holding a position are matters of prejudice and they cannot be convinced to alter their position when presented with more accurate premises or inferences. The style of presentation may be misleading in distinguishing between someone who is biased and someone who has strong opinions. Strong bias may pass unchallenged because of the style of presentation. For example, someone who is biased may disguise this by acting as if he has been forced into accepting a position against his will; that it is the last thing he would do if his hands were free (which they are). Conversely, someone who is open to a discussion of different perspectives may appear biased because of an overly strong assertion of a point of view. People with a point of view will try to offer a reason for their view. "Someone can be said to represent a point of view rather than a bias if s/he strives to (a) identify his/her interests; (b) open them to examination; (c) encourage discussion; and (d) take into serious consideration dissenting points of view" (MacLean, 1981, p. 148).

Focus on Common Goals. Fisher and Ury (1983) stress the importance of focusing on common goals, especially in contentious atmospheres. Focusing on common goals will be helpful in keeping anger and anxiety in reasonable bounds, even in response to people who are masters of giving others "aggro" (aggravation). Rather than dwelling on the problem person, the common goal can be reviewed. This focus encourages a consensual approach to decision making and an interest in understanding other points of view.

Increase Knowledge of Group Process. Many behaviors that occur in groups are the result of particular kinds of group process and structure. For example, groups have different leadership patterns and different norms. Being familiar with group process and structure increases your effectiveness in groups (see, for example, Feld & Radin, 1982). Knowledge of group process highlights the importance of setting an agenda at the beginning of the meeting to ensure that important topics are discussed. This information highlights the prevalence of the buddy-buddy syndrome and will perhaps encourage group members to select someone to be the guardian of agreed-on norms.

Know Whom You Are Dealing With. It helps to know whom you are dealing with—that is, to be familiar with preferred interactional styles of participants. It may not be possible to change a disliked or dysfunctional style; however, clear thinking skills and interpersonal competencies can be used to mute the effects of styles that compromise the quality of decision making. Group members can become more active in pointing out fallacies. Some people possess clear thinking skills as well as positive interpersonal competencies but use these only when they must in order to reach their goals. I have been quite amazed to see that someone who is usually attacking and demeaning in a discussion, and who makes use of dishonest strategies such as misrepresenting positions, can act quite differently (courteous, attentive, even ingratiating) in settings in which such strategies would be identified and quickly countered. Rather than assuming a pained patronizing expression when colleagues speak, there is attentive interest with an expression that wise words are being spoken.

The preferred style of some individuals is to make unsupported pronouncements and to act as if support is offered for the pronouncement when it is not. This method is used mostly by those who occupy a power position in the group—taking advantage of participants' reluctance to question a person in such a role. Pronouncers may assume a patronizing or offended stance if asked to support their pronouncements. Some people try to encourage others to go along with a position by forecasting negative outcomes if disliked options are selected. A colleague may say that if cognitive-behavioral methods are used rather than lithium to treat depression, the patient may make another suicide attempt. The question is: Is there any evidence that such an attempt would be more likely if the former method were used? If others are not swayed by one negative forecast, additional scare tactics may be invoked to create fear and worry. Intimidators may first try to neutralize disliked positions (for example, by using patronizing responses) and if this fails, they may then try to intimidate participants.

Seeking solutions to difficult clinical questions may be hampered by naysayers who may comment, "it won't work," "we've tried that in the past and it failed," "there's no time," "we don't have the resources," "you don't understand our system," or "that's the way we've been doing it for years." Typically, no evidence or only weak support is provided for such statements. Such statements may be made not because a solution is not desired, but because no possible solution can be envisioned. If this is so, providing a feasible option may result in a more constructive participation.

Encourage Helpful Group Practices. Agreeing on an agenda is useful in clarifying the goals of a meeting and increasing the probability that they are met. Agreement on an agenda offers an opportunity to reaffirm decisions to pursue certain goals if people get off the track. Another method that can be used to upgrade the quality of case conferences is to establish norms, such as (1) no one should interrupt another speaker, (2) no one person should hog the floor, (3) speakers are responsible for describing how points raised relate to the topic being discussed, and (4) pronouncements should be accompanied by supporting reasons. Agreement on a case presentation format will decrease discussion of extraneous data and help to ensure inclusion of data that increase the accuracy of decisions, such as information about environmental factors related to presenting problems. Another helpful norm is to take a vote on controversial issues; otherwise a consensus in favor of a position may be assumed when there is none, or there may be a consensus, but in favor of a competing position. One group member can be selected to introduce alternative perspectives in groups in which there tends to be premature closure and to remind the group that they should not attack (or ignore) people who introduce different views but respond to points raised in a thoughtful manner. This role can be assumed by a different person each month.

Enhance Clear Thinking Skills. Being familiar with formal and informal fallacies increases the likelihood that you can identify them and move the discussion to sounder points. Having names or numbers for the fallacies helps in recognizing them and may even be of value in discouraging a fallacy with humor. When I pointed out to one of my colleagues, who had the habit of distorting positions and then attacking the distorted version, that he had just committed number 19 of Thouless's (1974) list of thirty-eight dishonest tricks of debate, everyone laughed and he dropped his strawman argument. Case conferences provide one of many opportunities to hone clear thinking skills and related interpersonal competencies. Examples of informal fallacies are bound to occur. A "fallacy or stratagem of the week" can be selected for special focus.

Try to Understand Other Points of View. Clearly understanding the basis for other points of view helps in identifying flaws in positions. If this guideline had been used by participants in the case conference described earlier in this chapter, the true culprit may have been identified as being responsible for the abuse of Lindy and subsequent abuse avoided. Cogent counterarguments can be offered only if other views are understood. A focus on common goals encourages attention to other perspectives. We are less likely to blame others for actions, statements, and styles that we do not like if we try to see things from their perspectives. Empathic reactions increase recognition of environmental factors that influence others (Regan & Totten, 1975) and are positively related to accuracy in judging others (Davis, 1981).

Arguments and Discussions

There is general agreement that disagreements and differences of opinion are inevitable; however, many clinicians do not learn to discuss differences in a helpful fashion. For those who lack skills and positive experiences with discussions of differences, disagreements may create feelings of anxiety or anger. For example, students in the School of Social Welfare at Berkeley had been interested for years in forming a panel of clinicians with different perspectives and having these individuals discuss a case or some common questions. Some instructors who were approached turned them down on the grounds that a discussion of differences would be divisive. The terms *discussion* and *debate* seemed to be associated with *oppositional, destructive,* and *confrontational,* rather than with *inquiring* and *open.*

Some people react to disagreements as if these are altercations or may lead to altercations or fights. The term *argument* as used in lay language typically refers to a disagreement between two people—emotions are high, language may be abusive. There is disregard for the feelings of others. Winning is the object rather than finding the truth, and there is a resistance to new ideas. Discussions, dialogues, and debates are centered on issues rather than on people. The purpose of a discussion is not to protect the self-esteem of the head of the psychology department, it is to determine if Mr. Richards is ready to be discharged from the hospital or whether Mr. Sansom, who is dying of AIDS, requires a more protective setting. The emphasis should be on finding the correct or best solution to client problems. There is an openness to new ideas rather than a resistance to these no matter what their source—whether offered by

a low-power person, such as a social worker in a medical conference, or by a high-power person, such as the head physician on a
service unit; emotion is at a functional level.

Summary

One setting in which clinical decisions are made, discussed,
or rubber-stamped is case conferences. The case conference has been
the subject of some excellent and lively critiques, such as the classic
chapter by Meehl, in which he identified a number of characteristics
that dilute the quality of decisions made, including the tolerance for
feeble inferences and rewarding gold and garbage alike. Factors that
encourage the use of low-level appeals and irrelevant statements
include the buddy-buddy syndrome (people are reluctant to hurt or
embarrass others), a feeling of powerlessness, social anxiety, lack of
effective social skills, vested interests, ideological biases, and failure
to recognize fallacies. Rather than being a setting in which there is
a reasoned discussion of different alternatives, case conferences may
reflect emotive denunciations and pitches for or against particular
individuals.

Effective interpersonal skills such as considering other perspectives and assuming the best about the intentions of others are
an important complement to clear thinking skills. An emphasis on
collaboration rather than confrontation will encourage consideration and acceptance of divergent viewpoints. Other steps that can
be taken to increase effectiveness in case conferences include learning to identify and counter fallacies (such as polarized thinking,
straw person arguments, and appeals based on emotion rather than
reason) and encouraging helpful group practices, such as setting
agendas.

12

Overcoming Personal Obstacles to Critical Thinking

Lack of self-knowledge is one obstacle to effective reasoning. Other knowledge impediments include lack of topical knowledge and lack of procedural knowledge (Nickerson, 1986a). Self-knowledge includes familiarity with resources and limitations of reasoning processes in general as well as knowledge of personal strengths and limitations that influence decision making. Awareness of personal responses to certain kinds of clients or client behavior helps avoid unconstructive countertransference. Blau (1988) argues that psychotherapeutic errors may occur because of character flaws or neurotic conflicts on the part of clinicians. Errors of character pathology that he identifies include inappropriate intimacy between clients and clinicians, breaches of confidentiality, lying to clients, and not seeking consultation when it is called for. Both rehabilitative as well as preventative restraints are recommended in such instances in the form of selecting two senior colleagues, one to serve as a therapist and one to serve as a supervisor, to prevent the repetition of errors. Errors related to neurotic traits include becoming too busy to properly conduct practice, being inappropriately confrontative, overresponding to threats, not setting appropriate limits, and not dealing with depletion. Errors due to neurotic characteristics are presumed to reflect the fears, anxieties, and inappropriate or inadequate coping responses of the clinician, which in turn reflect the clinician's life-style.

Lack of interest in having a carefully thought out position or a wish to appear decisive may compromise the quality of clinical reasoning, as may a preference for mystery over mastery. Other obstacles to clear thinking include a low tolerance for ambiguity, a tendency to make premature judgments, unrealistic expectations, and a desire for quick success (Adams, 1974). Obstacles to the full development of intelligence identified by Sternberg (1987) include the following (pp. 212–213):

- Lack of motivation
- Lack of impulse control
- Lack of perseverance, or perseveration
- Inability to translate thought into action
- Talk of completing problems but lack of follow-through
- Failure to initiate
- Procrastination
- Distractability and lack of concentration
- Inability to delay gratification
- Spreading oneself too thick or too thin
- Capitalizing on the wrong abilities
- Lack of product orientation
- Fear of failure
- Misattribution of blame
- Excessive self-pity
- Excessive dependency
- Wallowing in personal difficulties
- Inability or unwillingness to see the forest from the trees
- Lack of balance between critical, analytic thinking and creative, synthetic thinking
- Too little or too much self-confidence

Attitudes considered critical for clear thinking included intellectual curiosity, intellectual honesty, objectivity, intelligent skepticism, open-mindedness, conviction of universal cause-and-effect relationships, disposition to be systematic, flexibility, and decisiveness (Burton, Kimball, and Wing, 1960). A comparison of subjects who were good and poor problem solvers revealed that good problem solvers were more attentive to detail and more aggressive, confident, and tenacious. Poor problem solvers relied on unreasoned guessing and self-justification, and they did not attend to detail (Bloom & Broder, 1960). Although some argue that there are different personal styles of decision making, so far there is little evidence for cross-situational consistency of style—perhaps because of variability in task requirements in different situations (Wright, 1985). Persistence and immersion in a task are two characteristics of creative thinkers (Weisberg, 1986). Baron (1981) suggests the traits of precision, efficiency, and originality as important cognitive styles. The term *style* refers to a way of approaching problems that is used in many different situations (Yinger, 1980). A preferred style may not influence all areas; for example, a clinician may be imprecise about goals, but be quite precise about scheduling appointments. Being sensitive to the feelings, level of knowledge, and degree of sophistication of others, as well as seriously considering the points of view of others, are also important (Ennis, 1987).

Recognize Signs of Depletion

Burnout has been a popular topic in the literature on psychotherapy. Symptoms of burnout include cynicism, depression, a loss of motivation and energy, a numbing of feeling. Burnout results from an imbalance between the strains of clinical practice and available skills and resources for handling these strains—it is sometimes referred to as an overload (Blau, 1988). Indications of burnout include sleepiness during sessions; drifting attention; being late for therapy sessions with increasing frequency; annoyance with patients; overzealous relief at the end of the work day; feelings of relief when a client cancels; sardonic or humorous references to patients; psychophysiological responses; increased irritability with staff, family and clients; and disillusionment with the work of psychotherapy (p. 284).

These indicators can be used as signs that something should be changed in one's personal or work life to create a more positive balance. For example, one cause of overload is not evaluating progress with clients; it is easy to become discouraged when clinical effectiveness is not assessed (Gambrill, 1983). Seeking new material through attending professional conferences and reading is one source of renewal suggested by Blau (1988). The topics addressed in this chapter identify other ways in which overload can be reduced and personal obstacles to critical thinking reduced.

Increase Effective Reactions to Uncertainty and Ambiguity

Clinical practice is highly probabilistic in both the assessment and intervention phases. Consider the following questions: How accurate is this client's self report? Will this treatment be more (or less) effective than another? How long should follow-up services be provided in order to maintain gains? Time limits the amount of information that can be gathered. Intervention plans must often be chosen in the face of uncertainty due to lack of data about the effectiveness of different methods. Uncertainty breeds a temptation to deny this tendency, perhaps fearing that recognition of it would stifle needed action. Inflated estimates of judgmental accuracy may in part be an adaptive reaction to the high degree of uncertainty that often exists in clinical practice; this overconfidence encourages needed action despite uncertainties concerning outcomes (Fischhoff, 1975).

How uncertainty is handled influences the quality of clinical decisions. It can be denied or ignored; that is, clinicians can (and often do) act as if a higher degree of certainty is warranted than is the case. Choice of this option may result in overlooking alternative, more accurate accounts. Recognizing the uncertainty involved in making clinical decisions and taking steps to reduce it is the approach recommended here. Steps that can be taken to decrease uncertainty include drawing on information in the professional literature and using multiple sources of assessment (see Chapter Eight). Making precise predictions and comparing these with client progress will improve the accuracy of future estimates. Acknowledging uncertainty does not mean that clinical decisions are not made; it means that they are made in spite of uncertainty, taking whatever steps possible to decrease it.

View Errors and Lack of Success as Learning Opportunities

Assumptions may not be questioned because of fears about discovering errors. Clinical errors and lack of success are inevitable in professional practice. Skill in troubleshooting is one of the cluster of skills that distinguishes novices from experts. Responding to setbacks as opportunities to learn focuses attention on problem solving. Reactions to feedback are influenced by how secure people feel; secure individuals are more receptive to both positive and negative feedback than are insecure people (Snyder & Clair, 1977; see also Chanowitz & Langer, 1985).

We tend to attribute our successes to our own efforts and abilities and our failures to external influences such as luck or test difficulty (see, for example, Davis and Davis, 1972). Excuses are especially likely to occur when we consider ourselves responsible for a negative outcome but still want to believe that we are good people. Excuses can be defined as "explanations or actions that lessen the negative implications of an actor's performance, thereby maintaining a positive image for oneself and others" (Snyder, Higgins, & Stucky, 1983, p. 45). For example, if an incorrect clinical decision is made one or more of the following accounts could be offered:

- It was impossible to get all the information.
- This was an unusually difficult case; anyone would have had trouble.
- I was pressed for time.
- I didn't have the authority to make a decision.
- I was tired.
- My graduate education didn't prepare me for this kind of case.

Examples of excuses astrologers offered when they made a wrong statement about a client include the following (Dean, 1986–1987, p. 173):

1. Client does not know himself.   } This shifts the blame from astrology to the participants.
2. Astrologer is not infallible.

3. Another factor is responsible.   } This puts the blame on the ambiguity of the birth chart.
4. Manifestation is not typical.

Excuses serve many functions, including preserving self-esteem, smoothing social exchanges, and helping people to live with their limitations. They function as self-handicapping strategies if they reduce options for achieving valued clinical goals. To the extent to which the excuses relieve clinicians from assuming undue responsibility for clients and encourage reasonable risk taking, they are helpful. To the extent to which they prevent clinicians from recognizing limitations that could be altered (through, for example, keeping up with practice-related research) or prevent them from using available knowledge of content and procedures, they are not helpful.

Reframing strategies attempt to mute the negative effects of an action. Harm may be underestimated ("He wasn't really harmed"), victims may be derogated ("He's not really worth helping"), or the source of the negative feedback may be attacked ("My supervisor doesn't have experience with such cases.") The third strategy is encouraged by our tendency to question the accuracy of negative feedback. Acts of omission may be excused by denying there was any need for action, as in the famous Kitty Genovese case in which witnesses who observed the slaying of a young woman did not become involved; they said they thought it was a "lovers' quarrel" or that it was not their responsibility (Rosenthal, 1964).

Transformed responsibility excuses emphasize decreased responsibility for an act. For example, consensus-raising tactics may be used; a clinician can protest that others would have acted in the same way. He can say that he was coerced or shortcomings can be attributed to others to avoid threats to himself—that is, projection can be used (Snyder, Higgins, & Stucky, 1983, p. 97). Use of projection is illustrated by research that shows that when people receive negative feedback they describe others as having the negative characteristics (Holmes, 1978, p. 40). A temporary inconsistency in performance may be appealed to in order to decrease responsibility. Variations include the intentionality plea (p. 41) ("I didn't mean to do it") and effort-lowering statements ("I didn't try"). (For a detailed description of different kinds of accounts, see Semin & Manstead, 1983.) Excuses may save time in the short term, but cost time in the long run. For example, not evaluating practice and not keeping up with practice-related research saves time in the short run but may cost time in the long run both for clients and clinicians because the most effective intervention methods may not be chosen. For further discussion of fear of failure on the part of clinicians see Kottler and Blau, 1989.

Enhance Stress-Management Skills

Stress may result from too much work, personal problems, a job that is boring or too demanding in terms of the match between required and available skills, or an oversensitivity to negative evaluations (see Table 13). Too little or too much interest, anxiety, or anger can get in the way of making accurate decisions. Excessive interest in an outcome may interfere with the careful weighing of

Table 13. Sources of Stress and Remedies.

Source	*Remedy*
• Negative thoughts	• Replace with positive task-oriented thoughts
• Ineffective social skills	• Acquire effective skills
• Overwork	• Plan more manageable work load (for instance, delegate responsibility), acquire needed resources
• Fatigue	• Check balance between work and recreation
• Lack of positive feedback from colleagues	• Arrange support group
• Lack of self-reinforcement for accomplishments	• Increase self-reinforcement
• Muscle tension	• Use relaxation skills
• Lack of knowledge	• Acquire needed information
• Lack of clinical skills	• Acquire helpful skills
• Lack of positive feedback from clients	• Enhance evaluation skills
• Lack of needed resources	• Problem-solve to determine if added resources can be acquired

evidence and make it difficult to manage impatience, anxiety, or anger. Both behavioral and cognitive coping skills can be of value in avoiding and regulating arousal (see Table 14). Situations initially appraised as threatening can be reframed as unimportant by asking questions such as "Does this really matter?" and "Will it make any difference ten years from now?" Ignoring minor irritations and acquiring skills in requesting behavior changes and responding to criticism will be helpful in avoiding reactions of anger that interfere with clear thinking skills. Expressing anger in an abusive manner only makes matters worse (Averill, 1982). See other sources for further detail (for example, Burns, 1980; Hazaleus & Deffenbacher, 1986; Matteson & Ivancevich, 1987; Novaco, 1975).

Increase Relationship Skills

Clinical practice involves exchanges with clients, significant others, fellow workers, clerical help, and various other professionals who may become involved in a case. The quality of skills for handling the social situations that arise influences the quality of decisions made. The importance of the clinician's relationship skills has been highlighted by research in psychotherapy (Garfield & Bergin, 1986). Premature termination by clients is often related to mistakes in how clinicians interact with clients (Herron & Rouslin, 1984; Levinson, McMurray, Podell, & Weiner, 1978). Examples of mistakes described by Kottler and Blau (1989, pp. 80–81) are shown below.

- Distracting mannerisms or facial expressions
- Poor attending skills and eye contact
- Difficulty following and focusing the direction of the client's statements
- The use of closed-ended questions and an interrogative style that puts the client on the defensive
- Frequent interruptions of the client's natural stream of expression
- Noting surface messages of the client's verbalizations rather than deeper-level messages

Table 14. Coping Skills Used by Hospice Nurses.

Rational Action
Came up with a couple of different solutions
Accepted my limitations
Did what I knew had to be done
Tried to learn from the situation
Discussed the situation with peer or team member
Drew on past experience of similar situation
Tried not to act too hastily
Told myself I had done well
Told myself that I was not responsible

Fantasized Action
Wished that I could change the way I felt
Wished that I could change what happened
Imagined a better time or place than the one I was in
Wished that the situation would go away or be over
Wished I were a stronger person

Emotional Avoidance
Kept my feelings to myself
Tried to forget the whole thing

Professionalism
Assured myself that the dying are needy
Told myself that dying is a natural process
Chose my words carefully with the patient

Emotional Response
Took deep breaths and/or mediated
Waited to see what would happen

Anticipated Coping
Anticipated difficulty and prepared myself emotionally
Talked to someone to find out more about the situation
Made up a plan of action and followed it
Tried to appreciate some humorous aspect of the situation
Asked someone I respected for advice and followed it
Examined my goals regarding the patient
Just took one step at a time

Conflicted Behavior
Avoided being with people for a while
Slept more than usual
Felt better by eating, drinking or smoking
Turned to some other activity to take my mind off things
Sought emotional support from family and friends

Table 14. Coping Skills Used by Hospice Nurses, Cont'd.

Meditation
Prayed
Hoped a miracle would happen
Looked for the "silver lining"
Rediscovered what is important in life
Examined my goals regarding the patient
Focused on what I might learn about life from the patient
Blamed myself
Talked to a patient about my feelings

Concerned Behavior
Went over the problem trying to understand it
Talked to someone who could do something

Source: Adapted from Chiriboga, Jenkins, & Bailey, 1983, p. 297.

- Relying exclusively on the content of communications rather than on affect or process
- Using excessive self-disclosure and inappropriately putting the focus on oneself
- Exaggerated passivity in therapeutic style
- Difficulty tolerating silence
- Appearing unduly cold, aloof, and wooden in appearance
- Appearing too friendly, seductive, and informal
- Being aggressive or punitive in confrontations

Negative outcomes such as an intensification of symptoms may be directly related to inappropriate or ineffective ways of relating to clients (Strupp & Hadley, 1985).

Effective social skills can be used to avoid conflicts as well as to resolve these in a constructive manner. Clear description of the exact nature of a conflict (for example, what does each party want, what indicators will be used to determine whether goals are met) is helpful (Filley, 1975; Fisher & Ury, 1983; Fleming, Fleming, Roach, & Oksman, 1985). A troubleshooting checklist for reviewing situations is offered in Exhibit 3. Examples of relevant social skills include praising others and offering encouragement; offering criticism in a constructive manner; disagreeing with others in a nonabrasive manner; supporting positive alternatives to negative

Exhibit 3. Troubleshooting Checklist.

_____ 1. Were my goals achievable? Did I focus on common goals?

_____ 2. Did I plan how to achieve my goals?

_____ 3. What thoughts and behaviors did I attend to? Were they relevant or irrelevant? Distracting or helpful?

_____ 4. What should I have done more of?

_____ 5. What should I have done less of?

_____ 6. Did I consider other perspectives?

_____ 7. Were special skills required that I don't have?

Source: Adapted from Gambrill & Stein, 1983, p. 159.

behaviors; requesting changes in annoying behavior without becoming unpleasant and effectively responding to criticism (see also Chapter Eleven).

Some clinicians overreact when they are criticized; they become anxious or angry and are less able and willing to consider alternative views. Confrontational rather than cooperative methods may be used to persuade colleagues to accept favored positions. Questions raised by clients about the effectiveness of proposed methods or degree of progress may be met with defensive responses rather than informed answers. Oversensitivity to negative feedback decreases the likelihood that divergent views will be shared or defended in the face of criticism and increases the likelihood of overreactions to criticism. Excessive reactions to negative evaluation or to being ignored may be related to unrealistic expectations, such as expecting to please everyone. Schlenker and Leary (1982) make a persuasive argument that all social anxiety is related to excessive fear of negative evaluation. The main reason people do not speak up in case conferences is because of a concern about what others will think of their ideas, of their style of presentation, or of the way they look. Women are more likely than men to be concerned with pleasing others, which may get in the way of expressing opinions. Focusing on the benefits of taking an active role in creating and critiquing knowlege will encourage participation; independence of judgment is one characteristic of creative individuals (Weisberg, 1986). Emotional reactions can be regulated by keeping things in perspective. "Whenever you are in doubt or when the self becomes too much with you, try the following expedient: Recall the face of the poorest and most helpless man you have ever seen and ask yourself if the step you contemplate is going to be of any use to him . . . Then you will find your doubts and your self melting away" (Ghandi in Burgess, 1984, p. 38). Cultivation of high self-esteem is an adaptive coping strategy even though the grounds for it are not totally accurate. People who have high self-esteem overestimate their competence in comparison with other people's estimates (Lewinsohn, Mischel, Chaplin, & Barton, 1980). In contrast, people who are depressed and who have low self-esteem rate their social competence more poorly than do nondepressed individuals; however, their ratings are closer to those given by others. Thus, denial can be a useful coping strategy (Lazarus, 1983). Social anxiety may be related to a lack of social skills. If this is the case, the most effective way to alter such reactions is to acquire and use helpful skills. One advantage of being a clinician is that clinical assessment skills can be used to determine how to achieve a desired change, such as decreasing social anxiety.

Increase Awareness of Transference and Countertransference Effects

Clinical decisions are made in a social context—one that is prone to transference and countertransference effects. One of the goals of clinical training programs is to help clinicians appreciate the role of transference effects (how clients may respond to clinicians based on their past experiences) and become aware of how they relate to different clients (countertransference effects). Not recognizing such effects may result in clinical errors such as misattributing a lack of progress to environmental obstacles rather than to relationship factors. (See also Strupp & Hadley, 1985.) Kottler and Blau (1989) discuss a number of errors that may result from lack of awareness of countertransference effects, including premature termination of treatment by clinicians due to an unrecognized dislike for clients. Thus, either underinvestment or overinvestment by clinicians in clients may result in less than optimal clinical decisions. Examples of errors described by Herbert Strean in one of his cases that he attributed to his negative attitude toward a client appear below (cited in Kottler & Blau, 1989, p. 132).

- He lost his objectivity and let himself be pulled into the client's manipulative ploys.
- Because of feelings of threat, jealousy, and competition, he perpetuated a continual power struggle.
- He often made the "correct" interpretation or said the "right" words, but in a tone of voice that was more hostile than empathic.
- He spent much of the time trying to prove to the client (flashbacks to his father) that he knew what he was doing.
- Although he was aware that his countertransference feelings were getting in the way, he could not monitor or confront them sufficiently, nor did he seek supervision or therapy to resolve them.
- He retreated behind the mask of cold, objective analyst in order to be punitive rather than adopting a posture of empathy and support.

Lack of appreciation of transference or dependency issues in the client-clinician exchange may result in premature termination (Herron & Rouslin, 1984).

Decrease Unrealistic Expectations

Clinicians are not immune to nurturing unrealistic expectations. These may relate to colleagues ("I have to please everyone"), as well as to clients ("I have to help everyone"). Ellis has offered a variant on his classic list of irrational assumptions that applies to practitioners:

- "I have to be successful with all of my clients practically all of the time.
- I must be an outstanding therapist, clearly better than other therapists I know or hear about.
- I have to be greatly respected and loved by all my clients.
- Since I am doing my best and working so hard as a therapist,

my clients should be equally hardworking and responsible, should listen to me carefully and should always push themselves to change.

• Because I am a person in my own right, I must be able to enjoy myself during therapy sessions and to use these sessions to solve my personal problems as much as to help clients with their problems." (Cordes, 1983, p. 22)

Clinicians who endorse statements such as "I must be successful with all my clients" are prone to stress induced burnout (Deutsch, 1984). Unrealistic beliefs may be due to expectations for success that cannot be realized because individual counseling is not relevant for altering presenting problems (such as homelessness). Waiting for an ideal alternative may result in unnecessary delays in choosing among options that are available (Corbin, 1980). Encouraging realistic expectations increases readiness to seek consultation at appropriate times (when stuck or concerned about a high-risk possibility such as potential suicide).

Improve Time-Management Skills

People who are productive engage in more metaplanning than do their less productive colleagues. Close inspection of a work schedule often reveals room for improvement (Maher & Cook, 1985). Helpful guidelines include the following:

1. Distinguish between tasks that must be done and discretionary tasks that do not have to be completed on a given day.
2. Delegate responsibilities to others.
3. Select a pleasing variety of tasks each day—some that can be easily accomplished and some that will be more challenging.
4. Arrange some distraction-free time each day.
5. Make realistic daily plans.
6. Allow time for recording between interviews.

Stressors differ in how easily they can be controlled. Some clinicians assume that their work days must have a crisis mentality; this attitude will interfere with systematic attention to cases. A closer examination may reveal that some distraction-free time can be arranged; rearranging a schedule or making trades with co-workers may offer some time-outs from phone calls and other interruptions.

Feeling disorganized may be a result of not planning the day in terms of priorities: what must be done versus what could be done (discretionary activities)—being careful not to overload the "must do" category. Arranging the day so that planned activities can be completed offers a sense of achievement and sometimes permits a free period at the end of the day in which some discretionary activity can be selected. If procrastination is a problem, self-management skills can be acquired to overcome this. The Premack Principle can be used to increase desired behaviors; high-probability behaviors can be used to reinforce low-probability behaviors (Premack, 1959). Rather than having a cup of coffee before starting a disliked task (such as recording), a modest amount of recording should first be completed (close to baseline). If delegating responsibility is difficult, the reasons for this can be explored. Taking advantage of a personal computer will take up time in the beginning but will save time in the long run.

Improve Self-Management Skills

The first ten obstacles to the full development of intelligence described at the beginning of this chapter are directly related to a lack of self-management skills. Self-management involves rearranging the environment and behavior in order to attain valued goals. Steps include identifying specific goals, planning how to achieve these, and monitoring progress. For example, if a clinician wants to be more consistent and timely in replying to referral sources— thanking them and offering information concerning progress—he could take advantage of the Premack Principle (see description above) and have readily available such helpful tools as notes and stamps. Precommitment strategies can be used to avoid future temptations such as momentary moods and distractions (Hogarth, 1981). For example, a commitment could be made to spend one hour each week reading the professional literature, and this time could be protected from interruptions by careful planning. Self-regulatory skills such as self-monitoring are a critical component of effective problem solving. Self-change methods have been used to help clients with a wide range of presenting problems; clinicians can also take advantage of these methods (Karoly & Kanfer, 1982; Meichenbaum & Turk, 1987; Watson & Tharp, 1985).

Encourage an Openness to Revising Beliefs

Of all the beliefs about why people think, feel, and act as they do, what is aberrant, what is normal, and what can be done to change behavior, some are based on sound reasons, others are based on unsupported hunches or misinformation. That is, beliefs vary in their accuracy. Some clinicians believe that growing up with an alcoholic parent usually results in a damaged adult. Does it? At a recent presentation on children of schizophrenic parents, the presenter made the comment that growing up with a schizophrenic parent inevitably results in damage to the person. Data concerning invulnerable children (children who to do well despite very difficult environments) were dismissed by the presenter with the statement, "I don't believe it's possible." Here we see an example of the preeminence of personal opinion over positions supported by empirical evidence. Many writers stress the relationship between effective reasoning and an attitude toward the truth. Effective reasoning "presupposes a questioning attitude, an openness to both arguments and facts, and a willingness to modify one's beliefs in the light of evidence that they should be modified. In other words, it presupposes a commitment to the truth insofar as the truth can be ascertained" (Nickerson, 1986a, p. 12). An aspect of this commitment is the understanding that all beliefs should be reexamined from time to time, and that there may be no correct answers for some questions, or no way to find out what the answers are. "That is not to say that reasoning serves no purpose in such cases, but simply to suggest that some issues must be decided on the basis of preferences, tastes, weakly held opinions regarding what the truth might be. The reasonable person will surely reason about such issues, but having reasoned, will recognize the tenuous nature of the basis of any conclusions drawn or decisions reached" (Nickerson, 1986a, pp. 12–13).

To offer high-quality services, new knowledge will have to be used and old material that is no longer useful will have to be winnowed out. Basic to this process is a willingness to challenge ideas and conceptions, a view of knowledge as tentative, and a view of theories as tools rather than dogma to be guarded. People differ in how open they are to examining their beliefs. This topic has been of interest in psychology for many years, as illustrated by Rokeach's book—*The Open and Closed Mind* (1960). Those with closed minds are more limited in their reactions to messages than are individuals with open minds. They are limited to alternatives one and four in the list below (Hayakawa, 1978, p. 232): "1. he may accept the speaker and accept his statement; 2. he may accept the speaker but reject his statement; 3. he may reject the speaker but accept his statement; 4. he may reject the speaker and reject his statement." There is indeed a relationship between dogmatism and making uncritical inferences (Tobacyk & Milford, 1982). There also is a relationship between rigidity, intolerance of ambiguity, and stress (see, for example, Hellman, Morrison & Abramowitz, 1987).

Intuitive beliefs are often remarkably difficult to modify—not only in social contexts but in others as well. For example, many students emerge from introductory physics courses with their original incorrect ideas of motion unchanged and with new knowledge incorporated into old intuitive beliefs so as to preserve these ideas and beliefs (McCloskey, 1984). "Intuitive conceptions are consistent ideas reliably held by the reasoner, which differ from scientific conceptions held by experts" (Linn, 1986, p. 167). Properties of beliefs that influence how difficult it may be to alter them include strength (confidence in a belief—willingness to act on a belief), longevity (how long it has been held), and value (how important it is to us). The stronger a belief, the more it is valued, and the longer it has been held, the harder it will be to change. These factors are not necessarily related to accuracy (Nickerson, 1986a, pp. 23-24). Public commitment to a belief makes it more resistant to change (Levy, 1977). Once a belief is formed, we are likely to fall prey to a confirmation basis—a selective search for confirming data.

Beliefs differ in their plausibility (their credibility or compellingness), as well as in how well they are formulated and how accessible they are in consciousness. Data tend to be interpreted in ways that make it consistent with current self-constructs; information that is not consistent tends to be resisted (Markus, 1977).

Whether a belief is true or false may have great or little impact on the tenability of other beliefs. If knowlege of a subject is quite limited, inconsistencies in beliefs may not be recognized. One way to avoid inconsistencies is not to recognize them; to simply add new beliefs without altering old ones. This has been called the *add on* principle (Harmon, 1986). The principle of *negative undermining* states that we should stop believing something whenever we do not have adequate justification to do so (Harmon, 1986, p. 39). Since clinicians do not keep track of their justifications, they often fail to use this principle. The principle of *positive undermining* states, "you should stop believing something whenever you believe that your reasons for believing it are not good" (p. 39). Clinicians are also influenced by the principle of *clutter avoidance*—the mind should not be cluttered with trivialities (Harmon, 1986, p. 55).

Practice-related beliefs are often difficult to alter because they are linked to a world view; a preferred approach to understanding reality. Conceptions of behavior and how it can be changed form a basic part of beliefs about the nature of human beings and thus have emotional connotations attached to them. If an alternative conception is proposed that deviates from an accepted view in significant ways, the new perspectives may be rejected out-of-hand. The strength of feelings about different views can be seen by reactions to Skinner's views. The more clearly an issue or situation is described, the easier it is to identify related beliefs. Often, it is only when specific situations are considered that differences emerge. For example, clinicians may agree on the value of client self-determination, but disagree as to how this should be implemented in specific cases.

A willingness to question beliefs requires a certain level of self-esteem, as well as curiosity and an interest in discovering what is true. A disinterest in examining practice beliefs may be related to a reluctance to accept responsibility for decisions made. Attributing responsibility for decisions to someone or some other entity (a supervisor, the legal system, the administration) relieves clinicians from assuming responsibilities. It is not unusual to hear clinicians say, "I don't make decisions in my practice. I help clients make their own decisions." This stance overlooks the social-influence process inherent in clinical practice (see, for example, Truax, 1966; Wills,

1982). The belief on the part of clinicians that they do not really make decisions is a key indicator of a sense of powerlessness that develops when someone lacks decision-making skills.

Encouraging Compatible Values

Use of effective clinical decision-making skills may require changes in the value of given incentives. Values that encourage clear thinking include an interest in mastery over mystery, a focus on identifying accurate accounts rather than on winning and being right, and an appreciation for originality rather than for maintaining the status quo. These preferences also increase the likelihood of creative solutions to problems, as does tolerance for differences (Perkins, 1988). Some clinicians read what they feel like reading, giving little thought to the potential clinical usefulness of material. That is, they value entertainment more than gaining knowledge that can help them to help their clients. Some are more concerned with appearing expert than they are with learning from their colleagues.

Changing a Preference for Mystery to One for Mastery. When this attitude is couched in such bold terms (a preference for mystery over mastery), no clinician may admit to it. However, some clinicians do have such a preference, and the aim of this book is to encourage clinicians to look and see what is; not to merely believe in what they would like to be true. One major indicator of such a preference is a disinterest in practice-related research findings that, if implemented, would improve the quality of clinical services. A preference for mystery and apparent profundity in contrast to clear descriptions and evaluation of programs that partially help people explains the neglect by clinicians of research-based data concerning the effectiveness of different kinds of intervention programs. "If a solution can actually be found, it is often judged to have little value, regardless of its practical importance for people's lives" (Thompson, 1988, p. 400). "Findings that would be considered fascinating, if not unprecedented, in other areas of the applied sciences are viewed as pedestrian" (p. 400). A distaste for clear description of procedures and outcomes is partially the result of training that emphasizes mystery over mastery. That is, some clinicians receive a miseducation in which an empirically based practice framework is not accurately described (Todd and Morris, 1983).

A distinterest in using procedural knowledge is often accompanied by absolutism—a search for final answers. This disinterest is also related to the false belief that use of content and procedural knowledge does not allow room for individual creativity. On the contrary, creativity in clinical practice is essential to fill in the gaps in knowledge. A search for final answers is at odds with an empirical approach in which there are no final answers. In opting for all, some clinicians opt against knowing what is known (see discussions of essentialism in Chapter Four).

A preference for mystery over mastery is probably one of the major reasons for the imposter syndrome, the feeling on the part of therapists that they are not therapists. Gibbs and DeVries found that about a fifth of a sample of sixty-two clinicians frequently feel like fakes (DeAngelis, 1987, p. 14). If clinicians do not possess and apply available empirically based content and procedural knowledge concerning problems they address, perhaps they do misrepresent themselves.

Encourage a Willingness to Examine Practice Skills

What people say that they do or know does not necessarily match their behavior. I often have been told "I already do that" when I am discussing the topic of identifying clear objectives. Observation usually reveals that the speaker does not have these skills. A belief that a skill is already available will get in the way of acquiring new competencies. Arranging opportunities to assess the quality of clinical skills offers useful feedback. A clinician who is skilled in a certain assessment or intervention method can review a colleague's use of this method and offer feedback on the fidelity of programs. Colleagues should be selected who are skilled in offering constructive feedback—that is, who know how to identify specific skills related to use of a particular assessment or intervention method and who offer specific feedback concerning helpful changes.

Increasing Self-Efficacy

Effective performance requires skill as well as a history of successful use of skills. "A lack of confidence in our ability to solve problems can manifest itself in a variety of ways; for example, it may be reflected by a lack of interest, a fear of exploring new domains, or a fear of criticism. These feelings can interfere with solving problems and can prevent us from engaging in activities that might improve our problem-solving skills . . . The tendency to avoid new areas becomes especially strong when others are performing well while we experience considerable difficulty. A common way to define such difficulties is simply to assume we are inept or slow and others are talented. An alternative perspective is that *everyone* experiences difficulty when first learning about a new area . . . " (Bransford & Stein, 1984, p. 123). Over the past years, considerable attention has been devoted to examining the influence of judgments of efficacy on performance (Bandura, 1986). Performance efficacy refers to the beliefs that a certain behavior can be performed. Outcome efficacy is a judgment of the likely effect of a behavior. A valued goal may not be pursued because required skills are not available or because of a history that use of skills will not lead to success in achieving a given outcome. Success in real-life situations is the most influential source of efficacy expectations; for example, clinicians who have been effective in helping depressed clients will have high self-efficacy in this area. Judgments of efficacy influence motivation—how long we persist at a task and how much effort we make. Perceptions of self-efficacy influence thoughts and emotions as well. Self-efficacy is not necessarily correlated with available skills. For example, Collins (1982) examined the role of different levels of mathematical efficacy on the performance of children at different levels of mathematical ability. Ability did contribute to performance; however, perceived self-efficacy also influenced behavior. Children who viewed themselves as having high mathematical self-efficacy discarded faulty strategies earlier, reworked more problems they had failed, were more accurate, and had more positive attitudes toward mathematics than did children with lower mathematical self-efficacy. Self-efficacy can be enhanced by acquiring additional skills; it will be diminished by magnifying negative qualities and minimizing positive qualities.

Low levels of outcome efficacy pose an obstacle to clinical decision making in several ways. Helpful views may not be presented in a case conference or may be presented in an ineffective manner. Just as the boldness with which comments are made does not necessarily reflect their soundness, so too, the diffidence with which comments are made does not necessarily reflect a lack of cogency. Low self-efficacy is associated with negative affect, which reduces the quality of problem solving. Positive emotions encourage flexibility and creativity and also enhance helpfulness and generosity, which will add to effectiveness in both client interviews and case conferences (see Isen, 1987). Low self-efficacy increases vulnerability to fears of negative evaluation and embarrassment (Edelmann, 1987, p. 130). Both extremes of self-esteem, excessive and limited, may interfere with clear thinking by encouraging a reluctance to examine beliefs. Evaluations of personal efficacy and self-esteem are not necessarily related (Bandura, 1986). If a clinician is effective in certain situations but does not value his or her particular skills, that clinician may still have low self-esteem.

Many people have a "let me out of here" approach when confronting difficult problems. "Over time, the let me out of here approach can result in self-fulfilling prophecies. For example, people who initially have difficulty solving math problems may come to believe that they have no math ability; they may therefore avoid situations in which they must deal with math problems. Since these people receive little practice with math because they avoid it, their initial hypothesis about not being able to solve math problems is quite likely to come true. In general, it seems clear that people who avoid dealing with problems place limitations on themselves that are not necessarily there to begin with" (Bransford & Stein, 1984, p. 4). Mental escapes such as drifting while reading or listening may be signs of the "let me out of here" attitude. "It can be very difficult to focus attentively on a problem while concerned with competing thoughts about personal problems or about fears that we may fail" (p. 6). Fatigue that is a natural result of hard work may be misperceived as reflecting personal limitations.

Reviewing Compromises

Many clinicians give up trying to stay abreast of practice-related research. Such research has increased substantially, and it is simply not possible to keep up with all relevant research related to many problem areas. It is even difficult for busy practitioners to keep up with research findings in one area. Consider the topic of parent-child interaction. Articles related to parents and children appear in well over fifty journals, and scores of books appear on this topic each year. Some clinicians have given up trying to keep up with practice-related research even in their area of specialty. Excuses may include: "It's not possible." "No one does it," or "There's nothing I can learn." Keeping up with research findings is difficult; guidelines are described in Chapter Three. Another way to give up is not to evaluate client progress in any systematic way, to accept a feeling of what works rather than gathering data to explore degree of progress. Some clinicians believe that evaluation will be very time consuming or that it cannot offer helpful information. Neither of these beliefs are true (see Chapter Ten).

One of the pleasures of being a professional is the promise of continued learning. Efforts to systematically improve practice competencies may be abandoned because of a lack of effective learning skills, including identification of specific goals, intermediate steps, and progress indicators (see Chapter Three). Incorrect beliefs about the conditions required for learning may get in the way. Clinical training programs differ greatly in opportunities they offer to evaluate whether skills have been acquired. Everyone gets stuck sometimes; plans are not successful or the assessment picture is cloudy. Consultation may have been eagerly used when it was readily available (for example, during an internship), but may no longer be sought.

The realities of practice may result in changes in what clinicians hope to accomplish. These changes are sometimes negative; there is an erosion of ideals once held as a result of the day-to-day realities of practice. Ashton and Webb (1986) studied teachers' sense of efficacy and its relation to student achievement and found marked changes over a few years, even in idealistic students. "As a student, Linda was full of vitality and fueled by a sense of purpose and personal efficacy. The teacher we observed had none of these characteristics. She went through her days mechanically and no longer spoke of social problems or individual development as motivating her work. Linda appeared unaware that her teaching had become just the kind of monotonous activity she had once been determined to avoid. Her classroom was drab, without decorations or examples of students' work. Visitors could not easily tell what subject was taught in her room and could see no physical evidence that those who worked within its walls shared a common commitment to their daily activities" (Ashton & Webb, 1986, p. 56).

Ideals about what can be accomplished may become tarnished over the years and be replaced by a pessimistic view (see discussion of dispositional bias in Chapter Nine). Clinicians may abandon once-valued goals, such as taking small steps to rectify inequities in service delivery. For example, the elderly do not receive their share of community mental health services. Although reactions such as depression and bereavement are common among the elderly, people 65 years old or older comprise only 10 percent of clients at community mental health services. Personal control tends to be abandoned when performance demands and risks associated with this control are viewed as excessive; it is under these circumstances that control is relinquished to others (Bandura, 1986, p. 449). Perhaps more commonly, it may be assumed that no one can alter conditions that contribute to problems such as unemployment, homelessness, and lack of adequate medical care for the uninsured. Appreciation of structural as well as personal causes of personal and social problems is critical in selecting appropriate levels of intervention and identifying opportunities for change.

Designing a Plan of Action

Identifying misconceptions is one matter. Getting rid of their influence is another. Clinicians typically carry out everyday tasks with the help of scripts (Schank and Abelson, 1977)—that is, sequences that are run off relatively automatically in specific contexts—for example, greeting clients, ending interviews, or requesting services from other professionals. Questioning these scripts takes time and requires effort. If new information is simply added to old information, both the old and the new will be used; "misconceptions must be altered in some way by demonstrating their falseness" (Green, McCloskey, & Caramazza, 1985, p. 137). Enhancing the quality of clinical decisions requires changes in thoughts and actions when in clinical situations. The thoughts and actions that are related to beliefs must be reviewed and altered in order to change the frequency of statements that encourage these beliefs; that is, there must be some "deep processing" (see Chapter Three). If, for example, the tendency is to focus on pathology and to neglect client assets, then client assets will not be explored unless clinicians believe it is important to do so and learn to incorporate skills in their everyday practice that are compatible with this belief.

Summary

Clear thinking may be compromised by a lack of self-knowledge. Self-knowledge includes familiarity with resources and limitations of reasoning processes, as well as knowledge of personal strengths and limitations that influence decision making. In addition to limitations of knowledge, there are also attitudinal obstacles that compromise the quality of reasoning. These include carelessness, lack of interest in having a carefully reasoned position on a matter, a wish to appear decisive, and a vested interest in a certain outcome. Factors that interfere with sound decision making include a preference for mystery over mastery, unconstructive reactions to mistakes and lack of success, a low tolerance for ambiguity and disorder, and a desire for quick success.

Effective stress-management and time-management skills are important in providing a facilitative setting for making decisions. Interpersonal skills are essential for managing the social exchanges that often are involved in making clinical decisions. Perhaps the most important obstacle is a lack of openness to examining competencies and the credibility of beliefs. This reluctance may be related to excessively low or high self-efficacy and the use of handicapping excuses. Lack of understanding of the relationship between personal preferences for certain practice perspectives and social and cultural values and incentives is an obstacle to self-examination of beliefs. Many obstacles to clear thinking, such as procrastination and distractibility, are related to a lack of effective self-managment skills. Guidelines describing how to alter the personal obstacles discussed in this chapter are available and, indeed, many clinicians often use these with their clients.

13

Maintaining
Critical Thinking Skills

Both personal and environmental obstacles may chip away at clear thinking skills. Clinicians continue to be bombarded with low-level appeals from professional newsletters, colleagues, and the media. Guidelines for maintaining helpful attitudes and skills are discussed in this chapter. These offer an agenda for developing a self-management program to enhance the quality of clinical decisions.

Generalizing and Maintaining Clear Thinking Skills

Having clear thinking skills does not mean that they will be used. The distinction between learning and performance is just as true in the area of clinical reasoning as in other areas. It is just as important to arrange for the maintenance of new skills as it is to develop them in the first place. Research highlights the importance of *transfer training*—that without such training the use of new skills is often confined to the specific situations in which training was first offered. A clinician may be able to solve a problem in one context through use of a rule of thumb but may fail to apply this rule in other situations in which it could be of value. Some instructional methods, such as discovery learning, which require review and revision of plans (Linn, 1986), are better than others in encouraging generalization. In this kind of learning the emphasis is on the

350

process rather than on the product of problem solving. Including a variety of different kinds of situations and acquiring useful self-management skills (such as asking "How am I doing?") encourages transfer (Belmont, Butterfield, & Ferretti, 1982; Stokes & Baer, 1977).

Remember the Benefits of Clear Thinking. Both clinicians and clients will benefit from use of clear thinking skills. Remembering the benefits of clear thinking—especially the long-term ones such as making accurate clinical predictions and increasing skills in handling more complex problems—will encourage clinicians to take advantage of clear thinking skills. Lack of knowledge about fallacies and persuasion strategies leaves clinicians vulnerable to their influence. Advertisers, politicians, professional organizations, and colleagues take advantage of these tactics everyday—with or without intention.

Focus on Process. Research concerning personal control supports the advantages of focusing on process (How can I do it?) rather than outcome (Can I do it?) (Langer, 1983). Focusing on outcome is likely to increase anxiety and draw attention away from exploring how problems can be solved. On the other hand, a process orientation encourages active involvement in grappling with problems and, consequently, a greater optimism about probable success since some new ideas for resolving a problem will be generated. A focus on outcome encourages self-induced incompetence—the belief that there is no relationship between behavior and outcomes of concern—and this orientation encourages a mindless approach to problems. "Since the attention of outcome-oriented individuals is directed toward the goal of the task and their own ability to accomplish it, they may be relatively 'mindless' concerning actual methods of performing the task, at least in comparison to process-oriented individuals. The latter individuals, in contrast, focus their attention on methods of task performance and are probably more mindful about different feasible solutions" (Langer, 1983, p. 131).

Increase Helpful Feedback. Perhaps in no other profession is so much of practice a true unknown, with so few opportunities for what occurs to be checked by others. Although this may seem like an advantage, it is the precise opposite. Disadvantages that result from the privacy of therapy and its results range from lost opportunities to gain corrective feedback from colleagues to the practice of outright quackery and sexual abuse of clients. As more is known about what works with what problem, the private nature of clinical practice poses more of a potential disadvantage to clients. Monitoring progress will improve the quality of decisions since detailed ongoing data on which to base decisions will be available. Methods that can be used to keep track of progress are described in a number of sources (see, for example, Barlow, Hayes & Nelson, 1984; Bloom & Fischer, 1982). Colleagues who have content and procedural knowledge about an assessment or intervention method can offer coaching in how to improve treatment fidelity and client participation based on observation of interviews or on review of audio or videotapes of these meetings.

Encourage Goals and Beliefs That Are Compatible with Clear Thinking. For some people, it is more important to avoid doubt and to appear consistent than it is to discover the best answer to a question. Many people do not believe in the value of thinking. "If people do not believe that thinking is useful, they will not think. This is perhaps the major argument one hears against thinking about things like nuclear war, religion, and morals: 'These matters are beyond me. They are best left to experts who are capable of thinking about them—if anyone'" (Baron, 1985b, p. 259).

Beliefs that encourage clear thinking include the following (p. 254): thinking often leads to better results; difficulties often can be overcome through thinking; good thinkers are open to new possibilities and to evidence against possibilities they favor; and nothing is wrong with being undecided or uncertain for a while. Beliefs that discourage clear thinking include: changing one's mind is a sign of weakness; being open to alternatives leads to confusion and despair; quick decision making is a sign of strength or wisdom; truth is determined by authority; we cannot influence what happens to us by trying to understand things and weigh them; and intuition is the best guide to making decisions.

An interest in being informed encourages use of clear thinking skills, as do curiosity and a "will to doubt." Only when beliefs are explicit can their credibility be examined. One of the most sturdy findings in the area of human judgment is that we are often unaware of how we are influenced. We may even change our opinions without knowing that we have done so. For example, listeners' opinions on bussing of school children could be altered from pro to con or from con to pro by an eloquent speaker, without listeners realizing that their opinion had shifted (Goethals & Reckman, 1973). Clearly describing the reasoning process involved in making a clinical decision increases the likelihood of avoiding errors and identifying the values that influence decisions.

Arrange a Supportive Environment. Unless there are prompts and incentives to use clear thinking skills, they linger in abeyance. Even the strongest repertoire can be eroded in an unsupportive environment. Arranging and maintaining a supportive environment will be easier with expertise in contingency analysis (skill in identifying and rearranging the relationships between behaviors and environmental events). Prompts and incentives should be provided for skills that encourage high-quality decision making, such as writing clear, up-to-date records; reliance on strong rather than weak sources of assessment data; and evaluation of progress. Clear description of goals and intermediate steps, involvement of kindred spirits in support groups, planning and evaluation of progress will increase the likelihood of success. If competencies start to drift downward, contingency analysis skills can be used to discover how to reverse the trend. Helpful questions include: What consequences support desired behaviors? What events punish these? How can opportunities for reinforcement of clear thinking skills be increased? What prompts can be arranged? Are necessary tools available? Are competing behaviors reinforced? Are personal obstacles getting in the way (see Chapter Twelve)? A reminder to question initial assumptions can be placed on the desk, and a heading for alternative hypotheses can be included on recording forms. Positive incentives can be arranged for behaviors that encourage clear thinking, and punishing consequences can be removed.

Some clinicians forgo having a voice in what happens in an organization or in their community because they believe that politics are beneath them. This decision will be a welcome one to those who wield power. Women may not receive guidance in office politics and may believe that it should not be necessary to seek to persuade their colleagues to be in favor of or against certain positions, or that it is not compatible with a woman's role. Skill in recognizing various kinds of political tactics is useful in anticipating and exerting countercontrol against these.

Politics—the effort to gain or maintain power—is an integral part of life; political action is often necessary to achieve desired goals. Political skills are important, especially skills in working with others toward a mutually valued aim, such as enhancing the quality of services offered to clients. As in any other area of human endeavor, efforts can be conducted with integrity or without scruples. Clinicians have a choice about how to react in settings in which low-level appeals are tolerated or even encouraged. Conditions that undermine and compromise the quality of decisions can be ignored; disliked situations can be tolerated with little or no effort made to improve matters. On the other hand, steps can be taken to create a more supportive environment. Such action is not easy but it is far more satisfying than just complaining. For example, if there is a policy against observation of interaction between clients and significant others in real-life settings such as home and school, and you believe this policy increases the probability of the fundamental attribution error, you can lobby to change the policy. Results of studies showing that observation of interaction between clients and significant others in real-life settings can provide useful data can be shared with colleagues. A request is more likely to receive a favorable reaction if it first involves a small change. Counterarguments should be prepared for anticipated objections, and the support of colleagues can be sought. If many people work together to achieve a change, it is more likely to occur than if one person pursues it alone. Monthly meetings can be held to review clinical decisions with other clinicians who prefer reasoned discussion rather than empathic or ideological explanations. Reaping the payoffs of clear thinking in greater success with clients will be a major incentive for maintaining clear thinking skills.

Understanding organizations—how they work, how they change, and why change is often difficult—will offer valuable information about options. Both the formal as well as the informal system can be examined to explore why certain patterns of behavior occur and why others do not. The informal system refers to contingencies that operate between individuals that are not formally codified in writing. Some of these operate in the form of informal rules such as: keep records general to protect confidentiality. An example of a formal rule would be the written requirement that there must be a written service agreement in each case. Even though a written regulation exists, implementation may not reflect its intention. For example, written service agreements may be present but may not contain the ingredients that facilitate case planning and clarify expectations, such as description of specific objectives and progress indicators.

Clinicians also have a choice as to how involved they become in their professional organizations; they can, for example, take active steps to enhance the extent to which such organizations are influential in improving the quality of clinical practice. Professional organizations can assume greater responsibility for clarifying vague ethical guidelines related to clinical competence. Professionals are mandated by their organizations to work within codes of ethics created by these organizations. Typically these codes are vague, requiring (and allowing) varied and discretionary interpretations. Take for example the statement in the NASW Code of Ethics (National Association of Social Workers, 1980) that "The social worker should accept responsibility or employment only on the basis of existing competence or the intention to acquire the necessary competence." What criteria are to be used to evaluate competence? Does "competence" imply being up-to-date with practice-related empirical literature and use of this information in making clinical decisions?

Cultivate Realistic Expectations. Use of clear thinking skills will enhance recognition of the limits and potentials of clinical practice. The expectation to succeed all the time can be satisfied by ignoring lack of success. Presenting problems differ in how much success can be achieved even by expert clinicians. It is unrealistic to expect clinicians to resolve problems such as poverty, lack of access to medical care, and lack of job opportunities that are the result of structural factors that would require drastic redistribution of resources. An understanding of the structural factors related to presenting problems protects clinicians from assuming potentials for change via counseling and therapy that simply do not exist.

Plan Personal Experiments. George Kelley (1955) suggested that clients approach change as personal experiments—trying out a new path for a limited time to determine if it is more productive and more pleasing. Personal experiments can be designed to enhance decision-making skills. These are more likely to succeed if self-management skills are available to identify clear goals and progress indicators and to plan a step-by-step way to achieve goals. Being one's own personal change agent is not easy. However, there are guidelines that can be used to make this a successful adventure (Neuringer, 1981; Watson & Tharp, 1985).

Practice Clear Thinking Skills. Both everyday life and clinical practice offer a myriad of opportunities to practice clear thinking skills—reading the newspaper and professional journals, watching TV, attending case conferences. Watching how other people handle situations in which fallacies occur will yield new options. Having names for the different kinds of fallacies makes it easier to identify them. Practice helps to make the use of thinking skills more automatic.

As Tuchman (1988) has said, we are a public that is brought up on deception through advertising. Structural factors related to personal and social problems often are not even mentioned in newspaper reports or professional sources, which focus on "blaming the victim." Real sources of control are often masked (see Chapter Two). The fact that a few companies control almost all of the major media sources is not encouraging in terms of presentation of views that are not compatible with vested interests (Bagdikian, 1987). Foucault (1981) has emphasized the extent to which sources of influence are not necessarily consciously used. That is, there may not be a conspiracy to suppress information about structural sources of control. Conspiracy or not, the public media influence accepted views of both clinicians and clients about the factors that are related to personal and social problems.

Take Advantage of Helpful Tools and Training Programs. Tools that can be used include diagrams, flow charts, contingency tables, decision trees, and computers. Note taking and reminders can be helpful in remembering needed information. Perkins (1987) suggests putting up a poster that lists important components of a *thinking frame* (a guide to organizing and supporting thought processes) (p. 47). Effective *metadecision skills* (decisions about which strategies to use in making decisions and how much time to devote to a decision) will save time and effort. A variety of aids can be used to manage information overload and to decrease the cost of making informed decisions. Time can be saved by taking advantage of computer testing and graphing of data concerning progress. Even brief programs can be helpful in counteracting error-producing strategies. Fong, Kravitz, and Nisbett (1986) found that brief instruction concerning the law of large numbers helped subjects to improve their statistical reasoning. Experts' judgments can be improved by training in how to ignore irrelevant data (Gaeth & Shanteau, 1984). One especially helpful tool is a valuable *schema,* a useful way of analyzing a problem. Lack of helpful schemas is one of the main reasons why people do not think more carefully about issues and tasks (Baron, 1985b). One example of a useful schema is contingency analysis (see definition given earlier). Most clinicians do not have this schema available.

Use Helpful Rules of Thumb. Many rules of thumb have been described in previous chapters. Those mentioned below are highlighted in terms of general usefulness.

1. *Look for disconfirming evidence.* Make it a habit to search for disconfirming evidence such as counterexamples and counterarguments. Bromley (1977) recommends inclusion of an Alternative Hypotheses heading in clinical records. This will help to counter the influence of initial assumptions which may be incorrect.

2. *Try to understand other people's points of view.* Understanding other points of view has several advantages. One is identifying flaws in preferred positions. If this rule of thumb had been used by participants in the case conference described in Chapter Eleven, the person actually responsible for the abuse

of Lindy may have been identified earlier and subsequent abuse might have been avoided. Misunderstandings are less likely and cogent counterarguments are more likely when other perspectives are understood. A focus on common goals encourages attention to other positions.

3. *Avoid the fundamental attribution error.* The tendency of clinicians to attribute the problems of clients to dispositional causes has been often noted in this book. This tendency deflects attention from environmental factors related to client concerns and thus may result in incorrect clinical inferences. One way to combat this bias is to enhance empathic reactions—that is, to "put yourself in other people's shoes" (Regan and Totten, 1975). Another is to become informed about environmental causes of personal problems.

4. *Be careful how you use language.* Different meanings for words and failure to clarify these can result in clinical errors and muddled discussions. Both spoken and written language in clinical settings (such as written records and case conferences) should be used to inform. As Nickerson (1986a) points out, "It is never inappropriate to ask what someone means by a specified word in a particular context" (p. 130).

5. *Watch out for vivid data.* The more vivid are the data the more caution should be exercised in assigning it weight. Clinicians tend to overlook the importance of nonoccurrences that may be very important. Make it a habit to ask about events that did not occur.

6. *Beware of personally relevant data.* One of the themes throughout this book is the influence of emotions and self-interest on judgments. "Perhaps there are no greater impediments to effective reasoning than those that derive from a confusion between reasoning and rationalizing, or, to make the same distinction in other terms, between weighing evidence on the one hand and defending a position or making a case on the other. This is the problem of our frequent failure, perhaps our inability, to assess evidence objectively and without bias when we have a vested interest in the outcome of a debate" (Nickerson, 1986b, p. 362). Researchers in the area of thinking emphasize the need for deep processing of new

ways of thinking, especially when there are strong incentives for maintaining current biases and prejudices—what Paul (1987) refers to as "activated ignorance" (p. 134)—that may neutralize new ways of thinking. Without deep processing, new knowledge about reasoning probably will be used to bolster current biases and prejudices. Emotional and personally relevant material can be used as a reminder to be especially vigilant. Being informed about research related to the influence of mood and arousal on judgments increases the likelihood that this potential source of error will be avoided.

7. *Complement clear thinking skills with knowledge.* Familiarity with relevant knowledge in a domain is critical in making accurate decisions. "The first rule of effective reasoning is to get your facts straight" (Nickerson, 1986a, p. 132). Clear thinking skills, as well as good intentions and supportive skills, may be enough when little is known about how to help a client with a problem (that is, when either nothing is known or research indicates that it does not matter what is done as long as you talk and listen to the person). Offering support is not enough, however, when more can be done. For example, I recently saw a client who had been seeing a therapist for depression for over a year. She reported that her therapist was using supportive counseling, and that there was no focus on acquiring skills that could be used in daily life to decrease depression. A careful assessment revealed many specific changes that could be made to decrease her depression; that is, far more help than supportive counseling was needed and available. Effective learning skills make it possible to gain maximum payoff for time spent locating and understanding practice-related content (see Chapter Nine).

8. *Ask about test accuracy.* Many clinical errors result from reliance on unreliable and invalid psychological tests. Questions of concern here include, How sensitive is the test? What is the false-positive rate? What is the false-negative rate?

9. *Ask about the other three cells.* Many writers emphasize the importance of asking about all four cells of a four-cell contingency table. Clinicians tend to pay attention to the present-present cell and to ignore the other three cells. This results in

overestimates of the effectiveness of intervention methods and overestimates of pathology.

10. *Ask questions with a high payoff value.* Questions differ in the likelihood that helpful information will be revealed by the answers. Asking questions that have maximum utility will save time. One helpful question is "What's missing?" Often what is not discussed is most important in understanding factors related to personal problems.

11. *Move beyond the illusion of understanding.* Some practice assumptions contribute real understanding; others merely provide a feeling of understanding and are unlikely to be helpful when applied to real-life clinical problems. Acceptance of beliefs based on a feeling of understanding is encouraged by the expectation that everyone should have explanations on hand for almost anything without significant effort being exerted to arrive at these accounts. Pressures on clinicians, often self-imposed, to appear more expert than is warranted encourage this tendency. Acceptance of beliefs only because they make sense may result in a fragmented eclectic approach to practice—that is, an unintegrated, unsupported package of assumptions that is used to make clinical decisions rather than a cohesive practice theory with empirical support.

12. *Catch reemerging falsehoods.* Certain key beliefs discourage acquisition and maintenance of clear thinking skills. One of the most common and hardy is the belief that reason and caring are incompatible. The rational individual is painted as cold, unfeeling, and missing the boat in relation to understanding the qualitative, subjective, rich-textured side of life. It is argued that one cannot be a clear thinker and a caring person at the same time. Reason and passion are pitted against one another as if they were adversaries. An argument can be made that caring without careful reasoning is not caring at all, especially in professions such as social work, psychology, psychiatry, and counseling. "A passionate drive for *clarity,* accuracy, and fair-mindedness, a fervor for getting to the bottom of things, to the deepest route issues, for listening sympathetically to opposition points of view, a compelling drive to seek out evidence, an intense aversion to contradiction,

sloppy thinking, inconsistent application of standards, a devotion to truth as against self-interest—these are essential commitments of the rational person" (Paul, 1987, p. 142).

Another hardy falsehood is that because there is no such thing as total objectivity (our interpretations of the meanings of events intrudes between what is in the world and what we see), the scientific method is no better than and, in fact, is not as valuable as a subjective intuitive approach in identifying credible assumptions. Objective methods are painted as sterile, narrow, and unfaithful to reality, and subjective methods are presented as rich, meaningful, and representative of reality. Objective methods are often discussed as if their use entails the belief that total objectivity is possible. In fact, the elaborate methodology involved in the scientific method arose because of concern with the very issue the subjectivists claim is ignored in an empirical approach—that is, a concern to tease out biasing effects in order to identify and eliminate inaccurate alternative explanations (see Chapter Four). Objective and subjective methods of inquiry differ in the kinds of questions that can be answered and in the kinds of answers that are offered. The scientific method is more appropriate for assessing the credibility of assumptions. This is not to say that subjective methods do not have value (Gambrill & Barth, 1980) (see Chapter Three).

Another falsehood that keeps people uninformed is the belief that clear thinking is difficult. This view is often accepted because of personal goals (for example, to decrease effort, to avoid indecision and failure). A related falsehood is the belief that immersion in a subject is required to critically evaluate its claims. On the contrary, knowledge of clear thinking skills can be applied to any area if methods used to arrive at assumptions are clearly described.

Some clinicians believe that the therapeutic process is essentially unknowable, implying that it is useless to try to identify specific elements that contribute to success. In moments of discouragement, it may be tempting to slip back into this old belief and to abandon efforts to discover what is knowable in this complex area. A belief that there are no answers will discourage a search for answers; "any advance, personal or scientific, depends on the assumption that what is not yet known is knowable" (Langer, 1983, p. 119). Indeed, research concerning therapy has yielded a great deal of information about the helping process (see, for example, Garfield & Bergin, 1986; Wills, 1982). The influence of Basagalia in changing the pattern of service delivery to psychiatric patients in Italy offers an example of what is possible to achieve (Basaglia in Scheper-Hughes & Lovell, 1987).

The belief that, if errors are inevitable there is no use trying to avoid them, will also reappear in various forms. The need to act encourages excessive belief in the appropriateness of these actions. Errors are part and parcel of continued refinement of clinical skills and are more likely to be avoided if the possibility of error is accepted.

Reviewing Your Career

A mismatch between available skills and problems to be solved may result in either a mentality of powerlessness or an unrealistic sense of omnipotence. Nattering (complaining without really trying to improve things) is an indicator of the former. Indicators of the latter include a renunciation of any attempt to draw on empirically based knowledge and a view of therapy as an art. The distinction between collective and individual ignorance is overlooked by clinicians who accept the latter path. One of the striking characteristics about the field of psychotherapy is the compartmentalization of standards; clinicians who view therapy as an art protest that they would not want their dentists or doctors to rely solely on this approach.

Many clinicians quite successfully and happily pursue careers in private practice. How effective they are in terms of offering the best service that could be provided to their clients is another question. Others may choose this form of practice after becoming disenchanted with the potential for success in agency-based practice. Clinical students usually start graduate education with ideals and enthusiasm, believing that they can achieve greater success than former helpers who were perhaps less motivated, received less adequate training, and cared less. After encountering more limited progress than was hoped for, they may revise their expectations downward—especially in relation to social reform goals. Original standards may become dimmer, harder to recall, or even forgotten, as new less hopeful ones replace them. Sources to blame for this change include "crummy" agencies, lack of resources, lack of time, and heavy caseloads. Clinicians may decide that clients are really worse off than they thought—sicker and harder to change. Graduate training encourages this view. Blaming the client or the agency removes responsibility from clinicians' shoulders (Ryan, 1976). Previous interests in increasing equity in the world by helping the many people who struggle under conditions of poverty, poor housing, high-crime neighborhoods, and poor education may be abandoned as it becomes obvious that personal counseling services result in little or no headway in decreasing these problems. Clinicians who work in agencies in which most presenting problems are related to such structural obstacles and who emphasize dispositional attributions often believe, with good reason, that they are providing a Band-Aid function; no real changes are possible that can indeed improve the quality of life for clients. Clients are often unappreciative—especially in nonvoluntary settings such as child protection agencies. Many clinicians believe that nothing can be done about social conditions and the personal problems they create until there are large societal and economic changes. One reason professionals focus on dispositional attributions for client's problems and ignore environmental causes is a lack of resources to change environmental sources of problems. These influences may encourage a move into private practice—that is, a move to working with the "ready-to-be-helped."

The kinds of excuses described above overlook opportunities for change that can be made within the constraints of a given setting, as well as small steps that can be taken outside work—for example, lobbying legislators. They also reflect a resignation to a less than optimal work life. Clinicians may be too invested to quit (Teger, Cary, Katcher, & Hillis, 1980). A review of career goals, as well as the promise and limits of personal counseling, may encourage a redistribution of effort in terms of a balance between private clinical practice with middle-class clients and participation in collective efforts to secure meaningful changes in service-delivery patterns for less advantaged people.

Reviewing Preferred Practice Theories

Not all answers to a question are equally good. Clinical decisions are more likely to be accurate if practice theories are selected that, on the whole, offer sound causal assumptions (justified beliefs) about presenting problems. Often, there are many routes to a given end, and as long as a theory directs attention to a successful route, a positive outcome will result. Some clinicians do not distinguish between theories of different quality—embracing weak ones as readily as strong ones (Meehl, 1978). A theory consists of a set of concepts and proposed interrelationships that are of value in understanding a broad array of phenomena. Confusing theories of different breadths of application can result in frustration, as efforts are made to apply a poorly developed narrow model to events that are too complex to be handled within such a limited framework. Understanding the historical context in which practice theories develop (the larger picture) is useful in stepping above everyday practice concerns to see if preferred practice theories complement personal and professional values.

The Beneficiaries of Clear Thinking

Clinical decision making is an ethical as well as a practical enterprise. Clinical decisions affect people; they offer or limit opportunities for clients and significant others to enhance the quality of their lives. The history of the interpersonal helping professions clearly indicates the need for boundaries on the individual discretion of clinicians in the selection of objectives (making sure that these are in the client's interests), in the selection of procedures (choosing those that, while least intrusive, are most effective and efficient), and in assurance of accountability by monitoring progress. As more effective methods are developed, lack of knowledge about these methods becomes more problematic.

Clients will benefit from clear thinking skills by selection of effective assessment and intervention methods. Clinicians will benefit from increased success in helping clients improve the quality of their lives. Whether colleagues will be thankful will depend on skills in diplomacy, their own attitudes toward truth, and on the other personal and environmental obstacles discussed in Chapters Eleven and Twelve. They are more likely to support clear thinking if common goals are emphasized. How about superiors? A quote from Nickerson (1987) is apt here. "I believe that often, when people in positions of authority (parents, teachers, managers, military leaders) say that they wish that the people over whom they have authority (children, students, employees, subordinates) could think, they mean that they wish their charges or subordinates were more skillful at accomplishing goals set, or at least endorsed, by their superiors. Seldom do they have in mind a concept of thinking that is sufficiently broad to include the questioning of the goals themselves and the authorities that have set them" (p. 34).

Use of sound decision-making methods can move clinical practice farther along the continuum of effectiveness, which includes deterioration effects, neither harming nor helping, and offering the best help that could be attained anywhere. Many clients are content with half the glass when they could have, if not the whole glass, as least three-quarters. Reviews of the effectiveness of psychotherapy show that, although clients often do not get what they came for, they still believe that the experience was valuable (Zilbergeld, 1983). They would probably be even happier if they also attained their goals.

Summary

Maintaining clear thinking skills should not be left to chance. Transfer of new skills to other areas can be facilitated by developing useful self-management skills, by focusing on the process rather than on the product of thinking, and by practicing skills in many different situations. Reviewing the benefits of clear thinking and remembering the daily prevalence of deception (such as suppressed information), both in the mass media and in professional sources, serve as a reminder to take advantage of clear thinking skills in day-to-day clinical practice. Increasing the quality of feedback about degree of progress offers more fine-grained data on the accuracy of clinical decisions. Arranging a supportive environment and cultivating realistic standards of success will also be helpful in maintaining clear thinking skills. Professional organizations can take more effective steps to upgrade the quality of clinical decisions and to ensure that competent services are offered for the benefit of clients. Rules of thumb such as asking, "What's the accuracy of this test?" as well as tools such as visual representations of problems can be used. Continued cultivation of helpful attitudes and values, such as an interest in accurate accounts of reality rather than in winning a point, will be helpful.

Increasing the quality of clinical reasoning skills may encourage a reconsideration of the potential of pursuing valued goals that have been abandoned; this may result also in a change in preferred practice theories. Most importantly, it will enhance the quality of services offered to clients.

References

Abercrombie, M.L.J. (1960). *The anatomy of judgement.* New York: Basic Books.

Abramovitz, C. V., & Dokecki, P. R. (1977). The politics of clinical judgement: Early empirical returns. *Psychological Bulletin, 84,* 460–476.

Abramowitz, S. I., Berger, A., & Weary, G. (1982). Similarity between clinician and client: Its influence on the helping relationship. In T. A. Wills (Ed.), *Basic processes in helping relationships.* Orlando, FL: Academic Press.

Abramowitz, S. I., & Murray, J. (1983). Race effects in psychotherapy. In J. Murray & P. R. Abramson (Eds.), *Bias in psychotherapy.* New York: Praeger.

Adams, J. L. (1974). *Conceptual blockbusting: A guide to better ideas.* New York: W. H. Freeman.

Adler, J. E. (1987). On resistance to critical thinking. In D. N. Perkins, J. Lochhead, and J. Bishop (Eds.), *Thinking: The second international conference.* Hillsdale, NJ: Erlbaum.

Advertisement. (1988, January-February). *Social Work, 33,* p. 73.

Advertisement for professional liability insurance. (1987, April). *NASW News, 32,* 17.

Ainslie, G. (1975). Specious reward: A behavioral theory of impulsiveness and impulse control. *Psychological Bulletin, 82,* 463–496.

Albert, S., Fox, H. M., & Kahn, M. W. (1980). Faking psychosis on the Rorschach: Can expert judges detect malingering. *Journal of Personality Assessment, 44,* 115–119.

American Psychiatric Association (1980). *Diagnostic and statistical manual of mental disorders* (3rd. ed.). Washington, DC: American Psychiatric Association.

American Psychiatric Association (1987). *Diagnostic and statistical manual of mental disorders* (3rd ed. rev.). Washington, DC: American Psychiatric Association.

Anderson, J. R. (Ed.). (1981). *Cognitive skills and their acquisition.* Hillsdale, NJ: Erlbaum.

Anthony, E. J., & Cohler, B. J. (1987). *The invulnerable child.* New York: Guilford.

Arkes, H. (1981). Impediments to accurate clinical judgment and possible ways to minimize their impact. *Journal of Consulting and Clinical Psychology, 49,* 323–330.

Armstrong, J. C. (1980). Unintelligible management research and academic prestige. *Interfaces, 10,* 80–86.

Armstrong, J. C. (1982). Barriers to scientific contributions: The author's formula. *The Behavioral and Brain Sciences, 5,* 197–199.

Ashton, P. T., & Webb, R. B. (1986). *Making a difference: Teachers' sense of efficacy and student achievement.* New York: Longman.

Averill, J. (1982). *Anger and aggression: Implications for theories of emotion.* New York: Springer-Verlag.

Azrin, N. H., Philip, R. A., Thienes-Hontos, P., & Besalel, V. A. (1980). Comparative evaluation of the Job Finding Club with welfare recipients. *Journal of Vocational Behavior, 16,* 133–145.

Badinter, E. (1980). *Mother love, myth and reality.* New York: Macmillan.

Bagdikian, B. H. (1987). *The media monopoly* (2nd ed.). Boston: Beacon Press.

Bandura, A. (1978). On paradigms and recycled ideologies. *Cognitive Therapy and Research, 2,* 79–103.

Bandura, A. (1986). *Social foundations of thought and action.* Englewood Cliffs, NJ: Prentice-Hall.

Banta, H. D. (1984). Embracing or rejecting innovations: Clinical diffusion of health care techniques. In S. Reiser and M. Anbar

(Eds.), *The machine at the bedside.* Cambridge, England: Cambridge University Press.

Barclay, C. R. (1986). Schematization of autobiographical memory. In D. C. Rubin (Ed.), *Autobiographical memory.* Cambridge, England: Cambridge University Press.

Bar-Hillel, M. (1983). The base-rate fallacy controversy. In R. W. Scholz (Ed.), *Decision making under uncertainty.* New York: Elsevier.

Barlow, D. H., Hayes, S. C., & Nelson, R. O. (1984). *The scientist practitioner: Research and accountability in clinical and educational settings.* New York: Pergamon Press.

Barlow, D. H., & Waddell, M. T. (1985). Agoraphobia. In D. H. Barlow (Ed.), *Clinical handbook of psychological disorders: A step-by-step treatment manual.* New York: Guilford.

Barocas, R., & Black, H. K. (1974). Referral rate and physical attractiveness in third grade children. *Perceptual and Motor Skills, 39,* 731–734.

Barocas, R., & Vance, F. L. (1974). Physical appearance and personal adjustment counseling. *Journal of Counseling Psychology, 21,* 96–100.

Baron, J. (1981). Reflective thinking as a goal of education. *Intelligence, 5,* 291–309.

Baron, J. (1985a). What kind of intelligence components are fundamental? In S. F. Chipman, J. W. Segal, & R. Glaser (Eds.), *Thinking and learning skills: Vol. 2. Research and open questions.* Hillsdale, NJ: Erlbaum.

Baron, J. (1985b). *Rationality and intelligence.* Cambridge, England: Cambridge University Press.

Barth, R. P., & Gambrill, E. (1984). Learning to interview: The quality of training opportunities. *The Clinical Supervisor, 2,* 3–14.

Batson, C. D. (1975). Attribution as a mediator of bias in helping. *Journal of Personality and Social Psychology, 72,* 455–466.

Batson, C. D., Jones, C. H., & Cochran, P. J. (1979). Attributional bias in counselors' diagnosis: The effects of resources on perception of need. *Journal of Applied Social Psychology, 9,* 377–393.

Batson, C. D., O'Quin, K., & Pych, V. (1982). An attribution theory analysis of trained helpers' inferences about clients' needs. In T.

A. Wills (Ed.), *Basic processes in helping relationships*. Orlando, FL: Academic Press.

Beck, A. T. (1976). *Cognitive therapy and the emotional disorders.* New York: International Universities Press.

Beck, A. T., Rush, A. J., Shaw, B. F., and Emery, G. (1979). *Cognitive therapy of depression.* New York: Guilford.

Beck, A. T., Steer, R. A., Kovacs, M., & Garrison, B. (1985). Hopelessness and eventual suicide: A 10-year prospective study of patients hospitalized with suicidal ideation. *American Journal of Psychiatry, 152,* 559–563.

Beck, P., Byyny, R. L., & Adams, K. S. (1981). *Case exercises in clinical reasoning.* Chicago: Yearbook Medical.

Beit-Hallahmi, B. (1987). The psychotherapy subculture: Practice and ideology. *Social Science Information, 26,* 475–492.

Belenky, M. F., Clinchy, B. M., Goldberger, N. R., & Tarule, J. M. (1986). *Women's ways of knowing: the development of self, voice and mind.* New York: Basic Books.

Belmont, J. M., Butterfield, E. C., & Ferretti, R. P. (1982). To secure transfer of training instruct self-management skills. In D. K. Detterman & R. J. Sternberg (Eds.), *How and how much can intelligence be increased.* Norwood, NJ: Ablex.

Bereiter, C., & Scardamalia, M. (1985). Cognitive coping strategies and the problems of "inert" knowledge. In S. F. Chipman, J. W. Segal, & R. Glaser (Eds.), *Thinking and learning skills: Vol. 2. Research and open questions.* Hillsdale, NJ: Erlbaum.

Berger, M., Jurkovic, G. J., & Associates. (1984). *Practicing family therapy in diverse settings: New approaches to the connections among families, therapists, and treatment settings.* San Francisco: Jossey-Bass.

Berger, P. L., & Luckman, T. (1966). *The social construction of reality.* New York: Doubleday.

Best, J. (1988). Missing children, misleading statistics. *Public Interest, 92,* 84–92.

Bishop, J. B., & Richards, T. F. (1984). Counselor theoretical orientation as related to intake judgements. *Journal of Counseling Psychology, 31,* 398–401.

Blackard, M. K., & Barsh, E. T. (1982). Parents' and professionals' perceptions of the handicapped child's impact on the family. *TASH, 7,* 62–70.

Blackmore, S. (1987). The elusive open mind: Ten years of negative research in parapsychology. *The Skeptical Inquirer, 11*(3), 244–255.

Blalock, H. M., Jr. (1984). *Basic dilemmas in the social sciences.* Beverly Hills, CA: Sage.

Blau, P. M. (1960). Orientation toward clients in a public welfare agency. *Administrative Science Quarterly, 5,* 341–361.

Blau, T. H. (1984). *The psychologist as expert witness.* New York: Wiley.

Blau, T. H. (1988). *Psychotherapy tradeoff: The technique and style of doing therapy.* New York: Brunner/Mazel.

Blenkner, M., Bloom, M., & Nielson, M. (1971). A research and demonstration project of protective services. *Social Casework, 10,* 483–499.

Bloom, B. S., & Broder, L. J. (1960). *Problem-solving processes of college students: An exploratory investigation* (Supplementary Educational Monograph No. 73). Chicago: University of Chicago Press.

Bloom, M., & Fischer, J. (1982). *Evaluating practice: Guidelines for the accountable professional.* Englewood Cliffs, NJ: Prentice-Hall.

Blum, J. (1978). *Pseudoscience and mental ability.* New York: Monthly Review Press.

Bond, M. H. (Ed.). (1986). *The psychology of the Chinese people.* New York: Oxford University Press.

Boren, J. H. (1972). *When in doubt, mumble: A bureaucrat's handbook.* New York: Van Nostrand Reinhold.

Borgida, E., & Nisbett, R. E. (1977). The differential impact of abstract vs. concrete information on decisions. *Journal of Applied Social Psychology, 7,* 258–271.

Bower, G. H., & Cohen, P. R. (1982). Emotional influences in memory and thinking: Data and theory. In M. S. Clark & S. T. Fiske (Eds.), *Affect and cognition.* Hillsdale, NJ: Erlbaum.

Bower, G. H., & Karlin, M. B. (1974). Depth of processing pictures of faces and recognition memory. *Journal of Experimental Psychology, 103,* 751–757.

Bowers, K. S. (1984). On being unconsciously influenced and informed. In K. S. Bowers & D. Meichenbaum (Eds.), *The unconscious reconsidered*. New York: Wiley.

Bowers, K. S. (1987). Intuition and discovery. In P. Stern (Ed.), *Theories of the unconscious and theories of the self*. Hillsdale, NJ: Analytic Press.

Bransford, J. D., & Stein, B. S. (1984). *The IDEAL problem solver: A guide for improving thinking, learning, and creativity*. New York: W. H. Freeman.

Brehmer, B. (1980). In one word: Not from experience. *Acta Psychologia, 45*, 223-241.

Brekstad, A. (1966). Factors influencing the reliability of anamnestic recall. *Child Development, 37*, 603-612.

Briar, S., & Miller, H. (1971). *Problems and issues in social casework*. New York: Columbia University Press.

Brim, O. G., & Hoff, D. B. (1957). Individual and situational differences in desire for certainty. *Journal of Abnormal and Social Psychology, 54*, 225-229.

Broad, W., & Wade, N. (1982). *Betrayers of the truth*. New York: Simon & Schuster.

Bromley, D. B. (1977). *Personality description and ordinary language*. New York: Wiley.

Bromley, D. B. (1986). *The case-study method in psychology and related disciplines*. New York: Wiley.

Brown, A. L. (1978). Knowing when, where, and how to remember: A problem of metacognition. In R. Glaser (Ed.), *Advances in instructional psychology* (Vol. 1). Hillsdale, NJ: Erlbaum.

Brown, A. L., & Campione, J. C. (1981). Inducing flexible thinking: A problem of metacognition. In M. Friedman, J. P. Das, & N. O'Connor (Eds.), *Intelligence and learning*. New York: Plenum.

Bryant, G. D., & Norman, G. R. (1980). Expressions of probability: Words and numbers. *New England Journal of Medicine, 302*, 411.

Buie, J. (1987, December). Newspaper's tone, errors irk sources. *APA Monitor, 18*, 23.

Buie, J. (1989, July). Psychologists defend reimbursement rights. *APA Monitor, 20*, 25.

Bunge, M. (1984). What is pseudoscience? *The Skeptical Inquirer,* *9*(1), 36–47.

Burgess, P. H. (1984). *The sayings of Mahatma Gandhi.* Singapore: Graham Brash.

Burnham, J. C. (1987). *How superstition won and science lost: Popularizing science and health in the United States.* New Brunswick, NJ: Rutgers University Press.

Burnham, J. C. (1988). *Paths into American culture: Psychology, medicine, and morals.* Philadelphia: Temple University Press.

Burns, D. (1980). *Feeling good: The new mood therapy.* New York: William Morrow.

Burton, W. H., Kimball, R. B., & Wing, R. L. (1960). *Education for effective thinking: An introductory text.* New York: Appleton-Century-Crofts.

Campbell, D. T., & Stanley, J. C. (1963). *Experimental and quasi-experimental design for research.* Chicago: Rand-McNally.

Campione, J. C. (1989). Assisted assessment: A taxonomy of approaches and an outline of strengths and weaknesses. *Journal of Learning Disabilities, 22,* 151–165.

Cantor, J. R., Zillmann, D., & Bryant, J. (1975). Enhancement of experienced sexual arousal in response to erotic stimuli through misattribution of unrelated residual excitation. *Journal of Personality and Social Psychology, 32,* 69–75.

Cantor, N. (1982). "Everyday" versus normative models of clinical and social judgment. In G. Weary & H. L. Mirels (Eds.), *Integrations of clinical and social psychology.* New York: Oxford University Press.

Carroll, L. (1946). *Alice in wonderland and through the looking glass.* Kingsport, TN: Kingsport Press.

Chanowitz, B., & Langer, E. J. (1980). Knowing more (or less) than you can show: Understanding control through the mindlessness-mindfulness distinctions. In J. S. Garber & M.E.P. Seligman, *Human helplessness: Theory and applications.* New York: Academic Press.

Chanowitz, B., & Langer, E. J. (1985). Self-protection and self-inception. In M. W. Martin (Ed.), *Self-deception and self-understanding.* Lawrence: University of Kansas Press.

Chapman, A. J., & Foote, H. C. (Eds.). (1977). *It's a funny thing, humor.* New York: Pergamon Press.

Chapman, L. J. (1967). Illusory correlation in observational report. *Journal of Verbal Learning and Verbal Behavior, 6,* 151–155.

Chapman, L. J., & Chapman, J. P. (1967). Genesis of popular but erroneous diagnostic observations. *Journal of Abnormal Psychology, 72,* 193–204.

Chapman, L. J., & Chapman, J. P. (1969). Illusory correlation as an obstacle to the use of valid psychodiagnostic signs. *Journal of Abnormal Psychology, 74,* 271–280.

Chase, W. G., & Ericsson, K. A. (1981). Skilled memory. In J. R. Anderson (Ed.), *Cognitive skills and their acquisition.* Hillsdale, NJ: Erlbaum.

Chase, W. G., & Simon, H. A. (1973). Perception in chess. *Cognitive Psychology, 1,* 55–81.

Chelton, L. G., & Bonney, W. C. (1987). Addiction, affects, and self-object theory. *Psychotherapy, 24,* 40–46.

Cherniss, C. (1986). Different ways to think about burnout. In E. Seidman & J. Rappaport (Eds.), *Redefining social problems.* New York: Plenum.

Chi, M.T.H., Feltovich, P. J., & Glaser, R. (1980). Categorization and representation of physics problems by experts and novices. *Cognitive Science, 5,* 121–152.

Chi, M.T.H., & Glaser, R. (1985). Problem solving ability. In R. J. Sternberg (Ed.), *Human abilities.* New York: W. H. Freeman.

Chipman, S. F., Segal, J. W., & Glaser, R. (1985). *Thinking and learning skills: Vol. 2. Research and open questions.* Hillsdale, NJ: Erlbaum.

Chiriboga, D. A., Jenkins, G., & Bailey, J. (1983). Stress and coping among hospice nurses: Test of an analytic model. *Nursing Research, 32,* 294–299.

Cialdini, R. B. (1984). *Influence: The new psychology of modern persuasion.* New York: Quill.

Ciminero, A. R., Calhoun, K. S., & Adams, H. E. (1986). *Handbook of behavioral assessment* (2nd ed.). New York: Wiley.

Cirino, R. (1971). *Don't blame the people.* New York: Random House.

Clark, M., Miller, L. S., & Pruger, R. (1980). Treating clients fairly:

Equity in the distribution of in home supportive services. *Journal of Social Service Research, 4,* 47–60.

Cohen, L. J. (1979). On the psychology of predictions: Whose is the fallacy? *Cognition, 7,* 385–407.

Collins, A. (1985). Teaching reasoning skills. In S. F. Chipman, J. W. Segal, & R. Glaser (Eds.), *Thinking and learning skills: Vol. 2. Research and open questions.* Hillsdale, NJ: Erlbaum.

Collins, J. L. (1982, March). *Self-efficacy and ability in achievement behavior.* Paper presented at the meeting of the American Educational Research Association, New York.

Colman, A. M. (1987). *Facts, fallacies and frauds in psychology.* London: Hutchinson.

Conner, J. M. (1985). Sex related differences and cognitive skills. In T. M. Shlechter & M. P. Toglia (Eds.), *New directions in cognitive science.* Norwood, NJ: Ablex.

Copi, I. M. (1961). *Introduction to logic* (2nd ed.). New York: Macmillan.

Corbin, R. M. (1980). Decisions that might not get made. In T. S. Wallsten (Ed.), *Cognitive processes in choice and decision behavior.* Hillsdale, NJ: Erlbaum.

Corcoran, K., & Fischer, J. (1987). *Measures for clinical practice: A sourcebook.* New York: Free Press.

Cordes, C. (1983, November). Don't be your most difficult client. *APA Monitor,* p. 22.

Dallas, M. E., & Baron, R. S. (1985). Do psychotherapists use a confirmatory strategy during interviewing? *Journal of Social and Clinical Psychology, 3,* 106–122.

Dangel, R. F., & Polster, R. A. (Eds.). (1984). *Parent training: Foundations of research and practice.* New York: Guilford.

Darley, J. M., & Gross, P. H. (1983). A hypothesis-confirming bias in labeling effects. *Journal of Personality and Social Psychology, 44,* 20–37.

Davidson, C. V., & Abramowitz, S. I. (1980). Sex bias in clinical judgements: Later empirical returns. *Psychology of Women Quarterly, 4,* 377–395.

Davis, L. E., & Proctor, E. K. (1989). *Race, gender & class: Guidelines for practice with individuals, families, and groups.* Englewood Cliffs, NJ: Prentice-Hall.

Davis, M. (1981). A multidimensional approach to individual differences in empathy. *JSAS Catalogue of Selected Documents in Psychology, 10,* 85.

Davis, W. L., & Davis, D. E. (1972). Internal-external control and attribution of responsibility for success and failure. *Journal of personality, 40,* 123–136.

Dawes, R. M. (1982). The value of being explicit when making clinical decisions. In T. A. Wills (Ed.), *Basic processes in helping relationships.* Orlando, FL: Academic Press.

Dawes, R. M., & Corrigan, B. (1974). Linear models in decision making. *Psychological Bulletin, 81,* 95–106.

Dawes, R. M., Faust, D., & Meehl, P. E. (1989). Clinical versus actuarial judgement. *Science, 243,* 1668–1674.

Dean, G. (1986–1987). Does astrology need to be true? Part I: A look at the real thing. *The Skeptical Inquirer, 11*(2), 166–185.

Dean, G. (1987). Does astrology need to be true? Part 2: The answer is no. *The Skeptical Inquirer, 11*(3), 257–273.

DeAngelis, T. (1987, July). Therapists who feel as if they're not therapists: The imposter syndrome. *APA Monitor, 18,* 14.

Decker, F. H. (1987). Psychiatric management of legal defense in periodic commitment hearings. *Social Problems, 34,* 156–171.

DeDombal, F. T., Leaper, D. J., & Horrocks, J. C. (1974). Human and computer-aided diagnosis of abdominal pain: Further reporting with emphasis on performance of clinicians. *British Medical Journal, 1,* 376.

DeRivera, J. (1985). Biological necessity, emotional transformation, and personal value. In S. Koch & D. E. Leary (Eds.), *A century of psychology as science.* New York: McGraw-Hill.

Deutsch, C. J. (1984). Self-reported sources of stress among psychotherapists. *Professional Psychology, 15,* 833–845.

Dewald, P. A. (1987). *Learning process in psychoanalytic supervision: Complexities and challenges.* New York: International Universities Press.

Dewey, J. (1933). *How we think* (rev. ed.). Boston: Heath.

Dillinger, D. (1988, March). Playing with prisoners' minds. *Fellowship, 54,* 18–20.

Dillon, R. F., & Sternberg, R. J. (Eds.). (1986). *Cognition and instruction.* Orlando, FL: Academic Press.

Dingwall, R., Eekelaar, J., & Murray, T. (1983). *The protection of children.* Oxford, England: Basil Blackwell.

D'Iulio, J. J., Jr. (1988). What's wrong with private prisons? *Public Interest, 92,* 66–83.

Dozier, D. M., & Rice, R. E. (1984). Rival theories on electronic newsreading. In R. E. Rice (Ed.), *The new media: Communication research and technology.* Beverly Hills, CA: Sage.

Dreyfus, H. L., & Dreyfus, S. E. (1986). *Mind over machine: The power of human intuition and expertise in the era of the computer.* New York: Free Press.

Duncan, B. (1976). Differential social perception and attribution of intergroup violence: Testing the lower limits of stereotyping blacks. *Journal of Personality and Social Psychology, 34,* 590–598.

Durlak, J. A. (1979). Comparative effectiveness of paraprofessional and professional helpers. *Psychological Bulletin, 86,* 80–92.

Eddy, D. M. (1982). Probabilistic reasoning in clinical medicine: Problems and opportunities. In D. Kahneman, P. Slovic, & A. Tversky (Eds.), *Judgment under uncertainty: Heuristics and biases.* New York: Cambridge University Press.

Edelmann, R. J. (1987). *The psychology of embarrassment.* New York: Wiley.

Edmondson, R. (1984). *Rhetoric in sociology.* New York: Macmillan.

Edwards, W., & Von Winterfeldt, D. (1986). On the cognitive illusions and their implications. In H. R. Arkes & K. R. Hammond (Eds.), *Judgement and decision making: An interdisciplinary reader.* Cambridge, England: Cambridge University Press.

Ehrenreich, B., & Ehrenreich, J. (1977). The professional managerial class. *Radical America, 11,* 7–31.

Einhorn, H. J. (1980a). Overconfidence in judgment. In R. A. Shweder (Ed.), *New directions for methodology in social and behavioral science: No. 4. Fallible judgment in behavioral research.* San Francisco: Jossey-Bass.

Einhorn, H. J. (1980b). Learning from experience and suboptimal rules in decision making. In T. S. Wallsten (Ed.), *Cognitive processes in choice and decision behavior.* Hillsdale, NJ: Erlbaum.

Einhorn, H. J. (1988). Diagnosis and causality in clinical and statistical prediction. In D. C. Turk & P. Salovey (Eds.), *Reasoning, inference and judgement in clinical psychology*. New York: Free Press.

Einhorn, H. J., & Hogarth, R. M. (1978). Confidence in judgement: Persistence of the illusion of validity. *Psychological Review, 85*, 395–416.

Einhorn, H. J., & Hogarth, R. M. (1985). Prediction, diagnosis, causal thinking in forecasting. In G. Wright (Ed.), *Behavioral decision making*. New York: Plenum.

Einhorn, H. J., & Hogarth, R. M. (1986). Judging probable cause. *Psychological Bulletin, 99*, 3–19.

Ellis, A., & Grieger, R. (1977). *Handbook of rational-emotive therapy*. New York: Springer.

Ellis, A., and Yeager, R. J. (1989). *Why some therapies don't work*. Buffalo, NY: Prometheus Books.

Ellis, M. (1987). *Practice assessment: The construction and negotiation of criteria on CSS and CQSW courses*. Unpublished master's thesis, Cranfield Institute of Technology.

Ellul, J. (1965). *Propaganda: The formation of men's attitudes*. New York: Vintage.

Elstein, A. S. (1988). Cognitive processes in clinical inference and decision making. In D. C. Turk and P. Salovey (Eds.), *Reasoning, inference, and judgement in clinical psychology*. New York: Free Press.

Elstein, A. S., & Bordage, G. (1979). Psychology of clinical reasoning. In G. C. Stone, F. Cohen, N. E. Adler, & Associates, *Health psychology—a handbook: Theories, applications, and challenges of a psychological approach to the health care system*. San Francisco: Jossey-Bass.

Elstein, A. S., Shulman, L. S., Sprafka, S. A., Allal, L., Gordon, M., Jason, H., Kagan, N., Loupe, M., & Jordan, R. (1978). *Medical problem solving: An analysis of clinical reasoning*. Cambridge, MA: Harvard University Press.

Emerson, R. M. (1969). *Judging delinquents: Context and process in juvenile court*. New York: Aldine.

Engel, S. M. (1982). *With good reason: An introduction to informal fallacies* (2nd ed.). New York: St. Martin's Press.

Ennis, B. J., & Litwak, T. R. (1974). Psychiatry and the presumption of expertise: Flipping coins in the courtroom. *California Law Review, 62,* 693-752.

Ennis, R. H. (1987). A taxonomy of critical thinking dispositions and abilities. In J. B. Baron & R. J. Sternberg (Eds.), *Teaching thinking skills, theory, and practice.* New York: W. H. Freeman.

Entwistle, N. (1987). A model of the teaching-learning process. In J.T.E. Richardson, M. W. Eysenck, & D. W. Piper (Eds.), *Student learning: Research in education and cognitive psychology.* Milton Keynes, England: Society for Research into Higher Education and Open University Press.

Evans, I. M., & Nelson, R. O. (1977). Assessment of child behavior problems. In A. R. Ciminero, K. S. Kalhoun, & H. E. Adams (Eds.), *Handbook of behavioral assessment.* New York: Wiley.

Eyberg, S. M., & Ross, A. W. (1978). Assessment of child behavior problems: The validation of a new inventory. *Journal of Clinical Psychology, 16,* 113-116.

Eysenck, H. J., & Nias, D.K.B. (1982). *Astrology: Science or superstition.* New York: St. Martin's Press.

Falbo, T., Hazen, M. D., & Linimon, D. (1982). The costs of selecting power bases or messages associated with the opposite sex. *Sex Roles, 8,* 147-157.

Falk, R. (1981). On coincidences. *The Skeptical Inquirer, 6,* 18-31.

Falloon, I.R.H., Boyd, J. L., & McGill, C. W. (1984). *Family care of schizophrenia.* New York: Guilford.

Faust, D., Hart, K., & Guilmette, T. J. (1988). Pediatric malingering: The capacity of children to fake believable deficits on neuropsychological testing. *Journal of Consulting and Clinical Psychology, 56,* 578-582.

Fearnside, W. W., & Holther, W. G. (1959). *Fallacy: The counterfeit of argument.* Englewood Cliffs, NJ: Prentice-Hall.

Fehrenbach, P. A., & O'Leary, M. R. (1982). Interpersonal attraction and treatment decisions in inpatient and outpatient psychiatric settings. In T. A. Wills (Ed.), *Basic processes in helping relationships.* Orlando, FL: Academic Press.

Feinstein, A. R. (1967). *Judgement.* Baltimore, MD: Williams & Wilkins.

Feld, S., & Radin, N. (1982). *Social psychology for social work and the mental health professionals.* New York: Columbia University Press.

Feltovich, P. J., Johnson, P. E., Moller, J. H., & Swanson, D. B. (1984). The role and development of medical knowledge in diagnostic expertise. In W. Clancy & E. H. Shortliffe (Eds.), *Readings in medical artificial intelligence: The first decade.* Reading, MA: Addison-Wesley.

Feyerabend, P. (1975). *Against method.* New York: Humanities Press.

Filley, A. C. (1975). *Interpersonal conflict resolution.* Glenview, IL: Scott, Foresman.

Fingarette, H. (1988). *Heavy drinking: The myth of alcoholism as a disease.* Berkeley: University of California Press.

Firestone, R. W., & Seiden, R. H. (1987). Microsuicide and suicidal threats of everyday life. *Psychotherapy, 24,* 31–39.

Fischhoff, B. (1975). Hindsight foresight: The effect of outcome knowledge on judgement under uncertainty. *Journal of Experimental Psychology: Human Perception and Performance, 1,* 288–299.

Fischhoff, B. (1982). Debiasing. In D. Kahneman, P. Slovic, & A. Tversky (Eds.), *Judgment under uncertainty: Heuristics and biases.* New York: Cambridge University Press.

Fischhoff, B., Goitein, B., & Shapira, Z. (1983). Subjective expected utility: A model of decision-making. In R. W. Scholz (Ed.), *Decision making under uncertainty.* New York: Elsevier.

Fischhoff, B., Slovic, P., & Lichtenstein, S. (1980). Knowing what you want: Measuring labile values. In T. S. Wallsten (Ed.), *Cognitive processes in choice and decision behavior.* Hillsdale, NJ: Erlbaum.

Fisher, R., & Ury, W. (1983). *Getting to yes: Reaching agreement without giving in.* New York: Penguin.

Fleming, D. C., Fleming, E. R., Roach, K. S., & Oksman, P. F. (1985). Conflict management. In C. A. Maher (Ed.), *Professional self-management: Techniques for special service providers.* Baltimore, MD: Brooks.

Foa, E. B., & Emmelkamp, P.M.G. (Eds.). (1983). *Failures in behavior therapy.* New York: Wiley.

Fong, G. T., Kravitz, D. H., & Nisbett, R. E. (1986). The effects of statistical training on thinking about everyday problems. *Cognitive Psychology, 18,* 253-292.

Forehand, R. L., & McMahon, R. J. (1981). *Helping the noncompliant child: A clinician's guide to parent training.* New York: Guilford.

Foster, S. L., Bell-Dolan, D. J., & Burge, D. A. (1988). Behavioral observation. In A. S. Bellack & M. Hersen (Eds.), *Behavioral assessment: A practical handbook* (3rd ed.). New York: Pergamon Press.

Foucault, M. (1981). *Power-knowledge: Selected interviews and other writings, 1972-1977.* New York: Pantheon.

Frank, J. (1974). *Persuasion and healing* (rev. ed.). New York: Schocken Books.

Franks, V., & Rothblum, E. D. (1983). *The stereotyping of women: Its effects on mental health.* New York: Springer.

Friedson, E. (Ed.). (1973). *Professions and their prospects.* Beverly Hills, CA: Sage.

From the president. (1986, November). *NASW News, 31,* 2.

From the president. (1987, April). *NASW News, 32,* 2.

Fromm, E. (1963). *Escape from freedom.* New York: Holt, Rinehart & Winston.

Gaeth, G. J., & Shanteau, J. (1984). Reducing the influence of irrelevant information on experienced decision makers. *Organizational Behavior and Human Performance, 33,* 263-282.

Gagne, R. M. (1977). *The conditions of learning* (3rd ed.). New York: Holt, Rinehart & Winston.

Gagne, R. M. (Ed.). (1987). *Instructional technology: Foundations.* Hillsdale, NJ: Erlbaum.

Gahagan, J. (1984). *Social interaction and its management.* London: Methuen.

Gambrill, E. (1983). *Casework: A competency based approach.* Englewood Cliffs, NJ: Prentice-Hall.

Gambrill, E. (1988). The state of the art in practice evaluation. In N. Gottlieb (Ed.), *Perspectives in direct practice evaluation.* Seattle: Center for Social Welfare Research, University of Washington, School of Social Work.

Gambrill, E., & Barth, R. P. (1980). Single-case study designs revisited. *Social Work Research and Abstracts, 16,* 15-20.

Gambrill, E., & Richey, C. (1988). *Taking charge of your social life.* Berkeley, CA: Behavioral Options.

Gambrill, E., & Stein, T. J. (1983). *Supervision: A decision making approach.* Beverly Hills, CA: Sage.

Gardner, M. (1957). *Fads and fallacies in the name of science.* New York: Dover.

Gardner, M. (1981). *Science: Good, bad and bogus.* Buffalo, NY: Prometheus.

Gardner, M. (1988). *The new age: Notes of a fringe watcher.* Buffalo, NY: Prometheus.

Garfield, S. L., & Bergin, A. E. (Eds.). (1986). *Handbook of psychotherapy and behavior change* (3rd ed.). New York: Wiley.

Gergen, K. J. (1987). Introduction: Toward a metapsychology. In H. J. Stam, T. B. Rogers, & K. J. Gergen (Eds.), *The analysis of psychological theory: Metapsychological perspectives.* Cambridge, MA: Hemisphere.

Gibbs, J. T., Huang, L. N., & Associates (1989). *Children of color: Psychological interventions with minority youth.* San Francisco: Jossey-Bass.

Gilligan, C. (1982). *In a different voice.* Cambridge, MA: Harvard University Press.

Glaser, R., & Chi, M.T.H. (1988). *Overview.* In M.T.H. Chi, R. Glaser, & M. J. Farr (Eds.), *The nature of expertise.* Hillsdale, NJ: Erlbaum.

Goethals, G. R., & Reckman, R. F. (1973). The perception of consistency in attitudes. *Journal of Experimental Social Psychology, 9,* 491-501.

Goffman, I. (1961). *Asylums.* New York: Anchor Press.

Goldberg, L. R. (1959). The effectiveness of clinicians' judgements: The diagnosis of organic brain damage from the Bender-Gestalt test. *Journal of Consulting Psychology, 23,* 25-33.

Goldberg, R. L. (1970). Man vs. model of man: A rationale, plus some evidence, for a method of improving on clinical inference. *Psychological Bulletin, 73,* 422-432.

Goldman, R. K., & Mendelsohn, G. A. (1969). Psychotherapeutic change and social adjustment: A report on a national survey of psychotherapists. *Journal of Abnormal Psychology, 74,* 164-172.

Goodman, G., & Doley, D. (1976). A framework for help-intended communication. *Psychotherapy: Theory, Research, and Practice, 13*, 106–117.

Gordon, B. (1989, February 14). Addict testifies on terrible power of crack cocaine. *San Francisco Chronicle*, pp. 1, A22.

Green, B. F., McCloskey, M., & Caramazza, A. (1985). The relation of knowledge to problem solving, with examples from kinematics. In S. F. Chipman, J. W. Segal, & R. Glaser (Eds.), *Thinking and learning skills: Vol. 2. Research and open questions*. Hillsdale, NJ: Erlbaum.

Greenfield, L. (1979). Engineering student problem solving. In J. Lochhead & J. Clement (Eds.), *Cognitive process instruction*. Philadelphia: Franklin Institute Press.

Greeno, J. G. (1978). Nature of problem-solving abilities. In W. K. Estes (Ed.), *Handbook of learning and cognitive processers: Vol. 5. Human information processing*. Hillsdale, NJ: Erlbaum.

Greeno, J. G. (1989). A perspective on thinking. *American Psychologist, 2*, 131–141.

Greenwald, A. G. (1980). The totalitarian ego: Fabrication and revision of personal history. *American Psychologist, 35*, 603–618.

Greist, J. H., Carroll, J. A., Erdman, H. P., & Wurster, C. R. (1987). *Research in mental health computer applications: Directions for the future* (Department of Health and Human Services Pub. No. (ADM) 87-1468). Rockville, MD: U.S. Department of Health and Human Services, National Institute of Mental Health.

Groen, J. G., & Patel, V. L. (1988). The relationship between comprehension and reasoning in medical experts. In M.T.H. Chi, R. Glaser, & M. J. Farr (Eds.), *The nature of expertise*. Hillsdale, NJ: Erlbaum.

Grunebaum, H., & Chasin, R. (1978). Relabeling and retraining reconsidered: The beneficial effects of a pathological label. *Family Process, 17*, 449–455.

Hagert, G., & Waern, Y. (1986). On implicit assumptions in reasoning. In T. Meyers, K. Brown, & B. McGonigle (Eds.), *Reasoning and discourse*. Orlando, FL: Academic Press.

Hall, D. F., Loftus, E. F., & Tousignant, J. P. (1984). Post-event information and changes in recollection for a national event. In G. L. Wells & E. F. Loftus (Eds.), *Eyewitness testimony: Psycho-*

logical perspectives. Cambridge, England: Cambridge University Press.

Hall, K. (1972). *Sex differences in initiation and influence in decision making among prospective teachers.* (Doctoral dissertation, Stanford University, Stanford, CA.) Dissertation Abstracts International, *33,* 3952-A.

Halloran, R. (1988, February 24). Byzantine stratagems made simple. *New York Times,* p. A-20.

Hamblin, C. L. (1970). *Fallacies.* London: Methuen.

Hand, D. J. (1985). *Artificial intelligence and psychiatry.* Cambridge, England: Cambridge University Press.

Harmon, G. (1986). *Change in view: Principles of Reasoning.* Cambridge, MA: MIT Press.

Hawkins, R. P. (1989). Developing potent behavior-change technologies: An invitation to cognitive behavior therapists. *The Behavior Therapist, 12,* 126–131.

Hayakawa, S. I. (1978). *Language in thought and action* (4th ed.). New York: Harcourt Brace Jovanovich.

Hayes, J. R. (1981). *The complete problem solver.* Philadelphia: Franklin Institute Press.

Hayes, S. C. (1981). Time series methodology and empirical clinical practice. *Journal of Consulting and Clinical Psychology, 49,* 193–211.

Hayes-Roth, F., Klahr, P., & Mostow, D. J. (1981). Advice taking and knowledge refinement: An iterative view of skill acquisition. In J. R. Anderson (Ed.), *Cognitive skills and their acquisition.* Hillsdale, NJ: Erlbaum.

Hazaleus, S. L., & Deffenbacher, J. L. (1986). Relaxation and cognitive treatment of anger. *Journal of Consulting and Clinical Psychology, 54,* 222–226.

Hellman, I. D., Morrison, T. L., & Abramowitz, S. I. (1987). Therapist flexibility/rigidity and work stress. *Professional Psychology, 18,* 21–27.

Herron, W. G., & Rouslin, S. (1984). *Issues in psychotherapy.* Washington, DC: Oryn Publications.

Higbee, K. L. (1977). *Your memory: How it works and how to improve it.* Englewood Cliffs, NJ: Prentice-Hall.

Hinton, J. W. (Ed.). (1983). *Dangerousness: Problems of Assessment and Prediction.* London: Allen & Unwin.

Hobbs, C. J., Wynne, J. M. (1989). Sexual abuse of English boys and girls: The importance of anal examination. *Child Abuse and Neglect, 13,* 195–210.

Hobbs, N. (1975). *The futures of children: Recommendations of the Project on Classification of Exceptional Children.* San Francisco: Jossey-Bass.

Hockey, R. (1984). Varieties of attentional state. In R. Parasuraman & D. R. Davies (Eds.), *Varieties of attention.* Orlando, FL: Academic Press.

Hodges, B. (1974). Effect of volume on relative weighting in impression formation. *Journal of Personality and Social Psychology, 30,* 378–381.

Hogarth, R. M. (1980). *Judgement and choice: The psychology of decision* (1st ed.). New York: Wiley.

Hogarth, R. M. (1981). Beyond discrete biases: Functional and dysfunctional aspects of judgemental heuristics. *Psychological Bulletin, 90,* 197–217.

Hogarth, R. M. (1987). *Judgement and choice: The psychology of decision* (2nd ed.). New York: Wiley.

Holland, J. H., Holyoak, K. J., Nisbett, R. E., & Thagard, P. R. (1986). *Induction: Processes of inference, learning, and discovery.* Cambridge, MA: MIT Press.

Hollingshed, A. B., & Redlich, R. C. (1958). *Social class and mental illness.* New York: Wiley.

Hollon, S. D., & Kendall, P. C. (1980). Cognitive self-statements in depression: Development of an automatic thoughts questionnaire. *Cognitive Research and Therapy, 4,* 382–395.

Holmes, D. S. (1978). Projection as a defense mechanism. *Psychological Bulletin, 85,* 677–688.

Horowitz, L. M., French, R., Lapid, J. S., & Weckler, D. (1982). Symptoms and interpersonal problems: The prototype as an integrating concept. In J. C. Anchin & D. J. Kiesler (Eds.), *Handbook of interpersonal psychotherapy.* Oxford, England: Pergamon Press.

Houts, A. C. (1984). Effects of clinician theoretical orientation and patient explanatory bias on initial clinical judgements. *Professional Psychology: Research and Practice, 15,* 284-293.

Houts, A. C., & Galante, M. (1985). The impact of evaluative disposition and subsequent information on clinical impressions. *Journal of Social and Clinical Psychology, 3,* 201-212.

Howlin, P., & Rutter, M. (1987). *Treatment of autistic children.* New York: Wiley.

Huber, R. B. (1963). *Influencing through argument.* New York: David McKay.

Huck, S. W., & Sandler, H. M. (1979). *Rival hypotheses: Alternative interpretations of data based conclusions.* New York: Harper & Row.

Huff, D. (1954). *How to lie with statistics.* New York: Norton.

Huston, K. (1986). A critical assessment of the efficacy of women's groups. *Psychotherapy, 23,* 283-290.

Hyman, R. (1961). On prior information and creativity. *Psychological Reports, 9,* 151-161.

Illich, I. (1976). *Medical nemesis.* New York: Pantheon.

Inhelder, B., Sinclair, H., & Bovet, M. (1974). *Learning and the development of cognition.* Cambridge, MA: Harvard University Press.

Isen, A. M. (1987). Positive affect, cognitive processes, and social behavior. In L. Berkowitz (Ed.), *Advances in experimental social psychology* (Vol. 20). Orlando, FL: Academic Press.

Isen, A. M., Shalker, T. E., Clark, M., & Karp, L. (1978). Affect, accessibility of material in memory, and behavior: A cognitive loop? *Journal of Personality and Social Psychology, 36,* 1-12.

Jacobs, J. (1985). "In the best interests of the child": Official court reports as an artifact of negotiated reality in children's assessment centers. *Clinical Sociology Review, 3,* 88-108.

Jacobson, R. B., & Humphrey, R. A. (1979). Families in crisis: Research and theory in child mental retardation. *Social Casework, 12,* 597-601.

James, W. (1975). *Pragmatism.* Cambridge, MA: Harvard University Press.

Jampata, V. C., Sierles, F., & Taylor, M. (1988). The use of DSM-III in the United States: A case of not going by the book. *Comprehensive Psychiatry, 29,* 39-44.

Janis, I. L., & Mann, L. (1977). *Decision making*. New York: Free Press.

Janson, D. (1988, April 22). End to suit denied in shooting death. *The New York Times*, pp. A1, B2.

Jennings, D. L., Amabile, T. M., & Ross, L. (1982). Informal covariation assessment: Data-based versus theory-based judgments. In D. Kahneman, P. Slovic, & A. Tversky (Eds.), *Judgment under uncertainty: Heuristics and biases*. New York: Cambridge University Press.

Jensen, D. D. (1989). Pathologies of science, precognition and modern psychophysics. *The Skeptical Inquirer, 13*, 147–160.

Johnson, D. M. (1972). *A systematic introduction to the psychology of thinking*. New York: Harper & Row.

Johnson, E. J. (1988). Expertise and decision under uncertainty: Performance and process. In M.T.H. Chi, R. Glaser, & M. J. Farr (Eds.), *The nature of expertise*. Hillsdale, NJ: Erlbaum.

Johnson, W. (1946). *People in quandaries: The semantics of personal adjustment*. New York: Harper & Row.

Johnson-Laird, P. N. (1983). *Mental models: Towards a cognitive science of language, inference, and consciousness*. Cambridge, MA: Harvard University Press.

Johnson-Laird, P. N. (1985). Logical thinking: Does it occur in daily life? Can it be taught? In S. F. Chipman, J. W. Segal, & R. Glaser (Eds.), *Thinking and learning skills: Vol. 2. Research and open questions*. Hillsdale, NJ: Erlbaum.

Jones, E. E., & Harris, V. A. (1967). The attribution of attitudes. *Journal of Experimental Social Psychology, 3*, 1–24.

Jones, E. E., & Nisbett, R. E. (1972). The actor and observer: Divergent perceptions of the cause of behavior. In E. E. Jones, D. E. Kanouse, H. H. Kelley, R. E. Nisbett, S. Valins, & B. Weiner (Eds.), *Attribution: Perceiving the causes of behavior*. Morristown, NJ: General Learning Press.

Jordan, J. S., Harvey, J. H., & Weary, G. (1988). Attributional biases in clinical decision making. In D. C. Turk & P. Salovey (Eds.), *Reasoning, inference, and judgement in clinical psychology*. New York: Free Press.

Jowett, G. S., & O'Donnell, V. (1986). *Propaganda and persuasion*. Newbury Park, CA: Sage.

Jungermann, H. (1983). The two camps on rationality. In R. W. Scholz (Ed.), *Decision making under uncertainty*. New York: Elsevier.

Kadushin, A. (1963). Diagnosis and evaluation for (almost) all occasions. *Social Work, 8,* 12–19.

Kadushin, C. (1969). *Why people go to psychiatrists*. New York: Atherton.

Kagle, J. D. (1984). *Social work records*. Homewood, IL: Dorsey.

Kahane, H. (1971). *Logic and contemporary rhetoric: The use of reason in everyday life*. Belmont, CA: Wadsworth.

Kahneman, D., & Tversky, A. (1973). On the psychology of prediction. *Psychological Review, 80,* 237–251.

Kahneman, D., & Tversky, A. (1982). Variants of uncertainty. *Cognition, 11,* 143–157.

Kaplan, M. (1983). A woman's view of DSM-III. *American Psychologist, 38,* 786–792.

Karoly, P., & Kanfer, F. H. (Eds.). (1982). *Self-management and behavior change: From theory to practice*. New York: Pergamon Press.

Kazak, A. E., & Marvin, R. S. (1984). Differences, difficulties and adaptation: Stress and social networks in families with a handicapped child. *Family Relations, 33,* 67–77.

Keisner, R. H. (1985). Self-fulfilling prophecies in psychodynamic practice. In G. Stricker & R. H. Keiser (Eds.), *From research to clinical practice*. New York: Plenum.

Keller, E. F. (1982). Feminism and science. *Signs, 7,* 589–601.

Kelley, G. A. (1955). *The psychology of personal constructs*. New York: Norton.

Kelley, H. H. (1950). The warm-cold variable of first impressions of persons. *Journal of Personality, 18,* 431–439.

Kendall, R. E. (1973). Psychiatric diagnoses: A study of how they are made. *British Journal of Psychiatry, 122,* 437–445.

Kenrick, D. T., & Gutierres, S. E. (1980). Contrast effects in judgements of attractiveness: When beauty becomes a social problem. *Journal of Personality and Social Psychology, 38,* 131–140.

Kent, R. N., & Foster, S. L. (1986). Direct observational procedures: Methodological issues in naturalistic settings. In A. R. Ciminero,

K. S. Calhoun, & H. E. Adams (Eds.), *Handbook of behavioral assessment* (2nd ed.). New York: Wiley.

Kessler, J. W. (1978). Potential errors in clinical practice. In J. S. Mearig (Ed.), *Working for children.* San Francisco: Jossey-Bass.

Kiesler, D. J. (1966). Some myths of psychotherapy research and the search for a paradigm. *Psychological Bulletin, 65,* 110–136.

Kirk, S., & Kutchins, H. (1988). Deliberate misdiagnosis in mental health practice. *Social Service Review, 62,* 225–237.

Kirk, S., Osmalov, M., & Fischer, J. (1976). Social workers' involvement in research. *Social Work, 21,* 121–132.

Kleinmuntz, B. (1984). The scientific study of clinical judgement in psychology and medicine. *Clinical Psychology Review, 4,* 111–126.

Klemp, G. O., & McClelland, D. C. (1986). What characterizes intelligent functioning among senior managers. In R. G. Sternberg & R. K. Wagner (Eds.), *Practical intelligence: Nature and origins of competence in the everyday world.* Cambridge, England: Cambridge University Press.

Knishinsky, A. (1982). *The effects of scarcity of material and exclusivity of information on industrial buyer perceived risk in provoking a purchase decision.* Unpublished doctoral dissertation, Arizona State University, Tempe.

Koberg, D., & Bagnall, J. (1976). *The universal traveler: A soft-system guide to creativity, problem-solving and the process of reaching goals.* Los Altos, CA: Kaufman.

Kohn, A. (1988). *False prophets: Fraud and error in science and medicine.* New York: Basil Blackwell.

Kopta, S. M., Newman, F. L., McGovern, M. P., & Sandrock, D. (1986). Psychological orientations: A comparison of conceptualizations, interventions, and treatment plan costs. *Journal of Consulting and Clinical Psychology, 54,* 369–374.

Korzybski, A. (1980). *Science and sanity: An introduction to non-aristotelian systems and general semantics* (4th ed.). Lakeville, CT: Institute of General Semantics.

Kottler, J. A., & Blau, D. S. (1989). *The imperfect therapist: Learning from failure in therapeutic practice.* San Francisco: Jossey-Bass.

Krantz, S. E., & Moos, R. H. (1988). Risk factors at intake predict nonremission among depressed patients. *Journal of Consulting and Clinical Psychology, 56,* 863–869.

Kruskal, W., & Mosteller, F. (1981). Ideas of representative sampling. In D. Fiske (Ed.), *New Directions for methodology of social and behavioral science: No. 9. Problems with language imprecision.* San Francisco: Jossey-Bass.

Kuipers, B., & Kassirer, J. P. (1984). Causal reasoning in medicine: Analysis of a protocol. *Cognitive Science, 8,* 363–385.

Kutchins, H., & Kirk, S. (1987). The reliability of the DSM-III: A critical review. *Social Work Research Abstracts, 22,* 3–12.

Lakoff, G., & Johnson, M. (1980). *Metaphors we live by.* Chicago: University of Chicago Press.

Landers, S. (1987, December). LD definition disputed. *APA Monitor,* p. 35.

Lang, P. J. (1977). Physiological assessment of anxiety and fear. In J. D. Cone & R. S. Hawkins (Eds.), *Behavioral assessment: New directions in clinical psychology.* New York: Brunner/Mazel.

Langer, E. J. (1975). The illusion of control. *Journal of Personality and Social Psychology, 32,* 311–328.

Langer, E. J. (1983). *The psychology of control.* Newbury Park, CA: Sage.

Langer, E. J., & Abelson, R. P. (1974). A patient by any other name . . . : Clinician group difference in labeling bias. *Journal of Consulting and Clinical Psychology, 42,* 4–9.

Lazarus, R. S. (1983). The costs and benefits of denial. In S. Breznitz (Ed.), *The denial of stress.* New York: International Universities Press.

Leahey, T. H., and Leahey, G. E. (1983). *Psychology's occult doubles: Psychology and the problem of pseudoscience.* Chicago: Nelson Hall.

Leiby, J. (1978). *A history of social welfare and social work in the United States.* New York: Columbia University Press.

Lemert, E. M. (1951). *Social pathology.* New York: McGraw-Hill.

Lenrow, P. (1978). Dilemmas of professional helping: Continuities and discontinuities with folk helping roles. In L. Wipse (Ed.), *Altruism.* Orlando, FL: Academic Press.

Lesgold, A., Rubinson, H., Feltovich, P., Glaser, R., Klopfer, D., & Wang, Y. (1988). Expertise in a complex skill: Diagnosing x-ray pictures. In M.T.H. Chi, R. Glaser, & M. Farr (Eds.), *The nature of expertise*. Hillsdale, NJ: Erlbaum.

Letter to the editor (1986, November). *NASW News*, p. 15.

Levinson, P., McMurray, L., Podell, P., & Weiner, H. (1978). Causes for the premature interruption of psychotherapy by private practice patients. *American Journal of Psychiatry, 135,* 826–830.

Levy, R. L. (1977). Relationship of an overt commitment to task compliance in behavior therapy. *Journal of Behavior Therapy and Experimental Psychiatry, 8,* 25–29.

Lewinsohn, P. M., Mischel, W., Chaplin, W., & Barton, R. (1980). Social competence and depression: The role of illusory self-perceptions. *Journal of Abnormal Psychology, 89,* 203–212.

Lewinsohn, P. M., Munoz, R. F., Youngren, M. A., and Zeiss, A. M. (1986). *Control your depression: Reducing depression through learning self-control techniques, relaxation training, pleasant activities, social skills, constructive thinking, planning ahead and more.* New York: Prentice-Hall.

Lichtenstein, S., Slovic, P., Fischhoff, B., Layman, M., & Coombs, C. (1978). Judged frequency of lethal events. *Journal of Experimental Psychology: Human Learning and Memory, 4,* 551–578.

Light, D. (1980). *Becoming psychiatrists*. New York: Norton.

Linn, M. C. (1986). Science. In R. F. Dillon & R. J. Sternberg (Eds.), *Cognition and instruction*. Orlando, FL: Academic Press.

Linton, M. (1982). Transformations of memory in everyday life. In U. Neisser (Ed.), *Memory observed: Remembering in natural contexts*. New York: W. H. Freeman.

Lipton, J. P., & Hershaft, A. M. (1985). On the widespread acceptance of dubious medical findings. *Journal of Health and Social Behavior, 26,* 336–351.

Lloyd-Bostock, S.M.A., & Clifford, B. R. (1983). *Evaluating witness evidence: Recent psychological research and perspectives*. New York: Wiley.

Lock, M. (1982). Popular conceptions of mental health in Japan. In A. J. Marsella and G. M. White (Eds.), *Cultural conceptions of mental health and therapy*. Norwell, MA: D. Reidel.

Loftus, E. (1979). *Eyewitness testimony*. Cambridge, MA: Harvard University Press.

Loftus, E. (1980). *Memory: Surprising new insights into how we remember and why we forget.* Reading, MA: Addison-Wesley.

Loftus, E., & Palmer, J. (1974). Reconstruction of automobile destruction: An example of the interaction between language and memory. *Journal of Verbal Learning and Verbal Behavior, 13,* 585–589.

Loftus, E. F., & Ketcham, K. E. (1983). The malleability of eyewitness accounts. In S.M.A. Lloyd-Bostock & B. R. Clifford (Eds.), *Evaluating witness evidence: Recent psychological research and new perspectives.* New York: Wiley.

Lord, C., Ross, L., & Lepper, M. R. (1979). Biased assimilation and attitude polarization: The effects of prior theories on subsequently considered evidence. *Journal of Personality and Social Psychology, 37,* 2098–2109.

McCloskey, M. (1984). Cartoon physics. *Psychology Today, 18* (4), 52–58.

McGee, P. E., & Goldstein, J. H. (1983). *Handbook of humor research: Vol.2. Applied studies.* New York: Springer-Verlag.

McGovern, M. P., Newman, F. L., & Kopta, S. M. (1986). Metatheoretical assumptions and psychotherapy orientation: Clinician attributions of patients' problem causality and responsibility for treatment outcome. *Journal of Consulting and Clinical Psychology, 54,* 476–481.

Machado, L. A. (1980). *The right to be intelligent.* Oxford, England: Pergamon Press.

Mackie, J. L. (1974). *The cement of the universe: A study of causation.* Oxford, England: Clarendon Press.

MacLean, E. (1981). *Between the lines: How to detect bias and propaganda in the news and everyday life.* Montreal: Black Rose Books.

McLellan, D. (1986). *Ideology: Concepts in social thought.* Minneapolis: University of Minnesota Press.

McNeil, B. J., Pauker, S. G., Sox, H. C., Jr., & Tversky, A. (1982). On the elicitation of preferences for alternative therapies. *New England Journal of Medicine, 306,* 1259–1262.

McReynolds, P. (1989). Diagnosis and clinical assessment: Current status and major issues. In M. R. Rosenzweig & L. W. Porter (Eds.), *Annual Review of Psychology, 40,* 83–108.

Maguire, G. P., & Rutter, D. R. (1976). History-taking for medical students. I. Deficiencies in performance. *Lancet, 11*, 556–560.

Maher, C. A., & Cook, S. A. (1985). Time management. In C. A. Maher (Ed.), *Professional self-management: Techniques for special service providers.* Baltimore, MD: Brooks.

Mahoney, M. J. (1977). Publication prejudices: An experimental study of confirmatory bias in the peer review system. *Cognitive Therapy and Research, 1*, 161–175.

Manning, N. P. (Ed.). (1985). *Social problems and welfare ideology.* Aldershot, England: Gower.

Marinucci, C. C. (1989, February 19). Last call for alcohol. *The New York Times,* p. D-1.

Marketing: A lifeline for private practice. (1987, October). *NASW News, 32,* 5.

Markus, H. (1977). Self-schemata and processing information about the self. *Journal of Personality and Social Psychology, 35,* 63–78.

Marlatt, G. A., & Gordon, J. R. (Eds.). (1985). *Relapse prevention: Maintenance strategies in the treatment of addiction.* New York: Guilford.

Martin, G., & Pear, J. (1988). *Behavior modification: What it is and how to do it* (3rd ed.). Englewood Cliffs, NJ: Prentice-Hall.

Maslach, C., & Pines, A. (1979). "Burn out": The loss of human caring. In A. Pines & C. Maslach, *Experiencing social psychology* (pp. 245–252). New York: Random House.

Masson, J. S. (1988). *Against therapy: Emotional tyranny and the myth of psychological healing.* New York: Atheneum.

Matteson, M. T., & Ivancevich, J. M. (1987). *Controlling work stress: Effective human resource and management strategies.* San Francisco: Jossey-Bass.

Mavissakalian, M., & Barlow, D. (1981). *Phobia: Psychological and pharmacological treatment.* New York: Guilford.

Mays, D. T., & Franks, C. M. (Eds.). (1985). *Negative outcome in psychotherapy and what to do about it.* New York: Springer.

Medawar, P. (1979). A bouquet of fallacies from medicine and medical science with a sideways glance at mathematics and logic. In R. Duncan & M. Weston-Smith (Eds.), *The encyclopedia of delusions: A critical scrutiny of current beliefs and conventions.* New York: Simon & Schuster.

Medawar, P. B. (1984). *Pluto's republic.* Oxford, England: Oxford University Press.

Medin, D. L. (1989). You have to almost know something in order to learn it. *Contemporary Psychology, 34,* 445–447.

Meehl, P. E. (1954). *Clinical versus statistical prediction: A theoretical analysis and a review of the evidence.* Minneapolis: University of Minnesota Press.

Meehl, P. E. (1960). The cognitive activity of the clinician. *American Psychologist, 15,* 19–27.

Meehl, P. E. (1973). Why I do not attend case conferences. In P. E. Meehl (Ed.), *Psychodiagnosis: Selected papers.* Minneapolis: University of Minnesota Press.

Meehl, P. E. (1978). Theoretical risks and tabular asterisks: Sir Karl, Sir Ronald and the slow progress of soft psychology. *Journal of Consulting and Clinical Psychology, 46,* 806–834.

Meichenbaum, D., & Asarnow, J. (1979). Cognitive behavior modification and metacognitive development: Implications for the classroom. In P. Kendall & S. Hollon (Eds.), *Cognitive behavioral interventions: Theory, research, and procedures.* Orlando, FL: Academic Press.

Meichenbaum, D., & Turk, D. C. (1987). *Facilitating treatment adherence: A practitioner's handbook.* New York: Plenum.

Mennerick, L. L. (1974). Client typologies: A method of coping with conflicts in the service worker–client relationship. *Sociology of Work and Occupations, 1,* 396–418.

Meyer, L. H., & Evans, I. M. (1989). *Nonaversive intervention for behavior problems: A manual for home and community.* Baltimore, MD: Brooks.

Michalos, A. C. (1971). *Improving your reasoning.* Englewood Cliffs, NJ: Prentice-Hall.

Milgram, S. (1963). Behavioral study of obedience. *Journal of Abnormal and Social Psychology, 67,* 371–378.

Miller, A. G., Gillen, B., Schenker, C., & Radlove, S. (1973). Perception of obedience to authority. *Proceedings of the 81st Annual Convention of the American Psychological Association, 8,* 127–128.

Miller, J. D. (1987). The scientifically illiterate. *American Demographics, 9,* 26–31.

Mills, C. W. (1959). *The sociological imagination*. New York: Grove Press.

Mischel, W. (1968). *Personality and assessment*. New York: Wiley.

Mischel, W. (1973). Toward a cognitive social learning reconceptualization of personality. *Psychological Review, 80*, 252–283.

Montenegro, M. (1988, December–January). Human subjects at risk of torture U.S. style: California. *NASW News, 14*, 5.

Moore, K. D. (1986). *Inductive arguments: A field guide*. Dubuque, IA: Kendall/Hunt.

Morawski, J. G. (1987). After reflection: Psychologists' uses of history. In H. J. Stam, T. B. Rogers, & K. J. Gergen (Eds.), *The analysis of psychological theory: Metaphysical perspectives*. New York: Hemisphere.

Morgan, R. F. (Ed.). (1983). *The iatrogenics handbook*. Toronto: IPI Publications.

Morgan, T. (1982). *Churchill: Young man in a hurry 1874–1915*. New York: Simon & Schuster.

Murray, D. (1984). *Write to learn*. New York: Holt, Rinehart & Winston.

Nadelmann, E. A. (1988). The case for legalization. *Public Interest, 92*(Summer), 3–31.

National Assessment of Educational Programs (NAEP). (1981). *Reading, thinking, and writing*. Denver, CO: Educational Commission of the States.

National Association of Social Workers. (1980). NASW code of ethics. *NASW News, 25*, 24–25.

National Campaign to Abolish the Lexington Women's Control Unit. (n.d.). *Buried alive in the Lexington Women's Control Unit*. Brooklyn, NY: National Campaign to Abolish the Lexington Women's Control Unit.

Nay, W. R. (1986). Analogue measures. In A. R. Ciminero, K. S. Calhoun, & H. E. Adams (Eds.), *Handbook of behavioral assessment*. New York: Wiley.

Nettler, G. (1970). *Explanations*. New York: McGraw-Hill.

Neuringer, A. (1981). Self-experimentation. *Behaviorism, 9*, 79–94.

Nickerson, R. S. (1985). Reasoning. In S. F. Chipman, J. W. Segal, & R. Glaser (Eds.), *Thinking and learning skills: Vol. 2. Research and open questions*. Hillsdale, NJ: Erlbaum.

Nickerson, R. S. (1986a). *Reflections on reasoning.* Hillsdale, NJ: Erlbaum.

Nickerson, R. S. (1986b). Reasoning. In R. F. Dillon & R. J. Sternberg (Eds.), *Cognition and instruction.* Orlando, FL: Academic Press.

Nickerson, R. S. (1987). Why teach thinking? In J. B. Baron & R. J. Sternberg (Eds.), *Teaching thinking skills: Theory and practice.* New York: W. H. Freeman.

Nickerson, R. S., Perkins, D. N., & Smith, E. E. (1985). *The teaching of thinking.* Hillsdale, NJ: Erlbaum.

Niemi, J. A., & Gooler, D. D. (Eds.). (1987). *New directions for continuing education: No. 34. Technologies for learning outside the classroom.* San Francisco: Jossey-Bass.

Nisbett, R. E., Borgida, E., Crandall, R., & Reed, H. (1976). Popular induction: Information is not necessarily informative. In J. S. Carroll & J. W. Payne (Eds.), *Cognition and social behavior.* Hillsdale, NJ: Erlbaum.

Nisbett, R. E., Krantz, D. H., Jepson, C., & Kunda, Z. (1983). The use of statistical heuristics in everyday inductive reasoning. *Psychological Review, 90,* 339-363.

Nisbett, R. E., & Lemley, R. N. (1979). *The evil that men do can be diluted, the good cannot.* Unpublished manuscript, University of Michigan, Ann Arbor.

Nisbett, R., & Ross, L. (1980). *Human inference: Strategies and shortcomings of social judgement.* Englewood Cliffs, NJ: Prentice-Hall.

Novaco, R. W. (1975). *Anger control: The development and evaluation of an experimental treatment.* Lexington, MA: Heath.

Novak, J. D., & Gowin, D. B. (1984). *Learning how to learn.* New York: Cambridge University Press.

Nye, M. J. (1980). N-rays: An episode in the history and psychology of science. *Historical Studies in the Physical Sciences, 11,* 125-156.

Orwell, G. (1958). Politics and the English language. In S. Orwell & I. Angus (Eds.), *The collected essays, journalism and letters of George Orwell: Vol. 4. In front of your nose, 1945-1950* (pp. 127-140). London: Secker & Warburg. (Original work published 1946)

Osborn, A. F. (1963). *Applied imagination: Principles and procedures of creative problem solving* (3rd ed.). New York: Scribner's.

Oskamp, S. (1965). Overconfidence in case-study judgements. *Journal of Consulting Psychology, 29*, 261–265.

Palincsar, A. S., & Brown, A. L. (1984). Reciprocal teaching of comprehension-fostering and comprehension-monitoring activities. *Cognition and Instruction, 1*, 117–175.

Parloff, M. B., Waskow, I. E., & Wolf, B. E. (1978). Research on therapist variables in relation to process and outcome. In S. L. Garfield & A. E. Bergin (Eds.), *Handbook of psychotherapy and behavior change: An empirical analysis* (2nd ed.). New York: Wiley.

Patel, V. L., Arocha, J. F., & Groen, G. J. (1986). Strategy selection and degree of expertise in medical reasoning. In *Proceedings of the eighth annual conference of the Cognitive Science Society.* Hillsdale, NJ: Erlbaum.

Patel, V. L., & Groen, G. J. (1986). Knowledge based solution strategies in medical reasoning. *Cognitive Science, 10*, 91–116.

Paul, G. L. (1986). *Assessment in residential treatment settings.* Champaign, IL: Research Press.

Paul, R. W. (1987). Critical thinking and the critical person. In D. N. Perkins, J. Lochhead, & J. Bishop (Eds.), *Thinking: The second international conference.* Hillsdale, NJ: Erlbaum.

Pepper, S. (1981). Problems in the quantification of frequency experiences. In D. Fiske (Ed.), *New directions for methodology of social and behavioral science: No. 9. Problems with language imprecision.* San Francisco: Jossey-Bass.

Perkins, D. N. (1985). General cognitive skills, why not? In S. F. Chipman, J. W. Segal, & R. Glaser (Eds.), *Thinking and learning skills: Vol. 2. Research and open questions.* Hillsdale, NJ: Erlbaum.

Perkins, D. N. (1987). Thinking frames: An integrative perspective on teaching cognitive skills. In J. B. Baron & R. J. Sternberg (Eds.), *Teaching thinking skills: Theory and practice.* New York: W. H. Freeman.

Perkins, D. N. (1988). Creativity and the quest for mechanism. In R. J. Sternberg & E. E. Smith (Eds.), *The psychology of human thought.* Cambridge, England: Cambridge University Press.

Perkins, D. N., Allen, R., & Hafner, J. (1983). Difficulties in every-day reasoning. In W. Maxwell (Ed.), *Thinking*. Philadelphia: Franklin Institute Press.

Petty, R. E., & Cacioppo, J. T. (1986). The elaboration likelihood model of persuasion. In L. Berkowitz (Ed.), *Advances in experimental social psychology* (Vol. 19). Orlando, FL: Academic Press.

Pfohl, S. J. (1978). *Predicting dangerousness: The social construction of psychiatric reality*. Lexington, MA: Heath.

Pilpel, R. H. (1976). *Churchill in America*. New York: Harcourt Brace Jovanovich.

Plous, S., & Zimbardo, P. G. (1986). Attributional biases among clinicians: A comparison of psychoanalysts and behavior therapists. *Journal of Clinical and Consulting Psychology, 54,* 568–570.

Polanyi, M. (1958). *Personal knowledge: Toward a post-critical philosophy*. Chicago: University of Chicago Press.

Pollio, H. R. (1979). Intuitive thinking. In G. Underwood & R. Stevens (Eds.), *Aspects of consciousness: Vol. 1. Psychological issues*. Orlando, FL: Academic Press.

Popper, K. R. (1959). *The logic of scientific discovery*. London: Hutchinson.

Popper, K. R. (1963). *Conjectures and refutations*. New York: Harper & Row.

Popper, K. R. (1977). On hypotheses. In P. N. Johnson-Laird & P. C. Wason (Eds.), *Thinking: Readings in cognitive science*. Cambridge, England: Cambridge University Press.

Popper, K. R. (1983a). The aim of science. In D. Miller (Ed.), *A pocket Popper*. London: Fontana Press. (Original work published 1957)

Popper, K. R. (1983b). The problem of induction. In D. Miller (Ed.), *A pocket Popper*. London: Fontana Press. (Original work published 1974)

Porter, N., & Geis, F. (1981). Women and nonverbal leadership cues: When seeing is not believing. In C. Mayo & N. M. Henley (Eds.), *Gender and nonverbal behavior* (pp. 39–61). New York: Springer-Verlag.

Premack, D. (1959). Toward empirical behavior laws, part 1: Positive reinforcement. *Psychological Review, 61*, 219-233.

Pressley, M., Borkowski, J. G., & O'Sullivan, J. T. (1984). Memory strategy instruction is made of this: Metamemory and durable strategy use. *Educational Psychologist, 9*, 94-107.

Prosser, M. (1987). The effects of cognitive structure and learning strategy on student achievement. In J.T.E. Richardson, M. W. Eysenck, & W. Piper (Eds.), *Student learning: Research in education and cognitive psychology*. Milton Keynes, England: Society for Research into Higher Education and Open University Press.

Pryor, J. B., & Kriss, M. (1977). The cognitive dynamics of salience in the attribution process. *Journal of Personality and Social Psychology, 35*, 49-55.

Pyszczynski, T., & Greenberg, J. (1985). Depression and preferences for self-focusing stimuli after success and failure. *Journal of Personality and Social Psychology, 49*, 1066-1075.

Pyszczynski, T., & Greenberg, J. (1987). Toward an integration of cognitive and motivational perspectives on social inference: A biased hypothesis-testing model. In L. Berkowitz (Ed.), *Advances in experimental social psychology* (Vol. 20). Orlando, FL: Academic Press.

Regan, D. T., & Totten, J. (1975). Empathy and attribution: Turning observers into actors. *Journal of Personality and Social Psychology, 32*, 850-856.

Renaud, H., & Estess, F. (1961). Life history interviews with one hundred normal American males: "Pathogenicity" of childhood. *American Journal of Orthopsychiatry, 31*, 796-802.

Rice, L. N., & Greenberg, L. S. (Eds.). (1984). *Patterns of change: Intensive analysis of psychotherapy process*. New York: Guilford.

Rieke, R., & Sillers, M. (1984). *Argumentation and the decision making process* (2nd ed.). Glenview, IL: Scott, Foresman.

Robbins, L. C. (1963). The accuracy of parental recall of aspects of child development and child-rearing practices. *Journal of Abnormal and Social Psychology, 66*, 216-270.

Robertiello, R. C., & Schoenewolf, G. (1987). *One hundred one common therapeutic blunders: Countertransference and counter-resistance in psychotherapy.* Northvale, NJ: Aronson.

Robertson, S. P., Black, J. B., & Lehnert, W. G. (1985). Misleading question effects as evidence for integrated question understanding and memory search. In A. C. Graesser & J. B. Black (Eds.), *The psychology of questions.* Hillsdale, NJ: Erlbaum.

Robitscher, J. (1980). *The powers of psychiatry.* Boston: Houghton Mifflin.

Rogers, C. R. (1957). The necessary and sufficient conditions of therapeutic personality change. *Journal of Consulting Psychology, 21,* 95–103.

Rokeach, M. (1960). *The open and closed mind.* New York: Basic Books.

Rosen, G. M. (1982). Self-help approaches to self-management. In K. R. Blankstein & J. Polivy (Eds.), *Self-control and self-modification of emotional behavior* (Vol. 7). New York: Plenum.

Rosenhan, D. L. (1973). On being sane in insane places. *Science, 179,* 250–258.

Rosenthal, A. M. (1964). *Thirty-eight witnesses.* New York: McGraw-Hill.

Rosenthal, R. (1988). *Experimenter effects in behavioral research.* New York: Irvington.

Ross, L., Amabile, T., & Steinmetz, J. (1977). Social roles, social control and biases in social perception processes. *Journal of Personality and Social Psychology, 35,* 485–494.

Ross, L., Greene, D., & House, P. (1977). The false consensus phenomenon: An attributional bias in self-perception and social perception processes. *Journal of Experimental Social Psychology, 13,* 279–301.

Ross, L., & Lepper, M. R. (1980). The perseverance of beliefs: Empirical and normative considerations. In R. A. Schweder (Ed.), *New directions for methodology of social and behavioral science: No. 4. Fallible judgment in behavioral research.* San Francisco: Jossey-Bass.

Ross, L., Lepper, M. R., & Hubbard, J. (1975). Perseverance in self perception and social perception: Biased attributional processes in the debriefing paradigm. *Journal of Personality and Social Psychology, 32,* 880–892.

Ross, W. D. (Trans. ed.). *The works of Aristotle*. Oxford, England: Clarendon Press. (Cited in Hamblin, 1970.)

Rubenstein, M. F. (1975). *Patterns of problem solving*. Englewood Cliffs, NJ: Prentice-Hall.

Runyan, W. M. (1977). How should treatment recommendations be made? Three studies in the logical and empirical bases of clinical decision making. *Journal of Consulting and Clinical Psychology, 45,* 552–558.

Ryan, D. (1987). The impermeable membrane. In J.T.E. Richardson, M. W. Eysenck, & W. Piper (Eds.), *Student learning: Research in education and cognitive psychology*. Milton Keynes, England: Society for Research into Higher Education and Open University Press.

Ryan, W. (1976). *Blaming the victim* (rev. ed.). New York: Vantage.

Rycroft, C. (1973). *A critical dictionary of psychoanalysis*. Towata, NJ: Littlefield, Adams.

Sacco, W., & Beck, A. T. (1985). Cognitive therapy for depression. In E. Beckman & W. R. Lober (Eds.), *Handbook of depression: Treatment, assessment, and research*. Homewood, IL: Dorsey Press.

Salancik, G. R., & Conway, M. (1975). Attitude inferences from salient and relevant cognitive content about behavior. *Journal of Personality and Social Psychology, 32,* 829–840.

Salovey, P., & Turk, D. C. (1988). Some effects of mood on clinicians' memory. In D. C. Turk & P. Salovey (Eds.), *Reasoning, inference and judgement in clinical psychology*. New York: Free Press.

Sampson, E. E. (1977). Psychology and the American ideal. *Journal of Personality and Social Psychology, 35,* 767–782.

Sanford, A. J. (1985). *Cognition and cognitive psychology*. Hove, East Sussex, Eng.: Erlbaum.

Sarbin, T. R. (1967). On the futility of the proposition that some people be labeled "mentally ill." *Journal of Consulting Psychology, 31,* 447–453.

Sarri, R. C. (1987). The female offender and the criminal justice system. In D. S. Burden & N. Gottlieb (Eds.), *The woman client: Providing human services in a changing world*. New York: Tavistock.

Schank, R., & Abelson, R. (1977). *Scripts, plans, goals, and understanding: An inquiry into human knowledge.* Hillsdale, NJ: Erlbaum.

Scheff, T. F. (1963). Decision rules, types of errors, and their consequences in medical diagnosis. *Behavioral Science, 8,* 97–107.

Scheff, T. J. (1984a). *Labeling madness* (2nd ed.). Englewood Cliffs, NJ: Prentice-Hall.

Scheff, T. J. (1984b). *Being mentally ill: A sociological theory* (2nd ed.). New York: Aldine..

Scheper-Hughes, N., & Lovell, A. M. (Eds.). (1987). *Psychiatry inside out: Selected writings of Franco Basaglia.* New York: Columbia University Press.

Schlenker, B. R., & Leary, M. R. (1982). Social anxiety and self-presentation: A conceptualization and model. *Psychological Bulletin, 92,* 641–669.

Schnelle, J. F. (1974). A brief report on invalidity of parent evaluations of behavior change. *Journal of Applied Behavior Analysis, 7,* 341–343.

Schoenfeld, A. H. (1982). Measures of problem-solving performance and of problem-solving instruction. *Journal for Research on Mathematics Education, 13,* 31–49.

Schopenhauer, A. (n.d.). The art of controversy. In A. Schopenhauer, *The essays of Arthur Schopenhauer* (T. B. Saunders, Trans.). New York: Wiley.

Schultz, T. (Ed.). (1989). *The fringes of reason: A whole earth catalog.* New York: Harmony Books.

Schur, E. M. (1971). *Labeling deviant behavior.* New York: Harper & Row.

Scriven, M. (1976). *Reasoning.* New York: McGraw-Hill.

Sedgwick, P. (1982). *Psycho Politics.* New York: Harper & Row.

Semin, G. R., & Manstead, A.S.R. (1983). *The accountability of conduct: A social psychological analysis.* Orlando, FL: Academic Press.

Shapiro, S. C. (1987). *Encyclopedia of artificial intelligence* (Vols. 1 and 2). New York: Wiley.

Shaughnessy, J. M. (1983). The psychology of inference and the teaching of probability and statistics: Two sides of the same coin.

In R. W. Scholz (Ed.), *Decision making under uncertainty.* New York: Elsevier.

Sherman, J. A. (1980). Therapist attitudes and sex-role stereotyping. In A. M. Brodsky & R. T. Hare-Mustin (Eds.), *Woman and psychotherapy: An assessment of research and practice.* New York: Guilford.

Shweder, R. A. (1977). Likeness and likelihood in everyday thought: Magical thinking in judgements about personality. *Current Anthropology, 18,* 637–658.

Shweder, R. A., & Miller, J. G. (1985). The social construction of the person: How is it possible? In K. J. Gergen & K. E. Davis (Eds.), *The social construction of the person.* New York: Springer-Verlag.

Sigel, I. E. (1979). On becoming a thinker. A psychoeducational model. *Educational Psychologist, 14,* 70–78.

Silverman, K. (1986). *Benjamin Franklin: The autobiography and other writings.* New York: Penguin.

Simon, H. A. (1983). *Reason in human affairs.* Oxford, England: Basil Blackwell.

Simon, H. A., & Chase, W. G. (1973). Skill in chess. *American Scientist, 61,* 394–403.

Singer, B., & Bernassi, V. A. (1981). Occult beliefs. *American Scientist, 69,* 49–55.

Sisson, J. C., Schoomaker, E. G., & Ross, J. C. (1976). Clinical decision analysis: The hazard of using additional data. In H. R. Arkes & K. R. Hammond (Eds.), *Judgement and decision making: An interdisciplinary reader.* Cambridge, England: Cambridge University Press.

Slovic, P., Fischhoff, B., & Lichtenstein, S. (1976). Cognitive processes and societal risk taking. In J. S. Carroll & J. W. Payne (Eds.), *Cognitive and social behavior.* Hillsdale, NJ: Erlbaum.

Slovic, P., Fischhoff, B., & Lichtenstein, S. (1982a). Response mode, framing, and information-processing effects in risk assessment. In R. M. Hogarth (Ed.), *New directions for methodology of social and behavioral science: No. 11. Question framing and response consistency.* San Francisco: Jossey-Bass.

Slovic, P., Fischhoff, B., & Lichtenstein, S. (1982b). Facts versus fears: Understanding perceived risk. In D. Kahneman, P. Slovic,

& A. Tversky (Eds.), *Judgment under uncertainty: Heuristics and biases.* New York: Cambridge University Press.

Slovic, P., Kunreuther, H., & White, G. F. (1974). Decision processes, rationality, and adjustment to natural hazards. In G. F. White (Ed.), *Natural hazards: Local, national, and global.* Oxford, England: Oxford University Press.

Smedslund, J. (1963). The concept of correlation in adults. *Scandinavian Journal of Psychology, 4,* 165–173.

Smith, C. R., and Hunsaker, D. M. (1972). *The bases of argument: Ideas in conflict.* Indianapolis, IN: Bobbs-Merrill.

Snyder, C. R., & Clair, M. S. (1977). Does insecurity breed acceptance? Effects of trait and situational insecurity on acceptance of positive and negative diagnostic feedback. *Journal of Counseling and Clinical Psychology, 45* (5), 843–850.

Snyder, C. R., Higgins, R. L., & Stucky, R. J. (1983). *Excuses: Masquerades in search of grace.* New York: Wiley.

Snyder, C. R., Shenkel, R. J., & Schmidt, A. (1976). Effects of role perspective and client psychiatric history on locus of problem. *Journal of Consulting and Clinical Psychology, 44,* 467–472.

Snyder, M., & Swann, W. B. (1978). Behavioral confirmation in social interaction: From social perception to social reality. *Journal of Experimental Social Psychology, 14,* 148–162.

Snyder, M., Tanke, E. D., & Berscheid, E. (1977). Social perception and interpersonal behavior: On the self-fulfilling nature of social stereotypes. *Journal of Personality and Social Psychology, 35,* 656–666.

Snyder, M., & Thomsen, C. J. (1988). Interactions between therapists and clients: Hypothesis testing and behavioral confirmation. In D. C. Turk & P. Salovey (Eds.), *Reasoning, inference, and judgement in clinical psychology.* New York: Free Press.

Snyder, R. E. (1966). Mammography: Contributions and limitations in the management of cancer of the breast. *Clinical Obstetrics and Gynecology, 9,* 207–220.

Sobell, M. B., & Sobell, L. C. (1982). Controlled drinking: A concept coming of age. In K. R. Blankstein & J. Polivy (Eds.), *Self-control and self-modification of emotional behavior.* New York: Plenum.

Spock, B. (1945). *Baby and child care.* New York: Pocket Books.

Staats, A. W., & Staats, C. K. (1963). *Complex human behavior: A systematic extension of learning principles.* New York: Holt, Rinehart & Winston.

Staff. (1985, August). Report on advocacy effects. *APA Monitor, 15,* 57.

Stanovich, K. E. (1986). *How to think straight about psychology.* Glenview, IL: Scott, Foresman.

Steadman, H. J., & Cocozza, J. J. (1974). *Careers of the criminally insane: Excessive control of deviance.* Lexington, MA: Heath.

Stein, T. J., & Gambrill, E. D. (1985). Permanency planning for children: The past and present. *Children and Youth Services Review, 7,* 83–94.

Sternberg, R. J. (1987). Teaching intelligence: The application of cognitive psychology to the improvement of intellectual skills. In J. B. Baron & R. J. Sternberg (Eds.), *Teaching thinking skills: Theory and practice.* New York: W. H. Freeman.

Sternberg, R. J., & Kagan, J. (1986). *Intelligence applied: Understanding and increasing your intellectual skills.* San Diego, CA: Harcourt Brace Jovanovich.

Sternberg, R. J., & Wagner, R. K. (Eds.). (1986). *Practical intelligence: Nature and origins of competence in the everyday world.* Cambridge, England: Cambridge University Press.

Stevens, P., Jr. (1988). The appeal of the occult: Some thoughts on history, religion, and science. *The Skeptical Inquirer, 12,* 376–385.

Stevenson, J. F., & Norcross, J. C. (1987). Current status of training evaluation in clinical psychology. In B. A. Edelstein & E. S. Berler (Eds.), *Evaluation and accountability in clinical training.* New York: Plenum.

Stokes, T. F., & Baer, D. M. (1977). An implicit technology of generalization. *Journal of Applied Behavior Analysis, 10,* 349–367.

Storms, M. (1973). Video-tape and attribution process: Reversing actors' and observers' points of view. *Journal of Personality and Social Psychology, 27,* 165–174.

Strauss, S., & Stavy, R. (1982). U-shaped behavioral growth: Implications for theories of development. In W. W. Hartup (Ed.), *Review of child development research* (Vol. 6). Chicago: University of Chicago Press.

Strong, P. M. (1979). *The ceremonial order of the clinic.* London: Routledge & Kegan Paul.

Strupp, H. H. (1958). The therapists' contribution to the treatment process. *Behavior Science, 3,* 34-67.

Strupp, H. H., & Hadley, S. W. (1985). Negative effects and their determinants. In D. T. Mays & C. M. Franks (Eds.), *Negative outcome in psychotherapy and what to do about it.* New York: Springer.

Stuart, R. B. (1970). *Trick or treatment: How and when psychotherapy fails.* Champaign, IL: Research Press.

Sue, D., & Sue, S. (1987). Cultural factors in the clinical assessment of Asian Americans. *Journal of Consulting and Clinical Psychology, 55,* 479-487.

Swann, W. B., Jr., & Guiliano, T. (1987). Confirmatory search strategies in social interaction: How, when, why, and with what consequences. *Journal of Social and Clinical Psychology, 5,* 511-524.

Szasz, T. S. (1961). *The myth of mental illness: Foundations of a theory of personal conduct.* New York: Harper & Row.

Szasz, T. S. (1970). *The manufacture of madness: A comparative study of the inquisition and the mental health movement.* New York: Harper & Row.

Tallent, N. (1983). *Psychological report writing* (2nd ed.). Englewood Cliffs, NJ: Prentice-Hall.

Tallent, N. (1988). *Psychological report writing* (3rd ed.). Englewood Cliffs, NJ: Prentice-Hall.

Taylor, S. E., & Fiske, S. T. (1975). Point of view and perceptions of causality. *Journal of Personality and Social Psychology, 32,* 439-445.

Taylor, S., Fiske, S., Close, M., Anderson, C., & Ruderman, A. (1979). *Solo status as a psychological variable: The power of being distinctive.* Unpublished manuscript, Harvard University. (Discussed in Gahagan (1984), p. 87.)

Teasdale, J. D., & Fogarty, S. J. (1979). Differential effects of induced mood on retrieval of pleasant and unpleasant events from episodic memory. *Journal of Abnormal Psychology, 88,* 248-257.

Teger, A. I., Cary, M., Katcher, A., and Hillis, J. (1980). *Too much invested to quit.* New York: Pergamon Press.

Temerlin, M. K. (1968). Suggestion effects in psychiatric diagnosis. *Journal of Nervous and Mental Disease, 147,* 349–357.

Terry, D. R. (1973). Structure of argument in debate. In D. R. Terry (Ed.), *Modern debate case techniques.* Skokie, IL: National Textbook.

Thompson, J. B. (1987). Language and ideology. *Sociological Review, 35,* 517–536.

Thompson, T. (1988). Retrospective review: Benedictus behavior analysis: B. F. Skinner's magnum opus at fifty. *Contemporary Psychology, 33,* 397–402.

Thorngate, W. (1986). The production, detection, and explanation of behavioral patterns. In J. Valsiner (Ed.), *The individual subject and scientific psychology.* New York: Plenum.

Thorngate, W., & Plouffe, L. (1987). The consumption of psychological knowledge. In H. J. Stam, T. B. Rogers, & K. G. Gergen (Eds.), *The analysis of psychological knowledge.* New York: Hemisphere.

Thouless, R. H. (1974). *Straight and crooked thinking: Thirty-eight dishonest tricks of debate.* London: Pan Books.

Tobacyk, J., & Milford, G. (1982). Criterion validity for Ellis' irrational beliefs: Dogmatism and uncritical inferences. *Journal of Clinical Psychology, 38,* 605–607.

Todd, J. T., & Morris, E. K. (1983). Misconception and miseducation: Presentations of radical behaviorism in psychology textbooks. *The Behavior Analyst, 6,* 153–160.

Toulmin, S. E., Rieke, R., & Janik, A. (1979). *An introduction to reasoning.* New York: Macmillan.

Trotter, R. J. (1986). The mystery of mastery. *Psychology Today, 7,* 32–38.

Trotter, W. F. (1916). *Instincts of the herd in peace and war.* London: Fisher Unwin.

Truax, C. (1966). Reinforcement and nonreinforcement in Rogerian psychotherapy. *Journal of Abnormal Psychology, 71,* 1–9.

Tuchman, B. W. (1984). *The march of folly: From Troy to Vietnam.* New York: Knopf.

Tuchman, B. (1989). In *Bill Moyers', A world of ideas: Conversations with thoughtful men and women about American life today and the ideas shaping our future.* New York: Doubleday.

Tufte, E. P. (1983). *The visual display of quantitative information.* Cheshire, CT: Graphics Press.

Turk, D. C., & Salovey, P. (1986). Clinical information processing: Bias inoculation. In R. Ingram (Ed.), *Information processing approaches to psychopathology and clinical psychology.* Orlando, FL: Academic Press.

Tversky, A., & Kahneman, D. (1971). Belief in the law of small numbers. *Psychological Bulletin, 76,* 105–110.

Tversky, A., & Kahneman, D. (1973). Availability: A heuristic for judging frequency and probability. *Cognitive Psychology, 5,* 207–232.

Tversky, A., & Kahneman, D. (1974). Judgement under uncertainty: Heuristics and biases. *Science, 185,* 1124–1131.

Tversky, A., & Kahneman, D. (1981). The framing of decisions and the psychology of choice. *Science, 211,* 453–458.

Tversky, A., & Kahneman, D. (1983). Extensionable versus intuitive reasoning: The conjunction fallacy in probability judgement. *Psychological Review, 90,* 293–375.

Valins, S., & Nisbett, R. E. (1972). Attributional processes in the development and treatment of emotional disorders. In E. E. Jones, D. E. Kanouse, H. H. Kelley, R. E. Nisbett, S. Vallins, & B. Weiner (Eds.), *Attribution: Perceiving the causes of behavior.* Morristown, NJ: General Learning Press.

Verhave, T., & Van Hoorn, W. (1984). The temperalization of the self. In K. J. Gergen & M. M. Gergen (Eds.), *Historical social psychology.* Hillsdale, NJ: Erlbaum.

Vygotsky, L. S. (1962). Thought and language. Cambridge, MA: MIT Press.

Wade, T. C., & Baker, T. B. (1977). Opinions and use of psychological tests: A survey of clinical psychologists. *American Psychologist, 32,* 874–882.

Wahler, R. G. (1980). The insular mother: Her problems in parent child treatment. *Journal of Applied Behavior Analysis, 13,* 207–219.

Wainer, H. (1976). Estimating coefficients in linear models: It don't make no nevermind. *Psychological Bulletin, 83,* 213–217.

Wakefield, J. (1987). Sex bias in the diagnosis of primary orgasmic dysfunction. *American Psychologist, 42,* 464–471.

Wallsten, T. S. (1983). The theoretical status of judgemental heuristics. In R. W. Scholz (Ed.), *Decision making under uncertainty.* New York: Elsevier.

Walter, H. I., & Gilmore, S. K. (1973). Placebo versus social learning effects in parent training procedures designed to alter the behavior of aggressive boys. *Behavior Therapy, 4,* 361–377.

Watson, D. L., & Tharp, R. G. (1985). *Self-directed behavior: Self-modification for personal adjustment* (4th ed.). Monterey, CA: Brooks/Cole.

Webster's new world dictionary (3rd college ed.). (1988). New York: Simon & Schuster.

Weiner, B. (1985). "Spontaneous" causal thinking. *Psychological Bulletin, 97,* 74–84.

Weinstein, C. E., & Rogers, B. T. (1985). Comprehension monitoring as a learning strategy. In G. d'Ydewalle (Ed.), *Cognition, information processing, and motivation.* New York: Elsevier.

Weinstein, N. D. (1980). Unrealistic optimism about future life events. *Journal of Personality and Social Psychology, 39,* 806–820.

Weisberg, R. (1986). *Creativity, genius and other myths.* New York: W. H. Freeman.

Weiss, J., & Brown, P. (1977). *Self-insight error in the explanation of mood.* Unpublished manuscript, Harvard University.

Wells, G. L., & Lindsay, R.C.L. (1983). How do people infer the accuracy of eyewitness memory? Studies of performance and a metamemory analysis. In S.M.A. Lloyd-Bostock & B. R. Clifford (Eds.), *Evaluating witness evidence: Recent psychological research and new perspectives.* New York: Wiley.

Wells, G. L., Lindsay, R.C.L., & Ferguson, T. J. (1979). Accuracy, confidence, and juror perceptions in eyewitness identification. *Journal of Applied Psychology, 64,* 440–448.

Wells, G. L., & Loftus, E. F. (1984). *Eyewitness testimony.* Cambridge, England: Cambridge University Press.

Westermeyer, J. (1987). Cultural factors in clinical assessment. *Journal of Consulting and Clinical Psychology, 55,* 471–478.

Whitehead, A. (1929). *The aims of education and other essays*. New York: Dutton.

Whitman, R. M., Kramer, M., & Baldridge, B. (1963). Which dreams does the patient tell? *Archives of General Psychiatry, 8*, 277–282.

Whitree v. New York State, 290 N.Y. 5. 2d 486 (Ct. Claims 1968).

Wiggins, J. (1984). Clinical and statistical prediction: Where are we and where do we go from here? *Clinical Psychology Review, 1*, 3–18.

Wilkins, L. T., Gottfredson, D. M., Robison, J. O., & Sadowsky, A. (1973). *Information selection and use in parole decision-making* (Supp. Rep. 5). Davis, CA: National Council on Crime and Delinquency Research Center.

Wilkins, W. (1986). Rhetoric and irrelevant criteria that disguise behavior therapy efficacy: Historical and contemporary notes. *Journal of Behavior Therapy and Experimental Psychiatry, 17*, 83–89.

Wills, T. A. (1978). Perceptions of clients by professional helpers. *Psychological Bulletin, 85*, 968–1000.

Wills, T. A. (1982). Nonspecific factors in helping relationships. In T. A. Willis (Ed.), *Basic processes in helping relationships*. Orlando, FL: Academic Press.

Wills, T. A., Weiss, R. L., & Patterson, G. R. (1974). A behavioral analysis of the determinants of marital satisfaction. *Journal of Clinical and Consulting Psychology, 42*, 802–811.

Wolf, F. M., Gruppen, L. D., & Bills, J. E. (1985). Differential diagnosis and the competing hypothesis heuristic: A practical approach to judgement under uncertainty and Bayesian probability. *Journal of the American Medical Association, 253*, 2858–2862.

Wolpe, J. (1986). Individualization: The categorical imperative of behavior therapy practice. *Journal of Behavior Therapy and Experimental Psychiatry, 17*, 145–154.

Wright, G. (1985). Decisional variance. In G. Wright (Ed.), *Behavioral decision making*. New York: Plenum.

Yinger, R. J. (1980). Can we really teach them to think? In R. E. Young (Ed.), *New Directions for teaching and learning: No. 3. Fostering critical thinking*. San Francisco: Jossey-Bass.

Zatz, M. J. (1984). Race, ethnicity, and determinate sentencing: A new dimension to an old controversy. *Criminology, 22,* 147–175.

Zegiob, L., Arnold, S., & Forehand, R. (1975). An examination of observer effects in parent-child interaction. *Child Development, 46,* 509–512.

Zilbergeld, B. (1983). *The shrinking of America: Myths of psychological change.* Boston: Little, Brown.

Ziskin, J. (1981). *Coping with psychiatric and psychological testimony* (3rd ed., two vols.). Venice, CA: Law and Psychology Press.

Name Index

A

Abelson, R., 348
Abelson, R. P., 250
Abercrombie, M.L.J., 163, 174, 192, 196
Abramovitz, C. V., 49
Abramowitz, S. I., 47, 49, 341
Adams, H. E., 204, 211
Adams, J. L., 326
Adams, K. S., 276
Adler, A., 238
Adler, J. E., 22
Ainslie, G., 17
Albert, S., 210
Allen, R., 13
Amabile, T., 225, 241
Anderson, C., 46
Anderson, J. R., 13
Anthony, E. J., 185
Aristotle, 108
Arkes, H., 278, 290
Armstrong, J. C., 59, 120
Arnold, S., 211–212
Arocha, J. F., 53
Asarnow, J., 76
Ashton, P. T., 347–348
Averill, J., 332
Azrin, N. H., 194

B

Badinter, E., 31
Baer, D. M., 351
Bagdikian, B. H., 356
Bagnell, J., 18
Bailey, J., 334n
Baker, T. B., 47, 210, 276
Baldridge, B., 49
Bandura, A., 36, 72, 182, 345, 346, 348
Banta, H. D., 60
Barclay, C. R., 206
Bar-Hillel, M., 231
Barlow, D. H., 55, 61, 81, 204, 211, 352
Barocas, R., 9
Baron, J., 11, 12, 17, 21, 327, 352, 357
Baron, R. S., 207
Barsh, E. T., 283
Barth, R. P., 63, 361
Barton, R., 336
Basaglia, F., 32, 33–34, 56, 60, 83, 85, 165, 166, 168, 362
Batson, C. D., 249, 250, 251, 252
Beck, A. T., 19, 88, 140, 219, 276
Beck, P., 276
Beit-Hallahmi, B., 31, 274
Belenky, M. F., 114

413

Bell-Dolan, D. J., 191
Belmont, J. M., 351
Bentham, J., 141
Bereiter, C., 75
Berger, A., 47
Berger, M., 36
Berger, P. L., 33
Bergin, A. E., 88, 332, 362
Bernassi, V. A., 58
Berscheid, E., 244
Besalel, V. A., 194
Best, J., 28, 281
Bills, J. E., 256
Black, J. B., 209
Blackard, M. K., 283
Blackmore, S., 152, 236
Blalock, H. M., Jr., 247
Blau, D. S., 331, 332, 336, 337
Blau, P. M., 39
Blau, T. H., 3, 4, 197, 325, 327, 328
Blenkner, M., 128
Bloom, B. S., 327
Bloom, M., 128, 352
Blum, J., 226
Bond, M. H., 35
Bonney, W. C., 105
Bordage, G., 279, 281n
Boren, J. H., 121
Borgida, E., 193, 243
Borkowski, J. G., 81
Bovet, M., 108
Bower, G. H., 43, 80
Bowers, K. S., 47, 253
Boyd, J. L., 19, 61
Bransford, J. D., 76, 77, 79, 81, 155,
    256, 258n, 290, 345, 346
Brehmer, B., 61
Brekstad, A., 206
Briar, S., 190
Brim, O. G., 44
Broad, W., 178, 180
Broder, L. J., 327
Bromley, D. B., 9, 101n, 107, 108,
    126, 260, 289n, 357
Brown, A. L., 63, 80, 256
Brown, P., 205
Bryant, G. D., 125
Bryant, J., 43
Buie, J., 35, 123, 158

Bunge, M., 56, 57n
Burge, D. A., 191
Burgess, P. H., 336
Burnham, J. C., 26, 68, 132
Burns, D., 332
Burt, C., 180
Burton, W. H., 326
Butterfield, E. C., 351
Byyny, R. L., 276

C

Cacioppo, J. T., 132
Calhoun, K. S., 204, 211
Campbell, D. T., 219
Campione, J. C., 12, 63, 80, 209, 256
Cantor, J. R., 43
Cantor, N., 165, 257n
Caramazza, A., 348
Carroll, J. A., 204
Carroll, L., 122
Cary, M., 363
Castro, F., 241
Chanowitz, B., 18, 98, 329
Chaplin, W., 336
Chapman, A. J., 317
Chapman, J. P., 7, 55, 227
Chapman, L. J., 7, 55, 227
Chase, W. G., 11, 16, 81, 224
Chasin, R., 163
Chelton, L. G., 105
Cherniss, C., 48
Chi, M.T.H., 14, 15, 53
Chipman, S. F., 13
Chiriboga, D. A., 334n
Churchill family, 266–268
Cialdini, R. B., 133–138, 175, 178
Ciminero, A. R., 204, 211
Cirino, R., 130, 132
Clair, M. S., 291, 329
Clark, M., 43, 276
Clifford, B. R., 203
Clinchy, B. M., 114
Close, M., 46
Cochran, P. J., 252
Cocozza, J. J., 273
Cohen, L. J., 279
Cohen, P. R., 43
Cohler, B. J., 185

Collins, A., 63
Collins, J. L., 345
Colman, A. M., 56
Conner, J. M., 114
Conway, M., 126
Cook, S. A., 338
Coombs, C., 192
Copi, I. M., 103
Corbin, R. M., 191, 266, 338
Corcoran, K., 209
Cordes, C., 338
Corrigan, B., 272
Crandall, R., 243

D

Dallas, M. E., 207
Dangel, R. F., 61
Darley, J. M., 173
Davidson, C. V., 49
Davis, D. E., 329
Davis, L. E., 49
Davis, M., 323
Davis, W. L., 329
Dawes, R. M., 232-233, 269, 272, 290
Dean, G., 283, 329
DeAngelis, T., 344
Decker, F. H., 37, 42, 198-201, 305, 318
DeDombal, F. T., 290
Deffenbacher, J. L., 332
DeRivera, J., 212
Deutsch, C. J., 338
DeVries, 344
Dewald, P. A., 64
Dewey, J., 75
Dillen, R., 202
Dillinger, D., 171
Dillon, R. F., 62
Dingwall, R., 24, 34, 35, 37, 38, 42, 186-188, 296, 307, 310, 315
D'Iulio, J. J., Jr., 32
Dokecki, P. R., 49
Doley, D., 1
Dozier, D. M., 82
Dreyfus, H. L., 16, 253
Dreyfus, S. E., 16, 253
Duncan, B., 172
Durlak, J. A., 54

E

Eddy, D. M., 276, 277, 278, 288
Edelmann, R. J., 346
Edmondson, R., 117
Edwards, W., 260
Eekelaar, J., 24, 296, 307, 315
Ehrenreich, B., 32
Ehrenreich, J., 32
Einhorn, H. J., 61, 84-85, 225, 233, 234-235, 236-237, 242, 245, 246, 265, 269, 276, 288, 291
Ellis, A., 56, 88, 140, 337
Ellis, M., 125
Ellul, J., 95
Elstein, A. S., 12, 13, 53, 54, 224, 243, 245-246, 265, 271, 275, 276, 279, 281n
Emerson, R. M., 37, 307, 315
Emery, G., 219
Emmelkamp, P. M., 3, 292
Engel, S. M., 141, 149, 150, 152, 153, 154, 157, 170
Ennis, B. J., 168
Ennis, R. H., 218, 327
Entwistle, N., 74
Erdman, H. P., 204
Ericsson, K. A., 81
Estess, F., 183
Euler, L., 173
Evans, I. M., 171, 206
Eyberg, S. M., 209
Eysenck, H. J., 283

F

Falbo, T., 316
Falk, R., 242
Falloon, I.R.H., 19, 61
Faust, D., 210, 269, 272, 290
Fearnside, W. W., 126
Fehrenbach, P. A., 48
Feinstein, A. R., 25, 124, 208
Feld, S., 320
Feltovich, P. J., 15, 16
Ferguson, T. J., 218
Ferretti, R. P., 351
Filley, A. C., 334
Fingarette, H., 91

Firestone, R. W., 121
Fischer, J., 72, 209, 352
Fischhoff, B., 192, 207, 208n, 247, 255, 270, 273, 274, 284, 288, 294, 328
Fisher, R., 320, 334
Fiske, S. T., 46, 243
Fleming, D. C., 334
Fleming, E. R., 334
Foa, E. G., 3, 292
Fogarty, S. J., 43
Fong, G. T., 357
Foote, H. C., 317
Forehand, R. L., 204, 211, 212
Foster, S. L., 191, 204, 212
Foucault, M., 356
Fox, H. M., 210
Frank, J., 49
Franklin, B., 210, 317
Franks, C. M., 3
Franks, V., 174
French, R., 246
Freud, S., 66, 69, 70, 119, 120, 155, 177, 238, 239
Friedson, E., 130
Fromm, E., 23

G

Gaeth, G. J., 357
Gagne, R. M., 62, 73
Gahagan, J., 240
Galante, M., 9
Gambrill, E., 63, 266, 293, 317, 327, 335n, 361
Gandhi, M., 336
Gardner, M., 56, 60, 178, 236
Garfield, S. L., 88, 332, 362
Garrison, B., 276
Geis, F., 317
Genovese, K., 330
Gergen, K. J., 32
Gibbs, J. T., 163
Gibbs, 344
Gillen, B., 243
Gilligan, C., 32
Gilmore, S. K., 204
Glaser, R., 13, 14, 15, 53
Goethals, G. R., 353

Goffman, I., 7
Goitein, B., 270, 273
Goldberg, L. R., 14
Goldberg, R. L., 271
Goldberger, N. R., 114
Goldman, R. K., 48
Goldstein, J. H., 317
Goodman, G., 1
Gooler, D. D., 82
Gordon, B., 28
Gordon, J. R., 61, 181
Gottfredson, D. M., 273
Gowin, D. B., 258
Graumann, 32
Green, B. F., 348
Greenberg, J., 10, 43
Greenberg, L. S., 88
Greene, D., 244
Greenfield, L., 78
Greeno, J. G., 12, 73, 89, 94, 114, 253, 255, 256
Greenwald, A. G., 204
Greist, J. H., 204
Grieger, R., 88, 140
Groen, J. G., 15, 53, 224–225
Gross, P. H., 173
Grunebaum, H., 163
Gruppen, L. D., 256
Guiliano, T., 10
Guilmette, T. J., 210
Gutierres, S. E., 138

H

Hadley, S. W., 3, 50, 334, 336
Hafner, J., 13
Hagert, G., 77
Hall, D. F., 202, 255
Hall, K., 317
Hamblin, C. L., 108, 140, 159
Hand, D. J., 256
Harmon, G., 342
Harris, V. A., 241
Hart, K., 210
Harvey, J. H., 44, 261, 292
Hawkins, R. P., 293
Hayakawa, S. I., 118, 124, 125, 341
Hayes, J. R., 256
Hayes, S. C., 204, 293, 352

Hayes-Roth, F., 78
Hazaleus, S. L., 332
Hazen, M. D., 316
Hellman, I. D., 341
Herron, W. G., 50, 332, 337
Hershaft, A. M., 59, 180
Higbee, K. L., 81
Higgins, R. L., 329, 330
Hillis, J., 363
Hinton, J. W., 273
Hitler, A., 92, 170
Hobbs, C. J., 91
Hobbs, N., 7, 79, 168
Hockey, R., 42
Hodges, B., 182
Hodgson, R., 61
Hoff, D. B., 44
Hogarth, R. M., 17, 45, 192, 225, 233,
    234–235, 265, 269, 283, 285, 286,
    287, 288, 290, 294, 339
Holland, J. H., 105
Hollingshed, A. B., 49
Hollon, S. D., 218
Holmes, D. S., 330
Holmes, S., 248
Holther, W. G., 126
Holyoak, K. J., 105
Horowitz, L. M., 246
Horrocks, J. C., 290
House, P., 244
Houts, A. C., 9, 47
Howlin, P., 61
Huang, L. N., 163
Hubbard, J., 84
Huber, R. B., 106
Huck, S. W., 92
Huff, D., 40, 216
Humphrey, R. A., 248
Hunsaker, D. M., 197
Huston, K., 177
Hyman, R., 80

I

Illich, I., 33
Inhelder, B., 108
Isen, A. M., 43, 44, 346
Ivancevich, J. M., 332

J

Jacobs, J., 37–38
Jacobson, R. B., 248
James, W., 109
Jampata, V. C., 167
Janik, A., 98
Janis, I. L., 18, 44
Janson, D., 143
Jenkins, G., 334n
Jennings, D. L., 225, 228
Jensen, D. D., 59, 230
Jepson, C., 21, 257
Johnson, D. M., 61
Johnson, E. J., 14
Johnson, M., 181, 240
Johnson, P. E., 15, 16
Johnson, S., 42
Johnson, W., 116
Johnson-Laird, P. N., 13, 66, 93
Jones, C. H., 252
Jones, D., 202
Jones, E. E., 241, 242
Jordan, J. S., 44, 261, 292
Jowett, G. S., 129
Jung, C. G., 144
Jungerman, H., 45
Jurkovic, G. J., 36

K

Kadushin, A., 298
Kadushin, C., 50
Kagan, J., 11
Kagle, J. D., 220
Kahane, H., 141, 142, 153, 170, 175,
    176
Kahn, M. W., 210
Kahneman, D., 9, 44–45, 66, 195,
    243, 282, 285, 286, 287
Kanfer, F. H., 340
Kant, I., 42
Kaplan, M., 174
Karlin, M. B., 80
Karoly, P., 340
Karp, L., 43
Kassirer, J. P., 224
Katcher, A., 363
Kazak, A. E., 185, 248, 283

Keisner, R. H., 244
Keller, E. F., 114
Kelley, G. A., 356
Kelley, H. H., 192
Kelly, 107
Kendall, P. C., 218
Kendell, R. E., 190, 224
Kenrick, D. T., 138
Kent, R. N., 212
Kessler, J. W., 3
Kiesler, D. J., 18
Kimball, R. B., 326
Kirk, S., 72, 167, 219
Klahr, P., 78
Kleinmuntz, B., 270
Klemp, G. O., 11
Knishinsky, A., 137
Koberg, D., 18
Kohn, A., 56, 180
Kohut, H., 69
Kopta, S. M., 44, 50
Korzybski, A., 171
Kottler, J. A., 331, 332, 336, 337
Kovacs, M., 276
Kramer, M., 49
Krantz, D. H., 21, 257
Krantz, S. E., 236, 246
Kravitz, D. H., 357
Kriss, M., 247
Kruskal, W., 215
Kuipers, B., 224
Kunda, Z., 21, 257
Kunreuther, H., 282
Kutchins, 167, 219

L

Lakoff, G., 181, 240
Landers, S., 165
Lang, P. J., 292
Langer, E. J., 18, 98, 242, 250, 329,
    351, 362
Lapid, J. S., 246
Layman, M., 192
Lazarus, R. S., 336
Leahey, G. E., 236
Leahey, T. H., 236
Leaper, D. J., 290
Leary, M. R., 335

Lehnert, W. G., 209
Leiby, J., 30
Lemert, E. M., 165
Lenrow, P., 22
Lepper, M. R., 10, 84, 246, 260
Lesgold, A., 15, 61
Levinson, P., 332
Levy, R. L., 341
Lewinsohn, P. M., 336
Lichtenstein, S., 192, 207, 208n, 247,
    274, 281, 284, 288, 294
Light, D., 60
Lincoln, A., 193
Lindsay, R.C.L., 203, 218
Linimon, D., 316
Linn, M. C., 341, 350
Linton, M., 204, 206
Lipton, J. P., 59, 180
Litwak, T. R., 168
Lloyd-Bostock, S.M.A., 203
Lock, M., 35
Loftus, E. F., 80, 126, 202, 203, 209,
    254, 255
Lord, C., 10, 78, 246
Lovell, A. M., 32, 33, 34, 49, 56, 60,
    83, 85, 165, 166, 168, 184, 362
Luckman, T., 33

M

McClelland, D. C., 11
McCloskey, M., 341, 348
McGee, P. E., 317
McGill, C. W., 19, 61
McGovern, M. P., 44, 50
Machado, L. A., 13
Mackie, J. L., 235
MacLean, E., 95, 129, 142, 178, 179,
    320
McLellan, D., 112
McMahon, R. J., 204, 212
McMurray, L., 332
McNeil, B. J., 274
McReynolds, P., 167, 168, 169, 231
Maguire, G. P., 207
Maher, C. A., 338
Mahoney, M. J., 246
Mann, L., 18, 44
Manning, M. P., 33

Manstead, A.S.R., 330
Marinucci, C. C., 29
Markus, H., 341
Marlatt, G. A., 61, 181
Martin, G., 246, 253
Marvin, R. S., 185, 248, 283
Marx, K., 238, 239
Maslach, C., 23, 48
Masson, J. S., 144, 162
Matteson, M. T., 332
Mavissakalian, M., 61
Mays, D. T., 3
Medawar, P. B., 56, 58, 59, 62
Medin, D. L., 15
Meehl, P. E., 7, 50, 163, 182, 185, 269, 272, 290, 296–304, 324, 364
Meichenbaum, D., 5, 76, 83, 340
Mendeleef, D. I., 162
Mendelsohn, G. A., 48
Mennerick, L. L., 162
Meyer, L. H., 171
Michalos, A. C., 40, 141, 146, 148, 149, 151, 157, 159, 160, 169, 176, 177, 178, 181, 302
Milford, G., 341
Milgram, S., 243
Miller, A. G., 243
Miller, H., 190
Miller, J. D., 20, 58
Miller, J. G., 31
Miller, L. S., 276
Mills, C. W., 27, 29
Minuchin, S., 20
Mischel, W., 167, 204, 210, 226, 336
Moller, J. H., 15, 16
Montenegro, M., 170
Moore, K. D., 104n
Moos, R. H., 236, 246
Morawski, J. G., 31
Morgan, R. F., 3, 163
Morgan, T., 266
Morris, E. K., 180, 344
Morrison, T. L., 341
Mosteller, F., 215
Mostow, D. J., 78
Murray, D., 79
Murray, J., 49
Murray, T., 24, 296, 307, 315

N

Nadelmann, E. A., 168
Nay, W. R., 211
Nelson, R. O., 204, 206, 352
Nettler, G., 109, 111n, 112, 113
Neuringer, A., 356
Newman, F. L., 44, 50
Nias, D.K.B., 283
Nickerson, R. S., 12, 13, 14, 54, 77, 88, 89, 93, 94, 95, 97, 99, 100, 102, 103n, 105, 106, 146, 255, 325, 340, 341, 358, 359, 365
Nielson, M., 128
Niemi, J. A., 82
Nisbett, R. E., 21, 45, 46, 47, 105, 128, 192, 193, 194, 206, 228, 229, 234, 236, 237, 238, 241, 242, 243, 247, 248, 257, 286, 287, 357
Norcross, J. C., 62
Norman, G. R., 125
Novaco, R. W., 332
Novak, J. D., 258
Nye, M. J., 179

O

O'Donnell, V., 129
Oksman, P. F., 334
O'Leary, M. R., 48
O'Quin, K., 249, 252
Orwell, G., 121, 122, 129
Osborn, A. F., 259
Oskamp, S., 191, 286
Osmalov, M., 72
O'Sullivan, J. T., 81

P

Palincsar, A. S., 63
Palmer, J., 209
Parloff, M. B., 49
Patel, V. L., 15, 53, 224–225
Patterson, G. R., 182
Pauker, S. G., 274
Paul, R. W., 359, 361
Pear, J., 246, 253
Pearson, K., 226
Pepper, S., 215

Perkins, D. N., 12, 13, 21, 61, 65, 224, 255, 343, 357
Petty, R. E., 132
Pfohl, S. J., 37, 305, 306
Pfungst, O., 235
Philip, R. A., 194
Pilpel, R. H., 266
Pines, A., 23, 48
Plouffe, L., 68, 69, 70, 71, 72
Plous, J., 239
Podell, P., 332
Polanyi, M., 253
Pollio, H. R., 253
Polster, R. A., 61
Popper, K. R., 59, 60, 96, 105, 111, 238–239
Porter, N., 317
Premack, D., 339
Pressley, M., 81
Proctor, E. K., 49
Prosser, M., 74
Pruger, R., 276
Pryor, J. B., 247
Pych, V., 249, 252
Pyszczynski, T., 10, 43

R

Rachman, S., 61
Radin, N., 320
Radlove, S., 243
Razran, 134
Reckman, R. F., 353
Redlich, R. C., 49
Reed, H., 243
Regan, D. T., 261, 323, 358
Renaud, H., 183
Rice, L. N., 88
Rice, R. E., 82
Richey, C., 317
Rieke, R., 98, 317
Roach, K. S., 334
Robbins, L. C., 206
Robertiello, R. C., 3
Robertson, S. P., 209
Robison, J. O., 273
Rogers, B. T., 74, 76
Rogers, C. R., 26, 134, 274
Rokeach, M., 23, 341

Rosen, G. M., 147
Rosenhan, D. L., 7, 163, 167
Rosenthal, A. M., 330
Rosenthal, R., 246
Ross, A. W., 209
Ross, J. C., 219
Ross, L., 10, 45, 46, 47, 84, 128, 192, 194, 206, 225, 228, 229, 236, 237, 238, 241, 243, 244, 246, 247, 248, 260, 286, 287
Rothblum, E. D., 174
Rouslin, S., 50, 332, 337
Rubenstein, M. F., 255
Ruderman, A., 46
Runyan, W. M., 264
Rush, A. J., 219
Rutter, D. R., 207
Rutter, M., 61
Ryan, W., 167, 363
Rycroft, C., 120

S

Sacco, W., 19
Sadowsky, A., 273
Salancik, G. R., 126
Salovey, P., 43, 259–260
Sampson, E. E., 32
Sandler, H. M., 92
Sandrock, D., 50
Sanford, A. J., 173n
Sarbin, T. R., 240
Sarokin, Judge, 143
Sarri, R. C., 274
Scardamalia, M., 75
Schank, R., 348
Scheff, T. F., 166
Scheff, T. J., 7, 30, 42, 165, 184
Schein, E., 171
Schenker, C., 243
Scheper-Hughes, N., 32, 33, 34, 49, 56, 60, 83, 85, 165, 166, 168, 184, 362
Schiller, J., 42
Schlenker, B. R., 335
Schmidt, A., 249
Schnelle, J. F., 204, 292
Schoenewolf, G., 3
Schoenfeld, A. H., 11

Schoomaker, E. G., 219
Schopenhauer, A., 157
Schultz, T., 236
Schur, E. M., 240
Scriven, M., 79, 88, 89, 105, 106, 107, 113, 172, 319
Sedgwick, P., 2, 7, 28, 35, 38, 85, 119, 168, 184
Segal, J. W., 13
Seiden, R. H., 121
Semin, G. R., 330
Semmelweiss, I. P., 178
Shalker, T. E., 43
Shanteau, J., 357
Shapira, Z., 270, 273
Shapiro, S. C., 15
Shaughnessy, J. M., 58
Shaw, B. F., 219
Shenkal, R. J., 249
Sherman, J. A., 174
Shweder, R. A., 31, 228
Sierles, F., 167
Sigel, I. E., 75, 108
Sillers, M., 317
Silverman, K., 210, 317
Simon, H. A., 11, 16, 20, 92, 224
Sinclair, H., 108
Singer, B., 58
Sisson, J. C., 219
Skinner, B. F., 69, 154, 342
Slovic, P., 192, 207, 208n, 247, 274, 282, 284, 288, 294
Smedslund, J., 231, 232n
Smith, C. R., 197
Smith, E. E., 12, 255
Snyder, C. R., 249, 291, 329, 330
Snyder, M., 9, 10, 49, 50, 207, 244
Snyder, R. E., 277, 278n
Sobell, L. C., 151
Sobell, M. B., 151
Sox, H. C., Jr., 274
Spock, B., 206
Staats, A. W., 126
Staats, C. K., 126
Stanley, J. C., 219
Stanovich, K. E., 223, 235
Stavy, R., 61
Steadman, H. J., 273
Steer, R. A., 276

Stein, B. S., 76, 77, 79, 81, 155, 256, 258n, 290, 345, 346
Stein, T. J., 266, 335n
Steinmetz, J., 241
Sternberg, R. J., 11, 12, 62, 326
Stevens, P., Jr., 20, 58
Stevenson, J. F., 62
Stokes, T. F., 351
Storms, M., 249
Strauss, S., 61
Strean, H., 336–337
Strong, P. M., 39
Strupp, H. H., 3, 9, 50, 334, 336
Stuart, R. B., 126
Stucky, R. J., 329, 330
Sue, D., 163
Sue, S., 163
Swann, W. B., Jr., 10, 207
Swanson, D. B., 15, 16
Szasz, T. S., 2, 30, 184, 240

T

Tallent, N., 212–214, 222n
Tanke, E. D., 244
Tarule, J. M., 114
Taylor, M., 167
Taylor, S. E., 46, 243
Teasdale, J. D., 43
Teger, A. I., 363
Temerlin, M. K., 128
Terry, D. R., 91
Thagard, P. R., 105
Tharp, R. G., 340, 356
Thienes-Hontos, P., 194
Thompson, J. B., 41, 112
Thompson, T., 343
Thomsen, C. J., 9, 10, 49, 50, 244
Thorngate, W., 60, 68, 69, 70, 71, 72
Thouless, R. H., 24, 68, 118, 120, 122, 127, 128, 141, 146, 155–156, 322
Tobacyk, J., 341
Todd, J. T., 180, 344
Totten, J., 261, 323, 358
Toulmin, S. E., 98, 100, 101, 105, 153
Tousignant, J. P., 202, 255
Trotter, W. F., 174

Truax, C., 26, 49, 342
Tuchman, B. W., 44, 356
Tufte, E. P., 216, 217n
Turke, D. C., 5, 43, 83, 259–260, 340
Tversky, A., 9, 44–45, 66, 195, 243, 274, 282, 285, 286, 287

U

Ury, W., 320, 334

V

Valins, S., 234
Vance, F. L., 9
Van Hoorn, W., 31
Verhave, T., 31
Von Winterfeldt, D., 260

W

Waddell, M. T., 55, 61, 81
Wade, N., 178, 180
Wade, T. C., 47, 210, 276
Waern, Y., 77
Wagner, R. K., 12
Wahler, R. G., 224
Wainer, H., 272
Wakefield, J., 49
Wallsten, T. S., 45
Walter, H. I., 204
Waskow, I. E., 49
Watson, D. L., 340, 356
Watson, J. B., 154
Weary, G., 44, 47, 261, 292
Webb, R. B., 347–348
Weckler, D., 246
Weiner, B., 243

Weiner, H., 332
Weinstein, C. E., 74, 76
Weinstein, N. D., 274
Weisberg, R., 13, 94, 253, 327, 335
Weiss, J., 205
Weiss, R. L., 182
Wells, G., 203, 218
Westermeyer, J., 163
White, G. F., 282
Whitehead, A., 75
Whitman, R. M., 49
Wiggins, J., 270, 271n, 272
Wilkins, L. T., 273
Wilkins, W., 8
Wills, T. A., 39, 48, 49, 50, 54, 182, 342, 362
Wing, R. L., 326
Wolf, B. E., 49
Wolf, F. M., 256
Wolpe, J., 258
Wright, G., 327
Wurster, C. R., 204
Wynne, J. M., 91

Y

Yeager, R. J., 56
Yinger, R. J., 42, 191, 327

Z

Zatz, M. J., 274
Zegiob, L., 211–212
Zilbergeld, B., 3, 61, 292, 365
Zillmann, D., 43
Zimbardo, P. G., 239
Ziskin, J., 214

Subject Index

A

A priorism fallacy, 151
Abstraction levels: and data collection, 193; of language, 118, 130–131, 163
Accident fallacy, 153
Accuracy: of assumptions, 223–263; of causal assumptions, 255–262; of decisions, 53; decreases in, 9–11; of predictions, 288–290; retrospective and predictive, 279; of tests, 359
Action plans, for clinicians, 348–349
Actuarial judgment, for prediction, 268–273, 289–290
Ad hominem argument: and appeals to pseudoauthority, 177; fallacy of, 144–147
Affirming the consequence error, 102
Agencies: clients viewed by, 39; clinician decisions and variables in, 36–43; conformity in, 41–42; contingencies in, 41; critical thinking in, 354–355, 363; and data collection, 195; and information access, 38–39; and power and status differences, 37–38, 41; stratagems in, 39–41

Ambiguity, reactions to, 328
American Psychiatric Association, 184
American Psychological Association, 35
Analogy: and credibility, 70; data from, 211; fallacy of inappropriate, 155–156; forced, 156; multiple, 259; for reasons, 90–91. See also Metaphors
Anchoring effects, and prediction, 286
Anger, as diversion, 157–158, 159
Appeals, irrelevant, fallacies of, 144–149
Archival data, 215
Arguments: ad hominem, 144–147, 177; analyzing, 105–107; circular, fallacy of, 150–151; discussions distinct from, 323–324; false though valid, 141–144; kinds of, 107–109; and reasoning, 98–105; soundness of, 102
Artificial intelligence, and expert thinking, 15–16
Asia, and social factors, 35–36
Assertions: bold, fallacy of, 128; and reasoning, 99–100
Assessment: and accuracy of causal assumptions, 255–262; aspects of,

223-263; background on, 223-225; and causal analysis, 234-237; of covariations, 225-233; and dispositional bias, 248-253; error sources in, 237-248; by experts and novices, 224, 228, 251, 253; and intuition, 253-254; and memory, 254-255; prediction related to, 269; summary on, 262-263; tools for, 256-257. *See also* Judgments

Assumptions: assessing accurately, 223-263; made explicit, 257-258; and reasoning, 99

Attitudes, of clinicians, 326-327

Attributions: fundamental errors of, 240-242, 358; and practice theories, 250

Authority: and ad hominem arguments, 144; appeals to pseudo-, fallacies of, 175-182; and begging the question, 149; and credibility, 70-71; imaginary, 180; of the many, 178; misleading aura of, 176-177; and persuasion, 135-136

Automatic Thoughts Questionnaire, 218

Availability: and data collection, 192-193; and fundamental attribution error, 242

B

Bad seed fallacy, 146

Bandwagon fallacy, 179

Barnum effect, 298

Base-rate data, for prediction, 277, 280-282, 288-289

Bayes's Theorem, 276-280, 289

Beck Depression Inventory, 210, 219, 284

Beck Hopelessness Scale, 276

Begging the question fallacy, 148, 149-153

Beliefs: and causal analysis, 236; for clear thinking, 352-353; clinician revision of, 340-343; and covariations, 225; facts distinct from, 97; opinions distinct from, 97-98;

and pathological set, 184-185; perseverance of, 84-85; personal, 42; practice-related, 342-343; superstitious, 285

Bender-Gestalt test, 14

Bias: confirmation, 78, 228, 230, 245-246; dispositional, 248-253; and emotional words, 124; hidden, sources of, 130; hindsight, 294; inoculation procedure for, 260; and reasoning, 95; in sample, 194-195; strong opinions distinct from, 319-320; temporary, 195; and visual distortions, 216-217

Blaming the victim, and classification fallacies, 167-168

Boston, subculture of psychotherapy in, 32

Bureau of Prisons, 170-171

Burnout signs, 327-328

C

California at Berkeley, University of, School of Social Welfare at, 323

Case conferences: arguments and discussions in, 323-324; aspects of, 296-324; background on, 296-297; characteristics of, 297-302; cheap shots in, 302-303; denunciations and pitches in, 306-307; effective, 316-323; empathy in, 322-323; example of, 307-316; goals in, 304-305, 320; group norms for, 321-322; participant styles in, 320-321; preparing for, 318-319; quality of discussion in, 303-306; summary on, 324

Case records, data from, 212-214, 220

Causal analysis, and assessment, 234-237

Causal assumptions, accuracy of, 2, 255-262

Cause: fallacy of false, 154; for reasons, 91-92

Central Intelligence Agency (CIA), 171

Certainty, alleged, fallacy of, 149

Chance fluctuations, and prediction, 287

Charitable approach, in learning, 79-80

Cheap shots, in case conferences, 302-303

Checklists, data from, 209-210

China: and brainwashing, 171; and social factors, 36

Choices: models of, 275-276; prediction and probability related to, 273-276

Circular argument fallacy, 150-151

Circumstantial evidence, 201

Claims or conclusion, and reasoning, 100

Clarity, for case conferences, 319, 322

Class: of clients, 49; and reasoning, 114-115

Classification: fallacies related to, 162-175; of people, 166-169; of procedures, 170-172

Clever Hans, 235

Clients: agency view of, 39; assessment of problems of, 223-263; class, race, and gender of, 49; clinicians in interaction with, 26, 47-50; fragility of, 301-302; predictions about, 264-295; YAVIS, 48

Clinical reasoning. *See* Critical thinking; Reasoning

Clinicians: action plans for, 348-349; and agency setting, 36-43; ambiguity and uncertainty for, 328; aspects of influences on, 26-52; attitudes of, 326-327; background on, 26-29, 325-327; barriers to critical thinking by, 325-349; beliefs revised by, 340-343; career review for, 362-364; clients in interaction with, 26, 47-50; compatible values for, 343-344, 352-353; compromises for, 346-348; coping skills for, 333-334; depletion signs for, 327-328; and dispositional bias, 248-253; errors as learning opportunities for, 328-331; larger picture for, 27-29; personal beliefs of, 42; personal experiments by, 356; political action by, 353-355; political, economic, and social influences on, 29-36; practice skills of, 344; practice theory review for, 364; psychological influences on, 43-47; and realistic expectations, 337-338, 355-356; relationship skills for, 332-336; rules of thumb for, 260-262, 357-362; self-efficacy of, 344-346; self-management skills for, 65, 339-340; as skeptical, 23-24; skill maintenance by, 350-366; stress-management skills for, 331-332; summary on, 51-52, 349; time-management skills for, 338-339; training of, 62-65, 183, 350-351; transference and countertransference for, 336-337; troubleshooting by, 259, 335

Coincidences, and assessment error, 242

Commitment, and persuasion, 135

Compartmentalization, decreasing, 299

Compassion, and reason, 300-301, 360-361

Compliance induction, strategies for, 132-134

Composition fallacy, 131

Comprehensibility of knowledge, 68-69

Compromises, for clinicians, 346-348

Computers: as assessment tools, 256; for data collection, 204, 210; and information access, 81-82; as time savers, 357

Conclusions, premises and, 103

Conferences. *See* Case conferences

Confirmation bias: and assessments, 228, 230, 245-246; and learning, 78

Confusion, fallacies of, 158-160

Consensus: fallacy of, 150, 178; information, 243-244, 284

Consequence, error of confirming, 102

Consistency: and differential weight of sign, 299; fallacy of, 147; and fundamental attribution error, 240–242; and illusory correlations, 229; and persuasion, 134–135; and reasoning, 96

Content, structure distinct from, 246–247

Context, and fallacies, 124–125

Contingency analysis, in clinical training, 64

Contingency table, and assessment, 231, 261, 359–360

Continuing education, need for, 83–84, 347

Continuum fallacy, 174

Contradictions: in case conferences, 305, 306; in false dilemma, 170; as implications, 102

Contrast effect, and persuasion, 138

Coping skills, for clinicians, 333–334

Correlations, illusory, and covariations, 227–229

Countertransference, for clinicians, 336–337

Covariations, assessment of, 2, 225–233

Creativity, and reasoning, 93–94

Credibility: of knowledge, 69–71; and reasoning, 97

Critical thinking: accuracy decreased in, 9–11; aspects of refining, 1–25; and assessment of client problems, 223–263; background on, 1–8; barriers to, 8–9, 325–349; benefits of, 17–20, 351, 364–365; and case conferences, 296–324; compatible values for, 343–344, 352–353; and content and procedural knowledge, 53–87; costs of, 20–23; and data collection, 190–222; expert and novice approaches to, 14–17; and fallacies, 140–189; generalizing skills in, 350–362; influences on, 26–52; and language, 116–132;

maintaining skills in, 350–366; and persuasion strategies, 132–138, 139; practicing, 356; and predictions, 264–295; process focus for, 351; and reasoning, 88–115; rules of thumb in, 260–262, 357–362; as skill, 11–13; summary on, 24–25, 365–366; supportive environment for, 353–355; tools and training for, 357–362

Criticism, fallacy of ignoring, 153

Crummy criterion fallacy, 302

Cultural relativism, and optimism, 186–187

Cultures, rights- and duty-based, 31

D

Data: irrelevant, 285–286; redundant, 286

Data collection: aspects of, 190–222; background on, 190–191; and evidence types, 197–203; influences on, 192–196; and missing items, 219; recording information for, 220–222; sources for, 203–215; and statistics, 215; summary on, 220, 222; and value of data, 216–219; and visual distortions, 216–217. See also Information

Debriefing, failure of, 84–85

Decision making. See Critical thinking

Decision trees, for accuracy of prediction, 288–289

Decisions, accurate, defined, 53

Denunciations, in case conferences, 306–307

Description: errors in, 2; inference distinct from, 195–196

Diagnostic and Statistical Manual (DSM-II), 257

Diagnostic and Statistical Manual (DSM-III): and assessment, 230, 237, 246; and classification, 164, 165, 166, 167, 168, 169, 183

Diagnostic and Statistical Manual—Revised (DSM-III-R), 164, 168

Dilemma, false, and classification fallacies, 169–170
Discussions: arguments distinct from, 323–324; quality of, 303–306. *See also* Case conferences
Dispositional bias, assessment of, 248–253
Diversions, fallacies with, 157–158
Division fallacy, 131

E

Economics, and clinician decisions, 32–35
Elitism fallacy, 181
Eloquence fallacy, 131–132
Emotional language fallacy, 122–124, 131, 150, 158
Emotions: and clinician decisions, 43–44; in clinician relationships, 335–336; and personal relevance, 358–359; positive, cultivating, 259–260
Empathic explanations, and reasoning, 109–111, 113
Empathy: in case conferences, 322–323; use of, 357–358
Empiricism, and credibility, 70
Environment: attention to, 261; and clinician decisions, 42–43; for critical thinking, 353–355
Equivocation, and confusion, 159–160
Error: acceptance of, 272–273; in assessment stage, 5; examples of, 2; indicators of, 4–5; in intervention stage, 5–6; as learning opportunity, 328–331; psychotherapeutic, 325; results of, 3–4; sources of, 133, 237–248, 280–288; in strategies for decision making, 6–7
Essentialism, and reasoning, 111
Euphemisms, fallacy of, 145–146
Evidence: disconfirming, 357; doubtful, fallacy of, 141–142; kinds of, 197–203; and reasoning, 94–95; standards of, 301; suppressed, fallacy of, 142–144; weighed, for prediction, 283

Example, fallacy of attacking, 148–149
Exclusion: for reasons, 92; inclusion tests confused with, 298–299
Expectations, by clinicians, 337–338, 355–356
Experience, limits of, 61–62
Experts: fallacies of supposed, 177; as witnesses, for data collection, 197–201
Experts and novices: assessments by, 224, 228, 251, 253; critical thinking by, 14–17; knowledge approached by, 54–55, 75, 76, 79, 80–81
Explanation: alternative, 260; naming distinct from, 245; and reasoning, 109–114
Extension forcing fallacy, 154

F

Facts: beliefs distinct from, 97; distorting, fallacies of, 153–156; evading, fallacies of, 149–153; in evidence, 201; overlooking, fallacy of, 153; and verbal propositions, 127
Faith, fallacy of appeal to, 181–182
Fallacies: avoiding, 140–189; background on, 140–141; of classification, 162–175; concept of, 140; of confusion, 158–160; with diversions, 157–158; of facts, 149–156; and false though valid arguments, 141–144; informal, 102, 128, 135–136, 141, 144, 153, 157, 176; of irrelevant appeals, 144–149; in language, 118–132; of optimism, 186–188; of overlooking facts, 153; pathological set related to, 182–186; of pseudo-authority appeals, 175–182; results of, 140; summary on, 160–161, 188–189
False cause fallacy, 235
False consensus effect, 243–244
Falsehoods, recurring, 360–362
Falsifiability, and reasoning, 96–97
Feedback: on critical thinking skills,

351–352; and data collection, 195; for prediction, 290–294

Firsthand reports, and data collection, 202–203

Framing of problem, and assessment error, 247, 259, 330

Framing of questions, importance of, 206–208

Freedom, responsibility related to, 23

Fundamental attribution error, and assessment, 240–242, 358

G

Gambler's fallacy, 287

Gender: of clients, 49; and reasoning, 114–115

Generalization: hasty, fallacy of, 153; for reasons, 91; and sample size, 193–194; unfounded, fallacy of, 151–152

Group process, in case conferences, 320

Guarantees, vacuous, fallacy of, 147–149

Guilt by association, fallacy of, 145–146

H

Hearsay evidence, 197

Hello-goodbye effect, 292

Hindsight bias, 294

Historical factors, and clinician decisions, 30–32

Hypothesis, and reasoning, 99

I

Ideological explanations, and reasoning, 110, 112–113

Ideas, presentation of, 317–318

Ignorance, fallacy of, 147–148, 157

Inclusion tests, exclusion tests confused with, 298–299

India, and social factors, 31, 35

Inference, description distinct from, 195–196

Information: access to, and agency policy, 38–39; access to, and knowledge, 81–83; consensus, 243–244, 284; contradictory, 305, 306; negative, 261; processing, and clinician decisions, 44–45; recording, 220–222; situational, 250–251; vivid, and clinician decisions, 46–47. *See also* Data collection

Intellectual competence, and reasoning, 89–90

Interpersonal skills, for case conferences, 316–317

Interventions: and perceived risk, 275; predictions about, 264–295

Intuition: and assessment, 253–254; and clinician decisions, 45; and objectivity, 361; revising, 341

Inventories, personality, data from, 209–210

Inverse, confusion of the, 232

Irrelevant thesis fallacy, 154–155

Israel, and reinforcement, 285

Italy, change in, 83, 362

J

Japan, and social factors, 35

Jargon: fallacy of, 120–122; and pseudoauthority, 177

Job Finding Club, 194

Judgments: accuracy decreased in, 9–11; actuarial, 268–273, 289–290; barriers to making, 8–9; tasks in, 1–2. *See also* Assessment

K

Knowledge: and active or passive learning, 73–80; aspects of, 53–87; background on, 53–54; and belief perseverance, 84–85; and clear thinking, 359; and clinical training programs, 62–65; concept of, 53; criteria for, 68–72; and experience, 61–62; expert and novice approaches to, 54–55, 75, 76, 79, 80–81; importance of, 54–56, 71;

inert, 75; and information access, 81–83; interest in, 71–72; and memory, 80–81; neglecting, 72; practice, assessing, 66–67; and reading decisions, 67–72; and reasoning, 94; scientific, 56–61; summary on, 85–87; use of, 83–84; usefulness of, 60

Korea, Democratic Republic of, and brainwashing, 171

L

Labels: and classification fallacies, 163, 164–166, 167–169; fallacy of, 124; negative and positive versions of, 184; and pathological set, 183; and stereotyping, 172–174

Language: and abstraction levels, 118, 130–131, 163; care in, 358; fallacies in, 118–132; functions of, 117–118; influence by, 116–118; sources of error in using, 133; summary on, 138–139

Learning: active or passive, 73–80; comprehension monitoring for, 76–77; conditions of, 63; and confirmation bias, 78; elaboration strategies for, 77; from errors, 328–331; summary on, 86

Lexington, Kentucky, women's prison in, 170–171

Liking, and persuasion, 134

Logic, and reasoning, 92–93, 102

Los Angeles, subculture of psychotherapy in, 32

M

Mastery, preference for, 343–344

Memory: and assessment, 254–255; improving, 81; and knowledge, 80–81; and prediction, 290; and self-reports, 206, 208–209; short- and long-term, 80

Mentoring, in clinical training, 63–64

Metacognition, skills in, 12, 15

Metaphors: fallacy of, 181; multiple, 259; and preconceptions, 240. *See also* Analogy

Michigan Alcohol Screening Test, 210

Minnesota Multiphasic Personality Inventory (MMPI), 44–45, 164, 268, 270

Moral character: and classification fallacies, 165; and historical factors, 30

Moral values, and pathological set, 183–184

Motivation: and clinician decisions, 44, 45; and data collection, 193; and interest in knowledge, 71; questionable, fallacy of, 146

Mysticism, and credibility, 69

N

Naming, explaining distinct from, 245. *See also* Labels

National Assessment of Educational Progress (NAEP), 79

National Association of Social Workers (NASW), 82, 122–123, 137n, 158, 170, 355

National Campaign to Abolish the Lexington Women's Control Unit, 171

Negative information, attention to, 261

New York City, subculture of psychotherapy in, 32

Newsspeak, fallacy of, 129–130

Nonoccurrences: and data collection, 195; ignoring, 248

Normative data, and pathological set, 185–186

O

Objectives, specific, for feedback, 293

Objectivity: fallacy of, 174; and intuition, 361

Observation, data collection from, 204, 211–212

Odds, prior and posterior, 278–279

Opinions: beliefs distinct from, 97–98; bias distinct from, 319–320

Optimism, fallacy of, 186–188

Outcomes, measures of, 291

Overconfidence, and assessment error, 245

P

Pathological set: and dispositional bias, 251–252; factors in, 182–186

Personality inventories, data from, 209–210

Persuasion tactics: for fear and anger, 159; influence of, 132–138, 139

Physiological measures, data from, 214–215

Point of view, and reasoning, 95

Political factors, and clinician decisions, 30–32

Popular sentiments, fallacy of, 176

Popularity, and irrelevant authority fallacy, 177

Power: in agencies, 37–38, 41; in case conferences, 302–303, 305–306

Practice theory: assessing, 66–67; and attributions, 250; and beliefs, 342–343; of clinicians, 344; reviewed, 364

Preconceptions: and clinician decisions, 45–46; and covariations, 226–227; errors from, 238–240

Predictions: accuracy increased for, 288–290; actuarial or clinical judgment for, 268–273; aspects of, 264–295; assessment related to, 269; background on, 264–266; and caseworker's report, 266–268; choice and probability related to, 273–276; error sources for, 2, 280–288; feedback for, 290–294; measures for making, 265–266; model for, 271–272; paradigm for, 270–271; and reasoning, 113–114; summary on, 294–295; test results for, 276–280

Predigested thinking, fallacy of, 119–120

Premack Principle, 339

Premises: and conclusions, 103; conversion error of, 102–103; and reasoning, 100, 102–103; relations between, 173

Presumptions, fallacies of, 170

Primacy effects fallacy, 128–129

Prisoners Rights Union, 170

Probabilities: choice and prediction related to, 273–276; compound, 232–233; conditional, 232–233, 287–288; and covariation, 229–233; joint, 284

Professional organizations: and clinician decisions, 35; ethical guidelines of, 355; and information access, 82–83

Progress indicators, for feedback, 292–293

Propaganda, and reasoning, 95

Provincialism fallacy, 178–179

Pseudoauthority appeals fallacies, 175–182

Psychological factors, for clinicians, 43–47

Psychological report, quality check of, 221–222

Psychotherapy: knowledge in, 54–56; social factors in, 49–50; subculture of, 31–32

Q

Questions: begging the, 148, 149–153; complex, leading, or trick, fallacy of, 152–153; as diversions, 157; importance of framing, 206–208; relevance of, 298, 360; of "what if," 261–262

R

Race, of clients, 49

Rationalism, and credibility, 69–70

Reading: deciding on, 67–72; habits for, 78–80; and remembering, 80–81

Reasoning: and analyzing arguments, 105–107; and arguments, 98–105; aspects of, 88–115; background on, 88–89; and compassion, 300–301, 360–361; components of, 88–89; deductive and inductive, 103–105; distinctions for, 92–98; and explanations, 109–114; gender and class influences of, 114–115; and intellectual competence, 89–90; and kinds of arguments, 107–109; and kinds of reasons, 90–92; summary on, 115

Reciprocity, and persuasion, 135

Reframing, as excuse for errors, 330

Regression effects, and prediction, 285

Reification fallacy, 125–126

Relationship skills, for clinicians, 332–336

Relevance: and assessments, 258; of data, 219; of questions, 298, 360

Reliability: of data, 218–219; and prediction, 284, 285

Reluctant evidence, 201

Repetition, conviction through, 127–128

Resemblance criteria, misuse of, 237–238

Residual rules, and labeling fallacies, 165

Resources: and dispositional bias, 252; scarce, responses to, 34–35

Responsibility: freedom related to, 23; transformed, 330–331

Rhetoric, concepts of, 117

Rigor, and compassion, 300–301, 360–361

Rorschach test, 227, 233

Rules: inconsistent use of, 247–248; of thumb, 260–262, 357–362

S

Sample bias, and data collection, 194–195

Sample size, and data collection, 193–194

San Francisco, crack cocaine use in, 28

Scarcity: and persuasion, 136–137; of resources, 34–35

Science: and pseudoscience, 56–61; and reasoning, 110, 111–112

Self-efficacy: of clinicians, 344–346; and costs of thinking, 21–22

Self-fulfilling prophecy, and assessment error, 244

Self-management skills: in clinical training, 65; for clinicians, 339–340

Self-monitoring, data from, 210–211

Self-report: data from, 204–209; for feedback, 292

Sign or symptom: differential weight of, 299; minimizing, 300; and probability, 233; for reasons, 91

Significant others, data from monitoring, 211

Situational information, discounting, 250–251

Slippery-slope fallacy, 175

Social factors, and clinician decisions, 35–36

Social proof: as diversion, 158; and persuasion, 137–138

Special pleading fallacy, 146–147

Speculation fallacy, 127

Spontaneity, role of, 19–20

Stanford University, confirmation bias study at, 78

Statements, types of, 101

Statistics: and actuarial judgment, 268–273, 289–290; for assessments, 256–257; evaluating, 215; neglect of, 299–300

Stereotyping: fallacy of, 172–174; and prediction, 282–283

Sterile study fallacies, 58

Stratagems, in agencies, 39–41

Straw persons fallacy, 153–154

Stress-management skills, for clinicians, 331–332

Structure, content distinct from, 246–247

Subjective utilities, and prediction, 274

Superstition, and prediction, 285
Symptom. *See* Sign or symptom

T

Testimonials: and data collection, 202–203; as feedback, 291–292
Tests: accuracy of, 359, sensitivity and specificity of, 276; for predictions, 276–280
Time-management skills, for clinicians, 338–339
Traditional wisdom, fallacies of, 178
Training: clinical, 62–65; for critical thinking, 357–362; and dispositional bias, 251; and pathological set, 183; transfer of, for skills, 350–351
Transference, for clinicians, 336–337
Troubleshooting skills: for assessment, 259; checklist for, 335
Truth, and reasoning, 95

U

Uncertain consequences fallacy, 302
Uncertainty, attention to sources of, 260
Undermining, negative and positive, 342
Understanding, illusion of, 360
United Kingdom: and caseworker's report, 266–268; child protective agencies in, 34; hysterectomies in, 2: imaginary authority in, 180; statistician in, 226
U.S. Department of Education, 164–165

Utility, and prediction, 283

V

Vagueness: and classification fallacies, 169; fallacy of, 125
Validity: of data, 219; illusion of, 286; and prediction, 283–284
Value, attributed indiscriminately, 297–298
Values: and assessment, 258–259; compatible, 343–344, 352–353; moral, 183–184
Venezuela, intelligence-increasing project in, 13
Visual distortions, and data collection, 216–217
Vividness: of analogies, and fallacies, 156; and assessment errors, 242–243, 253; care with, 358; and clinician decisions, 46–47; and data collection, 192–193, 216–217

W

Whitree v. *New York State*, and case records, 220
Will, fallacy of appeals to, 148
Wisdom, fallacies of traditional, 178
Wishful thinking fallacy, 148
Witnesses, expert, 197–201
Women: in case conferences, 316, 317, 335; and political tactics, 354
Words, and meanings, fallacies of, 124–125, 130. *See also* Language
Writing, learning from, 78–79